American Casebook Series

Hornbook Series and Basic Legal Texts

Nutshell Series

of

WEST PUBLISHING COMPANY

P. O. Box 3526

St. Paul, Minnesota 55165

March, 1978

ACCOUNTING

Fiflis and Kripke's Teaching Materials on Accounting for Business Lawyers, 2nd Ed., 684 pages, 1977 (Casebook)

ADMINISTRATIVE LAW

Davis' Cases, Text and Problems on Administrative Law, 6th Ed., 683 pages, 1977 (Casebook)

Davis' Basic Text on Administrative Law, 3rd Ed., 617 pages, 1972 (Text)

Davis' Police Discretion, 176 pages, 1975 (Text)

Gellhorn's Administrative Law and Process in a Nutshell, 336 pages, 1972 (Text)

Mashaw and Merrill's Introduction to the American Public Law System, 1095 pages, 1975 (Casebook)

Robinson and Gellhorn's The Administrative Process, 928 pages, 1974 (Casebook)

ADMIRALTY

Healy and Sharpe's Cases and Materials on Admiralty, 875 pages, 1974 (Casebook)

AGENCY—PARTNERSHIP

Crane and Bromberg's Hornbook on Partnership, 695 pages, 1968 (Text)

Henn's Cases and Materials on Agency, Partnership and Other Unincorporated Business Enterprises, 396 pages, 1972 (Casebook)

Seavey's Hornbook on Agency, 329 pages, 1964 (Text)

Seavey and Hall's Cases on Agency, 431 pages, 1956 (Casebook)

Seavey, Reuschlein and Hall's Cases on Agency and Partnership, 599 pages, 1962 (Casebook)

AGENCY—PARTNERSHIP—Continued

Steffen's Cases on Agency-Partnership, 3rd Ed., 733 pages, 1969 (Casebook)

Steffen's Agency-Partnership in a Nutshell, 364 pages, 1977 (Text)

ANTITRUST LAW

Gellhorn's Antitrust Law and Economics in a Nutshell, 406 pages, 1976 (Text)

Oppenheim and Weston's Cases and Comments on Federal Antitrust Laws, 3rd Ed., 952 pages, 1968, with 1975 Supplement (Casebook)

Oppenheim and Weston's Price and Service Discrimination under the Robinson-Patman Act, 3rd Ed., 258 pages, 1974 (Casebook)—reprint from Oppenheim and Weston's Cases and Comments on Federal Antitrust Laws, 3rd Ed., 1968

Posner's Cases and Economic Notes on Antitrust, 885 pages, 1974 (Casebook)

Sullivan's Handbook of the Law of Antitrust, 886 pages, 1977 (Text)

See also Regulated Industries, Trade Regulation

BANKING LAW

See Regulated Industries

BUSINESS PLANNING

Painter's Problems and Materials in Business Planning, 791 pages, 1975, with 1977 Statutory Supplement (Casebook)

CIVIL PROCEDURE

Casad's Res Judicata in a Nutshell, 310 pages, 1976 (Text)

LAW SCHOOL PUBLICATIONS — Continued

CIVIL PROCEDURE—Continued

Cound, Friedenthal and Miller's Cases and Materials on Civil Procedure, 2nd Ed., 1186 pages, 1974 with 1978 Supplement (Casebook)

Cound, Friedenthal and Miller's Cases on Pleading, Discovery and Joinder, 643 pages, 1968 (Casebook)

Ehrenzweig and Louisell's Jurisdiction in a Nutshell, 3rd Ed., 291 pages, 1973 (Text)

Federal Rules of Civil-Appellate-Criminal Procedure—West Law School Edition, 334 pages, 1977

Hodges, Jones and Elliott's Texas Cases and Materials on Texas Trial and Appellate Procedure, 2nd Ed., 745 pages, 1974 (Casebook)

Hodges, Jones, and Elliott's Texas Cases and Materials on the Judicial Process Prior to Trial in Texas, 2nd Ed., 871 pages, 1977 (Casebook)

Karlen's Procedure Before Trial in a Nutshell, 258 pages, 1972 (Text)

Karlen and Joiner's Cases and Materials on Trials and Appeals, 536 pages, 1971 (Casebook)

Karlen, Meisenholder, Stevens and Vestal's Cases on Civil Procedure, 923 pages, 1975 (Casebook)

Koffler and Reppy's Hornbook on Common Law Pleading, 663 pages, 1969 (Text)

McBaine's Cases on Introduction to Civil Procedure, 399 pages, 1950 (Casebook)

McCoid's Cases on Civil Procedure, 823 pages, 1974 (Casebook)

Park's Computer-Aided Exercises on Civil Procedure, 118 pages, 1976 (Coursebook)

Shipman's Hornbook on Common-Law Pleading, 3rd Ed., 644 pages, 1923 (Text)

Siegel's Hornbook on New York Practice, 1011 pages, 1978 (Text)

See also Federal Jurisdiction and Procedure

COMMERCIAL LAW

Bailey's Secured Transactions in a Nutshell, 377 pages, 1976 (Text)

Epstein and Martin's Basic Uniform Commercial Code Teaching Materials, 599 pages, 1977 (Casebook)

Henson's Hornbook on Secured Transactions under the U.C.C., 364 pages, 1973 (Text)

Murray's Commercial Law, Problems and Materials, 366 pages, 1975 (Coursebook)

COMMERCIAL LAW—Continued

Nordstrom and Clovis' Problems and Materials on Commercial Paper, 458 pages, 1972 (Casebook)

Nordstrom and Lattin's Problems and Materials on Sales and Secured Transactions, 809 pages, 1968 (Casebook)

Nordstrom's Hornbook on Sales, 600 pages, 1970 (Text)

Selected Commercial Statutes, 1144 pages, 1976

Speidel, Summers and White's Teaching Materials on Commercial and Consumer Law, 2nd Ed., 1475 pages, 1974 (Casebook)

Stone's Uniform Commercial Code in a Nutshell, 507 pages, 1975 (Text)

Uniform Commercial Code, Official Text with Comments, 816 pages, 1972

UCC Article Nine Reprint, 128 pages, 1976

Weber's Commercial Paper in a Nutshell, 2nd Ed., 361 pages, 1975 (Text)

White and Summers' Hornbook on the Uniform Commercial Code, 1086 pages, 1972 (Text)

COMMUNITY PROPERTY

Burby's Cases on Community Property, 4th Ed., 342 pages, 1955 (Casebook)

Huie's Texas Cases and Materials on Marital Property Rights, 681 pages, 1966 (Casebook)

Verrall's Cases and Materials on California Community Property, 3rd Ed., 547 pages, 1977 (Casebook)

COMPARATIVE LAW

Langbein's Comparative Criminal Procedure: Germany, 172 pages, 1977 (Casebook)

CONFLICT OF LAWS

Cramton, Currie and Kay's Cases-Comments-Questions on Conflict of Laws, 2nd Ed., 1021 pages, 1975 (Casebook)

Ehrenzweig's Treatise on Conflict of Laws, 824 pages, 1962 (Text)

Ehrenzweig's Conflicts in a Nutshell, 3rd Ed., 432 pages, 1974 (Text)

Goodrich and Scoles' Hornbook on Conflict of Laws, 4th Ed., 483 pages, 1964 (Text)

Scoles and Weintraub's Cases and Materials on Conflict of Laws, 2nd Ed., 966 pages, 1972 (Casebook)

CONSTITUTIONAL LAW

Engdahl's Constitutional Power in a Nutshell: Federal and State, 411 pages, 1974 (Text)

CONSTITUTIONAL LAW—Continued

Ginsburg's Constitutional Aspects of Sex-Based Discrimination, 129 pages, 1974 (Casebook)—reprint from Davidson, Ginsburg and Kay's Cases on Sex-Based Discrimination, 1974

Lockhart, Kamisar and Choper's Cases-Comments-Questions on Constitutional Law, 4th Ed., 1664 pages plus Appendix, 1975, with 1977 Supplement (Casebook)

Lockhart, Kamisar and Choper's Cases-Comments-Questions on the American Constitution, 4th Ed., 1249 pages plus Appendix, 1975, with 1977 Supplement (Casebook)—reprint from Lockhart, et al. Cases on Constitutional Law, 4th Ed., 1975

Lockhart, Kamisar and Choper's Cases and Materials on Constitutional Rights and Liberties, 4th Ed., 1244 pages plus Appendix, 1975, with 1977 Supplement (Casebook)—reprint from Lockhart, et al. Cases on Constitutional Law, 4th Ed., 1975

Miller's Presidential Power in a Nutshell, 328 pages, 1977 (Text)

Nowak, Rotunda and Young's Hornbook on Constitutional Law, 974 pages, 1978 (Text)

Vieira's Civil Rights in a Nutshell, 279 pages, 1978 (Text)

CONSUMER LAW

Epstein's Consumer Protection in a Nutshell, 322 pages, 1976 (Text)

Kripke's Text-Cases-Materials on Consumer Credit, 454 pages, 1970 (Casebook)

McCall's Consumer Protection, Cases, Notes and Materials, 594 pages, 1977, with 1977 Statutory Supplement (Casebook)

Schrag's Cases and Materials on Consumer Protection, 2nd Ed., 197 pages, 1973 (Casebook)—reprint from Cooper, et al. Cases on Law and Poverty, 2nd Ed., 1973

Selected Commercial Statutes, 1144 pages, 1976

Uniform Consumer Credit Code, Official Text with Comments, 218 pages, 1974

CONTRACTS

Calamari & Perillo's Cases and Problems on Contracts, approximately 1100 pages, August 1978 (Casebook)

Calamari and Perillo's Hornbook on Contracts, 2nd Ed., 878 pages, 1977 (Text)

Corbin's Text on Contracts, One Volume Student Edition, 1224 pages, 1952 (Text)

CONTRACTS—Continued

Freedman's Cases and Materials on Contracts, 658 pages, 1973 (Casebook)

Fuller and Eisenberg's Cases on Basic Contract Law, 3rd Ed., 1043 pages, 1972 (Casebook)

Jackson's Cases on Contract Law in Modern Society, 1404 pages, 1973 (Casebook)

Reitz's Cases on Contracts as Basic Commercial Law, 763 pages, 1975 (Casebook)

Schaber and Rohwer's Contracts in a Nutshell, 307 pages, 1975 (Text)

Simpson's Hornbook on Contracts, 2nd Ed., 510 pages, 1965 (Text)

COPYRIGHT

Nimmer's Cases and Materials on Copyright and Other Aspects of Law Pertaining to Literary, Musical and Artistic Works, 828 pages, 1971, with 1977 Supplement (Casebook)

See also Patent Law

CORPORATIONS

Hamilton's Cases on Corporations—Including Partnerships and Limited Partnerships, 998 pages, 1976, with 1976 Statutory Supplement and 1977 Case Supplement (Casebook)

Henn's Cases on Corporations, 1279 pages, 1974, with 1974 Statutes, Forms and Case Study Supplement (Casebook)

Henn's Hornbook on Corporations, 2nd Ed., 956 pages, 1970 (Text)

CORRECTIONS

Krantz's Cases and Materials on the Law of Corrections and Prisoners' Rights, 1130 pages, 1973, with 1977 Supplement (Casebook)

Krantz's Law of Corrections and Prisoners' Rights in a Nutshell, 353 pages, 1976 (Text)

Model Rules and Regulations on Prisoners' Rights and Responsibilities, 212 pages, 1973

Popper's Post-Conviction Remedies in a Nutshell, approximately 360 pages, April 1978 (Text)

CREDITOR'S RIGHTS

Epstein's Debtor-Creditor Relations in a Nutshell, 309 pages, 1973 (Text)

Epstein and Landers' Debtors and Creditors: Cases and Materials, 722 pages, 1978 (Casebook)

MacLachlan's Hornbook on Bankruptcy, 500 pages, 1956 (Text)

Riesenfeld's Cases and Materials on Creditors' Remedies and Debtors'

CREDITOR'S RIGHTS—Continued

Protection, 2nd Ed., 808 pages, 1975, with 1975 Statutory Supplement and 1977 Supplement Update (Casebook)

Selected Bankruptcy Statutes, 486 pages, 1974

CRIMINAL LAW AND CRIMINAL PROCEDURE

Cohen and Gobert's Problems in Criminal Law, 297 pages, 1976 (Problem book)

Davis' Police Discretion, 176 pages, 1975 (Text)

Dix and Sharlot's Cases and Materials on Criminal Law, 1360 pages, 1973 (Casebook)

Federal Rules of Civil-Appellate-Criminal Procedure—West Law School Edition, 334 pages, 1977

Grano's Problems in Criminal Procedure, 171 pages, 1974 (Problem book)

Heymann and Kenety's The Murder Trial of Wilbur Jackson: A Homicide in the Family, 340 pages, 1975 (Case Study)

Israel and LaFave's Criminal Procedure in a Nutshell, 2nd Ed., 404 pages, 1975 (Text)

Johnson's Criminal Law: Cases, Materials and Text on Substantive Criminal Law in its Procedural Context, 878 pages, 1975, with 1977 Supplement (Casebook)

Kamisar, LaFave and Israel's Cases, Comments and Questions on Modern Criminal Procedure, 4th Ed., 1572 pages, plus Appendix, 1974, with 1978 Supplement (Casebook)

Kamisar, LaFave and Israel's Cases, Comments and Questions on Basic Criminal Procedure, 4th Ed., 790 pages, 1974, with 1978 Supplement (Casebook)—reprint from Kamisar, et al. Modern Criminal Procedure, 4th Ed., 1974

LaFave's Modern Criminal Law: Cases, Comments and Questions, 789 pages, 1978 (Casebook)

LaFave and Scott's Hornbook on Criminal Law, 763 pages, 1972 (Text)

Loewy's Criminal Law in a Nutshell, 302 pages, 1975 (Text)

Uniform Rules of Criminal Procedure— Approved Draft, 407 pages, 1974

Uviller's The Processes of Criminal Justice: Adjudication, 991 pages, 1975, with 1977 Supplement (Casebook)

Uviller's The Processes of Criminal Justice: Investigation, 744 pages, 1974, with 1977 Supplement (Casebook)

CRIMINAL LAW AND CRIMINAL PROCEDURE—Continued

Vorenberg's Cases on Criminal Law and Procedure, 1044 pages, 1975, with 1977 Supplement (Casebook)

See also Corrections, Juvenile Justice

DECEDENTS ESTATES

See Wills, Trusts and Estates

DOMESTIC RELATIONS

Clark's Cases and Problems on Domestic Relations, 2nd Ed., 918 pages, 1974, with 1977 Supplement (Casebook)

Clark's Hornbook on Domestic Relations, 754 pages, 1968 (Text)

Kay's Sex-Based Discrimination in Family Law, 305 pages, 1974 (Casebook)—reprint from Davidson, Ginsburg and Kay's Cases on Sex-Based Discrimination, 1974

Krause's Cases and Materials on Family Law, 1132 pages, 1976 (Casebook)

Krause's Family Law in a Nutshell, 400 pages, 1977 (Text)

Paulsen's Cases and Selected Problems on Family Law and Poverty, 2nd Ed., 200 pages, 1973 (Casebook)—reprint from Cooper, et al. Cases on Law and Poverty, 2nd Ed., 1973

DRUG ABUSE

Uelmen and Haddox's Cases on Drug Abuse and the Law, 564 pages, 1974, with 1977 Supplement (Casebook)

EDUCATION LAW

Morris' The Constitution and American Education, 833 pages, 1974 (Casebook)

EMPLOYMENT DISCRIMINATION

Cooper, Rabb and Rubin's Fair Employment Litigation: Text and Materials for Student and Practitioner, 590 pages, 1975 (Coursebook)

Player's Federal Law of Employment Discrimination in a Nutshell, 336 pages, 1976 (Text)

Sovern's Cases and Materials on Racial Discrimination in Employment, 2nd Ed., 167 pages, 1973 (Casebook)—reprint from Cooper et al. Cases on Law and Poverty, 2nd Ed., 1973

See also Women and the Law

ENVIRONMENTAL LAW

Currie's Cases and Materials on Pollution, 715 pages, 1975 (Casebook)

Federal Environmental Law, 1600 pages, 1974 (Text)

ENVIRONMENTAL LAW—Continued

Hanks, Tarlock and Hanks' Cases on Environmental Law and Policy, 1242 pages, 1974, with 1976 Supplement (Casebook)

Rodgers' Hornbook on Environmental Law, 956 pages, 1977 (Text)

See also Natural Resources

EQUITY

See Remedies

ESTATE PLANNING

Casner and Stein's Estate Planning under the Tax Reform Act of 1976, 456 pages, 1978 (Coursebook)

Lynn's An Introduction to Estate Planning, 274 pages, 1975 (Text)

EVIDENCE

Broun and Meisenholder's Problems in Evidence, 130 pages, 1973 (Problem book)

Cleary and Strong's Cases, Materials and Problems on Evidence, 2nd Ed., 1124 pages, 1975 (Casebook)

Federal Rules of Evidence for United States Courts and Magistrates, 323 pages, 1975

Lempert and Saltzburg's A Modern Approach to Evidence: Text, Problems, Transcripts and Cases, 1231 pages, 1977 (Casebook)

McCormick, Elliott and Sutton's Cases and Materials on Evidence, 4th Ed., 1088 pages, 1971 (Casebook)

McCormick's Hornbook on Evidence, 2nd Ed., 938 pages, 1972 (Text)

Rothstein's Evidence in a Nutshell, 406 pages, 1970 (Text)

FEDERAL JURISDICTION AND PROCEDURE

Currie's Cases and Materials on Federal Courts, 2nd Ed., 1040 pages, 1975, with 1977 Supplement (Casebook)

Currie's Federal Jurisdiction in a Nutshell, 228 pages, 1976 (Text)

Federal Rules of Civil-Appellate-Criminal Procedure—West Law School Edition, 334 pages, 1977

Forrester and Moye's Cases and Materials on Federal Jurisdiction and Procedure, 3rd Ed., 917 pages, 1977 (Casebook)

Merrill and Vetri's Problems on Federal Courts and Civil Procedure, 460 pages, 1974 (Problem book)

Wright's Hornbook on Federal Courts, 3rd Ed., 818 pages, 1976 (Text)

FUTURE INTERESTS

See Wills, Trusts, and Estates

HOUSING AND URBAN DEVELOPMENT

Berger's Cases and Materials on Housing, 2nd Ed., 254 pages, 1973 (Casebook)—reprint from Cooper et al. Cases on Law and Poverty, 2nd Ed., 1973

Krasnowiecki's Cases and Materials on Housing and Urban Development, 697 pages, 1969, with 1969 Statutory Supplement (Casebook)

See also Land Use

INSURANCE

Keeton's Cases on Basic Insurance Law, 2nd Ed., 1086 pages, 1977

Keeton's Basic Text on Insurance Law, 712 pages, 1971 (Text)

Keeton's Case Supplement to Keeton's Basic Text on Insurance Law, approximately 350 pages, May 1978 (Casebook)

Keeton's Programmed Problems in Insurance Law, 243 pages, 1972 (Text Supplement)

INTERNATIONAL LAW

Friedmann, Lissitzyn and Pugh's Cases and Materials on International Law, 1205 pages, 1969, with 1972 Supplement (Casebook)

Jackson's Legal Problems of International Economic Relations, 1097 pages, 1977, with Statutory Supplement (Casebook)

Kirgis' International Organizations in Their Legal Setting, 1016 pages, 1977 (Casebook)

INTRODUCTION TO LAW

Dobbyn's So You Want to go to Law School, Revised First Edition, 206 pages, 1976 (Text)

Kinyon's Introduction to Law Study and Law Examinations in a Nutshell, 389 pages, 1971 (Text)

See also Legal Method and Legal System

JUDICIAL ADMINISTRATION

Carrington, Meador and Rosenberg's Justice on Appeal, 263 pages, 1976 (Casebook)

Nelson's Cases and Materials on Judicial Administration and the Administration of Justice, 1032 pages, 1974 (Casebook)

JURISPRUDENCE

Christie's Text and Readings on Jurisprudence—The Philosophy of Law, 1056 pages, 1973 (Casebook)

JUVENILE JUSTICE

Fox's Cases and Materials on Modern Juvenile Justice, 1012 pages, 1972 (Casebook)

Fox's Juvenile Courts in a Nutshell, 2nd Ed., 275 pages, 1977 (Text)

LABOR LAW

Gorman's Labor Law-Unionization and Collective Bargaining, 914 pages, 1976 (Text)

Oberer and Hanslowe's Cases and Materials on Labor Law—Collective Bargaining in a Free Society, 1091 pages, 1972, with 1972 Statutory Supplement, and 1975 Case Supplement (Casebook)

See also Employment Discrimination, Social Legislation

LAND FINANCE—PROPERTY SECURITY

Maxwell, Riesenfeld, Hetland and Warren's Cases on California Security Transactions in Land, 2nd Ed., 584 pages, 1975 (Casebook)

Nelson and Whitman's Cases on Real Estate Finance and Development, 1064 pages, 1976 (Casebook)

Osborne's Cases and Materials on Secured Transactions, 559 pages, 1967 (Casebook)

Osborne's Hornbook on Mortgages, 2nd Ed., 805 pages, 1970 (Text)

LAND USE

Beuscher, Wright and Gitelman's Cases and Materials on Land Use, 2nd Ed., 1133 pages, 1976 (Casebook)

Hagman's Cases on Public Planning and Control of Urban and Land Development, 1208 pages, 1973, with 1976 Supplement (Casebook)

Hagman's Hornbook on Urban Planning and Land Development Control Law, 706 pages, 1971 (Text)

See also Housing and Urban Development

LAW AND ECONOMICS

Manne's The Economics of Legal Relationships—Readings in the Theory of Property Rights, 660 pages, 1975 (Text)

See also Regulated Industries

LAW AND MEDICINE—PSYCHIATRY

King's The Law of Medical Malpractice in a Nutshell, 340 pages, 1977 (Text)

LEGAL RESEARCH AND WRITING

Cohen's Legal Research in a Nutshell, 3rd Ed., 415 pages, 1978 (Text)

LEGAL RESEARCH AND WRITING—C't'd

How to Find the Law With Special Chapters on Legal Writing, 7th Ed., 542 pages, 1976. Problem book available (Coursebook)

Rombauer's Legal Problem Solving—Analysis, Research and Writing, 3rd Ed., approximately 350 pages, May 1978. Problem Supplement available (Casebook)

Statsky's Legal Research, Writing and Analysis: Some Starting Points, 180 pages, 1974 (Text)—reprint from Statsky's Introduction to Paralegalism, 1974

Statsky and Wernet's Case Analysis and Fundamentals of Legal Writing, 576 pages, 1977 (Text)

Weihofen's Legal Writing Style, 323 pages, 1961 (Text)

LEGAL CLINICS

Cooper, Rabb and Rubin's Fair Employment Litigation: Text and Materials for Student and Practitioner, 590 pages, 1975 (Coursebook)

Freeman and Weihofen's Cases and Text on Clinical Law Training—Interviewing and Counseling, 506 pages, 1972 (Casebook)

LEGAL PROFESSION

Aronson's Problems in Professional Responsibility, 280 pages, 1978 (Problem book)

Mellinkoff's The Conscience of a Lawyer, 304 pages, 1973 (Text)

Mellinkoff's Lawyers and the System of Justice, 983 pages, 1976 (Casebook)

Pirsig and Kirwin's Cases and Materials on Professional Responsibility, 3rd Ed., 667 pages, 1976, with 1977 Supplement (Casebook)

LEGAL HISTORY

See Legal Method and Legal System

LEGAL METHOD AND LEGAL SYSTEM

Aldisert's Readings, Materials and Cases in the Judicial Process, 948 pages, 1976 (Casebook)

Fryer and Orentlicher's Cases and Materials on Legal Method and Legal System, 1043 pages, 1967 (Casebook)

Greenberg's Judicial Process and Social Change, 666 pages, 1977 (Coursebook)

Kempin's Historical Introduction to Anglo-American Law in a Nutshell, 2nd Ed., 280 pages, 1973 (Text)

Kimball's Historical Introduction to the Legal System, 610 pages, 1966 (Casebook)

LEGAL METHOD AND LEGAL SYSTEM
—Continued

Leflar's Appellate Judicial Opinions, 343 pages, 1974 (Text)

Mashaw and Merrill's Introduction to the American Public Law System, 1095 pages, 1975 (Casebook)

Murphy's Cases and Materials on Introduction to Law—Legal Process and Procedure, 772 pages, 1977 (Casebook)

Smith's Cases and Materials on the Development of Legal Institutions, 757 pages, 1965 (Casebook)

Statsky's Legislative Analysis: How to Use Statutes and Regulations, 216 pages, 1975 (Text)

LEGISLATION

Davies' Legislative Law and Process in a Nutshell, 279 pages, 1975 (Text)

Nutting and Dickerson's Cases and Materials on Legislation, 5th Ed., 744 pages, 1978 (Casebook)

Statsky's Legislative Analysis: How to Use Statutes and Regulations, 216 pages, 1975 (Text)

LOCAL GOVERNMENT

McCarthy's Local Government Law in a Nutshell, 386 pages, 1975 (Text)

Michelman and Sandalow's Cases-Comments-Questions on Government in Urban Areas, 1216 pages, 1970, with 1972 Supplement (Casebook)

Stason and Kauper's Cases and Materials on Municipal Corporations, 3rd Ed., 692 pages, 1959 (Casebook)

Valente's Cases and Materials on Local Government Law, 928 pages, 1975 (Casebook)

MASS COMMUNICATION LAW

Gillmor and Barron's Cases and Comment on Mass Communication Law, 2nd Ed., 1007 pages, 1974 (Casebook)

Zuckman and Gayne's Mass Communications Law in a Nutshell, 431 pages, 1977 (Text)

MORTGAGES

See Land Finance—Property Security

NATURAL RESOURCES LAW

Trelease, Bloomenthal and Geraud's Cases and Materials on Natural Resources Law, 1131 pages, 1965 (Casebook)

See also Environmental Law

OFFICE PRACTICE

Binder and Price's Legal Interviewing and Counseling: A Client-Centered Approach, 232 pages 1977 (Text)

OFFICE PRACTICE—Continued

Edwards and White's Problems, Readings and Materials on the Lawyer as a Negotiator, 484 pages, 1977 (Casebook)

Freeman and Weihofen's Cases and Text on Clinical Law Training—Interviewing and Counseling, 506 pages, 1972 (Casebook)

Shaffer's Legal Interviewing and Counseling in a Nutshell, 353 pages, 1976 (Text)

Strong and Clark's Law Office Management, 424 pages, 1974 (Casebook)

OIL AND GAS

Hemingway's Hornbook on Oil and Gas, 486 pages, 1971 (Text)

Huie, Woodward and Smith's Cases and Materials on Oil and Gas, 2nd Ed., 955 pages, 1972 (Casebook)

See also Natural Resources

PARTNERSHIP

See Agency—Partnership

PATENT LAW

Choate's Cases and Materials on Patent Law, 1060 pages, 1973 (Casebook)

See also Copyright

POVERTY LAW

Brudno's Poverty, Inequality, and the Law: Cases-Commentary-Analysis, 934 pages, 1976 (Casebook)

Cooper, Dodyk, Berger, Paulsen, Schrag and Sovern's Cases and Materials on Law and Poverty, 2nd Ed., 1208 pages, 1973 (Casebook)

Cooper and Dodyk's Cases and Materials on Income Maintenance, 2nd Ed., 449 pages, 1973 (Casebook)—reprint from Cooper et al. Cases on Law and Poverty, 2nd Ed., 1973

LaFrance, Schroeder, Bennett and Boyd's Hornbook on Law of the Poor, 558 pages, 1973 (Text)

See also Social Legislation

PRODUCTS LIABILITY

Noel and Phillips' Cases on Products Liability, 836 pages, 1976 (Casebook)

Noel and Phillips' Products Liability in a Nutshell, 365 pages, 1974 (Text)

PROPERTY

Aigler, Smith and Tefft's Cases on Property, 2 volumes, 1339 pages, 1960 (Casebook)

Bernhardt's Real Property in a Nutshell, 425 pages, 1975 (Text)

Browder, Cunningham and Julin's Cases on Basic Property Law, 2nd Ed., 1397 pages, 1973 (Casebook)

PROPERTY—Continued

Burby's Hornbook on Real Property, 3rd Ed., 490 pages, 1965 (Text)

Chused's A Modern Approach to Property: Cases—Notes—Materials, approximately 1150 pages, May 1978 (Casebook)

Cohen's Materials for a Basic Course in Property, approximately 600 pages, July 1978 (Casebook)

Donahue, Kauper and Martin's Cases on Property, 1501 pages, 1974 (Casebook)

Moynihan's Introduction to Real Property, 254 pages, 1962 (Text)

Phipps' Titles in a Nutshell, 277 pages, 1968 (Text)

Smith and Boyer's Survey of the Law of Property, 2nd Ed., 510 pages, 1971 (Text)

Uniform Eminent Domain Code, Official Text with Comments, 160 pages, 1975

Uniform Land Transactions Act, 1975 Official Text with Comments, 170 pages, 1976

See also Housing and Urban Development, Land Finance, Land Use

REAL ESTATE

See Land Finance

REGULATED INDUSTRIES

Morgan's Cases and Materials on Economic Regulation of Business, 830 pages, 1976 (Casebook)

Pozen's Financial Institutions: Cases, Materials and Problems on Investment Management, 844 pages, 1978 (Casebook)

White's Teaching Materials on Banking Law, 1058 pages, 1976, with 1976 Statutory Supplement (Casebook)

See also Mass Communication Law

REMEDIES

Cribbet's Cases and Materials on Judicial Remedies, 762 pages, 1954 (Casebook)

Dobbs' Hornbook on Remedies, 1067 pages, 1973 (Text)

Dobbs' Problems in Remedies, 137 pages, 1974 (Problem book)

Dobbyn's Injunctions in a Nutshell, 264 pages, 1974 (Text)

McClintock's Hornbook on Equity, 2nd Ed., 643 pages, 1948 (Text)

McCormick's Hornbook on Damages, 811 pages, 1935 (Text)

O'Connell's Remedies in a Nutshell, 364 pages, 1977 (Text)

Van Hecke, Leavell and Nelson's Cases and Materials on Equitable Remedies

REMEDIES—Continued

and Restitution, 2nd Ed., 717 pages, 1973 (Casebook)

Wright's Cases on Remedies, 498 pages, 1955 (Casebook)

York and Bauman's Cases and Materials on Remedies, 2nd Ed., 1381 pages, 1973 (Casebook)

REVIEW MATERIALS

Ballantine's Problems

Burby's Law Refreshers

Smith's Review

SECURITIES REGULATION

Ratner's Materials on Securities Regulation, 893 pages, 1975, with 1977 Supplement (Casebook)

Ratner's Securities Regulation in a Nutshell, 300 pages, 1978 (Text)

SOCIAL LEGISLATION

Brudno's Income Redistribution Theories and Programs: Cases-Commentary-Analysis, 480 pages, 1977 (Casebook) —reprint from Brudno's Poverty, Inequality and the Law, 1976

Cooper and Dodyk's Cases and Materials on Income Maintenance, 2nd Ed., 449 pages, 1973 (Casebook)—reprint from Cooper et al. Cases on Law and Poverty, 2nd Ed., 1973

Malone, Plant and Little's Cases on the Employment Relation, 1055 pages, 1974, with 1977 Supplement (Casebook)

See also Poverty Law

SURETYSHIP

Osborne's Cases on Suretyship, 221 pages, 1966 (Casebook)

Simpson's Hornbook on Suretyship, 569 pages, 1950 (Text)

TAXATION

Chommie's Hornbook on Federal Income Taxation, 2nd Ed., 1051 pages, 1973 (Text)

Chommie's Review of Federal Income Taxation, 90 pages, 1973 (Text)

Hellerstein and Hellerstein's Cases on State and Local Taxation, 4th Ed., approximately 1120 pages, April 1978 (Casebook)

Kragen and McNulty's Cases and Materials on Federal Income Taxation, 2nd Ed., 1107 pages, 1974, with 1977 Supplement (Casebook)

Kramer and McCord's Problems for Federal Estate and Gift Taxes, 206 pages, 1976 (Problem book)

Lowndes, Kramer and McCord's Hornbook on Federal Estate and Gift Taxes, 3rd Ed., 1099 pages, 1974 (Text)

TAXATION—Continued

McCord's 1976 Estate and Gift Tax Reform–Analysis, Explanation and Commentary, 377 pages, 1977 (Text)

McNulty's Federal Estate and Gift Taxation in a Nutshell, 343 pages, 1973 (Text)

McNulty's Federal Income Taxation of Individuals in a Nutshell, 2nd Ed., approximately 320 pages, May 1978 (Text)

Rice's Problems and Materials in Federal Estate and Gift Taxation, 3rd Ed., 474 pages, 1978 (Casebook)

Rice's Problems and Materials in Federal Income Taxation, 2nd Ed., 589 pages, 1971 (Casebook)

Rose and Raskind's Advanced Federal Income Taxation: Corporate Transactions–Cases, Materials and Problems, 955 pages, 1978 (Casebook)

Selected Federal Taxation Statutes and Regulations, 1321 pages, 1977

Soboloff's Federal Income Taxation of Corporations and Stockholders in a Nutshell, 374 pages, 1978 (Text)

TORTS

Green, Pedrick, Rahl, Thode, Hawkins, Smith, and Treece's Cases and Materials on Torts, 2nd Ed., 1360 pages, 1977 (Casebook)

Green, Pedrick, Rahl, Thode, Hawkins, Smith and Treece's Advanced Torts: Injuries to Business, Political and Family Interests, 544 pages, 1977 (Casebook)—reprint from Green, et al Cases and Materials on Torts, 2nd Ed., 1977

Keeton's Computer-Aided and Workbook Exercises on Tort Law, 164 pages, 1976 (Coursebook)

Keeton and Keeton's Cases and Materials on Torts, 2nd Ed., 1200 pages, 1977 (Casebook)

Kionka's Torts: Injuries to Persons and Property in a Nutshell, 434 pages, 1977 (Text)

Prosser's Hornbook on Torts, 4th Ed., 1208 pages, 1971 (Text)

Shapo's Cases on Tort and Compensation Law, 1244 pages, 1976 (Casebook)

See also Products Liability

TRADE REGULATION

Oppenheim and Weston's Cases and Materials on Unfair Trade Practices and Consumer Protection, 3rd Ed., 1065 pages, 1974, with 1977 Supplement (Casebook)

See also Antitrust, Regulated Industries

TRIAL ADVOCACY

Hegland's Trial and Practice Skills in a Nutshell, approximately 380 pages, May 1978 (Text)

Jean's Trial Advocacy (Student Edition), 473 pages, 1975 (Text)

McElhaney's Effective Litigation, 457 pages, 1974 (Casebook)

TRUSTS

See Wills, Trusts and Estates

WATER LAW

Trelease's Cases and Materials on Water Law, 2nd Ed., 863 pages, 1974 (Casebook)

See also Natural Resources

WILLS, TRUSTS AND ESTATES

Atkinson's Hornbook on Wills, 2nd Ed., 975 pages, 1953 (Text)

Averill's Uniform Probate Code in a Nutshell, 425 pages, 1978 (Text)

Bogert's Hornbook on Trusts, 5th Ed., 726 pages, 1973 (Text)

Clark, Lusky and Murphy's Cases and Materials on Gratuitous Transfers, 2nd Ed., 1102 pages, 1977 (Casebook)

Gulliver's Cases and Materials on Future Interests, 624 pages, 1959 (Casebook)

Gulliver's Introduction to the Law of Future Interests, 87 pages, 1959 (Casebook)

Halbach (Editor)—Death, Taxes, and Family Property: Essays and American Assembly Report, 189 pages, 1977 (Text)

Mennell's Cases and Materials on California Decedent's Estates, 566 pages, 1973 (Casebook)

Powell's Cases on Trusts and Wills, 639 pages, 1960 (Casebook)

Simes' Hornbook on Future Interests, 2nd Ed., 355 pages, 1966 (Text)

Turrentine's Cases and Text on Wills and Administration, 2nd Ed., 483 pages, 1962 (Casebook)

Uniform Probate Code, 5th Ed., Official Text With Comments, 384 pages, 1977

WOMEN AND THE LAW

Davidson, Ginsburg and Kay's Text, Cases and Materials on Sex-Based Discrimination, 1031 pages, 1974, with 1975 Supplement (Casebook)

See also Employment Discrimination

WORKMEN'S COMPENSATION

See Social Legislation

LEGAL PROBLEM SOLVING:
Analysis, Research and Writing

THIRD EDITION

By

MARJORIE DICK ROMBAUER
Professor of Law, University of Washington

AMERICAN CASEBOOK SERIES

ST. PAUL, MINN.
WEST PUBLISHING CO.
1978

Library of Congress Cataloging in Publication Data

Rombauer, Marjorie Dick.
    Legal problem solving.
    (American casebook series)
    First. ed. published in 1970 under title: Legal analysis and research.
    Includes bibliographical references and index.
    1. Legal research—United States. I. Title. II. Series.
KF240.R64   1978   340'.07'2073   78–3468
ISBN 0–8299–2002–1

Rombauer Leg.Prob.Solving 3rd Ed. ACB

1st Reprint—1979

To
E.R.R.

*

PREFACE TO THIRD EDITION

This course book is intended to provide a functional introduction to the analysis, research, and writing incident to research-oriented problem solving. It is directed primarily toward first-year law students, but has been written with the awareness that it may be used, as was the last edition, for paraprofessional courses and for self-teaching.

This edition has been expanded in several respects. A large number of footnotes and text notes have been added to provide additional information and additional sources of information for readers who are puzzled about or interested in learning more about particular subjects mentioned in the text. It is not intended that material cited in either form of notes be read in order to attain a general understanding of the text. Many footnotes in Part I also provide brief descriptions of basic types of legal publications and forms of published writings.

Part I again describes the skills required to work with court opinions, but with expansion of the explanatory material in Chapter 2 and addition of suggested exercises designed to permit immediate use, in manageable units, of the skills described. Court opinions provided for these exercises, together with opinions reproduced in text notes at the end of Chapter 3, provide background for examples used for illustrative purposes in Parts II and III and for samples of legal writing and oral argument included in the expanded Appendices.

Part II has again been expanded in this edition to provide a more comprehensive introduction to legal research. The order of Chapters 5 and 6 has been reversed to provide a smoother introduction to the functional steps in relation to preliminary analysis of a problem. Also, I have yielded to the urgings of instructors and students who used prior editions and have incorporated a number of illustrative pages from the research materials described in Chapters 4, 6, 7, and 8. Although the availability of such samples may delay the time when readers do what they ultimately must—examine the actual research materials—I now recognize that all who read this book may not have the research materials available for immediate examination.

Part III has also been expanded. Some introductory material on writing previously included in Chapter 2 has been moved to Chapter 10. A section on trial court arguments has been added to Chapter 11. Several examples have been added to both chapters.

I acknowledge my debt to Professor Marian G. Gallagher as a continuing source of inspiration and instruction and to Professors

Gallagher, Linda Hume, Virginia Lyness, Robert S. Hunt, and Charles Z. Smith, all of the University of Washington law faculty, who read and criticized portions of the revised text. I have been particularly aided by editorial assistance of Ms. Glenna S. Hall, class of '76, who also authored the memorandum reproduced in Appendix D. I did not accept all of my critics' suggestions; if I have erred, the fault is mine.

I am grateful for permission to quote from the works of several authors in addition to those quoted in earlier editions: from *On Law School Training in Analytic Skill*, 25 J.Legal Educ. 261 (1973), by Peter W. Gross, copyright 1972, Peter W. Gross; *The Doctrine of Stare Decisis*, 21 Wayne L.Rev. 1043 (1975), by E. M. Wise; *The Force of Precedent in the Lower Courts*, 14 Wayne L.Rev. 3 (1967), by Maurice Kelman; *Legal Writing: A Guide for Law Students* (1976), unpublished manuscript by Peter W. Gross, as reprinted in W. Statsky & R. Wernet, Jr., Case Analysis and Fundamentals of Legal Writing 411–16 (1977), copyright 1977, West Publishing Co.; from *Computer-Assisted Legal Research—An Analysis of Full-Text Document Retrieval Systems, Particularly the LEXIS System,* 1 ABF Research J. 175 (1976), by James A. Sprowl; from A Manual for Computer-Assisted Legal Research (1976), by James A. Sprowl; Book Review, 14 J.Legal Educ. 535 (1962), by Morton Gitelman, copyright 1962, American Association of Law Schools; Note, *Lucas v. Hamm*, 40 Texas L.Rev. 1046 (1962), by Estil A. Vance, Jr., copyright 1962, Texas Law Review; summary of argument in *Burns v. Alcala*, 43 U.S.L.W. 3409 (1975), copyright 1974, The Bureau of National Affairs, Inc.

I am also grateful to the several publishers who have granted permission to reproduce pages from their publications for illustrative purposes: Shepard's Citations, Inc. (from *Shepard's Indiana Citations,* Case Edition; *Shepard's Restatement of the Law Citations; Shepard's California Citations,* Case Edition; *United States Citations,* Case Edition; and *Shepard's Pacific Reporter Citations*)); The Lawyers Co-Operative Publishing Co./Bancroft-Whitney Co. (from volume 7 of *American Jurisprudence 2d*; *U. S. Supreme Court Digest, Lawyers' Edition;* \A. L. R. Blue Book of Supplemental Decisions; *ALR 2d and 3d Quick Index*)); Commerce Clearing House, Inc. (pages from *Poverty Law Reports*)); American Law Institute Publishers (from *Restatement (Second) of Torts* and Tentative Draft No. 4 of same); and West Publishing Co. (from volume 7 of *Corpus Juris Secundum; Washington Digest*; 238 South Eastern 2d advance sheet; *General Digest, Fifth Series; United States Code Annotated,* title 42).

M.D.R.

Seattle, Washington
April, 1978

ACKNOWLEDGMENTS

to

First Edition

Many former law students have worked with experimental versions of the various sections of this text and with sections which were abandoned. To them I must acknowledge my greatest debt, for their patience, their enthusiasms, their criticisms, and their numerous constructive suggestions. Particular thanks are due Rochelle K. Bancroft, Class of '72, University of Washington School of Law, for her critical appraisal of the final tentative version of this text.

Several faculty members have also worked with the various predecessor versions and contributed to the final text through criticisms and suggestions. Particular thanks are due Maurice E. Sutton, now a member of the firm of Jones, Grey, Kehoe, Bayley, Hooper & Olsen, Seattle, Washington, especially for the first draft of the suggestions that now comprise Section 7E, Oral Arguments, and to Virginia B. Lyness and Geoffrey Crooks, both now Assistant Professors, University of Washington School of Law, who have patiently suffered through use of some of my overly ambitious experimental versions.

I am also indebted to several other colleagues and former colleagues for their confidence, encouragement and advice, but particularly to Professor Lehan K. Tunks, who, both as Dean of the University of Washington School of Law and as a colleague, has been generous with time and encouragement, and to Professor Marian G. Gallagher, of the University of Washington School of Law, who has furnished inspiration both by instruction and example.

Finally, without the encouragement of my husband, Edgar R. Rombauer, attorney, this text surely never would have reached a final form.

One never knows where one's thoughts and words begin and others' leave off; I am no exception. Portions of this text undoubtedly reflect the influence of other texts which I used in teaching Legal Research and Writing courses in my early teaching years, particularly Professor Karl N. Llewellyn's classic, *The Bramble Bush;* Professor Edward D. Re's *Brief Writing and Oral Argument;* Professor Henry Weihofen's *Legal Writing Style,* and the definitive legal bibliography text, *Effective Legal Research,* by Professors Miles O. Price and Harry Bitner.

ACKNOWLEDGMENTS

I am grateful for permission to quote from the works of several authors: from a newspaper article on teaching methods by Professor Warren L. Shattuck; from *The Growth of American Law: The Law Makers,* by Professor James Willard Hurst, published by Little, Brown and Company, Copyright 1950 by James Willard Hurst; from "The Authority of Authority," by Professor John H. Merryman, which appeared in Volume 6 of the *Stanford Law Review* at page 613, Copyright 1954 by the Board of Trustees of the Leland Stanford Junior University; from *The Common Law Tradition: Deciding Appeals,* by Professor Karl N. Llewellyn, published by Little, Brown and Company, Copyright 1960 by Karl N. Llewellyn; from Comment, "Automated Legal Information Retrieval," which appeared in Volume 5 of the *Houston Law Review* at page 691, Copyright 1968 by the Houston Law Review, Inc.; and from Book Review, "A Uniform System of Citation," which appeared in Volume 67 of the *Columbia Law Review* at page 599, Copyright 1967 by the Directors of the Columbia Law Review Association, Inc.

MARJORIE DICK ROMBAUER

July, 1970

SUMMARY OF CONTENTS

SUMMARY OF CONTENTS

TABLE OF CONTENTS

PART II. PROBLEM ANALYSIS AND RESEARCH

TABLE OF CONTENTS

TABLE OF CONTENTS

APPENDICES

TABLE OF ILLUSTRATIONS

TABLE OF ILLUSTRATIONS

TABLE OF CASES

†

LEGAL PROBLEM SOLVING:

Analysis, Research and Writing

INTRODUCTION

This text is an introduction to a basic function of law-trained persons: solving legal problems. The problems with which lawyers must deal are infinitely varied, as are the possible solutions or answers, but many of the problems fall within one category: those requiring a reliable prediction of the probable legal consequences of a particular state of affairs. This text is primarily concerned with the skills required to work with this category of problems. Simplistically, reliable prediction requires identification of five problem elements (not necessarily in the order given): the raw facts, the law that may possibly control, the legal question or questions, the legally significant facts, and the law that will probably control. This text dissects the skills required to identify the last four elements and describes integrated use of these skills.

Part I of this text describes the basic skills required to identify the last three elements, assuming that the raw facts and the possibly controlling law have been identified. Developing these skills will be an objective of many of your law courses, even though a more obvious objective is to guide you toward knowledge and understanding of subject areas of law. The methods by which that law is taught, however, are designed to expose you to judges' and lawyers' use of these skills in solving problems and to give you seemingly endless opportunities to use them in answering isolated, sometimes microscopic, legal questions presented by given facts. For each course, the answers (or non-answers) to such questions should ultimately connect to give you an overview of the particular area of law, its background and development, its uncertainties, its strengths and weaknesses, and its possible and probable future. Incidentally, you will have begun to develop the skills described in Part I of this text. Thus Part I will supplement your other law courses by dissecting the skills learned from example and experience, with the ultimate objective of encouraging more refined and precise use of the skills.

Too frequently, law courses do not provide an opportunity for integrated use of the basic skills to solve complex legal problems. Therefore, Parts I and II of this text describe the interrelationship of these skills and their integrated use for such problem solving. Part

1

II of the text also describes the research materials and the research skills necessary to find the second problem-solving element, the possibly controlling law.

Finally, Part III describes specialized applications of communication skills.

This text is only incidentally concerned with the skills required to identify the first problem element, the raw facts (that is, the first collection of information about a problem). What happened will usually be tentatively determined through interviewing and investigating, skills that you may ultimately develop through experience, as well as through discovery proceedings, about which you will learn in a Civil Procedure course. If factual uncertainties are not thus eliminated, resort to court, administrative, arbitration, or other fact determination proceedings may be necessary. You will learn about methods used in such proceedings in Trial Practice, Evidence, Administrative Law, and other such courses. This is not to say that factual uncertainties are ignored in this text. One of the problem-solving skills that you must learn is the ability to work effectively within an elastic factual framework, that is, the ability to recognize when unknown facts are significant, when predictions are unreliable because they are based on factual assumptions or inferences, and when factual uncertainties are such that further work with a problem would probably be unproductive until additional information is obtained.

A prediction will not be sufficient to solve most problems. Once the probable legal consequences of a particular state of affairs are known, persons enmeshed in the problem must be advised how they can or should proceed. Advice must be communicated and implemented, which may require writing, drafting, counselling, negotiation, litigation, lobbying, or other activities. Some of the types of advice that may be given will necessarily be discussed or alluded to in this text; of the implementing activities, only writing and advocacy are discussed in detail.

Part I

INTERPRETING AND PREDICTING THE CONTROLLING LAW

Chapter 1

THE STARTING POINTS

SECTION 1A. OUR COURT SYSTEMS

Fifty-one systems operate within the United States, one system for each state and a system of federal courts that includes courts for the District of Columbia. Except under limited circumstances, each system is procedurally self-contained. The systems are somewhat similar in general structure and procedures, but variant names are sometimes attached to similar courts in the different systems.

The first court to which a legal dispute may be taken is called a court of original jurisdiction (a trial court). This may be a court of limited jurisdiction (for example, the federal court of claims or, in the state systems, justice court, traffic court, police court, family court) or a court of general jurisdiction (a court empowered to decide the bulk of disputes). In many states, as in Washington, the court of general original jurisdiction is called the superior court, but in New York, for example, it is called the supreme court; in Illinois, the circuit court; in Iowa, the district court. In the federal court system the general court of original jurisdiction is called the district court.[1]

---

1. C. Wright, Handbook of the Law of Federal Courts 7 (3d ed. 1976). Note that the federal district courts are said to be courts of limited jurisdiction in the sense that they can decide only such cases as are defined in congressional grants of jurisdiction and are within the federal judicial power as defined in the constitution. *Id.* at 17. They are general courts, however, in the sense that they hear the bulk of disputes arising within the federal jurisdiction.

Note that the word "jurisdiction" is used in two senses: to refer to what is here called a "court system" (e. g., the federal jurisdiction), and to refer to the power of a court or a court system to hear and decide particular disputes.

The party who loses in a trial court usually has a right to appeal to a higher court. Ordinarily the appeal or other request for review will be directed to an appellate court, whose function is to review the proceedings to determine whether the law has been correctly construed and applied. An appellate court does not receive evidence for the purpose of making factual determinations.[2] Within some state systems, however, the losing party in a trial before a court of limited jurisdiction may be required to appeal first to a court of general jurisdiction, where the party has the right to have the case completely retried, including the right to have the evidence heard again. This right to appeal both factual and legal determinations is called a right to a trial de novo. A party who loses after a trial de novo will then usually have the right to appeal to an appellate court. The appeal from a court of limited jurisdiction in other cases may be to some of the judges of the court of general original jurisdiction acting as appellate judges rather than as trial judges, as, for example, in the Appellate Term of the New York Supreme Court or the Appellate Departments of the California Superior Courts.

In about half the state court systems, the first and only review by an appellate court will be by the highest court within the state, usually called the supreme court (although in New York the highest court is called the court of appeals, and in Massachusetts, the supreme judicial court). In the federal system, although a decision of a district court may be reviewed directly by the highest court, the United States Supreme Court, more often it will be reviewed by the court of appeals of the appropriate circuit (a geographical subdivision of the United States), whose decision will be reviewed by the United States Supreme Court in only a very limited number of cases. Some states similarly have intermediate appellate courts, usually also called courts of appeal. (Again, however, there are name variations. In New York, for example, the intermediate court is called the appellate division, with four co-equal departments; in Maryland, it is called the court of special appeals.) A case commenced in a state court that presents a federal question may be reviewed by the United States Supreme Court under limited circumstances, but state appellate courts do not review federal court decisions, not even those decisions based on state law.[3]

---

2. Appellate courts also generally have some limited original jurisdiction, and evidence may be received in the exercise of that jurisdiction. For example, the Federal Constitution provides that the United States Supreme Court shall have original jurisdiction in cases in which a state is a party. U.S. Const. art. 3, § 2, cl. 2.

3. Under a procedure adopted by a few states in recent years, a federal court may certify to the highest court in the state a legal question presented in a pending case that is to be resolved under the law of that state, but this is still a comparatively new and unusual procedure. The usefulness of such a procedure is discussed in McKusick, *Certification: A Procedure for Cooperation Between State and Federal Courts*, 16 Maine L.Rev. 33 (1964).

SECTION 1B. OUR FORMS OF LAW

For purposes of this text, the law of the United States is classified by form as either precedent or written law. The precedent category includes all decisions in individual cases that may serve as authority for decisions in future cases. We will be primarily concerned with judicial precedents, that is, decisions of courts, but decisions of administrative officials and bodies acting in a quasi-judicial capacity to decide individual cases may also sometimes be precedents. The written law category includes, among other sources, constitutions and charters, legislation such as statutes and ordinances, administrative rules and regulations, executive orders, and court rules.

Many of our judicial precedents derive their significance from that portion of our legal system known as the common law system. Under this system, law is created by courts in the process of deciding disputes that are brought before them, because each decision becomes a precedent for the guidance of courts in deciding future similar cases. Simplistically,[4] the method works like this: Given a determination of the facts in a dispute, assuming no controlling written law, a court decides the case on the basis of what it believes the law is or should be. In determining what the law is or should be, it looks first to prior decisions resolving similar or analogous disputes and seeks to apply the underlying rules or principles that appear to have been established by those decisions. If the facts presented to the court include the same significant facts as appeared in a previously decided case, without additional facts that could be regarded as significant, the court frequently will bow to the authority of the decision in the prior case and follow it, reaching the same result in the pending case. In fact, under the doctrine of *stare decisis*, an appellate court will usually follow its prior decisions unless substantial considerations dictate a different result, while a subordinate court (for example, a trial court or an intermediate appellate court) is expected to follow the decisions of courts to which it is subordinate. If no prior decided case presented the same significant facts, the court will consider whether any prior decided case nevertheless has sufficient elements in common with the pending dispute to require or justify application of a rule or principle derivable from or underlying the decision in such prior case.

Even though a case before a court is clearly governed by written law, the court may nevertheless look to judicial precedents. Prior decisions may already have resolved questions about the meaning of the particular law or, if not, they may nevertheless furnish guidance in

---

4. How simplified this description is will become apparent to you when you read Chapter 2. Be certain that you understand the simplified explanations in this chapter, however, before you read on to learn about the ramifications.

determining what approach should be taken in determining its meaning.

The interrelations of our basic sources of written law and the common law decisional method have been described by one of our best-known jurists of the twentieth century, Benjamin Cardozo, who was briefly a New York trial court judge, then a member of the New York Court of Appeals, and finally a Justice of the United States Supreme Court:

> Our first inquiry should * * * be: Where does the judge find the law which he embodies in his judgment [decision]? There are times when the source is obvious. The rule that fits the case may be supplied by the constitution or by statute. If that is so, the judge looks no farther. The correspondence ascertained, his duty is to obey. The constitution overrides a statute, but a statute, if consistent with the constitution, overrides the law of judges. In this sense, judge-made law is secondary and subordinate to the law that is made by legislators. It is true that codes and statutes do not render the judge superfluous, nor his work perfunctory and mechanical. There are gaps to be filled. There are doubts and ambiguities to be cleared. * * *

> We reach the land of mystery when constitution and statute are silent, and the judge must look to the common law for the rule that fits the case. * * * The first thing he does is to compare the case before him with the precedents, whether stored in his mind or hidden in the books. * * * [I]n a system so highly developed as our own, precedents have so covered the ground that they fix the point of departure from which the labor of the judge begins. Almost invariably his first step is to examine and compare them. If they are plain and to the point, there may be need of nothing more. *Stare decisis* is at least the everyday working rule of our law. I shall have something to say later about the propriety of relaxing the rule in exceptional conditions. But unless these conditions are present, the work of deciding cases in accordance with precedents that plainly fit them is a process similar in its nature to that of deciding cases in accordance with a statute. It is a process of search, comparison, and little more. * * * It is when the colors do not match, when the references in the index fail, when there is no decisive precedent, that the serious business of the judge begins. He must then fashion law for the litigants before him. In fashioning it for them, he will be fashioning it for others.

> * * *

[T]he problem which confronts the judge is in reality a twofold one: he must first extract from the precedents the underlying principle, the *ratio decidendi*; he must then determine the path or direction along which the principle is to move and develop, if it is not to wither and die.

The first branch of the problem is the one to which we are accustomed to address ourselves more consciously than to the other. Cases do not unfold their principles for the asking. They yield up their kernel slowly and painfully. * * * Let us assume, however, that this task has been achieved, and that the precedent is known as it really is. * * * The problem remains to fix the bounds and the tendencies of development and growth, to set the directive force in motion along the right path at the parting of the ways.[5]

SECTION 1C. BASIC SKILLS REQUIRED TO WORK WITH JUDICIAL PRECEDENTS

Justice Cardozo has described generally how judges (and, hence, legal problem solvers) work with precedents. More specifically, your work with judicial precedents in problem solving will initially require use of three basic skills: analysis, evaluation, and synthesis.

Getting from the initial collection of information about a problem to a reliable prediction of the probable legal consequences first requires finding sources of law that may *possibly* control resolution of the problem. Such sources will frequently include precedents requiring interpretation. Interpretation of precedents requires, for the most part, analysis of reported appellate court opinions.[6]

Appellate courts usually report their decisions in opinions that explain how and why the particular decision was reached. Opinions of appellate courts in this country are usually printed, and it is these opinions that represent the influential precedents within our legal system. Trial courts may also write opinions for litigants who appear before them, but unless the decisions or opinions are generally reported (that is, regularly published for general distribution), they are rarely of any influence beyond the court from which they issue. Even when trial court opinions are generally reported, they will

---

5. From B. Cardozo, The Nature of the Judicial Process 14, 18–21, 28–30 (1921), copyright 1921 by Yale University Press, copyright renewed 1949. Reproduced with permission of the copyright owner.

6. The three words, "opinion," "decision," and "case," are sometimes used interchangeably to refer to precedents.

In this text, the three words are used in the following senses:

case—a dispute that has been taken before a court for resolution

decision—the result reached by a court in resolving a case before it

opinion—the official written statement of a case, the court's decision, and reasons for reaching its decision

usually have less authority value (that is, will be less persuasive) than opinions of appellate courts.

Analysis of appellate court opinions requires identification of their most important parts. Ideally, an opinion would contain at least five well-defined parts:

First, a statement of the significant facts of the dispute before the court—the facts that are necessary to an understanding of the dispute and of the court's decision, those that influenced the court's reasoning and decision.

Second, a statement of the relevant procedural details. This would include an explanation of the legal nature of the controversy and of the remedy sought (for example, an action for damages for breach of contract, an action for damages suffered as a result of defendant's negligence, a criminal prosecution for arson) and of the relevant procedural actions taken in the lower court (usually this would include only actions and rulings of the lower court that are alleged to have been erroneous and an indication of who prevailed in the lower court and at what point in the proceedings). For convenience, though it stretches the meaning of "procedure," the lower court's reasons for deciding as it did and the contentions of opposing counsel on appeal may be regarded as "relevant procedural details."

Third, a statement of the narrow legal question(s) or issue(s) that the appellate court was asked to resolve. If not expressly stated, the questions are frequently identifiable from the court's summary of why the lower court decided as it did or from the contentions of opposing counsel.

Fourth, a brief statement of the appellate court's decision, both procedural (for example, judgment for plaintiff is affirmed) and substantive (a "yes" or "no" answer for each question).

Fifth, an explanation of the court's reasoning in reaching its decision. This explanation might include what is sometimes treated as a sixth important part of an opinion: a statement of a general principle or rule assumed or found to preexist from which the court reasoned or a statement of the narrow rule that the court applied or developed in reaching its decision.

Unfortunately, courts may not only omit one or more of the ideal parts from their opinions, but they may also include statements not directly related to the questions that the court has been asked to resolve. Such extraneous statements are called "dicta" (plural) or "a dictum" (singular). For these and other reasons, analyzing opinions

to understand them and to determine their probable relevance may present a substantial intellectual challenge.

The prediction element of problem solving requires more than analysis of possibly controlling precedents, however. Having reached the point of believing that you understand how and why a court decided a case as it did, you must then sit in critical judgment on the court's conclusion and reasoning: you must evaluate the opinion. Recall that courts do not automatically follow precedents. Even under the stare decisis doctrine, a court may refuse to follow its prior decisions (assuming that to do so would not be inconsistent with precedents of a higher court) if other substantial considerations support a different result. A court not only may decline to follow a prior decision, it may also overrule it, that is, indicate its intent not to follow it in a particular case and in future cases. Therefore, prediction as to the *probably* controlling law requires an evaluation of clearly relevant precedents to determine whether they will be followed.

Factors that may prompt a court to refuse to follow a precedent will be discussed in detail later. For the present, it is sufficient to identify some of the questions that you might ask in evaluating an opinion: Is the result fair, just? Was there a better solution logically open to the court? Has the court adequately dealt with relevant precedents? Has the court expressed valid reasons for its conclusions? Is the court's reasoning consistent, logical? Is the court's solution of the problem practical, that is, will it work in actual practice? Has the court truly faced and decided the questions presented? In your early opinion reading you may tend to accept uncritically what courts write in opinions. You will find, however, that you will begin to have instinctive critical reactions as your knowledge and experience in opinion analysis grow.

You must also synthesize relevant opinions. In our problem-solving activities, we are rarely blessed with a single controlling precedent. Our legal system has generated precedents on infinite variations of factual patterns as well as inconsistent precedents for the same or similar factual patterns. Hence you cannot think in terms of reliance on a single precedent, but must be prepared to deal with multiple precedents that have relevance for a particular problem. The process of relating and combining relevant precedents is called synthesis. In synthesizing precedents you must first determine whether relevant decided cases were factually similar and whether they presented the same legal questions. If the facts were similar and the same questions were presented in the precedent cases, you must decide whether the decisions are consistent with each other. If they are consistent, should you formulate a synthesized rule that is broader or narrower than those you have concluded underlies decision of the individual cases? If two or more opinions appear to be incon-

sistent, you must return to the evaluative process and decide which one represents the better or more persuasive solution of the common problem (logically, practically, equitably).

At some point in the process of identifying the possibly controlling law and predicting the probably controlling law for a particular problem, you will have to identify the legal question or questions presented and the significant facts for the problem. As may already be apparent, your identification of significant facts and legal questions in the analysis of relevant opinions will help you to identify these elements in your problem.

SECTION 1D. "BRIEFING" OPINIONS

In most law schools in the United States, the "case method" of instruction is used for at least part of the first year of studies. Under this method, the basic course book collects excerpts from court opinions and other materials intended to lead students to their own conclusions as to the status of the law in the subject area and to an understanding of the background and possible future of the law in that area. Class preparation consists, to a great extent, of reading and analyzing, evaluating, and synthesizing the materials that appear in the course book. Law students customarily write out their analysis of an opinion in a summary form called a "brief" or a "digest" or an "abstract." The opinion brief (to be distinguished from the argumentative brief prepared for a court) serves as a handy record of opinion analysis for class reference and for subsequent review. Furthermore, writing out an analysis in some organized form is frequently a necessary step to understanding complex cases or reasoning. For many students, opinion briefing is also an important form of writing experience, a means of learning how to write their thoughts concisely and precisely and how to use their expanding legal language.

Opinion briefing is more than a type of study exercise, however, since one prepares a brief whenever one needs a written summary of opinion analysis for future reference. Attorneys write opinion briefs whenever they research a problem, unless it is a very simple problem.

There is no standard form for an opinion brief. A good starting form is the outline suggested by the parts of an opinion described in the preceding section, but the contents of an opinion brief will vary with the reasons for preparing it. More precisely, the reasons for reading and analyzing an opinion will dictate what you will be looking for and, hence, what you will want to record.

The ultimate reason for analyzing opinions is to be able to predict, on the basis of what courts have done in past cases, what a court will do in a current or future case. In analyzing for reasons of prediction, attention is focused on relating the contents of a particu-

lar opinion to a current problem. Are the facts the same or similar?
Are the questions presented the same or similar? Is the court's reasoning relevant to the current problem? For law study, on the other
hand, opinions are usually analyzed in the abstract, that is, without
reference to a particular problem. Objectives of analysis in the abstract include: (1) developing instinctive analytical and evaluative
reactions; (2) developing the ability to pinpoint legal questions; (3)
learning relevant considerations and the types of reasoning that are
persuasive to courts; (4) identifying past legal questions and how
courts have answered them; (5) gaining knowledge of "existing" law
(that is, currently recognized rules and principles, the reasons underlying their development, and the types of factual situations in which
they have been applied); and (6) identifying unsettled areas of law.
In the following chapters, discussion is primarily oriented toward
analysis and briefing in a problem-solving setting rather than in a
class-study setting. Your attention will be called to a few significant
variations in approach for the two settings.

NOTES

1. Some immediate knowledge of opinion reporting systems is
useful to permit you to begin translating opinion citations.

Until the beginning of the nineteenth century, the decisions of
appellate courts in this country were not generally published. Thereafter, private individuals and companies sometimes undertook to publish reports for individual courts. The need for authoritative reports soon became apparent. Some state legislatures authorized ap-
pointment of suitable official reporters to perform the reporting task.
Whether official or unofficial, the early reports were published under
the reporters' names, as was the custom in England. Each time the
reporter changed, the name of the set of reports changed. Thus, for
example, early Massachusetts court opinions were successively reported in Pickering (Pick.), Metcalf, Cushing (Cush.), Gray, and Allen.
These "nominative reports" were common until about 1840, when state
legislatures began authorizing publication of official reports under
their state names. By the late nineteenth century, official reports
for at least the highest court in each state were being published under the state names.

The history of federal court reporting is somewhat similar to
that of the state reports. The history of both is detailed in F. Hicks,
Materials and Methods of Legal Research ch. 5 (1923).

2. By 1887, the West Publishing Company had undertaken to
publish, in the National Reporter System, the opinions of all the
highest appellate courts, state and federal, and the opinions of some
intermediate appellate and trial courts as well. The National Reporter System now consists of thirteen units—four federal units, two
state units (the *California Reporter* and the *New York Supplement*)

and seven state-regional units. A state-regional unit reports the opinions of the courts of several states. For example, the *Northeastern Reporter* (N.E., N.E.2d) unit reports the opinions of courts in Illinois, Indiana, Ohio, New York, and Massachusetts. The other regional units are *Atlantic* (A., A.2d), *Northwestern* (N.W., N.W.2d), *Pacific* (P., P.2d), *Southeastern* (S.E., S.E.2d), *Southern* (So., So.2d), and *Southwestern* (S.W., S.W.2d). (Appearance of "2d" in the citation abbreviations parenthetically provided indicates a second series, not a second edition, though this is not necessarily true for citation abbreviations for other than opinion reports. A second edition replaces the former edition, but a second or third series usually continues from the time the preceding series left off, the appearance of a new series merely signalling some change in form or supplementary aids.) The volumes of the National Reporter System are usually the most prominent set of books in law library reading rooms, because they are generally shelved in the most accessible area, and the large number of similarly bound volumes in the system makes them almost impossible to overlook. Early state court report volumes may not be so immediately accessible.

3. The source or sources to which you will be cited for a state court opinion will depend to some extent on the date an opinion was handed down. The earliest state court opinions will usually be cited to nominative reports (for example, 2 Pick. 788). Some later nineteenth century state court opinions, those which pre-date the National Reporter System, will usually be cited only to official reports, identifiable by use of abbreviations for the state names (for example, 78 Ind. 225). Some recent state court opinions will be cited only to the National Reporter System, because beginning in the mid-1950's some states have stopped publishing official reports. Opinions that appear in both an official report and in the National Reporter System should be cited to both, with the year of decision as follows: Citizens' Loan, Fund & Savings Ass'n v. Friedley, 123 Ind. 143, 23 N.E. 1075 (1890). You will discover, however, that different courts and publishers have their own variant citation forms, including omission of the year of decision. When the year is omitted from opinion citations in sources that you use, you will nevertheless be able to identify the very old opinions from the information given in this text note and in text note 1, *supra*.

The most comprehensive guide for citation rules, forms, and abbreviations is A Uniform System of Citation (12th ed. 1976), commonly called the "Blue Book," published and distributed by the Harvard Law Review Association. This citation *Blue Book*, pages 100–42, also provides information about the names, levels, and opinion reports of federal courts and state appellate courts.

4. Primary authority (written law or precedents) may be only the starting authority on which a court relies. A wide variety of sec-

ondary material is also cited and discussed in judicial opinions. Three basic categories with which you should immediately become familiar are texts and treatises, Restatements of the Law, and law reviews (or law journals).

Treatises and texts cover one area or topic of law. They summarize principles, rules, and reasoning on which courts have relied, based on written law and on a synthesis of a large number of the reported opinions dealing with the topic. They may also contain critical and predictive commentary and suggested analyses of problems not yet considered in reported opinions. An example of a treatise is W. Jaeger, Williston on Contracts (3d ed. 1957) a multivolume treatise. An example of a student text is J. Calamari & J. Perillo, The Law of Contracts (2d ed. 1977). Student texts are, of necessity, less comprehensive than most treatises. An example of a student text that has acquired the reputation of a treatise, however, is W. Prosser, Handbook of the Law of Torts (4th ed. 1971).

A Restatement is similarly limited in coverage to a single area or topic of law. Several Restatements are currently in use. All are the product of intensive joint study by legal scholars, judges, and practitioners. Each includes rules stated in bold face type (commonly called "black-letter rules"), explanatory comments, and illustrative problems to which the rules should or should not be applied. To a very large extent, the black-letter rules have been synthesized from opinions of courts throughout the United States. An excellent example is the *Restatement of Contracts*, now being revised as *Restatement (Second) of Contracts*.

Law reviews are legal periodicals published by law schools, edited by law students. They contain articles written by legal scholars, judges, and practitioners and a large amount of material written by law students.

These and other secondary authorities will be discussed in detail in Part II. You can begin your acquaintance with these important secondary materials now by examining a volume of a treatise and a Restatement cited to you in one of your law courses and a copy of a law review or journal, particularly one published by your school.

5. A legal dictionary is a necessity. Particularly in early opinion reading you may be puzzled by many words that appear to have (and frequently do have) a technical legal meaning. A dictionary may give you at least a general meaning for such words. Modern comprehensive legal dictionaries are Ballentine's Law Dictionary (3d ed. 1969) (with pronunciations) and Black's Law Dictionary (Rev. 4th ed. 1968) (with a guide to pronunciations). Copies of one or both of these dictionaries are generally conveniently available in law libraries.

6. Several legal questions are usually presented in cases on appeal. In most course books, however, only excerpts from opinions

are printed, frequently to report the part dealing with only one legal question. To get some idea of the extent to which course book authors may have thus simplified opinion analysis for you, look at the full opinions for two or three edited opinions included in one or more of your course books.

7. On following pages are two appellate court opinions, reproduced exactly as reported in National Reporter volumes. The first opinion, *Citizens' Loan Fund & Savings Ass'n v. Friedley,* is reproduced from an early volume of the *Northeastern Reporter,* 23 N.E. 1075. The second opinion, *Hodges v. Carter,* is reproduced from a more recent volume of the *Southeastern Reporter,* 80 S.E.2d 144. Note common features of reported opinions as illustrated in these reproductions:

(a) *Case name.* Note that only one of multiple defendants is named in both opinions, as evidenced by use of *et al.* (an abbreviation of *et alius,* meaning "and another," or *et alii,* meaning "and others").

(b) *Name of the reviewing court and date the opinion was released.*

(c) *Headnotes.* The small-print paragraph that precedes the first opinion and the numbered paragraphs that precede the second opinion are called headnotes. Written by reporters or employees of publishers, headnotes cannot be relied on to accurately state the courts' decisions. They are merely handy research aids, useful for quick preliminary scanning of opinions and for indexing. The classification lines and numbers following the headnote numbers in the second opinion are part of a comprehensive indexing system for all published opinions of courts in the United States, both federal and state. This indexing system, called the Key Number System, is described in Chapter 7. If identified as a "Syllabus by the Court," however, meaning that they were written by the court, the summaries may have some authority value. *See, e. g.,* Baltimore & O. R. Co. v. Baillie, 112 Ohio St. 567, 148 N.E. 233 (1925) ("The syllabus of a case definitely states the law with reference to the facts upon which it is predicated * * *" 148 N.E. at 234); Note, *Trial Practice: Legal Effect of the Syllabus by the Court in Oklahoma,* 7 Okla.L.Rev. 116 (1954).

(d) *Name of the lower court whose decision is being reviewed.*

(e) *Concise summary of the case and of the ultimate procedural decision.* The concise summary does not appear in the very early National Reporter volumes (for example,

for the first opinion reproduced hereafter). The feature has been expanded in more recent National Reporter volumes.

(f) *Names of the parties' attorneys.*

(g) *Name of the judge who authored the opinion.*

Modern report and reporter volumes include additional features that will be noted hereafter.

FIRST SUGGESTED EXERCISE

Immediately following the first reproduced opinion is a sample brief thereof.[7] Before looking at the sample, read and analyze the first opinion carefully and prepare your own brief for critical comparison with the sample. Then analyze the second opinion and prepare a brief for it. Use a legal dictionary to determine the general meaning of any words with which you are unfamiliar. You may find that the description in this chapter of what you should look for in analyzing and briefing opinions is so general that you have questions about how to proceed. Nevertheless, you will be able to read the following chapter with more appreciation and understanding if you follow the procedure here suggested, because you will have specific questions for which you want to find answers.

This exercise is the first of five related exercises suggested in this and the following chapter. The exercises are designed to permit you to test your understanding of the descriptions of the basic skills set forth in these two chapters and to introduce you, in manageable units, to written report of your opinion analysis, synthesis, and evaluation.

(a) CITIZENS' LOAN, FUND & SAVINGS ASS'N OF BLOOMINGTON v. FRIEDLEY *et al.*

(b) (*Supreme Court of Indiana.* April 5, 1890.)

ATTORNEY—ERRONEOUS ADVICE.

(c) Before the supreme court of Indiana had decided that a mortgage executed by husband and wife on land held by them as tenants by entireties is void as to both of them, an attorney advised his client that such a mortgage was good. *Held* not such a mistake as would render the attorney responsible.

(d) Appeal from circuit court, Lawrence county; E. D. PEARSON, Judge.

(f) *Louden & Rogers,* for appellant. *Buskirk & Duncan,* for appellees.

(g) MITCHELL, C. J. This suit was instituted by the Citizens' Loan, Fund & Savings Association against Harmon H. Friedley, and the sureties on his bond, to recover money alleged to have been lost to the loan association on account of the negligence and want of skill of the defendant Friedley while acting as the attorney of the association. It is averred that the association made a loan of $400 to one of its shareholders in August, 1883, upon the faith of advice given by the appellee, its attorney, who certified to its officers, in writing, that the title to certain real estate, upon which the applicant for the loan proposed to execute a mortgage as security therefor, was perfect, and available to secure the loan applied for. It appears that the real estate was owned by the applicant and his wife as tenants by

---

7. The sample brief is longer than a brief prepared for class purposes might be. It has been prepared to illustrate the type of brief prepared for research-related purposes (for example, by including the *Dodge* citation) and to illustrate clearly the "parts" of an opinion as described in this chapter. Refinements will be suggested in Section 2D, *infra.* The "Rule of the Case" section of the sample will be explained in Section 2D also.

the entireties; that the loan was made in reliance upon the advice of the attorney; that the borrower subsequently died, his estate being insolvent; and that his widow successfully resisted a suit for the foreclosure of the mortgage subsequently brought by the association, her defense having been predicated upon the ground that she signed the note and mortgage merely as the surety for her husband.

It is insisted that the complaint shows that the association sustained loss in consequence of the ignorance, carelessness, or unskillfulness of its attorney, and that the latter, with his sureties, must therefore respond to it in damages for the amount lost. No neglect or want of skill appears, except that the attorney was mistaken as to the law applicable to the state of the title of the borrower, and its availability as a security for the loan. Attorneys are very properly held to the same rule of liability for want of professional skill and diligence in practice, and for erroneous or negligent advice to those who employ them, as are physicians and surgeons, and other persons who hold themselves out to the world as possessing skill and qualification in their respective trades or professions. Waugh v. Shunk, 20 Pa. St. 130. The practice of law is not merely an art. It is a science which demands from all who engage in it, without detriment to the public, special qualifications, which can only be attained by careful preliminary study and training, and by constant and unremitting investigation and research. But, as the law is not an exact science there is no attainable degree of skill or excellence at which all differences of opinion or doubts in respect to questions of law are removed from the minds of lawyers and judges. Absolute certainty is not always possible. "That part of the profession," said Lord MANSFIELD, in Pitt v. Yalden, 4 Burrows, 2060, "which is carried on by attorneys, is liberal and reputable, as well as useful to the public, when they conduct themselves with honor and integrity; and they ought to be protected where they act to the best of their skill and knowledge. But every man is liable to error; and I should be very sorry that it should be taken for granted that an attorney is answerable for every error or mistake, and to be punished for it by being charged with the debt which he has employed to recover for his client." Watson v. Muirhead, 57 Pa. St. 161; Mortgage Co. v. Henderson, 111 Ind. 24, 34, 12 N. E. Rep. 88. An attorney who undertakes the management of business committed to his charge thereby impliedly represents that he possesses the skill, and that he will exhibit the diligence, ordinarily possessed and employed by well-informed members of his profession in the conduct of business such as he has undertaken. He will be liable if his client's interests suffer on account of his failure to understand and apply those rules and principles of law that are well established and clearly defined in the elementary books, or which have been declared in adjudged cases that have been duly reported, and published a sufficient length of time to have become known to those who exercise reasonable diligence in keeping pace with the literature of the profession. Hillegass v. Bender, 78 Ind. 225, and cases cited; Pennington v. Yell, 11 Ark. 212; Goodman v. Walker, 30 Ala. 482; Weeks, Attys, §§ 284–289; Fenaille v. Coudert, 44 N. J. Law, 286; Gambert v. Hart, 44 Cal. 553. Thus, it has been said: "An attorney is liable for the consequences of his ignorance or non-observance of the rules of practice of the court he practices in,—for the want of care in the preparation of a cause for trial; while, on the other hand, he is not answerable for an error in judgment upon points of new occurrence, or of nice or doubtful construction." Chit. Cont. 482; Godefroy v. Dalton, 6 Bing. 460; Dearborn v. Dearborn, 15 Mass. 316. It is his own fault, however, if he undertakes without knowing what he needs only to use diligence to find out, or applies less than the occasion requires. A lawyer is without excuse who is ignorant of the ordinary settled rules of pleading and practice, and of the statutes and published decisions in his own state; but he is not to be charged with negligence when he accepts as a correct exposition of the law a decision of the supreme court of his own state; nor can he be held liable for a mistake in reference to a matter in which members of the profession possessed of reasonable skill and knowledge may differ as to the law, until it has been settled in the courts, nor if he is mistaken in a point of law on which reasonable doubt may be entertained by well-informed lawyers. Marsh v. Whitmore, 21 Wall. 178; Kemp v. Burt, 1 Nev. & M. 262.

Now, while it is quite true that section 5119, Rev. St. 1881, which took effect September 19, 1881, prohibited a married woman from entering into any contract of suretyship, and declared all such contracts void as to her, and while it had been thoroughly settled that a married woman who had joined in a mortgage of her separate property to secure the debt of her husband was to be regarded as his surety, (Leary v. Shaffer, 79 Ind. 567,) it had never been held, prior to the 23d day of January, 1884, when the judgment in Dodge v. Kinzy, 101 Ind. 102, was pronounced, that a mortgage executed by a husband and wife on lands held by them as tenants by entireties was void as to both of them. It cannot fairly be said, therefore, that, before the decision in Dodge v. Kinzy, supra, was made and promulgated, so as to have become known by those reasonably diligent in the profession, it was such a mistake to advise that a husband and wife might secure a debt of the former on his estate in lands held by himself and wife as tenants by the entireties as could only have resulted from the want of ordinary knowledge and skill, or from the failure to exercise reasonable care and caution. The error must be regarded as one into which any reasonably careful and prudent lawyer might have fallen, and therefore one for which the attorney was not liable. The judgment is affirmed, with costs.

———

SAMPLE BRIEF

<u>Citizens' Loan, Fund & Savings Ass'n v. Friedley</u>
(Ind. 1890)

Facts: It was averred that P loaned money to a man on the faith of D-
             attorney's advice that a husband and wife could give a mortgage on
             his estate in land that they owned as tenants by the entireties.
             Five months later the court held that a similar mortgage was void
             as to both husband and wife, in <u>Dodge v. Kinzy</u>, 101 Ind. 102. P's
             mortgage foreclosure action was defeated on the wife's defense
             that she had signed the mortgage as a surety.

Procedure: Action for damages for loss resulting from D's negligence and want
             of skill. J/D. P contended its complaint showed it suffered loss
             because of D's ignorance, carelessness, or unskillfulness.

Issues: (1) Was D-attorney's mistaken advice on a question not yet de-
             cided by the controlling court but subsequently decided adversely
             such as might be found to have resulted from want of ordinary
             knowledge and skill or from failure to exercise reasonable care?
             (2) Was the question one on which well-informed attorneys of
             reasonable diligence would have differed or had doubt?

Decision: (1) No, as limited by: (2) implicit finding that the law on the
             point was in doubt. J/D/Aff'd

Reasoning: <u>Principle stated</u>: An attorney impliedly represents that he pos-
             sesses the skill of and will exercise the diligence ordinarily
             possessed and exercised by well-informed attorneys in business of
             the character that he undertakes. <u>General rule stated</u>: An attor-
             ney will be liable for loss caused by failure to understand and
             apply rules and principles declared in statutes and decisions in
             his own state, published long enough to become known to attorneys
             who exercise reasonable diligence. <u>Dicta?</u>: An attorney may be
             liable for failure to understand and apply well-established rules
             and principles that are defined in elementary books and for ig-
             norance or non-observance of rules of pleading and practice of the
             court in which he practices, but will not be liable if he relies
             on a decision of the supreme court of his state.
                 The court reviewed the pre-<u>Dodge</u> law and concluded that al-
             though a statute prohibited a married woman from entering into con-
             tracts of suretyship and a court decision had settled that a mar-
             ried woman who mortgaged her separate property to secure a debt of
             her husband would be regarded as a surety, the Indiana court had
             not previously decided the point of law as to which D was mistaken.
             Therefore, the rule could not have become known to a reasonably
             diligent attorney.

<u>Rule of the case</u>: <u>An attorney will not be held liable for a mistake on a</u>
                     <u>point of law on which attorneys of reasonable skill and knowledge</u>
                     <u>may differ before it has been decided by the courts of his/her</u>
                     <u>state.</u>

(c) **1. Attorney and Client ☞107**

An attorney, who engages in the practice of law and contracts to prosecute an action in behalf of his client, impliedly represents that he possesses the requisite degree of learning, skill, and ability necessary to practice of his profession and which others similarly situated ordinarily possess, that he will exercise his best judgment in the prosecution of the litigation entrusted to him, and that he will exercise reasonable and ordinary care and diligence in the use of his skill and in the application of his knowledge to his client's cause.

2. Attorney and Client ☞109

An attorney who acts in good faith and in an honest belief that his advice and acts are well founded and in the best interest of his client is not answerable for a mere error of judgment or for a mistake in a point of law which has not been settled by the court of last resort in his state and on which reasonable doubt may be entertained by well-informed lawyers.

3. Attorney and Client ☞129(2)

In action by insured to recover compensation for losses resulting from alleged negligence in prosecuting insured's claims against insurers, evidence did not disclose breach of duty. G.S. § 58–153.

———◆———

239 N.C. 517

(a)   **HODGES v. CARTER et al.**
No. 21.

(b)   Supreme Court of North Carolina.
Feb. 24, 1954.

(e)   Action by insured to recover compensation for losses resulting from alleged negligence in prosecuting insured's claim against insurers. The Superior Court,
(d) Beaufort County, Chester R. Morris, J., entered judgment of involuntary nonsuit and insured appealed. The Supreme Court, Barnhill, C. J., held that no breach of duty was shown by the evidence.

Affirmed.

Civil action to recover compensation for losses resulting from the alleged negligence of defendant D. D. Topping and H. C. Carter, now deceased, in prosecuting, on behalf of plaintiff, certain actions on fire insurance policies.

On 4 June 1948 plaintiff's drug store building located in Belhaven, N. C., together with his lunch counter, fixtures, stock of drugs and sundries therein contained, was destroyed by fire. At the time plaintiff was insured under four policies of fire insurance against loss of, or damage to, said mercantile building and its contents. He filed proof of loss with each of the four insurance companies which issued said pol-

icies. The insurance companies severally rejected the proofs of loss, denied liability, and declined to pay any part of the plaintiff's losses resulting from said fire.

H. C. Carter and D. D. Topping were at the time attorneys practicing in Beaufort and adjoining counties. As they were the ones from whom plaintiff seeks to recover, they will hereafter be referred to as the defendants.

On 7 April 1949 plaintiff entered into a written contract of employment with defendants to prosecute an action against each of the insurers on the policy issued by it. The compensation to be paid was fixed on a contingent basis and defendants bound themselves "to do whatever may be necessary in order to bring the matters to a successful conclusion, to the best of their knowledge and ability."

On 3 May 1949 defendants, in behalf of plaintiff, instituted in the Superior Court of Beaufort County four separate actions —one against each of the four insurers. Complaints were filed and summonses were issued, directed to the sheriff of Beaufort County. In each case the summons and complaint, together with copies thereof, were mailed to the Commissioner of Insurance of the State of North Carolina. The Commissioner accepted service of summons and complaint in each case and forwarded a copy thereof by registered mail to the insurance company named defendant therein.

Thereafter each defendant made a special appearance and moved to dismiss the action against it for want of proper service of process for that the Insurance Commissioner was without authority, statutory or otherwise, to accept service of process issued against a foreign insurance company doing business in this State. When the special appearance and motion to dismiss came on for hearing at the February Term 1950, the judge presiding concluded that the acceptance of service of process by the Insurance Commissioner was valid

and served to subject the movants to the jurisdiction of the court. Judgment was entered in each case denying the motion therein made. Each defendant excepted and appealed. This Court reversed. Hodges v. New Hampshire Fire Insurance Co., 232 N.C. 475, 61 S.E.2d 372. See also Hodges v. Home Insurance Co., 233 N.C. 289, 63 S.E.2d 819.

On 4 March 1952 plaintiff instituted this action in which he alleges that the defendants were negligent in prosecuting his said actions in that they failed to (1) have process properly served, and (2) sue out alias summonses at the time the insurers filed their motions to dismiss the actions for want of proper service of summons, although they then had approximately sixty days within which to procure the issuance thereof.

Defendants, answering, deny negligence and plead good faith and the exercise of their best judgment.

At the hearing in the court below the judge, at the conclusion of plaintiff's evidence in chief, entered judgment of involuntary nonsuit. Plaintiff excepted and appealed.

(f) Allen, Allen & Langley, Kinston, for plaintiff-appellant.

Grimes & Grimes, Rodman & Rodman, and L. H. Ross, Washington, for defendant appellees.

(g) BARNHILL, Chief Justice.

This seems to be a case of first impression in this jurisdiction. At least counsel have not directed our attention to any other decision of this Court on the question here presented, and we have found none.

[1] Ordinarily when an attorney engages in the practice of the law and contracts to prosecute an action in behalf of his client, he impliedly represents that (1) he possesses the requisite degree of learn-

ing, skill, and ability necessary to the practice of his profession and which others similarly situated ordinarily possess; (2) he will exert his best judgment in the prosecution of the litigation entrusted to him; and (3) he will exercise reasonable and ordinary care and diligence in the use of his skill and in the application of his knowledge to his client's cause. McCullough v. Sullivan, 102 N.J.L. 381, 132 A. 102, 43 A.L.R. 928; In re Woods, 158 Tenn. 383, 13 S.W.2d 800, 62 A.L.R. 904; Great American Indemnity Co. v. Dabney, Tex. Civ.App., 128 S.W.2d 496; Davis v. Associated Indemnity Corp., D.C., 56 F.Supp. 541; Gimbel v. Waldman, 193 Misc. 758, 84 N.Y.S.2d 888; Annotation 52 L.R.A. 883; 5 A.J. 287, § 47; Prosser Torts, p. 236, sec. 36; Shearman & Redfield Negligence, sec. 569.

[2] An attorney who acts in good faith and in an honest belief that his advice and acts are well founded and in the best interest of his client is not answerable for a mere error of judgment or for a mistake in a point of law which has not been settled by the court of last resort in his State and on which reasonable doubt may be entertained by well-informed lawyers. 5 A.J. 335, sec. 126; 7 C.J.S., Attorney and Client, § 142, page 979; McCullough v. Sullivan, supra; Hill v. Mynatt, Tenn.Ch.App., 59 S.W. 163, 52 L.R.A. 883.

Conversely, he is answerable in damages for any loss to his client which proximately results from a want of that degree of knowledge and skill ordinarily possessed by others of his profession similarly situated, or from the omission to use reasonable care and diligence, or from the failure to exercise in good faith his best judgment in attending to the litigation committed to his care. 5 A.J. 333, sec. 124; In re Woods, supra; McCullough v. Sullivan, supra; Annotation 52 L.R.A. 883.

[3] When the facts appearing in this record are considered in the light of these controlling principles of law, it immediately becomes manifest that plaintiff has failed to produce a scintilla of evidence

tending to show that defendants breached any duty the law imposed upon them when they accepted employment to prosecute plaintiff's actions against his insurers or that they did not possess the requisite learning and skill required of an attorney or that they acted otherwise than in the utmost good faith.

The Commissioner of Insurance is the statutory process agent of foreign insurance companies doing business in this State, G.S. § 58–153, Hodges v. New Hampshire Insurance Co., 232 N.C. 475, 61 S.E.2d 372, and when defendants mailed the process to the Commissioner of Insurance for his acceptance of service thereof, they were following a custom which had prevailed in this State for two decades or more. Foreign insurance companies had theretofore uniformly ratified such service, appeared in response thereto, filed their answers, and made their defense. The right of the Commissioner to accept service of process in behalf of foreign insurance companies doing business in this State had not been tested in the courts. Attorneys generally, throughout the State, took it for granted that under the terms of G.S. § 58–153 such acceptance of service was adequate. And, in addition, the defendants had obtained the judicial declaration of a judge of our Superior Courts that the acceptance of service by the Commissioner subjected the defendants to the jurisdiction of the court. Why then stop in the midst of the stream and pursue some other course?

Doubtless this litigation was inspired by a comment which appears in our opinion on the second appeal, Hodges v. Home Insurance Co., 233 N.C. 289, 63 S.E.2d 819. However, what was there said was pure dictum, injected—perhaps ill advisedly—in explanation of the reason we could afford plaintiff no relief on that appeal. We did not hold, or intend to intimate, that defendants had been in any wise neglectful of their duties as counsel for plaintiff.

The judgment entered in the court below is

Affirmed.

Chapter 2

INTERPRETING AND PREDICTING THE COMMON LAW

SECTION 2A. INTRODUCTION

The decisional process and how it influences the skills needed to resolve legal problems have been generally described in Chapter 1. In this chapter we will examine more closely the basic skills required to work with problems that may be resolved within the common law framework.

SECTION 2B. THE COMMON LAW DOCTRINAL FRAMEWORK

Two doctrines are actually at work within the common law framework. The first is the doctrine of stare decisis, that is, a court will generally follow its prior decisions and a court is expected to follow decisions of the courts to which it is subordinate. The second, broader, one is the doctrine of precedents, that is, if a court within a similar legal system has previously considered and resolved a particular problem, its decision is worthy of consideration in resolution of future similar cases. These complementary doctrines create two types of authority value for judicial precedents—mandatory (those that a court should generally consider itself bound to follow) and persuasive (those that a court should consider and may be inclined to follow). All decisions not mandatory are merely persuasive. The concept of mandatory precedents carries over to problems governed by legislation, because many court opinions construe legislation.

What precedents are mandatory in a given case will depend on a determination of what law governs, namely, federal law or state law, and if state law, the law of which state? This text does not discuss the rules controlling this initial determination, which are generally

dealt with in Constitutional Law, Civil Procedure, Federal Jurisdiction, and Conflicts of Law texts.[1]   Note, however, that in a given case (the mandatory precedents may be those of a court or courts outside the jurisdiction (federal or state court system) within which a particular case is pending) Thus, for example, a state court may have to decide questions governed by federal law (as in a criminal prosecution under state law in which the defendant relies on federal constitutional protections), or a federal court may have to decide questions governed by state law (as in a diversity case, a case commenced in a federal court only because the parties are citizens of different states). The federal courts are said to be bound by state court decisions on non-federal questions.   Conversely, the state courts are bound by United States Supreme Court decisions on federal questions, though some state courts do not consider themselves to be bound by lower federal court decisions.[2]   All courts, however, face the same analytical hurdles in determining which pronouncements of controlling courts they are bound to follow as do lawyers who are trying to predict the law that will govern a problem.[3]

Assuming no complicating need to look to laws from outside the jurisdiction in which a case is pending, the mandatory precedents for a case on appeal will be prior decisions of the court before which the case is pending and of courts to which that court is subordinate, if any.   Prior to commencement of litigation "mandatory precedents" will include relevant decisions of the courts in the controlling jurisdiction.

Given a determination as to the governing jurisdiction, a court is "bound" to follow a precedent of that jurisdiction only if it is directly in point.   In the strongest sense, "directly in point" means that: (1) the question resolved in the precedent case is the same as the question to be resolved in the pending case, (2) resolution of that question was necessary to disposition of the precedent case, (3) the significant facts of the precedent case are also present in the pending

---

1. *E. g.*, A. Ehrenzweig and D. Louisell, Jurisdiction in a Nutshell 166–216 (3d ed. 1973) and A. Ehrenzweig, Conflicts in a Nutshell (3d ed. 1974), both examples of mini-textbooks prepared for student use.

2. See Comment, *The State Courts and the Federal Common Law*, 27 Alb.L. Rev. 73 (1963) (reviewing varying views of courts of Alabama, California, New York, and Pennsylvania and suggesting guidelines); 24 Vand.L. Rev. 627 (1971) (a Case Note on United States *ex rel.* Lawrence v. Woods, 432 F.2d 1072 (7th Cir. 1970)). The cited sources are examples of the two basic forms of student writing appear-

ing in law reviews.   "Recent Case Note" (or "Case Comment") form is discussed in Section 10B, *infra*.

3. C. Wright, Handbook of the Law of Federal Courts § 58 (3d ed. 1976): "Thus the federal judge * * * is free, just as his state counterpart is, to consider all the data the highest court of the state would use in an effort to determine how the highest court of the state would decide. * * * If there are no holdings from state courts, high or low, on the matter that the federal court is to decide, that court must look for other indications of the state law." (at 269–70).

case, and (4) no additional facts appear in the pending case that might be treated as significant. That a court may decline to follow a precedent because one of these requirements is not satisfied accounts for much of the energy that is devoted to minutely analyzing opinions and distinguishing cases.

The second factor required to make a precedent "binding"—that resolution of the question was necessary to disposition of the precedent case—requires further explanation. A basic premise of our legal system is that courts should decide only the cases presented to them. That courts create law for future cases is only incidental to their resolution of particular disputes. Therefore, if in deciding a particular dispute a court indicates what its decision would be if the facts or questions were other than those presented, a future court in the same jurisdiction would not be bound to decide a future case in accordance with the language not necessary to the court's resolution of the problem. It would be "dicta" or a "dictum."

Although a court is not "bound" to follow dicta from prior opinions, it may do so. For example, if it is apparent that argument on a question was presented to the court, even though the question was not presented in the facts of the case, dicta may be carefully reasoned; it may therefore be persuasive. Or, if the membership of a court has not substantially changed, the court may be inclined to follow its prior dicta; in fact, the dicta may have been purposely included to forewarn of the court's changed attitude toward a particular type of problem. Inclusion of dicta in an appropriately labeled section in your class briefs may therefore be useful. Looking forward to your problem-solving work, you may have to rely on dicta in your prediction of a court's solution of a problem. For example, given no prior decision on an issue, well reasoned dicta relevant to the issue may be persuasive to a court in a pending case in which the issue is presented. Dicta from an opinion of a higher court in the same jurisdiction may be more persuasive to a trial court than other forms of authority.

One additional detail of the common law doctrinal framework requires explanation at this point. As previously noted, a court may overrule its prior decisions. Ideally, an overruling is express, that is, the court discusses the overruled precedent and gives reasons for the decision to overrule it. An overruling may be implied, however; a court may reach a result in a pending case that is inconsistent with a directly-in-point mandatory precedent, without mentioning the precedent. An overruling by implication may be unintentional (for example, the prior precedent may not have been called to the attention of the overruling court), but it is an overruling nevertheless. The effect of any overruling is to deprive a precedent of its binding character within the deciding jurisdiction and reduce its persuasiveness in other jurisdictions as well. A similar effect follows from a

higher court's reversal of a lower court decision. Note a distinction, however: a *reversing* decision is a decision that a lower court committed error and reached the wrong result in the case being reviewed; an *overruling* decision is one that is inconsistent with a decision in a prior, different case.

SECTION 2C.   FACTORS THAT MAKE OPINION ANALYSIS DIFFICULT

Many factors make opinion analysis difficult. One factor that will make it most difficult at first is your lack of acquaintance with legal terms, particularly procedural terms. Perseverance in use of the legal dictionary in your early months of study will give you the necessary foundation in the language of the law. In early weeks, you will find that your reading of even a short opinion may require several trips through the dictionary in attempts to translate the definitions of technical words into non-legal words with which you are already familiar.

Language will be a continuing source of difficulty in another sense. The varying thinking habits and writing styles of judges produce varying degrees of ambiguity of the kinds that can be found in most written communications. Words have multiple meanings; the particular meaning intended may not be clear from the context, creating semantic ambiguity. Uncertainties of modification or reference, unresolved by the context, create syntactic ambiguity. Finally, inconsistencies may create contextual ambiguity, either internal (for example, inconsistent statements within an opinion) or external (for example, statements that are inconsistent with statements in an opinion of the same court in an analogous case).[4]

The quality of analysis in an opinion varies not only as a consequence of varying abilities of judges but also as a consequence of the methods of operation of appellate courts. Most appellate courts have more than one judge, and an opinion may have several contributors with only a single acknowledged author. The pressure for majority agreement of the judges may also contribute to lack of clarity, because lack of agreement on rationale, for example, may lead to an intentionally vague or ambiguous explanation. The press of time may prevent even the most competent judges from writing and organizing well. The fact that courts tend to write their opinions for readers with a background knowledge of relevant procedures and of the subject area under discussion creates difficulties not just for beginners in law study but even for experienced attorneys who happen not to have the assumed background knowledge.

---

4. The descriptions contained in this paragraph have been adapted from R. Dickerson, The Fundamentals of Legal Drafting § 3.3 (1965).

Disagreement among judges may create analytical problems, because there may not be a single opinion for a particular case. One judge, or more, may disagree with the decision of the majority of the judges on the court and may write a dissenting opinion, that is, an opinion explaining the reasons for disagreeing and perhaps explaining in detail what decision the dissenter would have reached—and why. One judge, or more, may agree with the decision of the majority but disagree with the reasoning of the majority and may therefore write a concurring opinion explaining the variant reasoning.

Occasionally you will find that there is not even an opinion of "the court," although "the court" may have reached a decision. For example, if, on a nine-judge court, four judges join for one opinion, two judges sign a concurring opinion agreeing with the result reached by the first four judges but stating different reasons, and the other three judges sign a dissenting opinion, there is no opinion of "the court" (a majority have not approved one opinion) but "the court" has reached a decision (four plus two judges agreed on the result). There may not even be a decision by "the court." For example, if four judges reach result x, four judges reach result y and one judge reaches result z, there is no decision to which a majority of the judges have agreed; since a majority have not decided that the lower court was wrong, the decision of the lower court would be affirmed.

Another source of difficulty is that dicta may not be easy to recognize. For example, does particular language state dicta or, rather, an alternative basis for deciding as the court did? Frequently counsel will present a series of arguments to a court. These arguments may present several questions, with several reasons for deciding in favor of counsel's client, any one of which would be sufficient to resolve the dispute. The court may nevertheless decide all questions, and it may properly do so if the questions are presented in the facts of the case.

Ultimately you will find that major analytical difficulties stem from the basic concepts of the common law doctrinal framework. What part of a prior opinion is the "decision" that a court may feel compelled to follow? How does one determine "the rules or principles that appear to have been established" by prior decisions? Is overly broad language to be treated as dicta? You will find no simple or certain answers to these and other questions. The discussion in the remainder of this chapter and in the Notes at the end of the chapter is intended to get you started toward your own answers to them.

SECTION 2D. OPINION ANALYSIS

The following discussion describes approaches to opinion analysis that may be used after you have read an opinion carefully enough to

have some general ideas and questions about its "parts." For convenience of expression, the singular is used for "question," "decision," and "rule," although opinions usually present more than one question, decision, and rule. Also for convenience, "appellant" is used to describe the party who sought review of a lower court decision, and "appeal" and "appealed" are used in relation to the review proceedings, although, technically, the words derived from "appeal" should be confined to use in relation to a review that is available as a matter of right rather than within the discretion of the reviewing court.[5] The two opinions reproduced at the end of the last chapter, *Citizens' Loan Fund & Savings Ass'n v. Friedley* and *Hodges v. Carter*, are used for illustrative purposes.

Facts. The significant facts in a decided case are those that affected the decision.[6] Identifying the significant facts is not simply a matter of copying from an opinion a coherent story about the dispute. To arrive at even a tentative conclusion as to what facts should be regarded as significant is impossible without having in mind a general idea of the question before the court, the result reached by the court, and the court's reasoning. Therefore, you must read an entire opinion before finally deciding which facts are significant (which suggests that underlining apparently significant facts in opinions in your course books on first reading is unwise).

Some facts are usually clearly not significant, for example, the particular individuals involved, dates, locations, and amounts. Even though such facts are *usually* not significant, however, do not assume that they never are. Note the *Citizens' Loan* case, for example, in which the date of the court's decision invalidating the type of mortgage approved by the defendant (after the defendant approved the mortgage) was significant. Some facts are clearly not significant because the court says that they do not affect the result (and that conclusion, with the court's explanation therefor, may be important to note as part of the court's reasoning). Other facts will usually be clearly significant, for example, those on which the court relies in its

5. The most common form of discretionary review is sought by way of a petition for a writ of certiorari. The court to whom the petition is addressed may refuse to grant the writ and thus refuse to review the lower court decision. See Chapter 11, footnote 9, *infra*.

6. "Significant" is not a term of art. Other words have been used to describe the particular facts of a case that affected or should have affected a decision. For example, they have been called the "material" facts, in Goodhart, *Determining the Ratio Decidendi of a Case*, 40 Yale L.J. 161 (1930), reprinted in Studying Law (A. Vanderbilt ed. 1955); the legally "operative" facts, in 3A C. Corbin, Contracts 2–3 (1960) ("When a contract bargain is made, we have a transaction between two or more specific parties. This transaction is a series of facts and events. * * * Any of these acts or events may affect the action of the courts in a given case. If they do affect it, they are legally operative facts * * *"); the legally "relevant" facts, in K. Llewellyn, The Bramble Bush 48 (1960); and the "key" facts in W. Statsky and R. Wernet, Jr., Case Analysis and Fundamentals of Legal Writing (1977).

reasoning, or those that are in some other way emphasized by the court. Facts that fall between these obvious extremes will appear in most opinions. You must attempt to decide whether these facts were mentioned in the opinion because the court regarded them as influential in reaching its decision. If so, they are "significant," as that term is defined herein. If you cannot decide whether certain facts were or were not significant, include them in your brief, perhaps with a parenthetical question mark, for later consideration.

In identifying the significant facts you will not only eliminate some details entirely as of no significance, but you will sometimes abstract others, that is, substitute general descriptive categories for particular facts. Thus, for example, you may question whether benefits described by a court as "federal military retirement benefits and benefits under the State Employees' Retirement System and the California National Guard retirement program" must be thus described or can appropriately be described as "federal and state retirement benefits" or as "governmental retirement benefits" or as "retirement benefits." The range of possible abstraction will sometimes be large, and its appropriate extremes may be subject to varying views. Therefore, exercise caution in abstracting facts in your early briefing. You can always subsequently abstract when you review a brief, but you may not recall enough specific details to permit you subsequently to un-abstract.

What should be treated as "fact" differs from the concept of "fact" as something having objective truth or reality. Depending on the stage of proceedings at which challenged action was taken by the trial court, unproved statements in pleadings of one of the parties may be accepted as facts (for example, averments in the plaintiff's complaint), or assumptions based on a view of evidence most favorable to one of the parties may be treated as facts, or written findings detailed by the trial judge after a careful review of the evidence and resolution of conflicts presented by, for example, various witnesses' testimony and inferences therefrom, may be considered the facts. These possibilities will be explained in a later discussion of procedure.

A fact-by-fact review of a court's summary of what happened in order to identify the significant facts is a necessary part of opinion analysis. Whether you will want to limit a fact section in a brief to a statement of only the significant facts will depend upon the particular opinion being analyzed. For example, if the events and details of a case are numerous and complicated, the facts section may be more comprehensive; it may include all information useful to understanding the case, outlined in chronological or other rational order as a preliminary step. The significant facts can then be underlined or they may be incorporated in the question statement. If the facts section of a brief is limited to a statement of only the facts thought to be significant, however, then all of them need not be repeated in the

statement of the question presented, so long as the question reflects dependence on the stated facts (most obviously by "on these facts * * *"). Or, if the significant facts in a particular case are few and simple, they may be incorporated in the question statement, and the facts section may be eliminated.

Procedure. Noting and understanding lower court procedural actions is important to accurate analysis of opinions. Who prevailed in the lower court and at what point in the proceedings must be known and understood to permit accurate statement of an appellate court's substantive decision as well as its procedural decision. The following discussion of the foundations of appellate review will explain this relationship between substance and procedure.

To obtain a reversal or modification of the trial court's decision on review, the appellant (the aggrieved party) must persuade the reviewing court that the trial court committed "reversible" (or, conversely, not harmless) error, that is, that the trial court made some mistake that affected the outcome of the case in a manner prejudicial to the appellant. An alleged error must be some mistaken procedural action or ruling. Assuming no purely accidental or arbitrary actions or rulings, and excepting questions about sufficiency of evidence, we must conclude that a trial court will commit error because of a mistake about the controlling law. Thus, the starting point for a successful appeal should be clear identification of each such alleged error and the underlying question of law. In practice, rules governing the form of appeal briefs (counsel's written arguments) have long required stylized identification of either the alleged errors (in Assignments of Error), or the alleged underlying questions (Questions Presented), or both.[7]

Possible errors range through the whole series of possible procedural actions and rulings in litigation. Until you learn details about these possibilities in Civil Procedure, Criminal Procedure, and Trial and Appellate Practice courses, you will have to educate yourself. Examining the procedures reported in each opinion that you analyze and seeking an explanation of them by consulting a legal dictionary or civil procedure text[8] will soon acquaint you with frequently recurring procedures. Within a few weeks you should develop instinctive recognition of what some common procedural actions generally entail and of the extent to which each may limit application of a substantive decision or may otherwise be important to an understanding of a particular opinion.

One respect in which knowledge of a procedural point may contribute to such understanding has already been mentioned, that is,

---

7. These requirements are discussed more fully in Section 11E, *infra*.

8. *See generally* M. Green, Basic Civil Procedure (1972) for a general overview, or F. James, Jr. & G. Hazard, Jr., Civil Procedure (2d ed. 1977) for more detailed discussion. Both are student texts.

the character of the "facts" on appeal. Thus, for example, if an action is dismissed prior to trial, no evidence will have been introduced from which the facts may be determined. Hence, the court must derive the "facts" from the written documents filed in the action. For example, a defendant may move for dismissal of a complaint on the ground that it fails to state a claim on which relief can be granted (or, in the terminology of other pleadings systems, may file a general demurrer, thus asserting that the complaint fails to state a cause of action). By a motion to dismiss or a general demurrer, the defendant asserts, in effect, that even though plaintiff could prove each fact stated in the complaint, there is no theory on which plaintiff would be entitled to relief. Thus, if the motion is granted (or the demurrer is sustained), the "facts" for purposes of review must be those averred (or alleged) in the complaint.

Facts may be uncertain even though evidence has been introduced. At the conclusion of a plaintiff's introduction of evidence, the defendant may move for a directed verdict on the ground that the plaintiff has failed to prove the facts necessary to support a claim on which relief can be granted, in effect asserting that even though all the evidence presented for the plaintiff and all favorable inferences to be drawn therefrom be accepted as true, there is no theory on which plaintiff is entitled to relief. If error is assigned to a court's granting such a motion, the facts for purposes of review must be derived from the most favorable view of the evidence from the plaintiff's viewpoint.

An action may go to trial and conclude with entry of judgment for one party or the other. If the action is a non-jury case, the judge will not only decide all procedural, evidentiary, and substantive law questions, but will also be the fact finder, that is, the judge will decide about credibility of witnesses, resolve any conflicts in the evidence, and so on. Under a common procedural requirement, the judge must then sign written Findings of Fact that state the significant factual conclusions thus found. On appeal, these findings become the accepted facts unless they are successfully challenged as unsupported by the evidence. On the other hand, if a case is tried before a jury, the jury is the finder of facts. The court must "charge" the jury, in "instructions," as to the relevant rules of law, the questions that the jury must decide, and what the verdict should be for the different possible resolutions of questions to be decided. Rarely, however, will a jury be required to answer the fact questions one by one in some tangible form that can be brought before an appellate court like a trial court's written findings of fact. Thus, on review of a jury case, an appellate court may have to state the "facts" by reviewing the evidence and assuming that conflicts in the evidence were resolved by the jury in favor of the winning party.

Sometimes an opinion is difficult to understand because the court fails to state the procedural point at which a case was disposed of in the lower court or to identify the procedural errors asserted on appeal. In the *Citizens' Loan* case, for example, the court does not even state directly for whom the lower court gave judgment—that judgment was for the defendant must be inferred from the appellate court's reasoning in relation to its affirmance of what the lower court did. From some of the court's discussion, however, it is possible to infer that the action had been terminated in the pre-trial stage, probably by dismissal of the complaint, because the court states the facts in terms of what was "alleged" and "averred," making no reference to testimony or other forms of evidence, and states defendant's contention as an insistence that "the complaint shows * * * "[9] The failure of courts to provide information about relevant lower court actions may require that you be alert for similar clues about what did happen.

As noted in Chapter 1, the reasoning of the lower court may be regarded as part of the procedural details. Sometimes that reasoning will point to the issue before the appellate court. Similarly, the summary of contentions of counsel on appeal may lead you to identification of a specific issue before the court or to a clearer understanding of the court's reasoning. You will soon find that for many opinions you will identify or infer the same contentions: that the present case is distinguishable from prior cases or that a prior decision should be overruled (or the converse, that a precedent is controlling and should not be overruled). If an attempted distinction appears to have some merit, it should be included in your brief, just as any argument that helps you to understand or to evaluate an opinion should be included in your brief.

The Issue (or Question) Before the Court. Analysis requires precise identification of the issue or issues decided. In the view taken of analysis and briefing up to this point in this text, the statement of the issue, with the decision-answer, stands for the substantive decision. That is, the substantive decision can be stated by restating the issue in affirmative form if the answer is "yes" or in negative form if the answer is "no." Hence, precise identification of the substantive decision requires precise identification of the question answered. After you have experience in opinion analysis and briefing you may find it more efficient to omit the issue statements in your briefs and to state the substantive decisions directly, although you may still have to identify the issues mentally in your analysis in order to be able to identify the decision. If the sample *Citizens' Loan* brief were

---

9. The validity of this inference is established by the brief on appeal filed by the appellant in the *Citizens' Loan* case: "The only question before this court then is, Did the court err in sustaining the demurrer to the amended complaint." Brief of Appellant at 4.

changed to this form, the issues would not be stated. Instead, the decision statement would be: D-attorney's mistaken advice on a question not yet decided by the controlling court but subsequently decided adversely was not such as might be found to have resulted from want of ordinary knowledge and skill or from failure to exercise reasonable care, the question being one on which well-informed attorneys of reasonable diligence would have differed or had doubt.

As previously indicated, court rules frequently require appellants to state Questions Presented in briefs on appeal. Ideally, counsel would precisely identify the questions, and the court would repeat each question in connection with the discussion thereof in its opinion. Unfortunately, neither counsel nor courts consistently rise above human failings, so careful analysis may be required in order to identify precise questions presented and ultimately, precise decisions.

In your early opinion analysis, you may find it helpful to think of each opinion as a discussion of a possible hierarchy of issues, each issue below the first stating a more specific view of the issue immediately above it. Here is a simple example of such a hierarchy:

Did the lower court err in entering judgment for D?

Had P and D entered into a contract?

Had D offered to sell?

Was D's statement that he would sell an offer if he made the statement in jest, with an undisclosed lack of intent to contract?

The first question is a correct statement of the procedural issue before the court in a substantial number of cases. But you must identify the substantive issue. Ask yourself, "Why was a question raised?" (In the example, because judgment for P was appropriate if P and D had entered into a contract. Why was there a question whether P and D had contracted? Because D contended that he had been jesting, that he did not really intend to offer to sell. Note how the assumed contentions contribute to formulation of the specific substantive issue.)

In your initial attempts to analyze opinions, try to identify the hierarchy of issues by asking the same "why" question until you arrive at the specific question that the court appears to answer. Sometimes you may thus identify an issue that was not even acknowledged by the court. The failure to discuss the issue that you have so identified may be a reason for criticizing the opinion in your evaluation of it.

At some level in the issue hierarchy, particularly in working with unexcerpted opinions, you will frequently find that an issue in the hierarchy branches into separable sub-issues. Thus, in the example given above, you might find that the second question branches

into an acceptance issue as well as an offer issue. Then you would have to ask the "why" question to identify the specific acceptance issue also.

Another way to attempt to identify questions more precisely than some courts do is to think about why the court discusses particular rules or concepts. For example, why did the court in the *Citizens' Loan* case discuss at such length the circumstances that would justify concluding that an attorney should be liable for client's losses? Because a question had been raised about what "rule of liability" (standard of conduct) should be applied? Or was the court merely reviewing the rules of liability to provide a background for its discussion of the more precise questions stated in the sample brief? The author of the sample brief concluded that the latter was the reason, because nothing in the court's discussion of the rule of liability intimated doubt about the rule. But, further, why did the court discuss the prior law on the question decided in *Dodge v. Kinzy*? The court's introductory language in the paragraph in which that law is discussed ("Now, while it is quite true * * * ") and, later, ("and while it had been thoroughly settled * * * ") may be acknowledgements of contentions by plaintiff's counsel that the *Dodge* decision was completely predictable, suggesting the second question stated in the sample brief.

Sometimes it will be necessary to go outside an opinion to get a reliable view of its meaning. Reading opinions cited in an opinion under study may provide insights to the court's view of the question presented or the extent of its decision. For example, for *Citizens' Loan*, reading the troublesome *Dodge v. Kinzy* opinion gives a more reliable view of the degree of uncertainty of the rule of law that had earlier defeated the plaintiff's recovery against the mortgaged property.[10] Just reading the original context of language quoted from

---

10. In Dodge v. Kinzy, 101 Ind. 102, 106–07 (1884), the court reasoned: Under a common law rule, a husband alone cannot execute a valid mortgage on land owned in the entireties because neither husband nor wife can dispose of any part of such an estate without consent of the other. A wife's signature as surety for a husband's separate debt is void because a statute prevents wives from entering into contracts of suretyship; therefore, where the wife purported to sign as surety, the signature was void. The husband's signature alone was necessarily insufficient, and the attempted mortgage was therefore ineffective. If the court was correct in its statement of the common law rule, was the decision in *Dodge* completely predictable? If the *Dodge* result was completely predictable, was the *Citizens' Loan* case correctly decided?

Similarly, the court's summary disposition of the second question presented in the *Hodges v. Carter* case seems less acceptable if one reads the prior, connected cases. In the first appeal, the court held that process could not be mailed, so the insurance companies had not been properly served. The court reasoned: "The wording of the statute *clearly* indicates that the legislature intended that process should be served in the manner other summonses are served. And, in this connection, it is noted that our statute prescribing procedure for the commencement of civil actions requires that 'summons must * * * be directed to the sheriff or other proper offices of the county' in which the defendant resides or may be found, and 'must be served by

a prior opinion or secondary authority may clarify the court's reliance thereon. If they are available, the parties' briefs filed with the court for an appeal may be a revealing source of information about the issues.[11] Use of external sources is particularly important to aid more reliable prediction in connection with research-related opinion analysis.

Just as the extent of abstraction that is appropriate in stating significant facts may be subject to varying views, what is an accurate statement of an issue before a court may be subject to varying views. In your early analysis and briefing, be cautious about abstracting in stating issues.

As already noted, the opinion excerpts in law course books frequently focus on only one or two of the issues presented in each case. When you work with unexcerpted opinions, you will have to do what each course book author has done in deciding what portions of opinions should be included in his or her book, that is, you will first have to decide which portions of the opinion relate to which issues. Then, if you are analyzing an opinion with a particular problem in mind, you will have to decide whether issues seemingly unrelated to your problem are truly unrelated so that you can safely ignore discussion of them.

Whenever you prepare a brief of an opinion dealing with multiple issues, number the issues and use corresponding numbers for the corresponding contentions, reasons, and rules. You may find it use-

the sheriff to whom it is addressed.' G.S. § 1–89. Hodges v. Home Ins. Co., 232 N.C. 475, 61 S.E.2d 372, 374 (1950) (emphasis added) cited in Hodges v. Carter as Hodges v. New Hampshire Fire Ins. Co.). In the second appeal, Hodges v. Home Ins. Co., 233 N.C. 289, 63 S.E.2d 819 (1951), the court held that a second action against the insurance companies, commenced after the insurance companies prevailed on the first appeal, had been commenced too late and was barred by the statute of limitations. The court made the following observation, which is apparently the language that triggered the malpractice suit: "At the time defendant entered its motion to dismiss the original action, the plaintiff still had more than sixty days in which to sue out an alias summons and thus keep his action alive. He elected instead to rest his case upon the validity of the service had. The unfortunate result is unavoidable." 63 S.E.2d at 822.

11. Thus, for example, the briefs filed in the *Citizens' Loan* case reveal that argument was presented on the second question stated in the sample brief relating to uncertainty in the law about which the defendant-attorney gave advice to the plaintiff. "The appellees cannot claim that Friedley was called upon for an opinion on some intricate and doubtful question of law." Brief of Appellant at 5. "It is true that this Court had decided in a number of cases * * * that a married woman was not liable as surety for her husband and that executing a mortgage for the debt of her husband on her separate real estate was not valid, but it had not before the case of Dodge v. Kinzy decided that a mortgage executed by husband and wife on the real estate held by entireties was void as to both and there was and is a difference of opinion among lawyers yet on the subject— and there was such doubt or uncertainty as would not make a lawyer liable in advance of the decisions of this Court for a mistake in judgment on this subject." Brief of Appellee at 6.

ful to prepare essentially separate briefs for each issue if the issues are unrelated.

Decision (or Holding or Point Decided). In its narrowest meaning, the decision of a court is merely a statement of the procedural action taken or directed with reference to the case before it, for example, judgment for plaintiff affirmed or judgment for defendant reversed, new trial directed. In this narrow sense, the decision does not directly answer the specific issue question that you should attempt to identify. "Decision" is also used in a broader sense, however, to describe the substantive result in a case, for example: D's statement that he would sell was an offer even though he made the statement in jest with an undisclosed lack of intent to contract. Even more broadly, it may refer to both the procedural and substantive results. The word "holding" is sometimes used interchangeably with "decision" in all these senses. In this text hereafter, unless the qualifying word "procedural" or "substantive" is added, both words are used to refer to the complete result.

Reasoning. If you consider the common law decisional process in simplified form, you will recognize that a court is faced with broad alternative possibilities each time it is required to decide a case that is not governed by written law: either it can apply an existing rule (that is, follow a precedent) or it can develop a new or variant rule (that is, refuse to follow a precedent or conclude that there is no precedent). Taking this simplified view, you can expect a court's reasoning to be of two types: justifying application of an existing rule (precedent justification) or justifying a result (policy justification—"policy" being used in a very broad sense to encompass any rational consideration not related to precedents).

It is easiest to identify a court's reasoning in an opinion that reports a decision in a novel case, one for which counsel concede there is no precedent. The court will usually go to great lengths to state policy justifications for the result it reaches. It may rely on social utility, ethical considerations, or general standards of justice. It may point to custom, to business practice, or to expediency. It may use negative "parade of horribles" reasoning (that is, that other available choices would lead to identified undesirable consequences). It may consider the logical structure of the law and fashion a result that fits in with other decisions in the general subject area. The court may also use precedent justifications by reasoning from a general principle or by analogy and thus justify application of an existing principle or rule.

If a court is faced with the argument that it should follow a precedent, however, the reasoning process may seem more complex. Ideally, when a court is faced with the argument that the decision or the rule underlying a prior decision should control the outcome of a

pending case, it should first compare the facts of the two cases. Following this comparison, it could reach one of at least four possible conclusions: [12]

1. It could conclude that the significant facts are identical and *apply* the precedent rule.

2. It could conclude that although the significant facts are not identical, they are sufficiently similar to justify the same result. In this event, it would apply and *extend* the rule to a new type of case by analogy.

    Note that for each of these first two possibilities, the basic "reason" for the court's reaching the conclusion to apply an existing rule is that the facts of the pending and precedent cases are identical or similar (precedent justifications). This is sufficient "reason" for a decision. The court's "reasoning" is its discussion of the precedent case(s) and the facts. But if opposing counsel has attacked the rule as well as its application to the case, the court should also state reasons justifying the rule (policy justifications).

3. It could conclude that the significant facts are not identical and that they are not sufficiently similar to justify the same result, that is, it would *distinguish* or *limit* the precedent and refuse to follow it, stating policy justifications for the result that it reaches.

4. It could conclude that the significant facts are identical but refuse to follow the precedent, stating policy justifications. The rejected precedent may be a mandatory precedent or merely persuasive. If the rejected precedent is a decision of the same court or a subordinate court and the court signals its intention not to follow it in the future, the precedent would be *overruled*. This fourth possibility is not open if the precedent is the decision of a higher court in the same jurisdiction, because only the deciding court or a higher court can *overrule* an existing precedent.

     A court's reasoning may seem even more complex in another type of case that you should early learn to recognize, one in which a court is faced with competing rules, principles, or analogies that lead to different results. In such a case, the court should give valid reasons for its decision to apply one rule, principle, or analogy rather than the competing one(s).

12. For a refined listing of sixty-four techniques actually used by courts in dealing with precedents, see K. Llewellyn, The Common Law Tradition: Deciding Appeals 77–91 (1960).

In your early opinion analysis efforts, you may find the following suggestion helpful. After reading an opinion, try to identify the court's pattern of reasoning in the abstract before analyzing its reasoning in detail. Here are some illustrative patterns:

No. 1   States a principle

Explains underlying reasoning

Finds no decisions refusing to apply principle

Discusses cases with very similar facts in which the principle has been applied

Applies principle

No. 2   States rules from secondary authority (*e. g.* a textbook)

States factual conclusion and inference therefrom that makes rule applicable

Applies rule

No. 3   Explains rules applicable in general problem area

Reaches factual conclusion that makes some of the rules inapplicable

Distinguishes cases in general problem area

Restates rules in general

Reaches another factual conclusion that makes some of the rules inapplicable

States result

No. 4   States generally accepted rule

Discusses criticism of rule by secondary authorities

Considers impact of rule in business community

Considers contrary alternative rule

Rejects generally accepted rule

Adopts alternative rule

Identification of a helter-skelter pattern such as is suggested by Illustration 3 may point up why you have difficulty understanding a particular opinion.

The Rule (or Underlying Principle or Ratio Decidendi). The "rule of a case" is a statement of what a decision may stand for with reference to future cases. It summarizes the controlling significant facts, the issue question, and its answer (that is, the substantive decision) in the form of a general statement that might be used to determine the outcome of a future case having similar facts.

The rule may have been established by prior decisions or stated in a secondary authority, and the court may simply announce its ap-

plication to these particular facts. Then you should ask yourself whether the announced rule really leads to the result reached. If not, then you should reformulate or refine the statement of the preexisting rule to state a rule of the case to reflect the deviant result. You should also ask yourself whether parts of the rule announced are dicta. If so, then the rule that you state for the case should be pruned to reflect only the portion applicable to the particular case. In either event, you may also wish to include in your brief the broader formulation of the rule as announced by the court, to be tested against other pertinent opinions that you may subsequently read. Note, for example, how these suggestions were used in preparation of the sample brief for the *Citizens' Loan* case. The court expressly stated affirmative principles and rules but developed a converse rule for the case in reaching a negative (no liability) decision. The affirmative principle and general rule are not dicta, however, because they established a possible basis for liability that was considered by the court. The rules labelled "dicta" are also worth including as defining other specific bases for liability in the problem area. (The rules appear to be dicta because the rule as to which the attorney was mistaken was apparently not stated in elementary texts or in a prior decision and because the attorney had not made a mistake in pleading or court practice.)

The court may state that the outcome in a case is dictated by a "principle." A "principle" differs from a "rule" only in breadth of generalization. Compare, for example, the principle and the general rule stated in the sample *Citizens' Loan* brief. A substantial number of rules may be developed under a principle. The following additional general rules (and many others) might be subsumed under the *Citizens' Loan* principle to summarize possible liability of an attorney for failure to act in accordance with the standard of conduct stated in the principle:

> An attorney will be liable for loss caused by the attorney's failure to take such steps to protect the client's right of appeal from an adverse decision in litigation as would be taken by well-informed attorneys.

> An attorney will be liable for loss caused by the attorney's failure to draft an enforceable document such as would be drafted by well-informed attorneys who deal with documents of that character.

Under each general rule, more specific rules can be subsumed.

The court may simply announce the result—the manner in which it has resolved the dispute—without stating or acknowledging that it has applied any rule or followed any precedent. Then you must exercise your developing analytical clairvoyance to phrase a rule describing the outcome of the case that should have general application to

future similar cases. Some would argue that the only "rule" that can be derived from such a decision is the exact decision and no more. Reliable "rules," they would say, can be derived only from the synthesis of two or more decisions. Recall, however, that one of the purposes of your practicing opinion analysis is to cultivate an ability to predict what a court may do with future cases. What better way to practice prediction than to speculate on the possible extreme to which a single decision can arguably be extended? When you try to state a rule for a case, you are always testing the possible reaches of the decision. Finally, a comprehensive brief should reflect the probable extremes of meaning with reference to future cases, from the narrowest meaning embodied in all the possibly significant facts and the decision, to the broadest rule that you believe can be said to underlie the decision.

Or, the court may simply cite a prior decided case as justification for its decision. Then you must analyze the opinion in the cited case to try to ascertain what rule or principle guided the decision in that case.

A Reminder and a Caveat. For convenience, the foregoing discussion of opinion analysis has been phrased in terms of identifying one question, one decision, one principle, one rule. Remember that one-question cases are unusual. The dangers of proceeding as though but one question must be identified for each opinion have recently been pointed out:

> [C]ases (as well as the excerpts treated by students) generally [present] a number of related issues. This means that where student case briefs seek complete and accurate statement of a case in terms of *one* issue, they typically adopt either of two courses. One course is statement of a compound issue stringing together "significant" propositions of law on which the rule of the case depends. (This is a style often used in case reporter headnotes.) A second course is selection of one of the sub-issues as the "key" issue. (This approach is often used in briefing cases for case method substantive law courses.)
>
> Neither is very helpful as a strategy of general application in thorough case analysis.[13]

Textual Reporting of Opinion Analysis. In reporting opinion analysis to someone else, you will usually use textual, narrative form rather than opinion-brief form. Nevertheless, the contents of the report (commonly called a case statement) will usually be the same: a statement of the significant "parts" of the opinion that are necessary to an understanding of the court's decision, but with emphasis on

13. Gross, *On Law School Training in Analytic Skill*, 25 J. Legal Educ. 261,   275 (1973). Copyright 1972, Peter W. Gross. Quoted with permission.

those parts that contribute most to understanding the relationship of the opinion to the problem or subject that you are discussing.

SECOND SUGGESTED EXERCISE

Reproduced as Appendix A is an excerpt from the opinion in Lucas v. Hamm, 56 Cal.2d 583, 15 Cal.Rptr. 821, 364 P.2d 685 (1961). Prepare a brief for the opinion after carefully analyzing it. Then rewrite the summary of your analysis in textual, narrative form, reporting the parts of the opinion in the order that seems most natural or logical to you.

SECTION 2E. OPINION EVALUATION

The purpose of evaluating an opinion in a problem-solving setting is to predict the authority value that will be accorded it. For a directly-in-point mandatory precedent, the purpose requires identification of weaknesses or strengths relating to the possibility of an overruling or limiting decision. For other precedents, the purpose requires identification of weaknesses or strengths relating to their persuasiveness as authorities. In general, courts may be more inclined to seize on weaknesses in persuasive precedents as justifications for refusal to follow than they would be to justify overruling on the basis of equivalent weaknesses in a directly-in-point, mandatory precedent. The benefits of stability in the law may be balanced against the substantive weaknesses of a mandatory precedent so that a court will continue to honor it even though it is based on what is concededly not the "best" rule.

In evaluating the substance of an opinion, you may use a two-pronged approach, based on the two basic types of reasoning that may be used by courts: (1) Are the court's precedent justifications adequate, that is, is the opinion technically valid? For example, has the court considered all the facts that you believe should have been treated as significant? Has the court decided the issues presented? When you have researched a problem, you will be fully acquainted with a representative sample of decisions in similar cases. You will then consider whether the court has adequately dealt with these relevant precedents. Has it recognized their strengths and weaknesses? Has it made valid factual comparisons and distinctions? Your evaluation of the court's comparisons and distinctions may be extended to include careful examination of all or many of the cases cited and discussed by the court. Additionally, you will want to consider the age, character, and quality of secondary authorities on which the court relied. (2) Has the court advanced valid policy justifications? Has it considered all possible conflicting policy considerations?

In predicting what law will probably control resolution of a particular problem, however, you will have to evaluate more than the substance of the opinion. Many factors will affect the authority val-

ue of a precedent.   Some of the factors that you should form the habit of noting are as follows:

What is the level of the deciding court within its jurisdiction? Many federal trial court opinions are reported; some state trial court opinions are reported, notably those of lower New York courts.   A trial court opinion has little *authority* value apart from the quality thereof, except in cases that will come before the same court.   In large part, the lack of persuasive authority value of a trial court decision is attributable to the fact that trial court decisions are usually rendered by a single judge, whereas appellate court decisions reflect the interaction of three or more judges.   Furthermore, at the appellate court level there is less pressure for quick decision, permitting greater time for reflection.   Thus, an opinion of the New York Court of Appeals, even though it has weaknesses, may carry substantial weight with the courts of other jurisdictions, while even a carefully reasoned trial court opinion may be passed over simply because it is a trial court opinion.   You should not ignore trial court opinions because of this possibility, however.   If you can find no other opinion in point, a carefully reasoned trial court opinion may carry more weight than secondary authority, and it will have obvious value if there is no secondary authority in point.   The opinions of even the lowest courts may be persuasive under some circumstances.   For example, during the 1960's a number of cases were litigated on questions related to the liability of a credit card holder for unauthorized purchases made under a lost or stolen credit card.   One of the earlier published opinions was from a New York municipal court,[14] a trial court of limited jurisdiction.   That opinion was cited by several appellate courts, and the court's decision and reasoning were influential.[15]

When was the case decided?   The older the decision, the more subject to scrutiny it will be, particularly if the trend of recent decisions in the problem area has been away from an established view or if related social attitudes have been changing.   For example, with re-

---

14.   Texaco, Inc. v. Goldstein, 34 Misc. 2d 751, 229 N.Y.S.2d 51 (Mun.Ct.1962), *aff'd* 39 Misc.2d 552, 241 N.Y.S.2d 495 (Sup.Ct., App. Term 1963) (per curiam). (Note the manner of identifying the lower courts in parentheses with the date.)

15.   *See, e. g.,* Sears, Roebuck & Co. v. Duke, 441 S.W.2d 521 (Tex.1969). (Note the manner of identifying the court when there is no official report.) The introductory signal, *"See,"* as used in this citation indicates that the cited opinion supports the statement in the text although it does not directly make the same statement.   "*E. g.*" means that there are other examples directly supporting the statement in the text.   Other useful introductory signals are described in the citation *Blue Book* at 6–8.   One cynic has described these signals thus:

"Which brings us to the rules that, more than all the others combined, have contributed to the *Blue Book's* notoriety: Introductory Signals. Damned as 'virtually cryptographic' by Mr. Wiener, the signals have been attacked as an ultra vires imposition of a full-blown theory of stare decisis.

cently changed attitudes toward protection of consumers, do you think that an early let-the-buyer-beware decision would be worth citing to a modern court?

Was the decision or reasoning divided? Appellate courts commonly have five, seven, or nine judges. Obviously a 5–4 decision is substantially less persuasive than a 9–0 decision. If a persuasive decision is closely divided, a court may treat the majority and dissenting opinions as worthy of equal consideration. If the decision or reasoning in a directly-in-point mandatory precedent is divided, possible subsequent changes in the composition of the court must be considered. For example, has one of the judges who signed a 5–4 majority opinion been replaced by a judge of unknown views? A recent 4–3 decision of the United States Supreme Court has produced substantial questions about the binding character of a decision by less than a majority of the full complement of judges, even though a majority of judges who heard the case were in agreement.[16]

Was the case considered by the whole court? Appellate courts sometimes sit in departments or panels of three or five judges, hearing only the most important cases en banc. An en banc decision may be more persuasive than a departmental decision. In intermediate appellate courts, the several judges may be divided into departments or divisions, with each case being heard by only one department or division. Given such division, the possibility that different departments or divisions are following inconsistent rules must be considered.

Does the opinion carry a full report of the case? Some opinions are sketchy, leaving unanswered obvious questions about what happened in the decided case. Such omissions may constitute a substantial weakness. Some appellate court decisions are reported in per curiam opinions, that is, opinions of the court without an acknowledged author. Many per curiams consist only of a statement of the

---

But the signals are back in all their glorious inscrutability. Use *no signal* when you've got the guts. Use *e. g.* when there are other examples you are too lazy to find or are skeptical of unearthing. Use *accord* when one court has cribbed from the other's opinion. Use *see* when the case is on all three's. Use *cf.* when you've wasted your time reading the case. Insert *but* in front of these last two when a frown instead of a smile is indicated. *See generally* and *see also* are retained with an apparent acknowledgment that there is no difference between the two. 'See' may also be used in a nonsignal sense, but 'must never be used in such a manner that it might be confused with the signal usage of the word.' "

Lushing, Book Review, 67 Colum.L.Rev. 599, 601–02 (1967) (footnotes omitted).

16. The decision was handed down in Fuentes v. Shevin, 407 U.S. 67, 92 S. Ct. 1983, 32 L.Ed.2d 556 (1972). Authorities are collected in Annot., 65 A.L.R.3d 504 (1975). (The A.L.R. series—American Law Reports—are annotated reports publishing selected court opinions, each followed by a textual annotation that collects, categorizes, and synthesizes other opinions discussing the same question or questions as the selected opinion.)

procedural decision, sometimes with a citation or citations to a precedent or precedents. Such a per curiam may sometimes give a clue to a court's attitudes on particular points, but more often per curiams lack authority value because the substantive decisions cannot be identified. If a lower court opinion has been published for a decision affirmed in a summary per curiam opinion, it may be argued that the higher court has thus adopted both the decision and reasoning of the lower court,[17] but the more expansive the lower court opinion is, the less persuasive this argument becomes.[18] Related and greater difficulties attach to summary dispositions on appeal, that is, appeals disposed of without a full briefing and oral argument by counsel.[19] Not only is the court's explanation for summary disposi-

17. Sacks, *Foreword to the Supreme Court, 1953, Term,* 68 Harv.L.Rev. 96, 102 (1954). Other problems with summary per curiams are discussed in Sacks at 99–103 and in Note, *Supreme Court Per Curiam Practice: A Critique,* 69 Harv.L.Rev. 707, 718–21 (1956). (Material in law reviews cited by a "Note" or "Comment" label and title, without an author's name, is student-authored material.)

18. *See,* Fusari v. Steinberg, 419 U.S. 379, 391, 95 S.Ct. 533, 540–41, 42 L. Ed.2d 521, 530–31 (1975) (concurring opinion). At least Chief Justice Burger disapproves of use of the lower court opinion to define the Court's judgment: "We might * * * make explicit what is implicit in some prior holdings. * * * When we summarily affirm, without opinion, * * * we affirm the judgment but not necessarily the reasoning by which it was reached." *Id.*

19. Some of the problems with summary affirmances are discussed in Note, *Summary Disposition of Supreme Court Appeals: The Significance of Limited Discretion and a Theory of Limited Precedent,* 52 Boston U.L.Rev. 373, 375–76 (1972) (distinguishing summary dispositions and summary per curiams), 404–15 (discussing the significance of a summary disposition as precedent). Recently it was observed in a majority opinion of the United States Supreme Court, "[T]hese * * * summary affirmances obviously are of precedential value * * * Equally obviously they are not of the same precedential value as would be an opinion of this Court treating the question on the merits."

Edelman v. Jordan, 415 U.S. 651, 671, 94 S.Ct. 1347, 1359, 39 L.Ed.2d 662, 677 (1974). But does this mean that summary affirmances are therefore not "binding" on lower courts, Jordon v. Gilligan, 500 F.2d 701 (6th Cir. 1974), or, rather, that although the Supreme Court may regard itself to be less bound by stare decisis principles for summary affirmances, lower courts cannot disregard them? Authorities are collected in Annot., 45 L. Ed.2d 791 (1976). (Like the A.L.R. series described *supra* in note 16, the Lawyers' Edition series are annotated reports, but only Supreme Court opinions—all of them—are reported therein.)

With increasing pressures on appellate courts from unmanageably heavy case loads, the courts have felt compelled to resort to summary dispositions, particularly by limiting or refusing to hear oral arguments, and short memorandum or per curiam opinions in an increasing number of cases. See the final report of the Commission on Revision of the Federal Court Appellate System, Structure and Internal Procedures: Recommendations for Change 41–53 (1975); P. Carrington, D. Meador & M. Rosenberg, Justice on Appeal 16–29, 31–43, 226–27 (1976). For samples of memorandum decisions (opinions), see *Id.* at 243–53. For a discussion of unpublished opinions as a response to the caseload problem and a survey of the extent to which this response is used in both federal and state courts with accompanying questions about precedent value, *see* Chanin, *A Survey of the Writing and Publication of Opinions in Federal and State Appellate Courts,* 67 Law l ib.J. 362 (1974).

tion lacking, but the court has not had the benefit of full assistance from counsel.

What was the quality of the arguments presented by counsel? Although oral arguments to appeal courts are rarely reported, counsel's briefs on appeal may be available. A law library frequently collects, at a minimum, briefs filed in cases decided by the United States Supreme Court and by the courts for the state and the federal circuit in which the library is located. A substantial weakness of a precedent may be that a particular line of precedents or reasoning was not presented to the court in counsel's briefs, and hence it cannot be presumed that it was considered by the court.

How has the decision been treated subsequently by the deciding court and other courts? Has it been cited favorably, followed, criticized, distinguished, limited, explained, questioned, overruled? In Chapter 7, a research tool that will supply answers to these questions, the citator, will be discussed.

Finally, recall that a comparative evaluation may be necessary. If you conclude that two or more lines of reasoning or competing rules are reflected in relevant opinions, you must decide which reasoning or rule is more persuasive or better.

THIRD SUGGESTED EXERCISE

Reproduced as Appendix B are excerpts from the opinion of the court and the dissenting opinion in Smith v. Lewis, 13 Cal.3d 349, 118 Cal.Rptr. 621, 530 P.2d 589 (1975). Carefully analyze both opinions and then write a textual report of the two opinions and an evaluation of the opinion of the court. In your evaluation, discuss first any of the nonsubstantive factors described in Section 2E that appear to be significant. Then discuss the adequacy of the court's treatment of the *Lucas* precedent (Appendix A) and any policy considerations that you think were or should have been influential. For an explanation of correct citation form, see Section 10G, *infra*.

SECTION 2F.　OPINION SYNTHESIS

Synthesis is essentially a process of comparing and relating precedents. In working with a particular problem, you will first select relevant mandatory precedents—those directly in point or analogous to the problem with which you are working. If you find more than one relevant precedent (as you frequently will), then you must compare the precedent cases and relate the opinions. From this process, this synthesis, you will derive a view of how the courts of the particular jurisdiction have dealt with your problem area. You will thus have a basis for predicting how your problem would be resolved by a court in that jurisdiction. If the synthesis of mandatory precedents does not yield a clear prediction, or if your evaluations

suggest weaknesses in the mandatory precedents, you may have to repeat the process with respect to relevant persuasive precedents.

You are already familiar with the simplest variety of synthesis if you have ever prepared an undergraduate term paper. This variety consists of drawing together reasons, conclusions, and other relevant material from several sources and weaving them together into a cohesive summary of an area of interest. The summaries of the rules for attorneys appearing in both the *Citizens' Loan* and *Hodges* opinions illustrate this type of synthesis. Given consistent treatment by a court or courts of the problem area in which you are interested, this variety of synthesis will suffice in your problem-solving work. Such consistency is an ideal, however. The ideal is not always realized when a given court has had to deal with a given problem area repeatedly over a period of years, with changing membership on the court. It is still less frequently realized by diverse courts from all parts of the country. Nevertheless, always start with the assumption that opinions dealing with common or analogous fact patterns and questions are consistent, particularly opinions of a given jurisdiction, and can be related to each other in some way that explains away apparent inconsistencies. The assumption may be wrong, but it will lead you to compare cases and resolution of questions more carefully.

Another variety of synthesis is more interesting and challenging, though modernly less commonly required. This variety requires tracing the growth of a particular approach to a given problem area from the first tentative gropings for a controlling principle to the formulation of a highly refined rule with detailed underlying reasoning. Thus, for example, the earliest relevant opinion might begin with a broadly phrased principle. Subsequent relevant decisions might add exceptions and refinements to suggest a somewhat limited rule. Later decisions might suggest further limiting factors, so that an even more refined rule must be stated. The reverse of this process might appear in a given line of precedents: in a series of precedents the court states narrow, seemingly divergent rules that can be explained by a governing principle.

You may be required to engage in such original and creative synthesis if no one has previously attempted to synthesize the particular collection of precedents that you select as relevant to a given problem. More often, the synthesis process will be partially or totally evaluative, that is, a check on a deciding court's own synthesis of precedents or a check on syntheses appearing in secondary materials. Even though you begin from an evaluative viewpoint, however, never forget that you may contribute something original. For example, you may recognize that a particular factor in a group of cases, not previously identified as significant, explains away apparent inconsistency between two groups of decisions. Consider the example suggested by Professor Oliphant in section 2G, *infra*.

Here is one way to approach the synthesis of seemingly inconsistent decisions. Starting with the assumption that they are actually consistent, compare them. Are the results truly inconsistent? Are the fact patterns of the cases similar, or are there some fact variations that might account for or suggest differing treatment by the court? Are the questions presented and resolved, both procedural and substantive, the same or analogous? If the facts and questions are the same or similar, look to the court's method of resolving the questions presented. Does the court appear to apply the same principle or rule? Is the reasoning inconsistent, or merely variant from opinion to opinion? If you identify significant differences in answer to one or more of these questions, you can group the opinions on the basis of the differences, and then review the same questions within each group.

The kind of synthesis suggested in the preceding paragraphs is a retrospective mental operation that follows collection and analysis of individual opinions. In actual problem solving, ideally, synthesis will be a progressive process accompanying analysis of individual opinions. That is, as you find and analyze relevant opinions you will note similarities and distinctions in fact patterns, questions presented, decisions, reasoning, and underlying rules and principles, so that when you have completed your research and accompanying opinion analysis, you will already have rationalized or grouped all the opinions. At least that is the end result toward which you should aim, because the ability to synthesize as you select relevant opinions will speed problem analysis and prediction.[20]

You will find examples of synthesis of varying quality in almost every opinion that you read—sometimes fully reported, but more often reported in the form of conclusions. Excellent examples of synthesis can be found in secondary authorities. The *Restatement of Contracts* is a classic example of rule synthesis. Each section of the Restatement states a rule or definition synthesized from opinions of courts throughout the United States, with accompanying comments that synthesize underlying reasoning and policies. Treatises and textbooks illustrate how principles, rules, and reasoning drawn from many individual opinions can be fused into a cohesive overview of courts' handling of particular types of problems.

Written Report of Synthesis. Without synthesis, a report on a group of cases presenting a common problem or issue would consist of textual statements of all the cases, a possibly unwieldy, monoto-

20. The process of synthesizing progressively—"matching the cases"—has been well described in a study-of-law context by Professor Karl Llewellyn, in Lecture III of The Bramble Bush (1960). The Bramble Bush collects a series of lectures delivered to students beginning the study of law. It is a short, instructive, and entertaining book that is well worth reading early in your law school career—particularly if you begin to feel that you do not understand what is expected of you in class and for class preparation.

nous recitation that would not give a reader an overall understanding of how a court or courts generally had dealt with the problem area. But, if you have analyzed a group of related opinions and concluded that the court in each instance reached the same result, stating all the cases is unnecessary. Rather, you might state the rule illustrated by the group of opinions, cite all of them, and then state fully only one case to illustrate the common factual pattern and a representative court's handling of it. Nothing more is needed if there are no significant factual or other differences among the cases and if the court or courts have used substantially similar reasoning.

Groups of cases and opinions are usually not so uniform, however, and the points of variation must therefore be identified. One technique is to report in groups based on the variable. For example, if all opinions in a group report the same result but report variant reasoning, the rule can be stated, the cases cited, and the illustrative case statement made; the cases can then be regrouped on the basis of the reasoning used (state one reasoning approach, cite supporting opinions; state second approach, cite supporting opinions).

Another approach to reporting variations is to use short, non-sentence parentheticals following the citation for each case. Thus, in the example given in the preceding paragraph, the variant reasoning of each court might be succinctly stated in non-sentence parentheticals following each citation after the illustrative case statement. Variant factual or procedural patterns might similarly be identified. Parentheticals may similarly be used to identify factors such as: (concurring opinion) (dictum) (5–4 decision) (per curiam).

FOURTH SUGGESTED EXERCISE

Prepare a synthesis on the law relating to liability of attorneys for negligence in performance of services as summarized and developed in *Citizens' Loan, Hodges, Lucas,* and *Smith.* Omit statements of the cases. Make your synthesis as comprehensive a survey of legal malpractice principles, rules, and reasoning as can be drawn from the four opinions and from the additional information about *Citizens' Loan* and *Hodges* reported in Section 2D. Use nonfootnoted form. For examples of nonfootnoted synthesis, see the summaries of law relating to liability set forth in each of the opinions. For other examples of synthesis style, see the case note on *Lucas v. Hamm* reproduced in Appendix C (particularly the second paragraph of the text and footnotes 1 and 2). (The note focuses on the portion of the court's opinion that is excerpted from *Lucas* as reproduced in Appendix A.)

SECTION 2G. THEORIES RELATED TO OPINION ANALYSIS

It has been suggested that a major difficulty in working with court opinions stems from the basic concepts of precedent and the

doctrine of stare decisis. What part of a prior opinion is the "decision" that a court may feel compelled to follow? How does one determine "the rules that appear to have been established" by prior decisions? Different writers have given different answers. To further complicate matters, they have used different terminology for similar ideas.

Compare the following discussions. How many different views are stated? Consider whether the author of this text appears to accept the view or views of one or more of these writers.

Mr. Henry Campbell Black wrote in 1912 for an early student hornbook:

The decision in a given case always is or should be concrete, as, that the plaintiff is or is not entitled to recover, that the judgment of the court below should be affirmed or reversed, that the prisoner should be discharged, the writ dismissed, etc. But this is not what is meant by the decision, as the term is used in relation to judicial precedents. Back of the particular judgment given lies the legal reason for giving it, or the juridical motive which caused the case to be decided as it was decided. This is called the "ratio decidendi." It is of course founded on the facts of the particular case, but is capable of being abstracted from them and generalized into the form of a proposition of law, or a series of such propositions, and, according to the theory of precedents, it is this doctrine or principle of law, held to govern the rights of the parties in a particular case and to determine the judgment which should be given therein, for which that case stands as an authority. The principle may or may not be explicitly set forth in the opinion of the court. Sometimes it is assumed, and the reasoning of the court is directed to the application of the rule to the special state of facts before it. Sometimes the rule is categorically or broadly stated. But it is not the very words of the court, but the underlying principle of law, which fixes the position of the decision as an authority. Even if the opinion of the court should be concerned with unnecessary considerations, or should state the proposition of law imperfectly or incorrectly, yet there is a proposition necessarily involved in the decision and without which the judgment in the case could not have been given; and it is this proposition which is established by the decision (so far as it goes) and for which alone the case may be cited as an authority.

It is important to be noticed, as a fundamental principle in the study of precedents, that it is the decision, that is, the judgment rendered in the case, and not the opinion of the court, which settles the point of law involved and makes the precedent. The decision is the conclusion of the court on the premises; the opinion sets forth the reasons of the determination, and usually states and explains them at greater or less length; and sometimes justifies and supports them by a copious citation of authorities and a wealth of argument, illustration, or analogy.[21]

21. H. Black, Handbook on the Law of Judicial Precedents 38, 39–40 (1912) (footnotes omitted). ("Hornbook" was the term used for an early series of student textbooks. The term is now used generally for any student textbook and also to describe elementary law—"hornbook law.")

Speaking to academicians in 1928, Professor Herman Oliphant argued for a more scientific approach to the study of cases:

[*Stare decisis*] asserts not one thing, but two. For one thing, it asserts that prior decisions are to be followed, not disregarded. But it also asserts that we are to follow the prior decisions and not something else.

* * *

The drift in our methods of dealing with legal problems which is upon us and is the subject of this discussion, concerns more intimately the second branch of the rule dealing with what it is in prior decisions which is to be followed. It is to be carefully noted that, when *stare decisis* is hereinafter mentioned, only this branch of the doctrine is referred to. It is in this quarter that innovation has been at work and is carrying us farther and farther toward treating this ancient doctrine as if it were *stare dictis* instead of *stare decisis*.

There seems to have been little critical study of this phase of the doctrine,—of just what it is in prior decisions which is to be followed. General statements that the decision is to be looked for, that dicta are of slight weight and offer no certain guide can be turned to at many places in the books and are familiar to all. Students beginning their law study are told these things in a general way and then are left to an apprenticeship among the cases to discover largely for themselves their fuller meaning. Yet this matter is the one most vital and difficult factor conditioning the soundness of their scholarship. It is because the word *decision* may mean any one of many things that it is perilous to leave the matter thus unarticulated.

What Does a Case Decide?

In the first place, a court, in deciding a case, may throw out a statement as to how it would decide some other case. Now if that statement is a statement of another case which is as narrow and specific as the actual case before the court, it is easily recognized as dictum and given its proper weight as such. In the second place the court may throw out a broader statement, covering a whole group of cases. But so long as that statement does not cover the case before the court, it is readily recognized as being not a decision, much less the decision of the case. It is dictum, so labeled and appraised. But in the third place, a court may make a statement broad enough to dispose of the case in hand as well as to cover also a few or many other states of fact. Statements of this third sort may cover a number of fact situations ranging from one other to legion. Such a statement is sometimes called the *decision* of the case. Thereby the whole ambiguity of that word is introduced and the whole difficulty presented.

If a more careful usage limits the word *decision* to the *action* taken by the court in the specific case before it, *i. e.*, to the naked judgment or order entered, the difficulty is not met; it is merely shifted. *Stare decisis* thus understood becomes useless for no decision in that limited sense can ever be followed. No identical case can arise. All other cases will differ in some circumstances,—in time, if in no other, and most of them will have differences which are not trivial. *Decision* in the sense meant in *stare decisis* must, therefore, refer to a proposition of law covering a group of fact situ-

ations * * * as a minimum, the fact situation of the instant case and at least one other.

To bring together into one class even this minimum of two fact situations however similar they may be, always has required and always will require an abstraction. If Paul and Peter are to be thought of together at all, they must both be apostles or be thought of as having some other attribute in common. Classification is abstraction. An element or elements common to the two fact situations put into one class must be drawn out from each to become the content of the category and the subject of the proposition of law which is thus applied to the two cases.

But such a grouping may include multitudes of fact situations so long as a single attribute common to them all can be found. Between these two extremes lies a gradation of groups of fact situations each with its corresponding proposition of law, ranging from a grouping subtending but two situations to those covering hosts of them. This series of groupings of fact situations gives us a parallel series of corresponding propositions of law, each more and more generalized as we recede farther and farther from the instant state of facts and include more and more fact situations in the successive groupings. It is a mounting and widening structure, each proposition including all that has gone before and becoming more general by embracing new states of fact. For example, A's father induces her not to marry B as she promised to do. On a holding that the father is not liable to B for so doing, a gradation of widening propositions can be built, a very few of which are:

    1. Fathers are privileged to induce daughters to break promises to marry.

    2. Parents are so privileged.

    3. Parents are so privileged as to both daughters and sons.

    4. All persons are so privileged as to promises to marry.

    5. Parents are so privileged as to all promises made by their children.

    6. All persons are so privileged as to all promises made by anyone.

There can be erected upon the action taken by a court in any case such a gradation of generalizations and this is commonly done in the opinion. Sometimes it is built up to dizzy heights by the court itself and at times, by law teacher and writers, it is reared to those lofty summits of the absolute and the infinite.

Where on that gradation of propositions are we to take our stand and say "This proposition is the decision of this case within the meaning of the doctrine of *stare decisis*?" Can a proposition of law of this third type ever become so broad that, as to any of the cases it would cover, it is mere dictum?

A Question of Double Difficulty

That would be difficult enough if it ended there. But just as one and the same apple can be thrown into any one of many groups of barrels according to its size, color, shape, etc., so also there stretches up and away

from every single case in the books, not one possible gradation of widening generalizations, but many. Multitudes of radii shoot out from it, each pair enclosing one of an indefinite number of these gradations of broader and broader generalizations. * * *

A student is told to seek the "doctrine" or "principle" of a case, but which of its welter of stairs shall he ascend and how high up shall he go? Is there some one step on some one stair which is *the* decision of the case within the meaning of the mandate *stare decisis*? That is the double difficulty.

* * *

But there is a constant factor in the cases which is susceptible of sound and satisfying study. The predictable element in it all is what courts have done in response to the stimuli of the facts of the concrete cases before them. Not the judges' opinions, but which way they decide cases will be the dominant subject matter of any truly scientific study of law.

* * *

One sampling of this proposed subject-matter of a real science of law must suffice. There are two lines of old cases involving the validity of promises not to compete. They are considered in square conflict. But when the opinions are ignored and the facts re-examined all the cases holding the promises invalid are found to be cases of employees' promises not to compete with their employers after a term of employment. Contemporary guild regulations not noticed in the opinions made their holding eminently sound. All the cases holding the promises valid were cases of promises by those selling a business and promising not to compete with the purchasers. Contemporary economic reality made these holdings also eminently sound. This distinction between these two lines of cases is not even hinted at in any of the opinions but the courts' intuition of experience led them to follow it with amazing sureness and the law resulting fitted life. * * * [22]

An English legal scholar, Arthur Goodhart, was troubled by the assumption underlying Professor Oliphant's position that judges decide cases on the basis of given sets of facts. He pointed out that facts are not constant. Judges reach conclusions on the basis of facts as *they* see them. He therefore attempted to state guiding rules (for determining the controlling principles) that were based in turn on rules for identifying the material (significant) facts:

In discussing the nature of a precedent in English law Sir John Salmond says:

> "A precedent, therefore, is a judicial decision which contains in itself a principle. The underlying principle which thus forms its authoritative element is often termed the *ratio decidendi*. The concrete decision is binding between the parties to it, but it is the abstract *ratio decidendi* which alone has the force of law as regards the world at large."

---

22. Oliphant, *A Return to Stare Decisis*, 14 A.B.A.J. 71, 72–73, 159 (1928) (footnotes omitted). Professor Oliphant was addressing the annual meeting of the American Association of Law Schools.

The rule is stated as follows by Professor John Chipman Gray:

"It must be observed that at the Common Law not every opinion expressed by a judge forms a Judicial Precedent. In order that an opinion may have the weight of a precedent, two things must concur: it must be, in the first place, an opinion given by a judge, and, in the second place, it must be an opinion the formation of which is necessary for the decision of a particular case; in other words, it must not be *obiter dictum.*"

Both the learned authors, on reaching this point of safety, stop. Having explained to the student that it is necessary to find the *ratio decidendi* of the case, they make no further attempt to state any rules by which it can be determined. It is true that Salmond says that we must distinguish between the concrete decision and the abstract *ratio decidendi*, and Gray states that the opinion must be a necessary one, but these are only vague generalizations. Whether it is possible to progress along this comparatively untrodden way in a search for more concrete rules of interpretation will be discussed in this paper.

*   *   *

Conclusion

The rules for finding the principle of a case can, therefore, be summarized as follows:

(1) The principle of a case is not found in the reasons given in the opinion.

(2) The principle is not found in the rule of law set forth in the opinion.

(3) The principle is not necessarily found by a consideration of all the ascertainable facts of the case and the judge's decision.

(4) The principle of the case is found by taking account (a) of the facts treated by the judge as material, and (b) his decision as based on them.

(5) In finding the principle it is also necessary to establish what facts were held to be immaterial by the judge, for the principle may depend as much on exclusion as it does on inclusion.

The rules for finding what facts are material and what facts are immaterial as seen by the judge are as follows:

(1) All facts of person, time, place, kind and amount are immaterial unless stated to be material.

(2) If there is no opinion, or the opinion gives no facts, then all other facts in the record must be treated as material.

(3) If there is an opinion, then the facts as stated in the opinion are conclusive and cannot be contradicted from the record.

(4) If the opinion omits a fact which appears in the record this may be due either to (a) oversight, or (b) an implied finding that the fact is immaterial. The second will be assumed to be the case in the absence of other evidence.

(5) All facts which the judge specifically states are immaterial must be considered immaterial.

(6) All facts which the judge impliedly treats as immaterial must be considered immaterial.

(7) All facts which the judge specifically states to be material must be considered material.

(8) If the opinion does not distinguish between material and immaterial facts then all the facts set forth must be considered material.

(9) If in a case there are several opinions which agree as to the result but differ as to the material facts, then the principle of the case is limited so as to fit the sum of all the facts held material by the various judges.

(10) A conclusion based on a hypothetical fact is a dictum. By hypothetical fact is meant any fact the existence of which has not been determined or accepted by the judge.[23]

The Goodhart views provoked an extended series of critical discussions that continued into the 1950's, when another scholar, Professor Julius Stone, sought to resolve the dispute:

Should we not, in the first place, try scrupulously to respect the distinction between that use of the term *ratio decidendi* which describes the process of reasoning by which decision was reached (the "descriptive" *ratio decidendi*), and that which identifies and delimits *the* reasoning which a later court is bound to follow (the "prescriptive" or "binding" *ratio decidendi*)?

Related to the distinction between the descriptive *ratio decidendi* and prescriptive *ratio decidendi,* are two approaches to the behaviour of courts as this bears on the problem of the *ratio decidendi.* One approach is that of the observer who seeks to describe and explain *as a matter of fact* how present decisions are related to prior decisions. The other approach seeks to establish from the behaviour of courts themselves, perhaps supplemented by assumed first principles, the limits within which, *as a matter of law,* a prior decision prescribes a binding rule for later decisions. It seeks (to use Professor Goodhart's term) to establish a "system" by which we can test what ground of decision of an earlier case is legally binding on the court in a later case.

* * *

Which of these attitudes is adopted by a particular inquiry is generally a matter of taste, or direction of intellectual interest. But it may also involve much more than that. To engage for example on an inquiry concerning *the* method, or even *the best* method, of discovery from the report of a single case what is "THE *ratio decidendi*" of that case, may also be an intellectually impermissible activity, unless at least two assumptions can be made. One of these is that there is normally ONE *ratio decidendi*, AND ONE ONLY, which explains the holding on the facts, and is as such bind-

23. Goodhart, *Determining the Ratio Decidendi of a Case,* 40 Yale L.J. 161–62, 182–83 (1930) (footnotes omitted). Reprinted by permission of the au-thor, The Yale Law Journal Company, and Fred B. Rothman & Company, from *The Yale Law Journal*, Vol. 40, pp. 161–183.

ing. The other is that such a *ratio decidendi*, assumed to exist, can be delimited from examination of the particular case itself. Professor Goodhart's paper of 1931 (originally published 1930), both by its general thesis and by its detailed argument, indulges both of these assumptions. It is, indeed, a model of their indulgence.

It is believed that the assumptions just stated will not bear examination, and the reasons for this belief may here be expanded as follows.

If the *ratio* of a case is deemed to turn on the facts in relation to the holding, and nine facts (a)–(j) are to be found in the report, there may (so far as logical possibilities are concerned) be as many rival *rationes decidendi* as there are possible combinations of distinguishable facts in it. What is more, each of these "facts" is usually itself capable of being stated at various levels of generality, all of which embrace "the fact" in question in the precedent decision, but each of which may yield a different result in the different fact-situation of a later case.

* * *

We here approach the very core of the difference between Professor Goodhart and the present writer concerning "the *ratio decidendi* of a case." * * * This is, that there is not (despite Professor Goodhart's theory) any one *ratio decidendi* which is necessary to explain a particular decision, and is discoverable from that decision.

For, once it is granted that "a material fact" of the precedent case can be stated at various levels of generality, each of which is correct for that case, any of these levels of statement is potentially a "material fact." Insofar as the *ratio decidendi* is determined by each "material fact," then what the precedent case yields must be a number of potentially binding *rationes* competing *inter se* to govern future cases of which the facts may fall within one level of generality, but not within another.

* * *

That the above submissions are correct can (with respect) also be inferred from Professor Goodhart's latest statement on the matter. He expresses himself, at the very end of his recent article, as in complete agreement with the present writer's view that "further decisions are frequently required" before the scope of "the *ratio decidendi* of a case" [Footnote omitted.] is finally determined. The least that this can mean is that the scope of the *ratio decidendi* of the precedent case will "frequently" not be determined or determinable until further decisions have been made; and that it will "frequently" be impossible to draw from "the facts treated by the judge as material and his decision as based on them" a single *ratio decidendi* that will serve as a useful basis for later judgment. If this is so, we must look in a single case not for the one single binding *ratio decidendi*, but rather for a range of alternative *rationes decidendi* competing *inter se* to govern future fact situations; and, as among these, only future decisions will show which is binding. All this involves critical admissions, which (it is ventured to submit) finally contradict Professor Goodhart's steady assumptions that there must be a single *ratio decidendi* of a case, ascertainable from within that case.[24]

24. Stone, *The Ratio of the Ratio Decidendi*, 22 Mod.L.Rev. 597, 600, 602–03, 607–608 (1959) (footnotes omitted). Copyright Modern Law Review Limited, London, 1959. Reproduced with permission of the publisher and the author.

In the meantime, an American law professor, Karl Llewellyn, had stated his views for the benefit of students beginning the study of law:

[It] now becomes our task to inquire into how the system of precedent which we actually have works out in fact, accomplishing at once stability and change.

We turn first to what I may call the orthodox doctrine of precedent, with which, in its essence, you are already familiar. Every case lays down a rule, the rule of the case. The express ratio decidendi is prima facie the rule of the case, since it is the ground upon which the court chose to rest its decision. But a later court can reexamine the case and can invoke the canon that no judge has power to decide what is not before him, can, through examination of the facts or of the procedural issue, narrow the picture of what was actually before the court and can hold that the ruling made requires to be understood as thus restricted. In the extreme form this results in what is known as expressly "confining the case to its particular facts." This rule holds only of redheaded Walpoles in pale magenta Buick cars. And when you find this said of a past case you know that in effect it has been overruled. Only a convention, a somewhat absurd convention, prevents flat overruling in such instances. It seems to be felt as definitely improper to state that the court in a prior case was wrong, peculiarly so if that case was in the same court which is speaking now. It seems to be felt that this would undermine the dogma of the infallibility of courts. So lip service is done to that dogma, while the rule which the prior court laid down is disembowelled. The execution proceeds with due respect, with mandarin courtesy.

Now this orthodox view of the authority of precedent—which I shall call the *strict* view—is but *one of two views* which seem to me wholly contradictory to each other. It is in practice the dogma which is applied to *unwelcome* precedents. It is the recognized, legitimate, honorable technique for whittling precedents away, for making the lawyer, in his argument, and the court, in its decision, free of them. It is a surgeon's knife.

It is orthodox, I think, because it has been more discussed than is the other. Consider the situation. It is not easy thus to carve a case to pieces. It takes thought, it takes conscious thought, it takes analysis. There is no great art and no great difficulty in merely looking at a case, reading its language, and then applying some sentence which is there expressly stated. But there is difficulty in going underneath what it said, in making a keen reexamination of the case that stood before the court, in showing that the language used was quite beside the point, as the point is revealed under the lens of leisured microscopic refinement. Hence the technique of distinguishing cases has given rise to the closest of scrutiny.   *   *   *

[W]hen you turn to the actual operations of the courts, or, indeed, to the arguments of lawyers, you will find a totally different view of precedent at work beside this first one. That I shall call, to give it a name, the *loose view* of precedent. That is the view that a court has decided, and decided authoritatively, *any* point or all points on which it chose to rest a case, or on which it chose, after due argument, to pass. No matter how broad the statement, no matter how unnecessary on the facts or the proce-

dural issues, if that was the rule the court laid down, then that the court has held. Indeed, this view carries over often into dicta, and even into dicta which are grandly obiter. In its extreme form this results in thinking and arguing exclusively from *language* that is found in past opinions, and in citing and working with that language wholly without reference to the facts of the case which called the language forth.

Now it is obvious that this is a device not for cutting past opinions away from judges' feet, but for using them as a springboard when they are found convenient. This is a device for *capitalizing welcome precedents.* And both the lawyers and the judges use it so. And judged by the *practice* of the most respected courts, as of the courts of ordinary stature, this doctrine of precedent is like the other, recognized, legitimate, honorable.[25]

Most recently, another American law professor summarized the foregoing views and then stated his own conclusions:

The correct view of the nature and scope of the *ratio decidendi* must proceed from the premise that it is neither the material facts of the case nor the rule of law as formulated by the court which form the authoritative element in a decision. The controlling question to be asked in determining the weight of a prior decision is whether the rationale of public policy underlying the first decision (which the first court tried to cast into the form of a proposition of law) is equally applicable in the second case. *A later case involving facts similar to those present in an earlier case should, as a general rule, be decided in consonance with the earlier case where both cases fall under the principle of public policy or justice which lay at the bottom of the earlier decision.* It is possible, however, that the policy rationale of the earlier case was inadequately or awkwardly stated by the judge, or that the verbal formalization chosen by him in spelling out the principle was either too broad or too narrow. The principle enunciated in the decision should not be broader than necessary to dispose of the legal problem before the court, but broad enough to include situations that cannot on any reasonable ground be distinguished from the facts at hand.

* * *

According to this view, a case is not controlling as a precedent for the sole reason that similarities and parallels between the facts of the earlier and later cases can be discerned. The *ratio decidendi* must be discovered by relating the facts of the two cases to a principle of legal policy which reasonably covers both situations. In many instances, this principle of policy will not spring into existence as a finished creature the first time it is expressed by a court. It will often have been stated by the court in a tentative and groping fashion, and its true import and scope will not be capable of being ascertained until other courts have had a chance to correct the inadequacies of the first formulation and to graft exceptions, qualifications, and caveats upon the principle. In this way the *ratio decidendi* of a case often develops its true and full meaning slowly and haltingly, and it may take a whole series of decisions involving variations of the situation presented in the first case until a full-blown rule of law, surrounded perhaps by a cluster of exceptions, replaces the tentatively and inadequately

25. The Bramble Bush 66–68 (1960). Copyright 1930, 1951 and 1960 by K. N. Llewellyn. Reproduced with permission of the copyright holder.

formulated generalization found in the initial decision. In short, a whole course of decisions will gradually mark out the outer limits of a legal principle left indeterminate by the first decision attempting to give form to it.[26]

SECTION 2H.   A CAVEAT

One of the dangers of the kind of description of mental skills that has been attempted in this chapter is that it creates the appearance of clarity and certainty for skills that are actually infinitely variable and that can be acquired only through experience. This point has been explained by one scholar as follows:

> Karl Llewellyn in *The Common Law Tradition* * * * gives a list, admittedly incomplete, of some sixty-four techniques for handling precedent, illustrated by reference to decided American cases: eight ways to * * * constrict a precedent, eight to stand by it, thirty-two to expand it, twelve ways to avoid it and four to kill it. * * *
>
> Judges, lawyers, sometimes even law students, use these techniques without having Llewellyn's list before them. For the most part, citation of authority is "an uncritical unreflective process," not necessarily or even usually engaged in with conscious reference to rules about the function of precedent. Insofar as it purports to state what must, may, or may not be done with previously decided cases, the doctrine of *stare decisis* cannot be disassociated from the prevailing craft tradition, the conventions, tacit as well as explicit, according to which lawyers argue points of law. The arguing or deciding of cases is, in other words, a matter of drawing on a complex of habits, experiences, and skills which are more or less the common property of people trained in a particular legal tradition. Those skills and habits cannot be adequately reduced to rule anymore [sic] than one can learn to be a connoisseur of art or of wine by reading a book and without ever seeing a picture or opening a bottle. It is not simply that practical experience is important. Rather, the necessary knowledge is largely implicit, learned from and constituted by particular instances of its exercise.[27]

NOTES

1. For a brief discussion of the views expressed in the material quoted in Section 2G, see E. Bodenheimer, Jurisprudence § 87 (Rev.

---

26. E. Bodenheimer, Jurisprudence 437–39 (Rev. ed. 1974). Copyright 1974 by the President and Fellows of Harvard College. Reproduced from earlier edition with permission of the publisher, Harvard University Press, and the author.

27. Wise, *The Doctrine of Stare Decisis*, 21 Wayne L.Rev. 1043, 1051–52 (1975) (footnotes omitted). Copyright 1975, Wayne Law Review. Quoted with permission.

ed. 1974). For a discussion of other views as well, see Comment, *Diverse Views of What Constitutes the Principle of Law of a Case,* 36 U.Colo.L.Rev. 377 (1964). For a short but very useful discussion of analyzing and briefing opinions for study-of-law purposes, see Gross, *On Law School Training in Analytic Skill,* 25 J.Legal Educ. 261, 271–83 (1973). For exhaustive discussions of analyzing and briefing opinions for problem-solving purposes, see W. Statsky and R. Wernet, Jr., Case Analysis and Fundamentals of Legal Writing chs. 6–20 (1977). For a novel approach to analyzing opinions on a mass basis, see Stayton, *An Easement to Decision: A Servitude Upon Judicial Legislation,* 35 Tex.L.Rev. 20 (1956). For the classic introduction to development of case skills in the law study setting, see K. Llewellyn, The Bramble Bush (1960). Another introductory book, F. Cooper, Living the Law (1958), is helpful in relating the study of law to the practice of law.

2. A trial court is expected to follow the decisions of the appellate courts in its jurisdiction. A trial judge could refuse to do so, however, and thus decide a case before it in a manner inconsistent with a directly-in-point mandatory precedent. What could the injured party do in such a case? Can you think of some factors that might operate to restrain trial judges from deliberately refusing to follow such a precedent? Can you think of some factors that might nevertheless lead a trial judge to refuse to follow such a precedent? One author has suggested the following answers to these questions:

> No simple blueprint can instruct a judge, high or low, in the astute performance of his craft; but our study of reasonably typical precedent situations prompts the following observations:
>
> 1. A rule of decision which is clear and unimpaired is authoritative. It is therefore to be applied by the lower judges, nolens volens. They are of course privileged to criticize and to suggest needful modifications. Indeed they should do so if convinced that the law is intolerable or seriously defective. But subordinate judges court censure if they reject controlling authority, whether openly or by techniques of evasion.
>
> 2. Judges must be alert to the fact that a rule can lose its force without formal repudiation. Absent a fair ground of logic or policy which serves to reconcile later with prior decisions, the lower courts should not shrink from declaring that an implied overruling has taken place and should in that event give full effect to the change.
>
> 3. When the case law is neither clear nor settled but obscure or erratic, there is strictly speaking no controlling authority. To characterize appellate decisions as nugatory is

not something that should be done hastily. However, when satisfied that there is no dispositive precedent despite colorably pertinent cases, the lower judge then has the duty, and the opportunity, to propound a sound rule of decision—one which not only resolves his present litigation but which stands a chance of promoting clarification and improvement on a larger scale.

The foregoing precedent situations require of the lower courts the diverse virtues of obedience, discrimination, and creativity. All are necessary. Each has its place.

Kelman, *The Force of Precedent in the Lower Courts*, 14 Wayne L. Rev. 3, 28 (1967). Quoted with permission. Consider the possible significance of these questions and answers for you as an attorney in a problem-solving role.

3. An instructor in political science recently questioned 342 undergraduate students and 10 judges in the same urban area about the factors that do or should enter into a judge's decision of a case. The responses are reported in Skogan, *Judicial Myth and Judicial Reality*, 1971 Wash.U.L.Q. 309. One of the factors inquired about was the importance of following the legal precedents established in the past, prefaced by the statement: "A judge must weigh a number of factors when he makes a decision in a case. For each of the following, indicate the extent to which you think they are factors that judges here in Milwaukee consider when they are making decisions." With respect to the importance of legal precedent, the responses were as follows:

	Judges	*Students*
Very important	20%	19%
Important	80%	48%
Don't Know	0%	7%
Unimportant	0%	22%
Very unimportant	0%	4%

How would you have responded to this question? What reasons can you advance on behalf of following precedents? Are these reasons of equal importance in all areas of law? Why or why not? The judges questioned in the Skogan survey were all trial court judges. Would this fact cause them to attach special significance to following precedents? Why or why not?

4. One of the reasons frequently advanced against the overruling of a precedent is that failure to follow a precedent would be unfair to those who have relied on it in planning their affairs. The argument assumes that an overruling decision must be given retrospective effect, that is, it must be applied to all cases subsequently coming before a court in the jurisdiction, even though the events giving rise

to a case occurred before the overruling decision. One response to this kind of reasoning is to give an overruling decision prospective effect only. See Comment, *Prospective Overruling—"Sunburst" Theory*, 18 Baylor L.Rev. 606 (1966). What objections may be raised to this approach? Consider, for example, Molitor v. Kaneland Community Unit Dist. No. 302, 18 Ill.2d 11, 163 N.E.2d 89 (1959) (5–2). The plaintiff, Thomas Molitor, was one of fourteen school children injured in a school bus accident. The lower court dismissed his complaint for damages on the ground that the school district was immune from tort liability under a common law rule based on the doctrine of sovereign immunity, except under limited circumstances as permitted by statute. Concluding that the common law rule was unjust and was unsupported by any valid reason in modern society, the court abolished the doctrine and overruled all prior contrary decisions, but limited its decision as follows:

> In here departing from *stare decisis* because we believe justice and policy require such departure, we are nonetheless cognizant of the fact that retrospective application of our decision may result in great hardship to school districts which have relied on prior decisions upholding the doctrine of tort immunity of school districts. For this reason we feel justice will best be served by holding that, except as to the plaintiff in the instant case, the rule herein established shall apply only to cases arising out of future occurrences. This result is in accord with a substantial line of authority embodying the theory that an overruling decision should be given only prospective operation whenever injustice or hardship due to reliance on the overruled decisions would thereby be averted. *   *   *

> Likewise there is substantial authority in support of our position that the new rule shall apply to the instant case. *   *   * At least two compelling reasons exist for applying the new rule to the instant case while otherwise limiting its application to cases arising in the future. First, if we were to merely announce the new rule without applying it here, such announcement would amount to mere *dictum*. Second, and more important, to refuse to apply the new rule here would deprive appellant of any benefit from his effort and expense in challenging the old rule which we now declare erroneous. Thus there would be no incentive to appeal the upholding of precedent since appellant could not in any event benefit from a reversal invalidating it.

> It is within our inherent power as the highest court of this State to give a decision prospective or retrospective application without offending constitutional principles. Great Northern Railway Co. v. Sunburst Oil & Refining Co., 287 U.S. 358, 53 S.Ct. 145, 77 L.Ed. 360.

> Although ordinarily the cases which have invoked the doctrine of prospective operation have involved contract or property rights or criminal responsibility, the basis of the doctrine is reliance upon an overruled precedent. Despite the fact that the instant case is one sounding in tort, it appears that the "reliance test" has been met here. We do not suggest that the tort itself was committed in reliance on the substantive law of torts, *i. e.*, the bus driver did not drive negligently in reliance on the doctrine of

governmental immunity, but rather that school districts and other municipal corporations have relied upon immunity and that they will suffer undue hardship if abolition of the immunity doctrine is applied retroactively. In reliance on the immunity doctrine, school districts have failed to adequately insure themselves against liability. In reliance on the immunity doctrine, they have probably failed to investigate past accidents which they would have investigated had they known they might later be held responsible therefor. Our present decision will eliminate much of the hardship which might be incurred by school districts as a result of their reliance on the overruled doctrine, and at the same time reward appellant for having afforded us the opportunity of changing an outmoded and unjust rule of law.

For the reasons herein expressed, we accordingly hold that in this case the school district is liable in tort for the negligence of its employee, and, all prior decisions to the contrary are hereby overruled.

163 N.E.2d at 96–98. See 14 Vand.L.Rev. 406 (1960). (The cited law review material is a Recent Case Note on the *Molitor* case. For a description of the purpose and form of this kind of law review material, see Section 10B, *infra*.) Both the author of the cited Note and a dissenting judge were concerned about the unfairness of the court's approach to the other children injured in the same accident. The court subsequently finessed this unfairness argument in Molitor v. Kaneland Community Unit Dist. No. 302, 24 Ill.2d 467, 182 N.E.2d 145 (1962) (plaintiffs included three siblings of Thomas Molitor), by finding that the first *Molitor* appeal had been a test case for these plaintiffs, too, and in Larson v. Kaneland Community Unit Dist. No. 302, 52 Ill.App.2d 209, 201 N.E.2d 865 (1964) (plaintiffs were also children injured in the same accident), by concluding that the plaintiffs had waived any claim they might have to recovery under the new rule by proceeding to judgment while appeals on the immunity rule were pending.

5. In reading opinions be aware of the authoring courts' analysis, synthesis, and evaluation of other court opinions. For example, after your first reading of an opinion for understanding of the problem before the court and for tentative identification of the "parts" of that opinion, review the opinion to consider the factors that the court takes into account in evaluating precedents. Also note the manner in which the court has discussed precedent opinions and how it has discussed opinions in relation to each other. This separate attention to courts' handling of precedents will aid your understanding of both the particular opinion and the factors that influence courts in resolving legal problems. It will also provide you with a developing awareness of the possible forms for much of your future legal writing, because discussion of analysis, synthesis, and evaluation of court opinions will be the nucleus of much of the legal writing that you will ultimately do.

FIFTH SUGGESTED EXERCISE

Prepare a casenote on *Smith v. Lewis* (Appendix B). For form, be guided by the casenote reproduced in Appendix C and by the description of this form of legal writing in Section 10B, *infra*. For substance, draw on the *Smith* opinions, on *Citizens' Loan, Hodges,* and *Lucas,* and on the additional information about *Citizens' Loan* and *Hodges* reported throughout Section 2D.

In all legal writing, the name of a case and its full citation should be given soon after the case is first mentioned. Case names may always be shortened by omitting the names of all but the first of multiple parties and by omitting the first names and initials of individual parties. Once you have given a case name and citation, in a continuing discussion you may refer to the case by the plaintiff's name or a shortened form of it. If the plaintiff's name is not distinctive (for example, if it is State or United States), the defendant's name or a shortened form of it may be used. For other citation rules, see Section 10G, *infra*.

In preparing your casenote, avoid the common writing errors discussed in Section 10F, *infra*.

Chapter 3

INTERPRETING STATUTES

SECTION 3A. INTRODUCTION

In this chapter we will examine preliminarily how a court's decisional approach to identifying and interpreting controlling law and, therefore, your approach, may differ if a problem is controlled by a statute rather than by the common law.

Statutes represent but one of several forms of written law. At the top of the hierarchy of written law is the Federal Constitution and treaties and laws made under the authority of the Constitution. Laws made under the Constitution include acts of Congress adopted within the ambit of authority described by the Constitution, interstate compacts (agreements entered into by states and approved by Congress), executive orders of the President, rules and regulations promulgated by federal administrative bodies acting under authority granted by Congress, and federal court rules. Within state jurisdictions is a similar hierarchy, excluding treaties but including, in addition, legislation of subordinate governmental units such as counties and cities.

In this text no attempt will be made to deal with problems involving treaties or interstate compacts, and in this chapter the discussion will be limited to problems governed by statutes. Much of what is said about statutes will have relevance for other forms of written law, but for future reference remember that distinctive approaches have developed around each form of written law.

Statutes are pervasive in our modern law. The bulk of federal law is derived from statutes enacted within the constitutional framework. In the states, statutes have been used to supplement, to clarify or to change single common law rules (for example, torts rules). They have been used in attempts to completely replace areas of the common law (for example, criminal law). They have been used to create and define completely new areas of law (for example, workmen's compensation). Statutes may even have an indirect impact on the common law. Thus, a court may decide that a statutory rule implementing a carefully reasoned policy is so salutary that it should be

applied in a case to which the statute clearly does not extend. For example, a statutory rule designed to govern sales of personal property may be adopted by a court to govern a sale of real property.

The possibility of working with a problem governed by a statute may have a certain appeal for you after your introduction to some of the uncertainties of working with the common law. The appearance of fewer uncertainties in working with statutes is deceptive, however. The scope of application of some statutes will be apparent merely from reading them, but this is equally true of some judicial precedents. On the other hand, uncertainties as to the meaning of many statutes will lead you right back into the judicial precedent labyrinth, because judicial construction may be necessary if the language or scope of application of a statute is not clear.

SECTION 3B.   HISTORY OF COURTS' CONSTRUCTION OF STATUTES

The history of the construction of statutes by courts has not always been one of advancement of the best interests of society. Construction should begin with the language of the statute. Courts long recognized that if the language were ambiguous, vague, or inconsistent, the purpose of the legislation (or the "intent of the legislature") should guide the construction thereof. But what if the language were not, in the abstract, ambiguous, vague, or inconsistent? During the early history of construction of statutes, a court's inquiry might go no further. If there was but one "plain meaning," the courts said, they must enforce the statute according to that plain meaning. They rationalized their attachment to the words used in a statute by saying that the "intent" of the legislature was best reflected in the language chosen. They thus refused to look beyond the seemingly unambiguous statute to extrinsic historical materials that might shed light on the purpose of the statute, suggesting quite a different meaning than a literal reading would suggest. A qualification of this "plain meaning" rule was recognized: if the "plain meaning" would lead to an absurd or totally unreasonable result, a court would look at extrinsic materials to guide its interpretation. Some courts nevertheless reached what could certainly be characterized as "absurd" results because of their assumption that words can have absolute meanings that must have been known by the legislators. After some erratic application of the "plain meaning" rule, the United States Supreme Court rejected it, emphasizing that the purposes of the legislation should be considered even though a statute seemed to apply unambiguously to a fact pattern. In other words, the Court affirmed that it would look beyond the language of the statute to determine the purposes of the legislation and to decide whether even a "plain meaning" was consonant with those purposes. State courts appear to have taken a similarly enlightened view. Nevertheless, some courts still tend

to write as though they can identify a "plain" (and hence, indisputable) meaning for particular language.[1]

Courts frequently characterize their search for external guidance to meaning as a search for the "intent of the legislature," rather than for "purpose." This phraseology clouds the inquiry. A legislature is not an entity capable of a common "intent." Whose "intent" is being sought then? that of a majority of legislators? of the members of the standing committee that reported the statute out? of the drafters? And, "intent" as to what? as to possible applicability of the statute to the specific factual pattern before the court? or something more general? The "purpose" phraseology can raise similar questions if "purpose" is thought to be related to applicability of a statute to a specific problem—or even to some kind of mental concurrence in a more general purpose. What should be sought, it would appear, is an understanding of the evil or mischief that the statute seems designed to correct, in light of the language used, the circumstances at the time of enactment, and information to be derived from the enactment process and documents produced in connection with that process.[2]

Just as early courts, through the plain meaning rule, sometimes imposed an arbitrary limitation on consideration of extrinsic materials, they also placed sometimes arbitrary limitations on the types of extrinsic materials that could be considered. Thus, for example, federal courts refused to consider reports of congressional debates. They also solved construction problems by arbitrary rules called "canons." For example, the courts developed rules calling for "strict" or "liberal" construction, depending on the character of the statute (for example, penal, remedial, or in derogation of the common law) or rules dignified by Latin phrases, such as *ejusdem generis* (of the same class) or *expressio unius est exclusio alterius* (expression of one excludes others)[3] that sometimes artifically limited the meaning of words. Some canons were logical guides to assigning meaning in the absence of other guidance. Unfortunately, the logical canons were sometimes invoked to reach results inconsistent with persuasive evidence of the purpose of particular legislation. The arbitrariness

---

1. *See* Murphy, *Old Maxims Never Die: The "Plain-Meaning Rule" and Statutory Interpretation in the "Modern" Federal Courts*, 75 Colum.L.Rev. 1299 (1975). For a more extended discussion of the "plain meaning rule" and the suggestion that it is not a single rule but has several variations, some quite acceptable, see R. Dickerson, The Interpretation and Application of Statutes 229–33 (1975).

2. *See* R. Dickerson, The Interpretation and Application of Statutes chs. 7 and 8 (1975) for a more sophisticated analysis. Professor Dickerson concludes

in part: "The necessity of assuming some actual subjective purpose includes only the necessity of assuming an immediate purpose exhausted by the statute. This purpose is best identified by the term 'legislative intent.' Being co-extensive with the problem of intended meaning, this concept normally furnishes, not a solution to, but a more helpful statement of, the problem." *Id.* at 101.

3. *See* J. Davies, Legislative Law and Process in a Nutshell 260–61 (1975) for a brief explanation of these and other canons.

or arbitrary application of canons contributed to the development of parallel inconsistent rules to escape the result of the earlier canons.[4] Courts still invoke canons as aids to construction, but their modern use is more often limited to interpreting statutes for which there are no legislative history materials (that is, materials related to the enactment process) or to justifying a result already suggested by a less arbitrary approach.

The history of courts' approaches to statutory construction is inextricably interwoven with the history of their attitude toward statutes as a source of law. In the definitive text on the history of major legal institutions in this country, Professor James Willard Hurst has reviewed the interaction of courts with legislatures as lawmakers. The following excerpt presents a summary of that interaction and also gives some additional information about modern courts' approaches to statutory construction.

Both trial and appellate courts were major lawmakers in United States history. In the first half of the nineteenth century, within the confines of a "judicial" power limited to disposition of particular disputes, the courts did the vast job of fashioning a body of common law for the main affairs of everyday life. They defined the bases of rights in real property; they laid the foundations for the law of business contracts and commercial instruments; they shaped rudimentary doctrine for such fields of new importance as the law of negligence or of the conflict of laws. From the logic and decisions of John Marshall, in the third quarter of the century the judges made good their title to pass on the constitutionality of legislation; and they used the power to such effect as to make it a material factor in the social balance of power. To 1937 judicial review continued to be a tangible influence on what the legislature did and how it did it, especially in regard to economic regulation. * * * [T]hrough the drama of judicial review, the courts made the idea of constitutional limitations one of the most powerful elements in our political thinking.

The task of statutory interpretation took on increasing importance in the role of the courts. This development paralleled the growing importance of judicial review in the late nineteenth century * * *

The interpretation of statutes offered a truly creative job for the judges. But the chances of events long obscured the creative opportunity. The legislature and its works fell far in popular standing in the second

---

4. A number of these "rules," as well as statements about the force of legislative history materials, have been gathered under the characterizations, "Thrust and Parry" (state courts handling of statutes) and "Thrust and Counterthrust" (federal courts handling of statutes) in K. Llewellyn, The Common Law Tradition: Deciding Appeals, *Appendix C,* 521–35 (1960). (Examples: *Thrust*: "Where various states have already adopted the statute, the parent state is followed." *Parry*: "Where interpretations of other states are inharmonious, there is no such restraint." *Id.* 523. *Thrust*: " 'The Court is not bound by an administrative construction.' " *Counterthrust*: " 'The construction given to a statute by those charged with the duty of executing it * * * ought not to be overruled without cogent reasons * * * and the administrative interpretation is of controlling weight unless plainly erroneous.' " *Id.* 534.).

quarter of the nineteenth century. But at the same time the newly forming states felt the urgent pressure of practical needs for law to meet their everyday needs and the everyday problems of the people. The response to this pressure afforded the first great manifestation of judicial lawmaking in the United States. Out of this period of policy leadership, the courts learned confidence in their own capacity to decide what was best for the community. For example, in the late nineteenth century, judges were not inclined to look favorably on legislation which, like the married women's property acts, changed doctrine which judges had made the law of the land. There was more involved than a conflict of policy ambitions. Social conservatism brought the full flowering of due process doctrine at the end of the century; the same impetus also inclined the courts, where they were not ready boldly to declare social legislation unconstitutional, to interpret it so restrictively as to narrow its effect.

These factors found expression in the abstract canons of statutory interpretation which liberally ornamented judicial opinions after the '70s: strict construction of statutes in derogation of the common law; strict construction of penal statutes, or of legislation that imposed "drastic" burdens, or of legislation that imposed special damages, or of legislation that could be fitted to one or another of various tags.

The effect was to put a primarily obstructive, if not destructive connotation on the process of statutory interpretation. And insofar as this was not the temper of approach, nineteenth-century lawmen tended to rate legislation or its proper handling as of secondary importance in the law. This depreciation of the statute book was promoted by the preeminence of case-made, judge-made law in the formative first half of the nineteenth century; and this was reinforced, first, by the office-apprentice system of legal education, and then by the spread of the case method in the law schools. Legislation was an intrusion on a symmetrical system of learning properly found only in the Reports. One could to general satisfaction summarily distinguish a cited case if he could brush it aside as merely "turning on the particular statute involved."

The slowness with which courts drew on the full resources of legislative history in the interpretation of statutes was a measure of their lack of interest or sympathy toward the legislative process; or, equally, it measured their failure to understand what was implied in a true effort to carry out their often-announced duty to find "the intention of the legislature." As late as 1897 a leading opinion of the Supreme Court of the United States noted "general acquiescence in the doctrine that debates in Congress are not appropriate sources of information from which to discover the meaning of the language of a statute passed by that body."

But it was in the trend of events that statutory interpretation should form one of the positive contributions of the courts to the making of law. Only the legislature—with its control of the purse, its powers of investigation, and its varied array of benefits and sanctions—could begin to cope with the demands made on government after the 1870's. But experience taught that the best-drawn statute was only the starting point of effective regulation; this was inevitable, out of the limits set by language and men's foresight, as well as by the infinite variety of events and causes. The measure of understanding, sympathy, and vigor with which the executive or the

judges implemented a statute decided how far it became a living fact of the community life.

Between about 1880 and 1920 legislation again became, as it once had been, the main growing point of the law in the United States. By 1920 administrative legislation shared this distinction. In either case, after 1880 the leadership in making general policy had passed from the courts; their creative opportunity had become the subordinate, but essential, task of imaginative, firm implementation of legislative policy.

The decisions after 1900 began to reflect a more affirmative and practical, a less negative and literal, approach, in response to the pressure of this shift in the political situation. Tangible witness of the change was in shifting techniques of interpretation. The canons of construction whose elaboration filled the pages of nineteenth-century treatises began to disappear from judges' opinions. After 1920 it became hard to assemble from the Digest any substantial citations to so familiar a late-nineteenth-century shibboleth as the rule that statutes in derogation of common law must be strictly construed. Before it had explicitly validated the change, in practice the Supreme Court of the United States began to drop the barriers to full use of the history of a statute as light upon its meaning. Where there had been absolutely phrased rules of competency that barred use of hearings, debates, committee reports, there appeared by the 1930's more or less explicit recognition that almost any official source contemporary with the passage of a statute might be used in its interpretation. The effect of such background evidence was to be gauged by its credibility, and not by its compliance with formal rules of competence.

Significant of the realism of the new approach was the particular weight given to materials that directly reflected how a modern legislature worked. This meant according particular attention, on the legislative side, to committee reports and to the remarks made in debate by leading committeemen; it meant, on the executive side, particular weight to executive messages and letters, in reflection of the executive's growing leadership in the legislative program; it meant, on the administrative side, attention to evidence of a long-continued, uniform, practical construction of the statute by men who, charged with immediate responsibility for effecting its objects, might be deemed aware of what was needed to make it work, men who oftentimes had sponsored the statute before the legislature as a response to their administrative experience.

In the law at least, mere technique guarantees no one result; there remains inescapably "the sovereign prerogative of choice." In 1940 as well as in 1890 the interpretation of statutes inevitably demanded that the courts share in making policy. One could still find examples—one was the restrictive interpretation of state statutes which curbed the use of the injunction in labor disputes—where judges hostile or distrustful toward the legislative judgment clearly shaped construction to minimize the effect of a statute. Only the naive could not see that in adroit hands the "history" behind an act might be read in different ways: The new technique of using legislative history in interpretation might widen, rather than narrow, the judge's discretion.

Nonetheless, the new approach lent itself less than the old to manipulation in the interests of the judge's personal values. It was most insistent

on a demonstrated basis in fact, for the interpretation given the legislation. And in any case its basic importance was that it showed a shift in the prevailing attitude toward statute law. Late-nineteenth-century judges rationalized their interpretations under abstract canons of construction which had no necessary relation, and required no showing of any specific relation, to the legislation in question. Clearly there was a drastic change in approach, when courts sought to view an act in terms of its own particular genealogy, and in effect to fashion their principle of construction from the materials of the statute's own environment and origins.

The change perhaps reflected the pragmatism which characterized thought in the United States after the turn into the new century. Certainly it evidenced a shift in the climate of opinion affecting the balance of power. Perhaps the judges merely shared the self-doubt of their generation. Perhaps they yielded more or less consciously to the weight of events which had thrust the initiative in policy on the legislative and executive branches. In any case, in the second quarter of the twentieth century judges plainly lacked the serene self-confidence and assurance of wisdom and rightness with which their predecessors had made a native common law and, firmly and sometimes arrogantly, had explicitly or under guise of interpretation wielded a veto over legislative judgment.[5]

SECTION 3C. ANALYSIS OF STATUTES AND CONSTRUING OPINIONS

Just as you seek to ascertain the meaning of court opinions through analysis, you must seek to ascertain the meaning (or possible alternative meanings) of a statute and its relevance and scope with respect to the subject area of a problem.

The starting point for analysis of a statute is the same as for analysis of an opinion: careful reading. Analysis of a statute is no more a simple "mechanical" skill than is analysis of a court's opinion. Present may be the same difficulties caused by the ambiguity of language—semantic, syntactic, and contextual ambiguities—and by the variant writing (drafting) skills of the authors of statutes. Ambiguities and inconsistencies may appear because of careless drafting or because, just as with opinions, a statute may have multiple authors. For example, different portions of a total act may have been drafted by different persons, and amendments suggested by the controlling legislative committee or by legislators on the floor may have been adopted. Similarly, the pressure for agreement may lead to intentional use of broad or vague language. Note one significant difference, however: no theory of dictum permits you to discount some language in a statute. All language in a statute should be treated as significant; if possible, the interpretation should give meaning to all the language without inconsistencies.

5. J. Hurst, The Growth of American Law: The Law Makers 185–89 (1950), Copyright © 1950 by James Willard Hurst. Reproduced with permission of the author.

To what sources you can turn to ascertain meaning after you have analyzed the language and structure of a statute is one of the significant things that you may expect to learn from the later discussion in this text about research on problems governed by legislation. Before reaching Part II of this text, however, you can learn a great deal about construction aids and how courts use them by being observant in reading opinions for your other law courses.

Your analysis of statutory-construction opinions will differ somewhat from analysis of opinions dealing with the common law.

In a sense, the issue [6] in every case requiring construction of a statute can be stated in the same form: Does [quoted language from the statute] mean—or include, or apply to—[a specific feature of the case before the court *or* a general class encompassing such a specific feature]? If you ask, "But why is there any problem?" you will usually not be led to a specific substantive issue but to a specific question about ambiguity (because of a word, a phrase, a sentence structure, a form of punctuation, or lack of punctuation), or about internally inconsistent language, or about an anomalous result (that is, application of the statute to the particular fact pattern seems unreasonable or inconsistent with the apparent purpose of the statute). Or, asking, "Why is there any problem?" may lead you to a specific issue about the construction approach to be used or about the extrinsic materials that should properly be consulted in construing the particular statute. Rarely will you be led to a substantive issue of the form that has previously been described in Section 2D, *supra*, though sometimes the specific issue may relate to a common law rule or concept if the court concludes that the legislature has relied on the common law in using a particular word in a statute. Nevertheless, the issue in the suggested form, together with what creates the construction issue (that is, the most specific issue that you can identify), should be identified for every construing opinion that you analyze, for reasons that should become apparent as you read on.

The "reasoning" to be found in opinions construing statutes also frequently seems unrelated to substantive matters. In a sense, the ultimate "reason" (conclusion) in such opinions—that a statute does or does not dictate a particular result—is akin to the "reason" that a precedent does or does not require a particular result. The basic reasoning of the court will be justifications for its conclusion that the language of the statute can or cannot reasonably be construed to extend to that fact pattern, just as for a common law decision the basic reasoning may be discussion of the factual similarities or dissimilarities of precedent cases. Once a court has settled the construction point—has decided what a statute means with reference to the partic-

---

6. Again, for convenience of expression, the discussion herein will proceed as though every opinion discussed only one issue.

ular factual pattern before the court—its inquiry frequently ends, and this accounts for the sparseness of reasoning relating to the substantive rule. In other words, you should not expect to find in an opinion construing a statute the kind of policy justifications for the rule or result that may be an important part of opinions in cases governed by the common law. A court is not expected to "justify" a statutory rule in this sense (as it usually will justify a common law rule that has been challenged), because the legislature has supposedly questioned and determined the social utility, practicability, consistency and justice of the rules that it adopts. Courts do sometimes invoke policy justifications for particular statutory constructions, however, either explicitly or implicitly. Thus, for example, given an evenly balanced construction question, a court may affirmatively state policy justifications that support one construction rather than the other or may rely on some policy through the negative approach that, as it is often stated, "The legislature could not have intended a result inconsistent with x policy."

If the issue for a particular opinion is formulated in the form suggested, then, given a "yes" or "no" answer, the decision is: [Quoted language from the statute] does—or does not—mean [the specific feature of the case]. From such a holding, frequently no meaningful substantive rule can be derived. Just as for an opinion explaining the construction of a private written document (for example, a contract, a will, or a lease), the decision may be so limited by the background of the particular case that you cannot formulate a useful rule extending beyond the distinctive ambiguity or inconsistency in that case. Thus, for example, a decision that in one statute the word "agreements" means "contracts" in a technical sense does not lead to a rule that "agreements" always means "contracts" when used in other statutes—even in the statutes of the same jurisdiction. Each construction issue and decision tends to be unique because of different contexts and different legislative histories. Hence, you must be particularly cautious in generalizing from decisions on interpretation questions. Nevertheless, many rules and principles have been and may be derived from opinions construing statutes, not only construction guidelines of the canon variety, but also generalizations about the meaning to be given particular words or types of provisions absent evidence of special meaning.

SECTION 3D. EVALUATION AND SYNTHESIS OF OPINIONS CONSTRUING STATUTES

Your evaluation of an opinion construing a statute will differ somewhat from your evaluation of an opinion dealing with a common law point. Consideration of the technical validity of the opinion will be necessary, but you will be looking for different factors. The starting point will be the language of the statute construed. What does

its language mean to you in relation to the fact pattern to which the court has applied or refused to apply it? Independent of any extrinsic interpretation aids, does the language fairly carry the meaning for which both counsel contended or that the court attached? What type of "meaning" is attached by the court? a common, lay meaning? a technical meaning drawn from non-legal sources? a meaning drawn from the common law? Is use of one of these "meanings" rather than one of the competing possibilities justified by the information before the court? What source is used as authority for this meaning? Is use of the particular source (for example, dictionary, testimony, the judges' own knowledge) justified? Does the court consider legislative history materials and other extrinsic interpretation aids, or does it resort to arbitrary or illogical use of construction canons? Is the court's construction consistent with what you know about the background of the statute? Does the court adequately deal with precedents interpreting the same or similar or related legislation?

Because a court is not expected to justify a statutory rule in a policy sense, the policy branch of evaluation will usually not be necessary in the same sense as for common law opinions. One exception to this generalization should be noted. If the support for alternative possible meanings leaves decisional leeway for a court, it is appropriate to consider whether the alternative chosen by the court was the "best," in the sense of consonance with policy considerations as well as with the purpose of the statute. Determining whether relevant policies are advanced by the legislative solution of the problem addressed by a statute (as opposed to the court solution of the interpretation question) is a different form of policy evaluation that is important for problems that can be solved by bringing about adoption of amending legislation.

The factors that affect authority value are essentially the same for statutory-construction precedents as for common law precedents, including the mandatory/persuasive dichotomy. The value of persuasive precedents may be more limited, however, because the limitation on extension of particular decisions to more generalized rules suggested in the preceding section operates even more strongly to preclude reliance on the construction of one legislature's language in construing another legislature's language. This will not always be true, however. For example, a state legislature will sometimes adopt a statute of a type already in force in another state or one enacted by Congress, perhaps adopting the same language throughout. If courts of the source state have already construed that statute, the construing opinions may be highly persuasive to the courts of the state for which the statute is later adopted. A court may even presume that the later adopting legislature was aware of the earlier construction and hence "adopted" it along with the statute. Another example:

Some types of comprehensive legislation, such as Workmen's Compensation Acts, have been enacted in many or all states, in many instances with the same language. The result is a body of construing precedents for such legislation from courts across the country, precedents that may be as diverse and inconsistent as a group of precedents on a point of common law. Courts will draw on this body of persuasive precedents as freely as they do in deciding questions of common law. The numerous adoptions of uniform state acts [7] (with one of which—the Uniform Commercial Code—you may already be familiar) have multiplied the legislation for which a substantial body of persuasive precedents of this type is available.

The synthesis process does not differ in the legislation setting. You may find it necessary in working with problems governed by statutes to synthesize with respect to two types of questions, however: questions about appropriate construction approaches and substantive questions about the meaning of a controlling statute.

NOTES

1. Professor Llewellyn has suggested, in his book, The Common Law Tradition: Deciding Appeals 371 (1960):

> [T]he *range* of techniques correctly available [to courts] in dealing with statutes is roughly equivalent to the range correctly available in dealing with case law materials.

What do you think he means? Do you agree?

2. Should a doctrine of precedents apply to decisions construing statutes? One court concluded, without authority, that the doctrine of stare decisis is not applicable to a case of statutory interpretation, reasoning that departure from the language of a statute through interpretation could result in judicial encroachment on legislative power, inhibiting constitutional checks and balances. Windust v. Department of Labor & Indus., 52 Wash.2d 33, 323 P.2d 241 (1958). A dissenter properly pointed out that stare decisis does apply in the field of statutory construction. 323 P.2d at 253. It is true that courts may permanently change the meaning of statutes through construction. As with any generalization, however, you may find that this statement goes too far. Is it not also true that the legislature has the ultimate interpretive power, since it can amend a statute to attempt to "correct" an unacceptable court interpretation? But what if the legislature does not amend a statute after a controversial or questionable interpretation by a court? Does the legislature, by inaction, "adopt" or "accept" the court's interpretation if it fails to "correct" the interpretation? What if the legislature reenacts an interpreted section without change or rejects a proposed amendment that would

---

7. The origin of uniform acts is explained in Section 8D *infra*.

have changed the court's interpretation? Has it thereby affirmatively put its stamp of approval on the court's interpretation so that the court should not overrule the interpretation?

3. Statutes are printed in comprehensive compilations commonly called codes but variantly titled from state to state. All statutes that have general application and are in force in the jurisdiction at the time a compilation is made are included, usually organized by subject matter. Commonly used subdivisions include titles, chapters, and sections. The current federal statutory compilation is the 1976 edition of the *United States Code*, cited by title (that is, major subdivision) number and section number, thus: 42 U.S.C. § 606(a) (1976). Official names for all state statutory compilations are included in the citation *Blue Book*, pages 101–42.

4. On federal constitutional questions, United States Supreme Court decisions are mandatory. Hence, initial work on constitutional questions is concentrated on analysis of the Court's opinions. This analysis requires no techniques not already discussed. It may more often try your patience, however. Supreme Court opinions on constitutional questions tend to be longer than other opinions, and their decisions and reasoning more often tend to be split dramatically. Evaluation of both precedent and policy justifications is necessary, and policy justifications may be regarded as reaching their highest form on significant constitutional points. Synthesis, too, reaches its highest form in working with long Supreme Court opinions.

5. On the extent to which stare decisis should control constitutional decisions, see Douglas, *Stare Decisis*, 49 Colum.L.Rev. 735–37, 747, 752–55 (1949); Long, *The Doctrine of Stare Decisis: Misapplied to Constitutional Law*, 45 A.B.A.J. 921 (1959); Noland, *Stare Decisis and the Overruling of Constitutional Decisions in the Warren Years*, 4 Val.L.Rev. 101 (1969); A. Goldberg, Equal Justice 74–97 (1971); Gordon, *A Quiet Revolution*, 1 Justice Magazine 12 (Mar.–Apr.1972). Probably the most quoted view on the subject is that of Mr. Justice Brandeis, dissenting in Burnet v. Coronado Oil & Gas Co., 285 U.S. 393, 406 (1931):

> *Stare decisis* is usually the wise policy, because in most matters it is more important that the applicable rule of law be settled than that it be settled right   *   *   *   This is commonly true even where the error is a matter of serious concern, provided correction can be had by legislation. But in cases involving the Federal Constitution, where correction through legislative action is practically impossible, this Court has often overruled its earlier decisions. [Footnotes omitted.]

6. For convenience of discussion, this text separates problems governed exclusively by the common law from problems governed ex-

clusively by written law. Problems cannot always be so neatly categorized, however. Rather, they tend to fall along a continuum, with problems for which only common law concepts are relevant at one end and problems for which only written law is relevant at the other end, with varying degrees of mix in between. That courts sometimes ignore the dichotomy is well illustrated in Peters v. Simmons, 87 Wash.2d 400, 552 P.2d 1053 (1976), reprinted in part in the following pages. Where does the statute of limitations begin and the common law end? Do you approve of the manner in which the court handled the problem? Is it significant that statutes of limitation in the state of Washington date back to the 1850's, prior to statehood? Is it significant that such statutes were derived from early English statutes? ("Statutes of limitations exist in all the states, and with few exceptions they have been copied from the one brought here by our ancestors in colonial times. * * * They are regarded as statutes of repose arising from the lapse of time and the antiquity of transactions, and they also proceed upon the presumption that claims are extinguished whenever they are not litigated in the proper forum within the prescribed period." Levy v. Stewart, 78 U.S. (11 Wall.) 244 (1870).) See generally, Traynor, *Statutes Revolving in Common-Law Orbits*, 17 Cath.U.L.Rev. 401 (1968).

PETERS v. SIMMONS

Supreme Court of Washington, 1976.
87 Wash.2d 400, 552 P.2d 1053.

WRIGHT, Associate Justice.

This is an appeal by plaintiffs from an order of the King County Superior Court dismissing their action for alleged malpractice against defendant, an attorney, on the basis that it was barred by the statute of limitations.

The issues dispositive of this appeal are: (1) Has this court acquired jurisdiction to entertain the instant appeal? (2) Does the statute of limitations for legal malpractice commence to run when the client discovers or, in the exercise of reasonable diligence, should have discovered that he or she had suffered an injury.

On May 19, 1969, plaintiffs sold their business, the Mercer Island Taxi Company, to Bellevue Enterprises, Inc. The purchase agreement drafted for them by defendant, an attorney, failed to include a guaranty clause or signature line for the signature of John Fisk, president of Bellevue Enterprises, Inc., as guarantor of the purchaser's obligation. Subsequently, Bellevue Enterprises, Inc., failed to make the required payments under the purchase agreement and defaulted.

On January 14, 1971, defendant filed an action entitled *"Peters v. Bellevue Enterprises, Inc. and John Fisk"* as a result of the default on the purchase agreement. On November 11, 1972, defendant withdrew as plaintiffs' counsel and consented to the substitution of other counsel. The cause

of action was dismissed. Plaintiffs' substituted counsel, who represents them on this appeal, then commenced another action entitled *"Peters v. Fisk."* On June 19, 1974, the court dismissed this action. The court found that, during the May 19, 1969, meeting, at which the purchase agreement was executed by the plaintiffs and by Fisk, defendant failed to inform either Fisk or the purchaser's attorney that Fisk's signature as a guarantor was required on the purchase agreement.

On July 17, 1974, plaintiffs filed the instant action against defendant for damages in the sum of $32,366.74, plus interest. The complaint for damages alleged that defendant had negligently drafted the purchase agreement. Defendant raised in his answer the affirmative defense that plaintiffs' action was barred by the 3-year statute of limitations, RCW 4.16.080,[1] because the negligent act upon which the complaint was based occurred on May 19, 1969. Defendant's motion for summary judgment of dismissal was granted on December 18, 1974, on the ground that the plaintiffs' action was barred by the statute of limitations.

Plaintiffs timely filed an appeal in the Court of Appeals from the order granting summary judgment of dismissal. On March 11, 1975, the superior court entered an amended order granting defendant's motion for summary judgment of dismissal. No appeal was taken from this order. The order was amended to reflect the fact that the superior court had taken into consideration plaintiffs' and defendant's briefs regarding the motion for summary judgment of dismissal and an affidavit of Delmer E. Peters. The affidavit verified the facts recited in the first three pages of plaintiffs' brief.

With respect to the first issue, defendant contends that (1) this court lacks jurisdiction to entertain the appeal because no notice of appeal was filed from the order of March 11, 1975, which is the judgment appealed from; and (2) the appeal properly should be dismissed as premature because it was filed before entry of final judgment.

* * *

* * * The appeal was not prematurely filed because the rights of the parties were finally determined by the order granting defendant's motion for summary judgment entered on December 18, 1974.

With respect to the primary issue, the plaintiffs contend that the court should adopt the rule that the 3-year statute of limitations, RCW 4.16.-080(3), does not begin to run until the facts have been discovered, or, in the exercise of reasonable diligence, should have been discovered. During oral argument, defendant agreed with the court that the failure of an attorney to perform properly legal services contracted for may constitute a breach of contract. The defendant also agreed that the failure to act as a reasonably prudent, diligent attorney in light of the standards of his or her profession may give rise to an action for negligence. The crux of defendant's argument, then, is simply that the statute of limitations begins to run on the date of the alleged act of malpractice.

This issue was last considered in Busk v. Flanders, 2 Wash.App. 526, 468 P.2d 695 (1970). The *Busk* case adhered to prior Washington law

---

1. RCW 4.16.080(3) requires that an action must be brought within three years "upon a contract or liability, express or implied, which is not in writing, and does not arise out of any written instrument."

which had adopted the traditional view that a malpractice suit is based on a breach of contract and that the statute of limitations begins to run from the time of the breach and not from the date of its discovery. Schirmer v. Nethercutt, 157 Wash. 172, 179–80, 288 P. 265 (1930); Cornell v. Edsen, 78 Wash. 662, 664–65, 139 P. 602 (1914).

This rather narrow and mechanistic viewpoint appears to have been engendered in part by the fact that the relation between an attorney and a client arises out of a contract. The analytical shortcoming of such a desire to categorize causes of action manifests itself most clearly in an action for legal malpractice. As conceded by defendant, an action for legal malpractice may be framed conceptually either as a tort or a breach of contract. Neel v. Magana, Olney, Levy, Cathcart & Gelfand, 6 Cal.3d 176, 98 Cal.Rptr. 837, 491 P.2d 421, 423 (1971). The failure to exercise the requisite skill, care and diligence necessary to the proper rendition of legal services may give rise to an action for breach of contract. Similarly, it may constitute a tort.

The discovery rule, *i. e.*, when a client discovers or in the exercise of reasonable diligence should have discovered an injury, has been extended in Washington and applied to a variety of actions for professional malpractice. The rule has been extended to physicians,[2] and surveyors.[3] Recently in Gazija v. Nicholas Jerns Co., 86 Wash.2d 215, 543 P.2d 338 (1975), the discovery rule was extended to insurance agents. The *Gazija* case noted that the rule has similarly been extended in various jurisdictions to accountants,[4] architects,[5] and most significantly to attorneys. Neel v. Magana, Olney, Levy, Cathcart & Gelfand, supra; Edwards v. Ford, 279 So.2d 851 (Fla. 1973); Hendrickson v. Sears, 365 Mass. 835, 310 N.E.2d 131 (1974). The primary reason for extending and applying the rule is because the consumer of professional services frequently does not have the means or ability to discover professional malpractice. It is apparent, then, that the statute of limitations in RCW 4.16.080(3) was not designed to compel, by the initiation of a lawsuit, the exercise of a right not discovered, or in the exercise of reasonable diligence, not discoverable within the time frame specified in the limitations statute. *See* Janisch v. Mullins, 1 Wash.App. 393, 399, 461 P.2d 895 (1969).

The resolution of the issue presented in the instant case does not lend itself to the task of simply counting the number of days that have passed since an alleged injurious act occurred. Rather, as noted in *Gazija*, whether or not to extend the discovery rule is a matter of judicial policy—the resolution of which turns, in part, upon the need, as expressed by the legislature, to bar stale claims. But this legislative policy must be balanced against the unfairness of cutting off valid claims under circumstances which constitute an avoidable injustice. There are additional compelling reasons for adopting the rule where legal malpractice is involved as exist in the case of other professional malpractice. Not to adopt the rule would be inconsistent with its application to other professions such as physicians, insurance agents and surveyors. As with other professions, the application of

2. Ruth v. Dight, 75 Wash.2d 660, 453 P.2d 631 (1969).

3. Kundahl v. Barnett, 5 Wash.App. 227, 486 P.2d 1164 (1971).

4. Moonie v. Lynch, 256 Cal.App.2d 361, 64 Cal.Rptr. 55 (1967).

5. Steel Workers Holding Co. v. Menefee, 255 Md. 440, 258 A.2d 177 (1969).

the occurrence rule ignores the fact that ultimately the client has little choice but to rely on the skill, expertise, and diligence of counsel.

In view of these considerations, we hold that the statute of limitations for legal malpractice should not start to run until the client discovers, or in the exercise of reasonable diligence should have discovered the facts which give rise to his or her cause of action.

The judgment of the trial court is reversed and the cause of action is remanded for a trial consistent with this opinion. It is so ordered.

STAFFORD, C. J., and ROSELLINI, HUNTER, HOROWITZ, HAMILTON, UTTER and BRACHTENBACH, JJ., concur.

7. The court's opinion in the *Peters* case is not representative of construction of more recently enacted statutes by state courts. Nevertheless, reliance on legislative history materials and other external sources will more often be found in opinions construing federal legislation than in those construing state legislation, in large part because a greater volume of such materials is available for federal legislation. A recent example of the Supreme Court's use of such materials is of interest because of the varying responses of lower federal courts to the interpretation problem. The case, Burns v. Alcala, 420 U.S. 575, 95 S.Ct. 1180, 43 L.Ed.2d 469 (1975), concerned a federal public assistance program under the Social Security Act, Aid to Families with Dependent Children (AFDC). The interpretation question was whether the term "dependent children" as used in that statute, 42 U.S.C. § 606(a) (1976), included children not yet born. An excerpt from the lower court opinion and the Supreme Court opinion are reproduced in the following pages. As you read that excerpt and then the Supreme Court opinion, consider whether the source of the disagreement among the lower courts was a question of construction (what does the statute mean) or of construction technique (how should the meaning be determined) or a combination of both.

The lower court, in Alcala v. Burns, 362 F.Supp. 180 (S.D.Iowa 1973), concluded that children not yet born were included, reasoning in part:

The plaintiffs argue that the Social Security Act contemplates coverage for the "unborn child" when it provides coverage for a "dependent child." It is first contended that the plain language of the statute implies they are to be included and that there is no indication in the statutory language that mothers with unborn children are to be excluded from coverage. They point to the definition by Webster's New International Dictionary (Second Edition Unabridged) which defines "child" as: "An unborn or recently born human being; fetus; infant; baby. * * *" The defendants argue just as ardently that the clear language of the Social Security Act constantly refers to children in being and that nowhere is "unborn child" referred to. The defendants argue that the customary meaning of the word "child" is that of a born person.

In any event, the Court does not find this venture into the plain meaning of the term "dependent child" extremely fruitful. It is obvious that the "plain language" of the statute is not as plain as both parties contend and is surely not conclusive for the plaintiffs or the defendants. It is ascertainable, however, that an "unborn child" is not specifically excluded by the language of the Act.

Given this ambiguity in the statute, the Congressional intent becomes more important and is a more fruitful inquiry. Title 42 U.S.C. Section 601 authorizes funds:

> "For the purpose of encouraging the care of dependent children in their homes * * * by enabling each state to furnish financial assistance and rehabilitation and other services, as far as practicable under the conditions in such State, to needy dependent children and the parents or relatives with whom they are living to help maintain and strengthen family life and to help such parents * * * to attain or retain capability for the maximum self-support and personal independence consistent with the maintenance of *continuing parental care and protection.* * * *" (Emphasis added).

Inclusion of the "unborn child" is consistent with the purposes of the Act above stated. The stipulated testimony of Dr. Roy Pitkin clearly states the additional needs of the child and mother during this prenatal period and the serious consequences that flow to the family if the nutritional and medical needs of the child are not met during this prenatal period. Meeting of these family needs is consistent with the purposes of the A.F.D.C. program stated above. As stated in Carleson v. Remillard, *supra*, 406 U.S. at 604, 92 S.Ct. at 1936:

> "We cannot assume here, anymore than we could in King v. Smith, *supra*, that while Congress 'intended to provide programs for the economic security and protection of *all* children,' it also 'intended arbitrarily to leave one class of destitute children entirely without meaningful protection.' 392 U.S., at 330, 88 S.Ct., at 2140."

The term "dependent child" is broad enough to encompass an "unborn child" and the coverage for "unborn children" is consistent with the purposes of the Social Security Act. No credible argument can be made that Congress intended to exclude "unborn children" from coverage under this Act. Therefore the Court concludes that coverage for "unborn children" is contemplated by the Social Security Act.

This conclusion is strengthened by a reading of the relevant regulations of the Department of Health, Education and Welfare. The Code of Federal Regulations, 45 C.F.R., Section 233.90 provides that:

> "(c)(2) Federal financial participation is available in:
>
> * * *
>
> (ii) Payments with respect to an unborn child when the fact of pregnancy has been determined by medical diagnosis. * * *"

Since 1946 it has been the policy of HEW that payments are authorized on behalf of "unborn children." The position of HEW, as stated in their ami-

cus brief filed by the defendants, is that Section 233.90(c)(2) is an optional program to the states and that just because these regulations *allow* coverage of unborn children does not dictate that coverage is required.

If, however, this so-called optional program of HEW is a valid program, the power to promulgate this Regulation would flow from the Social Security Act. As stated in the defendants' Brief on page 7:

> "However, it is equally clear that such regulations may not go beyond the limits of the Act or law on which such regulations are based. Townsend v. Swank, 404 U.S. 282, 92 S.Ct. 502, 30 L.Ed.2d 448 (1971)."

The fact that HEW has allowed payments to "unborn children" since 1946 under this Act and the fact that Congress has acquiesced in this position is a most convincing argument that the Social Security Act encompasses eligibility for the parent with an "unborn child." The Court again concludes that "unborn children" are eligible for A.F.D.C. benefits under the Social Security Act and that under the precedents of *King, Townsend* and *Remillard* and the Eighth Circuit cases of Rosen v. Hursh, 464 F.2d 731 (8 Cir. 1972) and Doe v. Gillman, 479 F.2d 646, No. 72–1605 (8th Cir., 1973), the defendants cannot enforce more strict eligibility requirements than those requirements in the Federal statute.

The court of appeals affirmed on appeal, holding that "the district court correctly concluded that the term 'dependent child' is broad enough to encompass an unborn child and that such coverage is consistent with the purposes of the Social Security Act." Alcala v. Burns, 494 F.2d 743, 746 (8th Cir. 1974). By the time the question reached the Supreme Court, the same general conclusion had been reached by the court of appeals for four other circuits and by at least fifteen other district courts, while the Court of Appeals for the Second Circuit and four district courts had reached a contrary conclusion. See citations collected in Parks v. Harden, 504 F.2d 861, 863, n. 4 (5th Cir. 1974). The Supreme Court agreed with the minority, 7–1, with Justice Douglas not taking part, Burns v. Alcala, 420 U.S. 575, 95 S.Ct. 1180, 43 L.Ed.2d 469 (1975). Note, in the following opinion, the types of informational sources to which the Court looked in supporting its conclusions. (Note also the reversal of the parties name in the title of the case. Under Supreme Court practice, the name of the party who sought review will appear first, regardless whether that party was the plaintiff or the defendant in the action. Note also the marginal numbers with the ⊥ symbol. The numbers identify the page numbers in the official—U.S.—reports; such identification of original pagination is sometimes called "star paging.")

⊥Mr. Justice POWELL delivered the opinion of the Court.

The question presented by this case is whether States receiving federal finan- ⊥576 cial aid under the program of Aid to Families with Dependent Children (AFDC) must offer welfare benefits to ⊥577 pregnant women for their unborn children. As the case comes to this Court,

the issue is solely one of statutory interpretation.

1

Respondents, residents of Iowa, were pregnant at the time they filed this action. Their circumstances were such that their children would be eligible for AFDC benefits upon birth. They applied for welfare assistance but were refused on the ground that they had no "dependent children" eligible for the AFDC program. Respondents then filed this action against petitioners, Iowa welfare officials. On behalf of themselves and other women similarly situated, respondents contended that the Iowa policy of denying benefits to unborn children conflicted with the federal standard of eligibility under § 406(a) of the Social Security Act, as amended, 42 U. S.C. § 606(a), and resulted in a denial of due process and equal protection under the Fourteenth Amendment.[1] The District Court certified the class and granted declaratory and injunctive relief. The court held that unborn children are "dependent children" within the meaning of § 406(a) and that by denying them AFDC benefits Iowa had departed impermissibly from the federal standard of eligibility. The District Court did not reach respondents' constitutional claims. 362 F.Supp. 180 (SD Iowa 1973). The Court of Appeals for the Eighth Circuit affirmed. 494 F.2d 743 (1974). We granted certiorari to resolve the conflict among the federal courts that have considered the question.[2] 419 U.S. 823, 95 S.Ct. 39, 42 L.Ed.2d 47. We conclude that the statutory term "dependent child" does not include unborn children, and we reverse.

II

[1] The Court has held that under § 402(a)(10) of the Social Security Act, 42 U.S.C. § 602(a)(10), federal partici-

pation in state AFDC programs is conditioned on the State's offering benefits to all persons who are eligible under federal standards. The State must provide benefits to all individuals who meet the federal definition of "dependent child" and who are "needy" under state standards, unless they are excluded or aid is made optional by another provision of the Act. New York Dept. of Social Services v. Dublino, 413 U.S. 405, 421–422, 93 S.Ct. 2507, 2516–2517, 37 L. Ed.2d 688 (1973); Carleson v. Remillard, 406 U.S. 598, 92 S.Ct. 1932, 32 L. Ed.2d 352 (1972); Townsend v. Swank, 404 U.S. 282, 92 S.Ct. 502, 30 L.Ed.2d 448 (1971); King v. Smith, 392 U.S. 309, 88 S.Ct. 2128, 20 L.Ed.2d 1118 (1968). The definition of "dependent child" appears in § 406(a) of the Act:

"The term 'dependent child' means a needy child (1) who has been deprived of parental support or care by reason of the death, continued absence from the home, or physical or mental incapacity of a parent, and who is living with his father, mother, grandfather, grandmother, brother, sister, stepfather, stepmother, stepbrother, stepsister, uncle, aunt, first cousin, nephew, or niece, in a place of residence maintained by one or more of such relatives as his or their own home, and (2) who is (A) under the age of eighteen, or (B) under the age of twenty-one and (as determined by the State in accordance with standards prescribed by the Secretary) a student regularly attending a school, college, or university, or regularly attending a course of vocational or technical training designed to fit him for gainful employment . . . ." 42 U.S.C. § 606(a).

The section makes no mention of pregnant women or unborn children as such.

Respondents contend, citing dictionary definitions,[3] that the word "child" can

---

1. The complaint was framed under 42 U.S.C. § 1983, and jurisdiction in the District Court was based on 28 U.S.C. § 1343(3). See Hagans v. Lavine, 415 U.S. 528, 94 S.Ct. 1372, 39 L.Ed.2d 577 (1974).

2. The cases are cited in Parks v. Harden, 504 F.2d 861, 863 n. 4 (CA5 1974).

3. *E. g.*, Webster's Third New International Dictionary (1961), which includes as one

be used to include unborn children. This is enough, they say, to make the statute ambiguous and to justify construing the term "dependent child" in light of legislative purposes and administrative interpretation.[4] They argue that both factors support their position in this case. First, paying benefits to needy pregnant women would further the purpose of the AFDC program because it would enable them to safeguard the health of their children through prenatal care and adequate nutrition. Second, for over 30 years the Department of Health, Education, and Welfare (HEW) has offered States an option to claim federal matching funds for AFDC payments to pregnant women.[5]

A

[2, 3] Several of the courts that have faced this issue have read *King, Townsend,* and *Carleson, supra,* to establish a special rule of construction applicable to Social Security Act provisions governing AFDC eligibility. They have held that persons who are arguably included in the federal eligibility standard must be deemed eligible unless the Act or its legislative history clearly exhibits an intent to exclude them from coverage in effect creating a presumption of coverage when the statute is ambiguous. See Carver v. Hooker, 369 F.Supp. 204,

210–215 (NH 1973), aff'd, 501 F.2d 1244 (CA 1 1974); Stuart v. Canary, 367 F.Supp. 1343, 1345 (ND Ohio 1973); Green v. Stanton, 364 F.Supp. 123, 125–126 (ND Ind.1973), aff'd sub nom. Wilson v. Weaver, 499 F.2d 155 (CA 7 1974). But see Mixon v. Keller, 372 F.Supp. 51, 55 (MD Fla.1974). This departure from ordinary principles of statutory interpretation is not supported by the Court's prior decisions. *King, Townsend,* and *Carleson* establish only that once the federal standard of eligibility is defined, a participating State may not deny aid to persons who come within it in the absence of a clear indication that Congress meant the coverage to be optional. The method of analysis used to define the federal standard of eligibility is no different from that used in solving any other problem of statutory construction.

[4, 5] Our analysis of the Social Security Act does not support a conclusion that the legislative definition of "dependent child" includes unborn children. Following the axiom that words used in a statute are to be given their ordinary meaning in the absence of persuasive reasons to the contrary, Banks v. Chicago Grain Trimmers, 390 U.S. 459, 465, 88 S.Ct. 1140, 1144, 20 L.Ed.2d 30 (1968); Minor v. Mechanics Bank of Alexandria, 1 Pet. 46, 64, 7 L.Ed. 47 (1828), and reading the definition of

---

definition of "child," "an unborn or recently born human being: *fetus, infant, baby.*" This, of course, is only one of many definitions for the word "child," and its use with reference to unborn children is not the most frequent. Webster's New International Dictionary (2d ed. 1957) qualified the definition quoted above by adding: "now chiefly in phrases. Cf. *with child, childbirth.*" Respondents have candidly furnished citations to other current dictionaries that do not indicate that the word "child" is used to refer to unborn children. Respondents acknowledge that reliance on dictionaries cannot solve the question presented in this case. At most, the dictionaries demonstrate the possible ambiguity in the term "dependent child."

4. See United States v. Southern Ute Indians, 402 U.S. 159, 173 n. 8, 91

S.Ct. 1336, 1343, 28 L.Ed.2d 695 (1971); Studebaker v. Perry, 184 U.S. 258, 269, 22 S.Ct. 463, 468, 46 L.Ed. 528 (1902); Merritt v. Welsh, 104 U.S. 694, 702–703, 26 L.Ed. 896 (1882).

5. The current regulation provides that "[f]ederal financial participation is available in . . . [p]ayments with respect to an unborn child when the fact of pregnancy has been determined by medical diagnosis." 45 CFR § 233.90(c)(2)(ii). Although the regulation itself does not say expressly that aid to unborn children is optional with the States, HEW's administrative practice makes clear that this regulation allows States to exclude unborn children from their AFDC programs. As of 1971 HEW had approved 34 state plans, including Iowa's, that furnished no aid to unborn children. 494 F.2d 743, 745 (CA8 1974).

"dependent child" in its statutory context, we conclude that Congress used the word "child" to refer to an individual already born, with an existence separate from its mother.

As originally enacted in 1935, the Social Security Act made no provision for the needs of the adult taking care of a "dependent child." It authorized aid only for the child and offered none to support the mother.[6] C. 531, § 406, 49 Stat. 629. The Act expressly contemplated that the first eligible child in a family would receive greater benefits than succeeding children, recognizing the lower per capita cost of support in families with more than one child, § 403(a), but the Act included no similar provision recognizing the incremental cost to a pregnant woman of supporting her "child." The Act also spoke of children "living with" designated relatives, § 406(a), and referred to residency requirements dependent on the child's place of birth. At § 402(b). These provisions would apply awkwardly, if at all, to pregnant women and unborn children. The failure to provide explicitly for the special circumstances of pregnant women strongly suggests that Congress had no thought of providing AFDC benefits to "dependent children" before birth.[7]

---

6. The Act was amended in 1950 to authorize payment for the needs of the child's caretaker. Act of Aug. 28, 1950, § 323, 64 Stat. 551.

7. A number of other provisions of the Act would be similarly inapplicable to unborn children. See Murrow v. Clifford, 502 F.2d 1066, 1075–1076 (CA3 1974) (Rosenn, J., concurring and dissenting).

8. The original definition of "dependent child" was: "a child under the age of sixteen who has been deprived of parental support or care by reason of the death, continued absence from the home, or physical or mental incapacity of a parent, and who is living with his father, mother, grandfather, grandmother, brother, sister, stepfather, stepmother, stepbrother, stepsister, uncle, or aunt, in a place of residence maintained by one or more of such relatives as his or their own home . . . ." § 406(a), 49 Stat. 629.

[6] The purposes of the Act also are persuasive. The AFDC program was originally conceived to substitute for the practice of removing needy children from their homes and placing them in institutions, and to free widowed and divorced mothers from the necessity of working, so that they could remain home to supervise their children. This purpose is expressed clearly in President Roosevelt's message to Congress recommending the legislation, H.R.Doc. No. 81, 74th Cong., 1st Sess., 29–30 (1935), and in committee reports in both Houses of Congress, S.Rep. No. 628, 74th Cong., 1st Sess., 16–17 (1935); H.R.Rep. No. 615, 74th Cong., 1st Sess., 10 (1935). See Wisdom v. Norton, 507 F.2d 750, 754–755 (CA 2 1974); Note, Eligibility of the Unborn for AFDC Benefits: The Statutory and Constitutional Issues, 54 B.U.L.Rev. 945, 955–958 (1974). The restricted purpose of the AFDC program is evidenced in the Act itself by the limitations on aid. The Act originally authorized aid only for children living with designated relatives.[8] The list of relatives has grown, *supra*, at 1183, but there is still no general provision for AFDC payments to needy children living with distant relatives or unrelated persons, or in institutions.[9]

[7] Congress did not ignore the needs of pregnant women or the desira-

---

9. The Act now authorizes, in addition to payments for children in the homes of designated relatives, foster care payments for children who have been removed from the homes of relatives. 42 U.S.C. § 608. It also provides financial support for child-welfare services, in a form different from the direct payments in the general AFDC program, for "homeless, dependent, or neglected children." 42 U.S.C. §§ 622, 625.

The statement of purposes in the Act, amended several times since 1935, still indicates that Congress has not undertaken to provide support for all needy children:

"For the purpose of encouraging the care of dependent children in their own homes or in the homes of relatives by enabling each State to furnish financial assistance and rehabilitation and other services, as far as practicable under the conditions in such State, to needy dependent children and the parents or relatives with whom they are liv-

bility of adequate prenatal care. In Title V of the Social Security Act, now codified as 42 U.S.C. §§ 701–708 (1970 ed. and Supp. III). Congress provided federal funding for prenatal and postnatal health services to mothers and infants, explicitly designed to reduce infant and maternal mortality.[10] See S.Rep. No. 628, *supra,* at 20. In selecting this form of aid for pregnant women, Congress had before it proposals to follow the lead of some European countries that provided "maternity benefits" to support expectant mothers for a specified period before and after childbirth. Hearings on S. 1130 before the Senate Committee on Finance, 74th Cong., 1st Sess., 182, 965–971 (1935). If Congress had intended to include a similar program in the Social Security Act, it very likely would have |584 done so explicitly rather than by relying on the term "dependent child," at best a highly ambiguous way to refer to unborn children.

B

[8] Respondents have also relied on HEW's regulation allowing payment of AFDC benefits on behalf of unborn children. They ask us to defer to the agency's long-standing interpretation of the statute it administers. Respondents have provided the Court with copies of letters and interoffice memoranda that preceded adoption of this policy in 1941 by HEW's predecessor, the Bureau of Public Assistance. These papers suggest that the agency initially may have taken the position that the statutory

phrase "dependent children" included unborn children.[11]

A brief filed by the Solicitor General on behalf of HEW in this case disavows respondents' interpretation of the Act. HEW contends that unborn children are not included in the federal eligibility standard and that the regulation authorizing federal participation in AFDC payments to pregnant women is based on the agency's general authority to make rules for efficient administration of the Act. 42 U.S.C. § 1302. The regulation is consistent with this explanation. It appears in a subsection with other rules authorizing temporary aid, at the option of the States, to individuals in the process of gaining or losing eligibility for the AFDC program. For example, one of the accompanying rules authorizes States to pay AFDC benefits |585 to a relative 30 days before the eligible child comes to live in his home. 45 CFR § 233.90(c)(2). HEW's current explanation of the regulation deprives respondents' argument of any significant support from the principle that accords persuasive weight to a consistent, long-standing interpretation of a statute by the agency charged with its administration. See FMB v. Isbrandtsen Co., 356 U.S. 481, 499–500, 78 S.Ct. 851, 862, 2 L.Ed.2d 926 (1958); Burnet v. Chicago Portrait Co., 285 U.S. 1, 16, 52 S.Ct. 275, 280, 76 L.Ed. 587 (1932).

Nor can respondents make a convincing claim of congressional acquiescence in HEW's prior policy. In 1972, in the context of major Social Security legisla-

---

ing to help maintain and strengthen family life and to help such parents or relatives to attain or retain capability for the maximum self-support and personal independence consistent with the maintenance of continuing parental care and protection . . . ." 42 U.S.C. § 601.

10. As Judge Weinfeld's opinion for the Second Circuit in Wisdom v. Norton, 507 F.2d 750, 755 (1974), points out, one of the major reasons for making welfare payments on behalf of an unborn child would be to enable its mother to purchase adequate prenatal care. The fact that Congress explicitly provided medical care for expectant mothers in

Title V is evidence "of a congressional intent *not* to include unborn children under AFDC but to provide for maternity care in a different section of the statute." *Id.,* at 755 n. 27.

11. At oral argument petitioners' counsel objected to the inclusion of these materials in respondents' brief, noting that they were not in the record and had not been authenticated. Tr. of Oral Arg. 43–45. Respondents suggested that at least some of the materials are proper subjects for judicial notice. In the view we take of the case these materials are not dispositive, and it is unnecessary to resolve their status.

tion, both Houses of Congress passed bills to revise the AFDC system. One section of the bill passed in the Senate would have amended the definition of "dependent child" expressly to exclude unborn children. H.R. 1, 92d Cong., 1st Sess. (1972) (as amended by Senate); 118 Cong.Rec. 33990, 33995 (1972); see S.Rep. No. 92–1230, pp. 108, 467 (1972). The House bill would have substituted an entirely new definition of eligibility under the Administration's "Family Assistance Plan." H.R. 1, 92d Cong., 1st Sess. (1972); 117 Cong.Rec. 21450, 21463 (1971). The accompanying committee report specified that under the new definition unborn children would not be eligible for aid. H.R.Rep. No. 92–231, p. 184 (1971). Both bills passed the respective Houses of Congress, but none of the AFDC amendments appeared in the final legislation, Pub.L. 92–603, 86 Stat. 1329, because the House and Senate conferees were unable to agree on the underlying principle of welfare reform. All efforts to amend AFDC were postponed for another session of Congress. See 118 Cong.Rec. 36813–36825, 36926–36936 (1972); Mixon v. Keller, 372 F.Supp., at 55. Under the circumstances, failure to enact the relatively minor provision relating to unborn children cannot be regard|586 ed as approval of HEW's practice of allowing optional benefits. To the extent this legislative history sheds any light on congressional intent, it tends to rebut the claim that Congress by silence has acquiesced in the former HEW view that unborn children are eligible for AFDC payments.[12]

C

In this case respondents did not, and perhaps could not, challenge HEW's policy of allowing States the option of paying AFDC benefits to pregnant women. We therefore have no occasion to decide whether HEW has statutory authority to approve federal participation in state programs ancillary to those expressly provided in the Social Security Act, see Wisdom v. Norton, 507 F.2d, at 756, or whether 42 U.S.C. § 1302 authorizes HEW to fund benefits for unborn children as a form of temporary aid to individuals who are in the process of qualifying under federal standards. See Parks v. Harden, 504 F.2d 861, 875–877 (CA 5 1974) (Ainsworth, J., dissenting).

⎿ III ⎿587

Neither the District Court nor the Court of Appeals considered respondents' constitutional arguments. Rather than decide those questions here, where they have not been briefed and argued, we remand the case for consideration of the equal protection and due process issues that were raised but not decided below.

Reversed and remanded.

Mr. Justice DOUGLAS took no part in the consideration or decision of this case.

Mr. Justice MARSHALL, dissenting.

As the majority implicitly acknowledges, the evidence available to help resolve the issue of statutory construction presented by this case does not point de-

---

12. Several of the courts that have adopted the position urged here by respondents have interpreted the action of the 92d Congress as evidence of a "belief that unborn children are currently eligible under the Act 'and that only by amending its language can their status as eligible individuals be altered.'" Parks v. Harden, 504 F.2d, at 872. See also Carver v. Hooker, 501 F.2d 1244, 1247 (CA1 1974); Wilson v. Weaver, 358 F.Supp. 1147, 1155 (N.D Ill.1973), aff'd, 499 F.2d 155 (CA7 1974). The House bill does not lend itself to this interpretation because it was not de-

signed to amend the existing AFDC structure but to create an entirely different system. The Senate bill was framed as an amendment to the eligibility provisions in § 406(a), but there is no evidence that its drafters believed unborn children were included in the existing definition of dependent children. It would be equally plausible to suppose that they thought HEW had misinterpreted the Act, and wanted to make the original intent clear. See Wilson v. Weaver, 499 F.2d, at 161 (Pell, J., dissenting).

cisively in either direction. When it passed the Social Security Act in 1935 Congress gave no indication that it meant to include or exclude unborn children from the definition of "dependent child." Nor has it shed any further light on the question other than to consider, and fail to pass, legislation that would indisputably have excluded unborn children from coverage.

The majority has parsed the language and touched on the legislative history of the Act in an effort to muster support for the view that unborn children were not meant to benefit from the Act. Even given its best face, however, this evidence provides only modest support for the majority's position. The lengthy course of administrative practice cuts quite the other way. Although the question is a close one, I agree with the conclusion reached by five of the six Courts of Appeals that have considered this issue,[1] and would accordingly affirm the judgment below.

The majority makes only passing reference to the administrative practice of 30 years' duration, under which unborn children were deemed eligible for federal AFDC payments where state programs provided funds for them. According to the majority, this longstanding administrative practice is deprived of any significant weight by HEW's present suggestion that it has always treated unborn children as being outside the statutory definition of "dependent child." The agency's characterization of its former position, however, misrepresents the history of the administrative practice.

As early as 1941 the Bureau of Public Assistance faced the problem of whether unborn children were covered by § 406 (a) of the Act. At that time, the Board determined that under the Act federal funds could be provided to the States for aid to unborn children. The agency's governing regulation in the HEW Handbook of Public Assistance Administration expressly included unborn children among those eligible for aid "on the basis of the same eligibility conditions as apply to other children." Pt. IV, § 3412(6) (1946). The language of the regulation and the inclusion of unborn children among five other classes of children eligible for AFDC payments under the definition of "dependent child" make it evident that the agency deemed unborn children to come within the terms of § 406(a) of the Act.[2]

This regulation remained unchanged until 1971, when it was placed in the Code of Federal Regulations as 45 CFR § 233.90(c)(2)(ii). Although its language was altered somewhat, the regulation still provided that, in electing States, federal participation would be available for unborn children once the fact of pregnancy was confirmed by medical diagnosis. It was only when a series of lawsuits were filed seeking to have AFDC made available to unborn children in those States that did not provide for them in their local AFDC plans that the agency contended that unborn children were not really within the eligibility provisions of § 406(a) after all.

After this Court's decisions in King v. Smith, 392 U.S. 309, 88 S.Ct. 2128, 20 L.Ed.2d 1118 (1968), Townsend v. Swank, 404 U.S. 282, 92 S.Ct. 502, 30 L. Ed.2d 448 (1971), and Carleson v. Remillard, 406 U.S. 598, 92 S.Ct. 1932, 32

---

1. Besides the court below, the Courts of Appeals holding that unborn children are within the eligibility terms of § 406(a) include the First, the Fourth, the Fifth, and the Seventh Circuits, see Carver v. Hooker, 501 F.2d 1244 (CA1 1974); Doe v. Lukhard, 493 F.2d 54 (CA4 1974); Parks v. Harden, 504 F.2d 861 (CA5 1974); Wilson v. Weaver, 499 F.2d 155 (CA7 1974). Only the Second Circuit has taken the opposite view, Wisdom v. Norton, 507 F.2d 750 (1974).

2. Among the other "situations within the scope of the [statutory] term 'deprivation' [of parental support or care]" were "Children Living With Both Natural Parents," § 3412 (1); "Children Living With Either Father or Mother," § 3412(2); and "Children of Unmarried Parents," § 3412(5). In discussing the eligibility of the last group, the regulations noted: "The act provides for the use of aid to dependent children as a maintenance resource available on equal terms to all children who meet eligibility conditions." *Ibid.*

L.Ed.2d 352 (1972), it appeared obvious that if any class of potential beneficiaries was within the Act's eligibility provisions, the States were required to provide aid to them. Thus, if HEW had chosen to stick with its previous interpretation that unborn children were within the eligibility provision of § 406(a), it would have had to require that all participating States grant benefits for unborn children. On the other hand, if it were determined that unborn children were not eligible under the Act, federal financing would not be available even in those States that provided |590 | AFDC payments for them. In order to preserve the status quo, the agency came up with the inventive solution of ascribing the "unborn children" regulation to its rulemaking power under § 1102 of the Act, and thus avoiding the mandatory effects of a finding of "eligibility" under § 406(a).

This ingenious but late-blooming tactical switch does little, in my view, to cancel out the effect of the long and consistent prior course of administrative interpretation of the Act. Since the agency's position in this case and related cases is evidently designed to preserve its authority to extend federal aid on an optional basis in spite of *King, Townsend,* and *Carleson,* I would view somewhat skeptically the agency's assertion that it has never deemed unborn children to be within the eligibility provisions of § 406(a).

Even if the agency's new position is not discounted as a reaction to the exigencies of the moment, the policies underlying the doctrine of administrative interpretation require more than simply placing a thumb on the side of the scale that the agency currently favors.[3] The agency's determination that unborn children are eligible for matching federal |591 aid was made early in the life of the program, and the administrators of the Act determined only a few years after the Act's passage that making AFDC payments available to unborn children was consistent with the statutory purposes. This contemporaneous and long-applied construction of the eligibility provision and purposes of the Act is entitled to great weight—particularly in the case of a statute that has been before the Congress repeatedly and has been amended numerous times. The majority contends that because of the details of the unsuccessful 1972 legislative effort to exclude unborn children from coverage, the respondents can claim little benefit from the natural inference that the statute still included them among those eligible for aid. This may be so, but in light of the history of the administrative interpretation of § 406(a), I cannot agree that the Act, in its present form, should be read to exclude the unborn from eligibility.

I dissent.

3. The reasons for assigning weight to an administrative agency's interpretation vary in part according to the role that Congress intended the agency to play in the lawmaking process. Where the act in question is an open-ended statute under which Congress did not "bring to a close the making of the law," but left the "rounding out of its command to another, smaller and specialized agency," FTC v. Ruberoid Co., 343 U.S. 470, 486, 72 S.Ct. 800, 809, 96 L.Ed. 1081 (1952) (Jackson, J., dissenting), the agency's shift in position, even at a late date, should be given substantial weight. See NLRB v. J. Weingarten, Inc., 420 U.S., at 265–266, 95 S.Ct., at 967–968; Phelps Dodge Corp. v. NLRB, 313 U.S. 177, 193–194, 61 S.Ct. 845, 852, 85 L.Ed. 1271 (1941). Plainly, however, Congress did not intend the term "dependent child" in this detailed and often-amended statute to be subject to re-examination and redefinition as the agency's perceptions of social needs changed. In cases such as this one, where the agency is intended merely to carry out the congressional mandate, a long-standing course of administrative interpretation is relevant primarily as a contemporaneous construction of the Act by persons dealing intimately with its terms on a day-to-day basis.

Part II

PROBLEM ANALYSIS AND RESEARCH

Chapter 4

THE LAW LIBRARY AND ITS BASIC RESOURCES

SECTION 4A. INTRODUCTION TO PART II

In Part I, we assumed that the possibly controlling law for a problem had somehow been identified, and then proceeded to examine the skills needed to interpret that law and predict what interpretation would probably control resolution of a problem. In Part II, we move on to examine the skills and publications needed to find the possibly controlling law. Note initially, however, that finding—research—cannot be neatly separated from interpreting what is found. Re-search on a legal problem must be guided by progressive, cumulating interpretation of what is found. Interpretation and prediction, on the other hand, are obviously strongly influenced by what is or is not found.

Effective legal research skills must begin with a working knowl-edge of the basic legal publications. Acquiring a working knowledge of legal materials, in turn, begins with memorizing information about numerous publications. It requires substantially more, however, be-cause you must also understand common limitations and deficiencies resulting in part from the human failings of those who prepare the materials and in larger part from the peculiarities of the common law doctrinal framework.

From this text you will learn in detail about only the basic legal materials. Their functions and contents are representative of Ameri-can legal materials, however, and, to some extent, of legal materials in English-speaking countries generally. Given knowledge of basic legal materials and their use, you should be prepared to identify other per-tinent publications when you need them and to acquaint yourself with how to use them efficiently. Of course, researching legal problems

should, and often does, carry the researcher beyond legal materials, but legal materials are the starting point.

This chapter will introduce you generally to law libraries and to the basic legal publications. Subsequent chapters deal with general research suggestions; with the interconnection of fact-gathering, analysis, and research in preliminary work with a problem; then with research on problems governed by the common law and by legislation, and, finally, with the frontiers of legal information retrieval.

SECTION 4B. INTRODUCTION TO LAW LIBRARIES

—By Marian G. Gallagher, Professor of Law and Librarian,
University of Washington School of Law

Law school libraries are organized and operated much like the undergraduate college and university libraries to which law students become accustomed before entering law school. Those circumstances which give rise to the rumor that law libraries are "different" can be described summarily with the observation that lawyers historically have been more dependent on their libraries than have the professionals in other disciplines, have demanded and supported better methods of information retrieval and have developed habits of library use unlike those of other people. Some standard library procedures therefore have undergone adjustment in law libraries to accommodate impatient lawyer researchers.[1] A few comments about law libraries in general follow, not to point out things that are "different," but because beginning law students are embarking on a career notably short of free time. There is a certain time-saving advantage in knowing where you are going.

Your use of the library will be different. No matter how much you used your undergraduate library, you will use your law library more. You will be a scholar in residence. Full time students who use it as a base for studying their own as well as the library's materials often spend the greater part of their waking hours there.

Your being in residence will give you a better opportunity to become acquainted with the library staff and they with you. Unless yours is a very large student body, or unless an automated circulation system demands it, you will not need to produce an I.D. card. For the traditional sign-a-slip circulation procedure, you will need only to

---

1. The information explosion now has generated impatience in the scholarly patrons of general libraries as well, with resulting adjustments through experiments in computerized information retrieval and bibliographic controls. With the planning for electronic linking of library resources of whatever discipline or location, standardization of procedures among libraries takes on new importance, and many law librarians anticipate the need to relinquish some lawyer-invented systems in the future as the price for plugging into the network.

practice legibility, against the day someone else wants the book you took home.

The collection and its arrangements. Law school library collections vary widely in size (from under 30,000 to over 1,000,000 volumes) and, beyond the basic books, in subject and jurisdictional emphasis. Whatever the scope of your school's collection, first priority will have been given to the acquisition of materials that support the curriculum. Unless you undertake independent research on an exotic topic, the collection should contain most of the books you will need. Until you begin independent research on any topic, the books you will use will have been cited to you by professors or by course materials. Of these cited materials, most of the texts, treatises, and restatements will be on reserve, the reports and perhaps the statutes will be on open stacks and the periodicals may be on closed stacks, on open stacks or on a combination. There is no standard "best" arrangement for law collections. Variations are dictated by patron use patterns and often by architectural accident. All copies of much used sets may not be shelved together in one place, and wherever the collection has outgrown available open shelf space, early volumes of sets, early editions of texts, and even whole parts of the collection may have been forced into locations accessible only to the library staff.

Whatever the arrangement, various directional aids will be available to you: charts of the open stack areas, stack labels, and written guides. The written guides invariably seem bent on telling you more than you need to know about using your law library, but a few minutes spent on that kind of pamphlet saves a great amount, later, in thrashing-about time.

Some law libraries have book catalogs; some have computer-generated book catalogs. A more recent development is COM format, catalogs on microfilm or microfiche, used with sophisticated reading machines.[2] Until these modern catalog forms are more widely used in law libraries, you will probably be using a card catalog to discover whether your library holds research materials cited in obscure footnotes and to uncover uncited materials pertinent to your inquiry. A law library card catalog works just like the one you used as an undergraduate. It may be a one-alphabet listing by author, subject and title or it may be a divided catalog, but the difference in convenience to a knowledgeable user is not worth comment. It is worth a student's time, however, to note whether the catalog covers all of the

2. For a fuller description of COM, see Spaulding, *A Primer on COM (Computer Output Microfilm), An Alternative to Computer Printout,* 7 Am. Libraries 468 (1976). For a survey of major trends and significant publications with respect to cataloging practices that portend the closing of card catalogs in the future, see Chan, *Year's Work in Cataloging and Classification: 1975,* 20 Lib. Resources Tech. Serv. 213 (1976).

law library's resources. Federal and international documents often are not represented by cards in the catalog, and state document listings sometimes are under-represented. Various types of legal and related materials may be listed in separate files (card files or printed checklists), and it is expected that serious researchers will heed the library's directional signs and how-to-use guides, to avoid missing important resources.

The staff. The size of law library staffs, like the size of book collections, varies among law schools. Generally the number of staff members who work in technical processes must outnumber those who work with greater visibility in circulation and reference, but all have as their primary objective making the library supportive of law students, and all are equally available when needed by law students. One or more of the professionals (in law libraries, this means persons with legal or librarianship degrees or with long and responsible experience) on a staff of any size will have responsibility in circulation and reference and will place priority on helping you locate needed materials speedily; if the staff is large enough, there may be help beyond the locating-materials point, not to the looking-it-up point but at least to the how-to-use point. The search for legal authority throughout your career will lead you into many dead ends, and a certain amount of that is necessary to the learning process. No professional law librarian, however, likes to see a law student charting his or her own misadventures, and all of them are approachable when you need help.

The library rules. The extent to which a collection can circulate outside of the library varies among law schools, and for a variety of reasons. The greater the demand for individual titles and particular types of materials, the less likely they are to circulate. Demand for some materials is seasonal, however, and books that usually are restricted to use in the library may be taken out at other times with staff permission. Restrictive stamps may be placed in volumes only as a reminder to you to request that permission. Those who adjust best to the system discover that the staff's permission ought to be obtained in advance of the borrowing—usually a simple procedure requiring a signature on book card or transaction slip and a clear statement of the length of time the book will be needed. Those who adjust best discover that the staff says "yes" oftener than it says "no" —insistence on the letter of the rules is confined to libraries with too-large student bodies or to those times when the actual or probable demand exceeds the supply.

Nevertheless, all libraries have rules, and it is assumed that all students will be acquainted with them (there are posted circulation policies, and often you will be given your own copy). Even aside from the fact that the circulation policy may point out the difference in time-due for Reserve books and Special Reserve books, or the gen-

erous amount of the penalty for removing looseleaf services from their reading alcove, familiarity with the policy makes it easier to request exceptions in a knowledgeable manner.

There also may be a fine schedule. Not all law school libraries bother with fines, because peer pressure (to say nothing of consideration for people one knows that well) encourages the average law student to share the library's resources. If your law library does have a fine schedule, it may not be applied automatically to all delinquents (as it would have to be applied by a library serving thousands of students). In all but the largest law schools, it is fairly easy for the circulation staff to notice, without doing extensive research into the subject, which students are habitually late in returning books; it is even more evident which students are late in returning books which are in demand (in the period before exams, or during writing assignments, for instance), and those students who do not fall into these absent-minded or desperate categories may complete their law school careers without having put the staff to the nuisance of preparing a fine notice.

The general rule. No written memorandum or How-to-Use-the-Library booklet can anticipate every student's questions about his or her law library or books. Your library staff will welcome questions.

SECTION 4C.   BASIC TYPES OF LEGAL PUBLICATIONS

Table I, on the following page, will give you a framework of reference within which to fit the several publications to be discussed in detail in the following chapters. Some of the types of publications included in the table have already been generally described in text notes and footnotes appearing in Part I of this text. Those publications and others are described in greater detail in the remainder of this section.

The three broad categories under which the publications are classified are defined as follows:

Primary materials are publications containing the "law," that is, judicial or quasi-judicial opinions and written law.

Search materials are publications containing indexes, tables, or other patterned research aids useful only for identifying and locating primary or other materials.

Secondary-search materials are publications containing textual analyses and syntheses of primary materials. The most useful materials of this type also contain critical commentary and discussions or predictions about what the law should or will be. These publications are usually referred to only as "secondary" materials, but because they also contain

citations to primary and other materials, the dual name is used herein to remind you that they will often serve a search function.

TABLE I

An Outline of Basic Publications

SEARCH	SECONDARY–SEARCH	PRIMARY
DIGESTS		COURT OPINIONS
American Digest System		Official Reports
Supreme Court Digests		National Reporters
West's Federal Practice		Advance Sheets
Digest 2d; Modern		
Federal Practice Digest;		
Federal Digest		
State Digests		
DICTIONARIES		
Ballentine's Law Dictionary		
Black's Law Dictionary		
Words and Phrases		
	ENCYCLOPEDIAS	
	American Jurisprudence 2d	
	Corpus Juris Secundum	
	TREATISES. TEXTS	
	ANNOTATED REPORTS	
	American Law Reports	
	Lawyers Edition	
	ALR Federal	
	LOOSE LEAF SERVICES	
PERIODICAL INDEXES		
Index to Legal Periodicals	LEGAL PERIODICALS	
Index to Foreign Legal		
Periodicals		
Index to Periodicals		
Related to Law		
RESTATEMENT IN COURTS	RESTATEMENTS	
ANNOTATED CODES		WRITTEN LAW
		Federal Constitution
		State Constitution
		Federal Statutes
		Statutes at Large
		Revised Statutes
		United States Code
United States Code Annotated		State Statutes
		State Codes
State Codes Annotated		
Uniform Laws Annotated		City and Other
		Local Codes
		Administrative Regulations
		Federal Register
		Code of Federal Regulations
		State Administrative
		Codes
		Executive Documents
		Federal Court Rules
		State Court Rules
		Local Court Rules
SHEPARD'S CITATORS		[B7687]

The two basic types of publications containing court opinions, *National Reporters* and *official reports,* have already been described in text notes following Chapter 1.   The distinction between the two is of interest to a researcher because of the different research aids provided by the two types of publications.   Both reporters and reports may be supplemented by *advance sheets,* temporary paperback publications of recent opinions not yet printed in hard cover volumes.

Digests are glorified indexes to reported opinions.   They consist of headnotes classified in an alphabetical arrangement of topics, sub-topics, and sub-sub-topics.   Digests to be discussed include the American Digest System, indexing opinions reported in the United States from 1658 to the present, and digests covering, respectively, United States Supreme Court opinions, all federal court opinions, opinions of states in National Reporter regions, and opinions of one state only. See Illustration 1.

The *legal encyclopedias* cover all fields of law.   Simplistic syntheses of reported opinions, without critical or predictive commentary, are organized under more than 400 legal and institutional topics, alphabetically arranged.   The encyclopedias discussed herein cover federal and state law, but encyclopedias covering the law of only one state are also available (for example, for California and New York).

Treatises and texts are more limited in scope, covering only one field or topic of law.   Like the encyclopedias, they contain textual syntheses (usually more reliable than those in the encyclopedias); in addition, the better treatises also contain critical and predictive commentary and suggested analyses of problems not yet considered in reported opinions.   They may be multivolume or single volume.   Types to be discussed include comprehensive treatises that discuss both state and federal law, the more basic and general student texts, and books particularly written for practitioners, emphasizing procedures and practice techniques as well as discussing the substantive law.

Restatements are similarly limited in coverage to a single field or topic of law.   The product of intensive joint study by scholars, judges, and practitioners, several Restatements are currently in use. Each includes black-letter rules, explanatory comments, and illustrative problems to which the rules should or should not be applied.   To a very large extent, the black-letter rules have been synthesized from opinions of courts throughout the United States.   The *Restatement in the Courts* is a multivolume index to court opinions and secondary sources that discuss or cite Restatement rules.

Annotated reports are publications reporting selected court opinions, together with textual "annotations" that summarize and synthesize other opinions discussing the same legal problems dealt with in the reported opinions.   Since these reports are of greatest value for

4A Pac D 2d—495   **ATTORNEY & CLIENT**   <key>107

For references to other topics, see Descriptive-Word Index

conduct of a client's affairs, even though no material or monetary damage may result.—In re Fraser, 523 P.2d 921, 83 Wash.2d 884.

An attorney should endeavor to spare client that frustration and anxiety which must be felt when client's cause is not pursued with reasonable diligence and promptness.—Id.

Attorney owes a duty to the ward, as well as to guardian who engages his services.—Id.

Wash. Standards of legal profession require undeviating fidelity of lawyer to his client and no exceptions can be tolerated.—Van Dyke v. White, 349 P.2d 430, 55 Wash.2d 601.

Wash. An attorney is in the highest degree responsible for protection of his client's interests.—Hood v. Cline, 212 P.2d 110, 35 Wash. 2d 192.

Wash. The relation of attorney and client is one of the strongest fiduciary relationships known to the law.—In·re Beakley, 107 P.2d 1097, 6 Wash.2d 410.

<key>107. —— **Skill and care required.**

Ariz. 1967. Attorney must act for his client in reasonably careful and skillful manner in light of his special professional knowledge.—Martin v. Burns, 429 P.2d 660, 102 Ariz. 341.

Attorney will not be held liable, while acting in good faith and in belief that his conduct is for the benefit of his client, for mere error of judgment or for mistake in point of law that has not been settled by highest court of jurisdiction and upon which reasonable lawyers differ.—Id.

best of his ability.—Pete v. Henderson, 269 P. 2d 78, 124 C.A.2d 487, 45 A.L.R.2d 58.

Cal. Regardless of whether claim is based on tort or breach of contract, attorney is not liable for every mistake he may make in his practice; he is not, in absence of express agreement, insurer of soundness of his opinions or of validity of instrument he drafts; and he is not liable for being in error as to question of law on which reasonable doubt may be entertained by well-informed lawyers.—Lucas v. Hamm, 364 P.2d 685, 56 C.2d 583, 15 Cal.Rptr. 821, certiorari denied 82 S.Ct. 603, 368 U.S. 987, 7 L.Ed.2d 525.

Colo. Attorney employed by two surviving directors of defunct corporation to enjoin issuance of tax deed on corporate land had duty to protect land against loss to end that assets might be available for creditors and stockholders of defunct corporation, and any title acquired by him was in trust for his clients.—Whatley v. Wood, 366 P.2d 570, 148 Colo. 349.

Colo. A lawyer does not guarantee results but merely undertakes to use his best skill and judgment.—Eadon v. Reuler, 361 P.2d 445, 146 Colo. 347.

Kan. 1969. Appointed counsel's duty to indigent client is basically the same as that owed to any client, and, in all cases, attorney must act with utmost honesty, good faith, fairness, integrity and fidelity, irrespective of client's ability to pay.—In·Phelps, 459 P.2d 172, 204 Kan. 16 ... Phelps

ILLUSTRATION I.

Key Number Digest Form

ILLUSTRATION 2.

Shepard's Citator Form

their annotations, they are classified as secondary-search sources even though they contain some primary material.

Looseleaf services. These services, also called topical law reports, collect in looseleaf form the text of statutes, administrative material, court opinions, and explanatory commentary for business, tax, and other subjects. The looseleaf form permits more convenient, frequent supplementation—weekly to monthly—than do most forms of publications. The special fields for which such services are provided tend to be those that have continuously changing laws, so that prompt and frequent supplementation and explanation are more than usually important.

An *annotated code* contains the statutes, and sometimes the constitution and court rules, of a given jurisdiction, together with an index to court opinions construing the legislation included. Annotated codes are classified as search publications even though they contain primary materials because they are of greatest value for their index to construing opinions. Note that "annotated" codes differ from "annotated" reports in that the former do not contain textual discussions. Rather, like the digest system, the annotated code indexing system is based on headnotes.

Shepard's Citators are patterned collections of citations to opinions, annotations, and selected legal periodicals wherein previously decided cases, legislation, legal-periodical articles, or Restatements are cited. They contain no text, merely columns of citations. Use of a Shepard's citator to find citing material is commonly called "Shepardizing." See Illustration 2.

SECTION 4D. COMMON FEATURES OF LEGAL PUBLICATIONS

Publications most useful in legal research will contain at least two of the following aids, illustrated in the pages following this section.

1. *A detailed index.* The most common and useful indexes include fact, legal-term, and legal-concept words, and words and phrases that have been defined by courts or secondary authorities. Many multivolume works have a double indexing system, a general index covering material in all volumes and an index for each volume, covering the titles or topics in that volume only. In a particular work, the volume indexes may be more detailed than the general index, or they may simply pick up from the general index the entries relevant to each volume. See Illustration 3.

2. *A detailed table of contents.* Two such tables are usually included in legal publications: a "Summary of Contents" (or "Analysis") that lists the chapters (or analogous "topic" or "title" divisions), followed by a "Table of Contents" (or "Sub-Analysis") that

lists the section, paragraph, or other sub-unit headings within the individual chapters, topics, or titles. See Illustrations 4 and 5.

3. *Prefatory summaries.* "Scope" notes or introductory paragraphs appearing at the beginning of divisions (such as chapters, topics, titles) of some publications describe the coverage of the divisions and may also cross-reference to coverage of related or excluded matters in other divisions. See Illustration 4. A preface may describe the coverage of a publication and how to use it.

4. *Citations to authorities and cross-references.* Almost all legal publications cite authorities for textual statements, though some cite more selectively than others. Most legal publications also include cross-citations to related discussions within each publication and in other relevant publications. See Illustration 6. In fact, two major law-book publishers, West Publishing Company and The Lawyers Co-Operative Publishing Co./Bancroft-Whitney Co., each publish a coordinated set of research materials for a research system that is based on the cross-citations within the system.

5. *Supplementation.* Methods of supplementation include "pocket parts" (current pamphlets slipped into a pre-prepared "pocket" on the inside of the back or front cover of each volume), separate current pamphlets, loose-leaf insertions at the front of volumes or at the front of divisions within volumes, and separate bound volumes. Supplements range from weekly through annual coverage. They are usually *cumulative*, that is, all previous supplementary materials are integrated in the current supplement. See Illustration 7. Not only is the text supplemented, with citations and cross-references, but indexes, tables, and other research aids are supplemented as well, a point to be remembered whenever you use a supplemented publication. New research features may be added in supplements.

In addition to or as a substitute for current supplementation, republication of useful and popular publications is common, either in full, through new editions, or in part, through revision and re-issue of individual volumes called "replacements" or "recompilations." Publication of new editions of large multivolume works volume by volume usually creates a research gap because index volumes are the last to be republished. The difficulties created by this gap may be minimized by temporary index pamphlets or by parallel reference tables cross-referencing from the old index or table of contents to new, but as yet unindexed, volumes.

Note that some new editions may be labelled "2d" (for example, *American Jurisprudence 2d* is a revision and republication of the earlier edition, *American Jurisprudence*). The "2d" designation is also used for another purpose, however: A publisher may decide to change the format or research features of a publication; to mark the changes, a new series will be started. Thus, for example, we have A.

L.R., A.L.R.2d, and A.L.R.3d, the *American Law Report* series. The later series do not replace the earlier series, but continue from the date the earlier series terminated.

6. *Tables.* A "Table of Cases" alphabetically lists the names of all cases cited and discussed in a publication and cites to the page numbers where each case is mentioned. Some publications include "Tables of Statutes" cited and discussed. "Parallel Reference Tables" convert citations for one published source to citations for another, for example, from an official report to a National Reporter volume. Parallel-reference tables are also available for conversion of a citation for one version of a legal source to a citation for an earlier or later version of the same source, such as a statute or a text. See Illustration 8. Tables of abbreviations appear in the front of many comprehensive sources.

The common features of legal publications just described dictate basic research approaches. Within a particular publication, you may be able to start with: (1) an index, in which case you must be able to analyze the problem to be researched with sufficient perception to choose appropriate words or phrases to lead to relevant material, or (2) a summary of contents and table of contents (or an analysis and subanalysis), in which case you must be able to analyze your problem with sufficient legal sophistication to choose an appropriate legal classification, and—to a lesser extent—you must have sufficient understanding of the scope of that legal classification to recognize appropriate legal concepts and subclassifications, or (3) a table of cases or statutes, in which case you must be able to analyze your problem sufficiently to recognize that a particular primary authority is relevant. Prefatory material will help you to ascertain whether a particular publication or topic that you have chosen is relevant. Cross-references and supplements will aid you in carrying your research forward.

NOTES

1. **A note about how to learn to use legal research materials almost painlessly.** One point on which it has been possible to get unanimous agreement among law students is that the dullest and least efficient way to learn details about legal research sources is through descriptive readings. Start with the assumption, then, that you want to do most of your learning about legal research sources other than through reading about them. The balance of the chapters in this Part II have been written to provide an overview for these "other" learning approaches. Here is a suggested procedure:

> **First,** examine the research source that you are to learn about next. Does it have each of the "common" research

INDEX

ATTORNEYS AT LAW—Cont'd

Lien of attorney—Cont'd
  construction of statutes, supra
  contracts, supra
  counterclaim or setoff, supra
  death of attorney, § 293
  debtors and creditors, supra
  dismissal of action by client, § 151
  enforcement of, §§ 302–308
  equitable remedies, §§ 283, 303
  execution, staying of, § 130
  extent of lien, § 284
  fraud or deceit, supra
  funds, supra
  independent legal action, enforcement in,
    § 304
  intervention by attorney, supra
  limitation to services in particular suit, § 285
  litigation, property recovered in, § 299
  loss of lien—
    charging lien, §§ 292–295
    retaining lien, §§ 278–280
  money, lien as attaching to, §§ 300, 301
  notice—
    adverse party's destruction of lien, § 305
    assignment without notice of lien, § 295
    charging lien, §§ 287, 288, 300
    compromise by client, § 294
    enforcement of lien, § 302
    motion by attorney to protect lien, § 306
    retaining lien, §§ 274, 277
  original action, enforcement in, § 302
  possession of property, lien dependent on,
    §§ 272, 281
  priority of lien, §§ 289–291, 307
  property subject to lien—
    charging lien, §§ 296–301
    retaining lien, §§ 273–275
  receivers, infra
  retaining on general lien, generally, §§ 272–
    280
  services and compensation protected by lien,
    § 276
  statutory basis, § 282
  successful defense of rights, lien for, § 286
  summary proceeding for malpractice, de-
    fense to, § 192
  waiver, § 292
Lien on title, negligence in overlooking of,
  § 173
Limitation of actions—
  admissions by attorney, effect of, § 122
  adverse interest in subject matter, § 165
  compensation, §§ 230, 231
  disciplinary proceedings, § 62
  dismissal of action by attorney as affected
    by running of, § 125
  malpractice, §§ 176, 184–187
Liquor.   Intoxicating liquor, supra
Loan to client, § 216
Lobbying services, § 228
Local rules and decisions, malpractice by non-
  observance of, § 169
Loss of work, extra compensation for, § 234
Lynching, disbarment for advocacy of, § 52
Mail, notice of lien by, § 288
Mail fraud, disciplinary proceeding in case
  of, § 50
Maintenance.   Champerty and maintenance,
  supra

ATTORNEYS AT LAW—Cont'd

Maintenance orders, lien of **attorney as at-**
  taching to, § 298
Malpractice—
  generally, §§ 167–200
  action or suit, recovery by, §§ 182–190
  appeal and error, supra
  appearance as unauthorized, § 179
  assistant, negligence of, § 181
  basis of liability, §§ 167–181
  briefs, contents of, §§ 20, 29
  burden of proof, § 188
  clients, liability to, §§ 167–195
  collection of claims, supra
  compensation, supra
  contract, action based on, §§ 167, 182, 185
  damages, elements of, §§ 167, 183, 190
  delegated authority, acting beyond scope of,
    § 178
  discretion of court, supra
  dismissal of action, supra
  errors of judgment, effect of, § 170
  evidence, supra
  form of remedy, § 182
  fraud, § 180
  funds, improper handling of, § 177
  initiating and conducting litigation, negli-
    gence in, §§ 171, 172, 176
  judgments or decrees, supra
  limitation of actions, §§ 176, 184–187
  nonobservance of local rules, § 169
  partner, negligence of, § 181
  pleadings, §§ 171, 183
  preparation of legal instruments, § 174
  questions of law and fact, § 189
  reasonable degree of care and skill, § 168
  recording and filing laws, infra
  summary proceedings, §§ 191–195
  third persons, liability to, §§ 193, 196–200
  title search, § 173
Marriage, agreements contrary to public policy, § 166
Marshals, liability for fees of, § 200
Master and servant—
  insurance adjuster, employment of, § 86
  solicitation of business, infra
  staff attorney, §§ 76, 82–84
  trust company's employment of attorney,
    § 76
Measure of compensation.   Compensation, supra
Memorandum note on judgment as notice of
  lien of attorney, § 288
Mental condition.   Incompetent or insane
  persons, supra
Mingling of client's funds with personal funds,
  § 177
Minimum fee schedules, § 246
Minors.   Children, supra
Misappropriation of property—
  generally, §§ 35, 36
  insanity as bar to disciplinary actions, § 59
  judge, misconduct of, § 47
  malpractice action, §§ 181, 182
  nonprofessional misconduct, § 44
  tax collector, attorney as, § 49
Misconduct of attorney—
  disbarment, suspension, or reprimand, supra
  knowledge of attorney imputed to client,
    § 111

1032

ILLUSTRATION 3.

Page from volume index, "Attorneys at Law" topic,
American Jurisprudence 2d

ATTORNEYS AT LAW

Scope of Topic: This article discusses the nature, status, and purpose of the office of attorney; the qualifications and admission to practice of attorneys; the creation and termination of the relation of attorney and client; the rights, privileges, duties, and disabilities arising from the office or relation; the authority of the attorney and his client's responsibility for his acts; the liability of the attorney to his client or to third persons; the compensation of attorneys and their rights to assert liens for their fees; and the punishment, suspension, or disbarment of attorneys.

Treated elsewhere are such matters as the authority of particular persons or classes of persons to employ an attorney (see, for example, BANKRUPTCY; CORPORATIONS; EXECUTORS AND ADMINISTRATORS; GUARDIAN AND WARD; HUSBAND AND WIFE; INFANTS; INCOMPETENT PERSONS; PUBLIC OFFICERS AND EMPLOYEES; RECEIVERS; TRUSTS), the general subject of champerty and maintenance (see CHAMPERTY AND MAINTENANCE), the right of an attorney to act as surety for his client (see SURETYSHIP), arguments of counsel (see TRIAL), attorneys' fees as costs (see COSTS), communications between attorney and client as being privileged (see WITNESSES), and an attorney's liability for, and the privilege attaching to, defamatory communications made regarding the subject of his employment (see LIBEL AND SLANDER).

✦ **Table of Parallel References see p vii.** ✦

I. INTRODUCTORY (§§ 1–7)

II. JUDICIAL SUPERVISION OF LEGAL PROFESSION
   A. ADMISSION TO PRACTICE (§§ 8–11)
   B. DISCIPLINARY PROCEEDINGS (§§ 12–72)
   C. JUDICIAL PREVENTION OF UNAUTHORIZED PRACTICE OF LAW (§§ 73–90)

III. ATTORNEY-CLIENT RELATIONSHIP
   A. CREATION AND NATURE (§§ 91–93)
   B. EFFECT OF RELATION ON TRANSACTIONS BETWEEN ATTORNEY AND CLIENT (§§ 94–99)
   C. AUTHORITY OF ATTORNEY (§§ 100–137)
   D. TERMINATION OF RELATIONSHIP (§§ 138–147)
   E. SUBSTITUTION OF ATTORNEYS (§ 148)
   F. RIGHT OF CLIENT TO SETTLE OR DISMISS (§§ 149–152)

IV. PRIVILEGES AND DISABILITIES OF ATTORNEY
   A. IN GENERAL (§ 153)
   B. REPRESENTATION OF CONFLICTING INTERESTS (§§ 154–159)
   C. ACQUIRING ADVERSE INTEREST IN SUBJECT MATTER OF LITIGATION OR EMPLOYMENT (§§ 160–165)
   D. AGREEMENT TO ACT CONTRARY TO PUBLIC POLICY (§ 166)

V. LIABILITY OF ATTORNEY FOR MALPRACTICE
   A. LIABILITY TO CLIENT (§§ 167–195)
   B. LIABILITY TO THIRD PERSONS (§§ 196–200)

35

ILLUSTRATION 4.

First page from "Attorneys at Law" topic, *American Jurisprudence 2d,* illustrating scope notes and summary of contents for topic.

40

ILLUSTRATION 5.

Page from "Attorneys at Law" topic, *American Jurisprudence 2d,*
illustrating detailed table of contents for topic

§ 167   ATTORNEYS AT LAW   7 Am Jur 2d

V. LIABILITY OF ATTORNEY FOR MALPRACTICE

A. LIABILITY TO CLIENT

1. BASIS OF LIABILITY

§ 167. Generally.

An attorney who fails in his duty, causing actual loss to the client,[16] is liable for the damages sustained.[17] Generally, however, the attorney's liability for damages is only to his client, the liability flowing only from the dereliction of a duty owed to the client.[18] And in an action against an attorney for malpractice, contributory negligence of the client in disregarding the legal advice of his attorney is a defense.[19]

Although a client has a cause of action ex contractu against an attorney who fails or neglects to perform legally permissible services which he expressly, or by implication, agrees to perform for the client,[20] it has been held that there can be no recovery of property placed in the hands of an attorney for use in the advancement of an illegal purpose,[21] such as compounding a felony.[1] Other decisions hold that because of the trust and confidence placed in the attorney, and his superior influence, the client is not in pari delicto with the attorney. Under this view the client may recover from the attorney whether the contract is still executory or has been executed.[2]

§ 168. Failure to exercise reasonable degree of care and skill.

His duty to his client requires an attorney to exercise the knowledge, skill, and ability ordinarily possessed and exercised by members of the legal profession[3]

---

16. Fitch v Scott, 3 How (Miss) 314.

17. National Sav. Bank v Ward, 100 US 195, 25 L ed 621; Citizens Loan Fund & Sav. Asso. v Friedley, 123 Ind 143, 23 NE 1075; Caltrider v Weant, 147 Md 338, 128 A 72; McLellan v Fuller, 220 Mass 494, 108 NE 180; McCullough v Sullivan, 102 NJL 381, 132 A 102, 43 ALR 928.
Annotation: 45 ALR2d 11, §§ 3 et seq.; 22 L ed 482.

An attorney is answerable in damages for any loss to his client which proximately results from a want of that degree of knowledge and skill ordinarily possessed by others of his profession similarly situated, or from the omission to use reasonable care and diligence, or from the failure to exercise in good faith his best judgment in attending to litigation committed to his care. Hodges v Carter, 239 NC 517, 80 SE2d 144.
An attorney is liable to his client for negligence in rendering professional services, the liability being imposed for want of such skill, prudence, and diligence as lawyers of ordinary skill and capacity commonly possess and exercise. Theobald v Byers, 193 Cal App 2d 147, 13 Cal Rptr 864.

18. National Sav. Bank v Ward, 100 US 195, 25 L ed 621; Lawall v Gorman, 180 Pa 532, 37 A 98.

19. Theobald v Byers, 193 Cal App 2d 147, 13 Cal Rptr 864, 87 ALR2d 986, reh den
146

(but holding that client was not guilty of contributory negligence as a matter of law).
Annotation: 87 ALR2d 994, § 3.

20. Weekley v Knight, 116 Fla 721, 156 So 625.

21. Jones v Henderson, 189 Ky 412, 225 SW 34, 20 ALR 1471.
Annotation: 20 ALR 1476, s. 26 ALR 98, 116 ALR 1021.

1. Jones v Henderson, supra (attorney and client, in entering into contract contrary to public policy, are in pari delicto, and neither can recover against the other); Holland v Sheehan, 108 Minn 362, 122 NW 1.
Annotation: 116 ALR 1023.

2. Re Sylvester, 195 Iowa 1329, 192 NW 442, 30 ALR 180; Berman v Coakley, 243 Mass 348, 137 NE 667, 26 ALR 92; Irwin v Curie, 171 NY 409, 64 NE 161.
Annotation: 20 ALR 1476, s. 26 ALR 98, 116 ALR 1025.

3. Wilcox v Plummer, 4 Pet (US) 172, 7 L ed 821; Hampel-Lawson Mercantile Co. v Poe, 169 Ark 840, 277 SW 29; Pete v Henderson, 124 Cal App 2d 487, 269 P2d 78, 45 ALR2d 58; People v Gerold, 265 Ill 448, 107 NE 165; Babbitt v Bumpus, 73 Mich 331, 41 NW 417; McCullough v Sullivan, 102 NJL 381, 132 A 102, 43 ALR 928.
Annotation: 45 ALR2d 63, § 2.

[7 Am Jur 2d]

ILLUSTRATION 6.

Pages from text of "Attorneys at Law" topic, *American Jurisprudence 2d*
(continued on following page)

ILLUSTRATION 6.

(continuation)

---

7 Am Jur 2d   ATTORNEYS AT LAW   § 169

similarly situated.[4] He is not bound to exercise extraordinary diligence, but only a reasonable degree of care and skill, having reference to the character of the business he undertakes to do.[5] Within this standard, he will be protected so long as he acts honestly and in good faith.[6]

Although it has been said that an attorney is liable to his client only for "gross negligence" or "gross ignorance" in the performance of his professional duties,[7] these terms apparently mean only want or absence of reasonable care, skill, and knowledge.[8]

§ 169. Nonobservance of local statutes, rules, and decisions.

In his professional activity, an attorney engages that he possesses and will use the reasonable legal knowledge that lawyers of ordinary ability and skill possess and exercise.[9] He is held liable for the consequences of his ignorance or nonobservance of the rules of the courts in which he practices,[10] or of the statutes and published decisions of his own jurisdiction.[11] However, it has been said that he is not held to the same degree of accountability for his ignorance of the laws of a foreign jurisdiction.[12]

It has been held that the failure to observe statutory requirements in the preparation of a security document, the failure to record it in the proper county, the failure to record it at all, or the failure to inform the client of the necessity for recordation constitute acts of negligence sufficient to hold an attorney liable to his client, if the negligence can be proved and damages can be shown to be the result of such acts or omissions.[12.5]

An attorney who undertakes the management of business committed to his charge thereby impliedly represents that he possesses the skill, and will exhibit the diligence, ordinarily possessed and employed by well-informed members of his profession in the conduct of the business he has undertaken. Citizens Loan Fund & Sav. Asso. v Friedley, 123 Ind 143, 23 NE 1075.

An attorney is liable for failure to perform his professional duty, whether or not the failure was intential or fraudulent. Cornell v Edsen, 78 Wash 662, 139 P 602.

The courts have consistently held that liability will be imposed on an attorney for want of such skill, prudence, and diligence as lawyers of ordinary skill and capacity commonly possess and exercise. Theobald v Byers, 193 Cal App 2d 147, 13 Cal Rptr 864, 87 ALR2d 986, reh den.

4. Hodges v Carter, 239 NC 517, 80 SE2d 144, 45 ALR2d 1.

5. Goodman v Walker, 30 Ala 482; Babbitt v Bumpus, 73 **Mich** 331, 41 NW 417; Glenn v Haynes, 192 **Va** 574, 66 SE2d 509, 26 ALR2d 1334; Ward v Arnold, 52 **Wash** 2d 581, 328 P2d 164.

An attorney engages that he will employ a degree of skill ordinarily adequate and proportioned to the business he assumes to handle. Cox v Sullivan, 7 Ga 144.

6. National Sav. Bank v Ward, 100 US 195, 25 L ed 621; Gilbert v Williams, 8 Mass 51; Babbitt v Bumpus, 73 **Mich** 331, 41 NW

417; Sjobeck v Leach, 213 **Minn** 360, 6 NW 2d 819; Hill v Mynatt (**Tenn**) 59 SW 163.

7. Pennington v Yell, 11 Ark 212; Babbitt v Bumpus, supra.

8. Goodman v Walker, 30 Ala 482; Glenn v Haynes, 192 **Va** 574, 66 SE2d 509, 26 ALR 2d 1334.

9. McCullough v Sullivan, 102 NJL 381, 132 A 102, 43 ALR 928.

An attorney is liable to his client if the latter's interests suffer on account of the attorney's failure to understand and apply those rules and principles of law that are well established and clearly defined in the elementary books or which have been declared in adjudged cases duly reported and published a sufficient length of time to have become known to those who exercise reasonable diligence in keeping pace with the literature of the profession. Citizens Loan Fund & Sav. Asso. v Friedley, 123 **Ind** 143, 23 NE 1075.

10. Goodman v Walker, 30 Ala 482; Citizens Loan Fund & Sav. Asso. v Friedley, supra; Hill v Mynatt (**Tenn**) 59 SW 163.

11. Citizens Loan Fund & Sav. Asso. v Friedley, 123 **Ind** 143, 23 NE 1075.

12. Fenaille v Coudert, 44 NJL 286.

12.5. Hampel-Lawson Mercantile Co. v Poe, 169 Ark 840, 277 SW 29 (chattel mortgagee's suit against its attorney for alleged negligence in filing the mortgage in wrong county, as result of which chattel mortgagee's lien was

147

§ 158   ATTORNEYS AT LAW

senting a defendant in a criminal proceeding outside the county where the county attorney serves, and the denial of defendant's choice of choice on such grounds was a violation of his Sixth and Fourteenth Amendment rights. Myers v State **(Miss)** 296 So 2d 695.

§ 159. Judicial restraints

p 141, n 12—Cord v Smith (CA9 Cal) 338 F2d 516, mandate clarified 370 F2d 418.

Annotation: 31 ALR3d 715, 720, § 3.

When it appears that an attorney represents conflicting interests or accepts a subsequent retainer adverse to an interest for which he was retained by a former client, the court in which the proceeding is pending should, upon timely motion by the former client who objects to such possible violation of his confidence, disqualify counsel from continuing with the conflicting representation of the subsequent client. Brasseaux v Girouard **(La App)** 214 So 2d 401, writ refused 253 La 60, 216 So 2d 307.

Additional case authorities for section:
Where each subpoenaed witness before grand jury was potential defendant, court received information that testimony of each might be expected to incriminate one or more of other witnesses, and extent of possible multiple cross-involvement in criminal activity was known to court but hidden from individual witnesses by requirements of secrecy, it was inappropriate for supervising judge to permit multiple representation of witnesses by single counsel. Pirillo v Takiff, 462 Pa 511, 341 A2d 896, reinstated (Pa) 352 A2d 11, cert den and app dismd 423 US 1083, 47 L Ed 2d 94, 96 S Ct 873.

§ 160. Generally

p 142, n 15—
As to disciplinary proceeding based upon attorney's purchase of client's property, see § 34.5, supra.

§ 166. Generally; nonenforceability

p 145, n 6—
Annotation: Validity and propriety of arrangement by which attorney pays or advances expenses of client. 8 ALR3d 1155.

p 145, n 8—McDearmon v Gordon & Gremillion, 247 Ark 318, 445 SW2d 488 (contract was unenforceable where attorney's fee in divorce case was entirely dependent upon his obtaining property settlement in specified minimum amount).
Salter v St. Jean **(Fla App)** 170 So 2d 94, holding that while an agreement for a contingent fee in domestic relations litigation is against public policy and unenforceable as it relates to alimony, support, or property settlements in lieu of alimony, such contingent fee agreements are enforceable when they relate solely to the return of a wife's separate property.

p 145—*Add following note 12:* A contract of employment between an attorney and a trustee in bankruptcy for fees based on a contingent basis is invalid.[12.5]

n 12.5—Official Creditors' Committee of Fox Markets v Ely (CA9 Cal) 337 F2d 461, cert den 380 US 978, 14 L Ed 2d 272, 85 S Ct 1342.

p 145, n 13—Cummings v Patterson, 59 Tenn App 536, 442 SW2d 640.

§ 167. Generally

Practice Aids: Attorney's negligence in connection

with estate, will, or succession matters. 55 ALR3d 977.
—Gillen, Legal malpractice. 12 Washburn LJ 3.
Symposium, Responsibilities and Liabilities of Lawyers and Accountants. 30 Bus Lawyer, March, 1975.

p 146, n 17—Lysick v Walcom, 254 Cal App 2d —, 62 Cal Rptr 640.
Ramp v St. Paul Fire & Marine Ins. Co. 263 La 774, 269 So 2d 239, 55 ALR3d 967.

Practice Aids: 14 Am Jur Trials 265. Actions Against Attorneys for Professional Negligence.

p 146, n 18—
Allegation that defendant attorney represented both plaintiff and his former wife was not sufficient to allege damage to plaintiff and suit against attorney was properly dismissed. Brosie v Stockton, 105 Ariz 574, 468 P2d 933.

p 146, n 19—Ishmael v Millington, 241 Cal App 2d 520, 50 Cal Rptr 592.

p 146—*Add paragraph after note 2:* An attorney's representation of two or more clients with adverse or conflicting interests constitutes such misconduct as to subject him to liability for malpractice, unless the attorney has obtained the consent of the clients after full disclosure of all the facts concerning the dual representation.[2.5]

n 2.5—
Annotation: 28 ALR3d 389, 394, § 4.

§ 168. Failure to exercise reasonable degree of care and skill

p 146, n 3—Cook v Irion **(Tex Civ App)** 409 SW2d 475.

p 147, n 6—Dorf v Relles (CA7 Ill) 355 F2d 488, 17 ALR3d 1433 (applying Illinois law).

p 147, n 8—Thompson v Erving's Hatcheries, Inc. **(Miss)** 186 So 2d 756.

Additional case authorities for section:
Attorney has duty to inform his client promptly of any new information important to him, including implicit obligation to inform him of attorney's failure to act at time sufficiently prior to running of statute of limitations to permit him to engage another attorney who could then take proper action on his behalf. Passanante v Yormark, 138 NJ Super 233, 350 A2d 497.

§ 170. Effect of errors of judgment

p 148, n 13—Cook v Irion **(Tex Civ App)** 409 SW2d 475.

p 148, n 15—Collins v Wanner **(Okla)** 382 P2d 105.

Additional case authorities for section:
Also recognizing that if an attorney acts in good faith he may not be held liable for a mere error of judgment:
Iowa—Baker v Beal (Iowa) 225 NW2d 106.

An attorney does not ordinarily guarantee the soundness of his opinions, and is not liabile for every mistake he may make in his practice, but he is expected, to possess knowledge of those plain and elementary principles of law which are commonly known by well-informed attorneys, and to discover those additional rules of law which may readily be found by standard research techniques. If the law on a

40

[7 Am Jur 2d Supp]

ILLUSTRATION 7.

Page from cumulative pocket part supplement, *American Jurisprudence 2d*

TABLE OF PARALLEL REFERENCES

This table shows where the subject matter of the various sections of articles in the first edition of American Jurisprudence is treated in American Jurisprudence 2d. It enables one to translate references in the Am Jur General Index, in the AM JUR FORMS books and in Am Jur PROOF OF FACTS as well as the many references to "Am Jur" in the reported cases in other legal publications, into references to Am Jur 2d.

When a particular subject matter is treated in another topic the title of the other topic is indicated.

The reader should always consult the volume index for detail and for matter not appearing in the first edition.

ATTORNEY GENERAL

AM JUR §§	AM JUR 2d §§	AM JUR §§	AM JUR 2d §§	AM JUR §§	AM JUR 2d §§
1	Scope note	8.5	15	16	19
2	1	9	9, 12, 15	17	22; CHARITIES
3	10, 24	10	13	18	18, 20
4	2	11	15	19	18
5	6, 24	12	16, 17	20	18
6	6, 9, 15	13	3	21	23, 24
7	4, 6, 25, 26, 27	14	8		
8	11, 12, 15, 18, 19	15	5		

ATTORNEYS AT LAW

AM JUR §§	AM JUR 2d §§	AM JUR §§	AM JUR 2d §§	AM JUR §§	AM JUR 2d §§
1	Scope note	33	207	65	155
2	2	34	138	66	156
3	73	35	140	67	100
4	88	36	139	68	112
5	1	37	141	69	134
6	3	38	142	70	124
7	4	39	143	71	127
8	5	40	144	72	104
9	CONTRACTS	41	146, 147	73	105
10	6	42	WAR	74	107
11	153	43	144	75	108
12	201	44	148	76	109
13	202	45	92	77	111
14	2	46	93	78	110
15	2	47	167	79	112
16	9, 10	48	94	80	113
17	90	49	95	81	116
18	89	50	97	82	114
19	8	51	96	83	179
20	8	52	98	84	179
21	11	53	99	85	120
22	8	54	37	86	120
23	8	55	37	87	117
24	8	56	227	88	120
25	83	57	41	89	118
26	8, 9	58	160	90	119
27	8	59	160	91	121
28	8	60	161	92	121
29	91	61	162	93	122
30	91	62	164	94	122
31	208	63	165	95	123
32	91	64	154	96	124

vii

ILLUSTRATION 8.

Page from parallel reference table, Volume 7 of
American Jurisprudence 2d

features described in Section 4D or some variant thereof? How is it classified and defined in Table I, Section 4C?

Then, read the discussion of the source in this text—but do your reading with volumes of the source at your elbow, so that you can turn to the source volumes immediately to examine any details described or mentioned in this text.

Finally, for each source, use the basic research approaches described in Section 6C, *infra,* to attempt to find material on a legal problem in which you are currently interested.

The suggested three-step procedure, used in connection with readings in this text, will give you a working knowledge of each source. But there is more. This text does not begin to describe all the useful variant details that you will find in many research sources. Many of these details you will learn by a process of osmosis, as you look at or use the sources. Others you may learn in class meetings, through discussion and lectures. Some you may learn from other readings assigned by an instructor or by doing your own research in legal bibliography. Several good legal bibliography books are available. Concise and basic is M. Cohen, Legal Research in a Nutshell (3d ed. 1978). More comprehensive books include How to Find the Law (M. Cohen ed. 7th ed. 1976); J. Jacobstein & R. Mersky, Fundamentals of Legal Research (1977); M. Price & H. Bitner, Effective Legal Research (3d ed. 1969) (currently being revised for publication in late 1978).

2. If you are not generally familiar with the contents and use of a card catalog, see How to Find the Law, *supra,* note 1, at 301–03.

3. Recent developments in computer-assisted legal research and in the forms of legal materials are discussed in Chapter 9, *infra,* and text notes following that chapter.

4. It is suggested in Section 4A, *supra,* that peculiarities of the common law doctrinal framework may result in limitations on the effectiveness of legal research materials. Identify as many such "peculiarities" as you can and suggest a limitation resulting from each.

5. Learning correct citation forms and abbreviations is a necessary nuisance. Hereafter in this text, citation abbreviations will be given parenthetically as research sources are named, and the abbreviations will thereafter frequently be used in place of the full titles. Absence of a citation abbreviation for a publication will indicate that that source is a search tool only and therefore not generally cited. You will ultimately conserve time if you memorize each abbreviation

as you learn about each source. As a starter, memorize the abbreviations for the National Reporter units reporting state court opinions:

The state-regional units:

P., P.2d
N.W., N.W.2d
S.W., S.W.2d
N.E., N.E.2d
A., A.2d
S.E., S.E.2d
So., So.2d

The state units: (Cite to both the state unit and the state-regional units, if an opinion appears in both.)

N.Y.S., N.Y.S.2d
Cal.Rptr.

In addition, note the abbreviations, contents, and form of citations in footnotes throughout this text. The contents and form conform generally to the contents and form prescribed in the citation *Blue Book,* described in text note 3 following Chapter 1, though spacing may vary from *Blue Book* form.

6. The National Reporter system includes five federal units. *The Supreme Court Reporter* (S.Ct.) reports opinions of the United States Supreme Court since 1882. The *Federal Reporter* (F., F.2d) currently reports opinions of the federal court of appeals as well as those of some lesser federal courts. Until 1932 federal district court opinions were also reported in the *Federal Reporter*, but since that year they have been reported in the *Federal Supplement* (F.Supp.). *Federal Rules Decisions* (F.R.D.) reports opinions dealing with federal rules of procedure that are not designated for publication in the *Federal Supplement*. Federal district court judges determine which of their opinions shall be published in the *Federal Supplement*. Vestal, *A Survey of Federal District Court Opinions: West Publishing Company Reports*, 20 Sw.L.J. 63, 77 (1966). Some district court opinions not published in these West reporters may be published in topical reports. Vestal, *Reported Federal District Court Opinions: Fiscal 1962*, 4 Houston L.Rev. 185, 185–90 (1966). Early lower federal court opinions (1789–1880) are collected in *Federal Cases* (F. Cas.), arranged alphabetically by case name and assigned sequential numbers. Citation is by number, thus: Bishop v. Stockton, 3 F.Cas. 453 (C.C.W.D.Pa.1843) (No. 1,440).

The most recent addition to the National Reporter System is *West's Military Justice Reporter* (M.J.) which reports opinions of the United States Court of Military Appeals and selected opinions of the Courts of Military Review.

7. Some state jurisdictions have appellate court opinions that are unreported (either unreported in fact or not officially designated

as "reported"), for which there may be special rules relating to authority value. See, for example, Note, *Selective Publication of Case Law*, 39 So.Cal.L.Rev. 608 (1966); Vestal, *Reported Opinions of the Federal District Courts: Analysis and Suggestions*, 52 Iowa L.Rev. 379, 392–97 (1966). What should be the authority value of an unreported opinion? (Copies may be obtained from official files or from counsel of record, for example, and citations thereto will occasionally appear in other published materials by case name, court, and docket number, *e. g., Tillman v. Endsley*, No. 73–1476–Civ.–CF (S.D.Fla. Oct. 1, 1973).) See Chanin, *A Survey of the Writing and Publication of Opinions in Federal and State Courts*, 67 Law Lib.J. 362 (1974); Jacobstein, *Some Reflections on the Control of the Publication of Appellate Court Opinions*, 27 Stan.L.Rev. 791 (1975).

8. Learn the locations of the publications you will be using. If a location diagram of your law school library is provided for you, find each of the publications listed in Table I on the diagram. If a diagram is not provided, you may find it useful to prepare your own diagram of locations of the basic publications described in this chapter, including locations of the several units of the National Reporter System.

Chapter 5

GENERAL RESEARCH SUGGESTIONS

SECTION 5A. INTRODUCTION

No simple mechanical formula for analyzing and researching all problems can be given you. The most effective and efficient approach will vary from problem to problem, depending on the nature of the problem, the analytical and procedural stage at which you become involved, your prior knowledge of the subject area, your prior experience in doing research generally, and how much time you may allot to researching the particular problem. Nevertheless, some general suggestions will be useful to you in your initial research efforts. This chapter is intended to provide a framework of suggestions. The following three chapters will fill in the framework.

No research system can exhaust all possibilities for all problems. Some research sources will always be omitted; something will always be missed. An exhaustive search cannot be justified for many problems. The research steps described in this chapter and the following chapters have been developed with these truisms in mind. The steps are designed to minimize the risk that the "something" missed in a search of a limited number of research sources is something crucial or significant.

SECTION 5B. SUGGESTED STEPS IN RESEARCH

Unless a researcher has prior knowledge about the area or areas of law in which a problem may be categorized, preliminary research and analysis is necessary to provide sufficient background to permit identification or understanding of questions to be researched. Secondary-search materials are the most useful starting points for such preliminary analysis, with emphasis on the *secondary,* summarizing function of this class of research books. A legal dictionary may also be useful as a starting point. Chapter 6 describes the books that will be most useful to you as a beginning researcher for this preliminary analysis phase of problem solving.

Given tentative formulation of the questions presented by a problem after preliminary research and analysis (or given background knowledge in the problem area that makes such preliminary analysis unnecessary) research must usually be directed first toward finding primary authority in the controlling jurisdiction and then, perhaps, toward finding persuasive authorities, both primary and secondary. The following suggested steps give a possible general outline for comprehensive search on a question. Research sources mentioned that are not described in Chapter 6 will be described in Chapters 7 and 8.

STEP 1. **The Search for Statutes or Other Written Law.** The first step is always to determine whether there is any controlling or relevant written law. This step is usually directed toward finding statutes, and may require searching for four basic types of material:

Statutes, in the controlling code or other available source.

Court opinions construing the relevant statutes, in an annotated code or other available source.

Secondary commentary in periodicals, annotated reports, treatises, or encyclopedias, or for court opinions construing similar legislation.

Legislative history materials.

Similar types of material may be sought for other types of written law also.

STEP 2. **The Search for Mandatory Precedents.** Assuming no controlling legislation, a search for mandatory precedents will require:

Preliminary search for opinions in the controlling state digest, state encyclopedia, Restatement annotations, local practice text, local periodical, or other local source.

A double-check search in a second of the above-listed sources if more than one is available.

Bringing the search down to date by:

(a) checking relevant advance sheets and

(b) Shepardizing relevant opinions in the appropriate Shepard's citator unit.

STEP 3. **The Search for Persuasive Precedents.** If mandatory precedents do not supply a clear answer, a search for persuasive precedents will require:

Preliminary search through one of the sources used for preliminary analysis (encyclopedia, treatise, Restatement, or legal periodicals), the American Digest System, the annotated reports, or a Shepard's regional-Reporter citator unit.

A double-check search in a second of the above-listed sources.

Bringing the search down to date by:

    (a) checking relevant advance sheets and, perhaps, the supplement to the American Digest System, and

    (b) Shepardizing relevant persuasive opinions in the appropriate Shepard's unit.

STEP 4. **The Search for Refinements of Your Analysis.** For the preceding three steps your attention has been focused for the most part on ascertaining the existing law, that is, the reasoning and rules applied in existing precedents. The fourth step should take you into materials that will support or show the errors of the doctrinal approach or approaches. As a minimum, it should include a search of the *Index to Legal Periodicals*. The library catalog may help you to identify additional sources. For many problems, a search of non-legal materials will be justified. Government documents, federal or state, may provide statistical and other data.

SECTION 5C. GENERAL RESEARCH SUGGESTIONS

Four research suggestions are of sufficient importance to be stated as black letter rules:

Never Assume the Absence of Relevant Legislation. Your preliminary analysis or background knowledge of a subject area may reveal that a particular problem on which you are working falls within an area commonly controlled by legislation. If not, do not assume that there is no controlling legislation. Note, for example, that the publishers of the encyclopedias do not attempt to collect all relevant statutes along with their report of case law, although they do cite and discuss federal statutes and statutes generally in force within the several states. Furthermore, each legislative session, both state and federal, produces new statutes. Increasingly, legislation has encroached on areas traditionally controlled by the common law, and federal legislation has encroached on areas traditionally governed by state law. Hence, you cannot safely assume the absence of relevant legislation.

To simplify your introduction to legal research, discussion of the essential Step 1, the search for statutes or other written law, is deferred in this text. In Chapter 7 it will be assumed that you have conducted a search and found no relevant written law for a problem on which you are working. Chapter 7, therefore, is devoted to Steps 2, 3, and 4, the steps necessary for comprehensive research on a question controlled by the common law. The research required for Step 1 will be discussed in Chapter 8. Do not let this order of presentation lead you to forget this first rule of research.

Research Separable Questions Separately.   When a problem presents more than one question, research those questions individually. You cannot research each question in isolation, since you must always analyze in the context of the whole problem.   However, much student frustration in early research efforts can be traced to an attempt to solve a multiquestion problem in one undirected foray through the books.   Much careless analysis by even experienced researchers can be traced to a similar undirected search.   You may avoid such frustration and faulty analysis if you will start your research on the question that logically should be answered first and pursue it to a conclusion.   If you locate material that will be helpful on another question, write the citation to it in separate notes and return to the material when you are researching that question.   If you find that you repeatedly encounter material relevant to more than one of your questions, consider whether you have formulated your questions too narrowly.

Until you become experienced in researching problems, you will find it helpful to rough draft your discussion and conclusion for each question immediately after completing your research on it, so that you can identify weaknesses in your analysis and gaps in your research while the details are still fresh in your mind.   Write out your conclusion even if it can be expressed in a single sentence and select your supporting authority in order to settle your mind on these points before going on to the next question.

Always Check the Latest Available Supplement(s) for Each Source That You Use When You First Use It.   *Remember that indexes are supplemented too.*   The ultimate objective of your search is to find the most recent authority or material available.   In working with any supplemented source, as soon as you find what appears to be a relevant section or statement therein, turn to the supplement for that section for a quick scan to ascertain whether recent commentary or citations have been added.   If significant new material does appear in the supplement, you may then save time that otherwise would have been wasted in working with dated text or citations.

Double Check Your Search Within Every Source That You Use.   You cannot be confident that one research approach to a particular source has led you to all relevant material therein because of the double danger (1) that you as a researcher have overlooked some relevant index entry or topic and (2) that a relevant word or topic has been placed at an unexpectable point within the source.   Therefore, particularly in your early research efforts, double check by using both the index and topic approaches in sources for which both approaches can be used.   Or, if you are led to a particular source by a cross-reference from another source, nevertheless use the index or the topic approach to verify whether the cross-reference was exhaustive of the subject in which you are interested.

SECTION 5D. NOTES RECORDING YOUR RESEARCH

Detailed notes are necessary whenever you undertake research on anything other than a simple problem with the expectation that your research will extend beyond one quick session. The longer the period of time over which your research may be expected to extend, the more detailed the notes should be. Scan apparently relevant material in each source before you begin taking notes; you may thus avoid taking extensive notes on tangential material when later pages disclose directly-in-point discussion. Head up every page of notes with the name of the problem and the date.

Minimal notes include:

Notes that record your opinion analysis and evaluation. For opinions that preliminary investigation indicates may be pertinent, always note:

—The name and full citation.

—The court of decision if it is not the highest court in its jurisdiction. (In National Reporter volumes, the name of the deciding court is given below the name of each case; the hierarchy of courts whose opinions are reported in each National Reporter volume is identifiable from the listing of each state's courts and judges at the front of each volume.)

—The date of decision.

—A brief of the relevant portion, including nature of action, issues related to your problem, significant facts for those issues, decisions on those issues and any principles, rules, and reasoning related to your problem area.

—In your briefs, include also the names and citations of crucial authorities on which the courts relied. (This inclusion will mark a significant difference between class study briefing and research briefing. Analysis and evaluation of authorities relied on become important in the evaluation of many court opinions; therefore, you need a record of the crucial citations.)

—The headnote number and, if you are working with a National Reporter volume, the digest key number and topic for each relevant portion of the opinion. (The headnote number appears first—1, 2, 3; the key number and topic appear as part of the heading of each note in the modern reporter volumes, thus: **5. Attorney and Client ☞107**

Begin making evaluation notes for opinions as soon as you have sufficient background to be critical. (Being "critical" means noting good points as well as weak points.)

If preliminary reading suggests that an opinion cited in your notes is not relevant, briefly indicate why it is not relevant near its citation in your notes.

Notes that accurately record the language of written law. The crucial language of statutes and other written law should be copied, by hand or machine, not paraphrased. For long, complex sections, a skeletal outline of provisions also may be necessary for accurate analysis.

Notes that record your coverage. Frequently your research will be done during disconnected periods stretching over days or weeks. To avoid retracing your steps or failing to check some source or portion of a source, make the following types of notes:

> List secondary authorities checked, including references to sections, page numbers, and footnotes scanned or read, with a brief notation of relevancy of coverage. Use some symbol to indicate supplements checked. Always note the date of basic volumes and of any supplements; you will need this information for later citation.

> List all units of search tools checked (for example, digest key numbers and units in which checked, *Index to Legal Periodical* volumes and subjects checked) and briefly indicate degree of relevancy.

> Indicate with an "s" or some other symbol the Shepardizing of each opinion on which you intend to rely.

Notes that keep you honest. Plagiarism includes the use, without acknowledgment of source, of someone else's ideas as well as such use of another's written language. Avoid such appropriation of another's ideas by noting the source of each non-original idea in your notes. Similarly, prominently identify copied language in your notes —perhaps by circled quotation marks—and write down the page number where the language appears (you will need the page number for later citation). When you paraphrase someone else's language only slightly, note this, too, for later rewriting should you decide to use the basic thought expressed; thus, you can avoid borderline plagiarism. Finally, note the context of language copied for quoting; you may thus avoid later inadvertent misrepresentation of the impact of the language.

NOTES

1. For other general introductory suggestions on system in research and on note taking during research, see Vom Baur, *How to Look up Law and Write Legal Memoranda—Revisited,* 11 Prac.Law, May 1965 at 23, 25–34; J. Jacobstein & R. Mersky, Fundamentals of Legal Research 501–04 (1977); The Research Group, Inc., Basic Legal Research Techniques 1–4 (3d ed. 1975).

2. Apart from the official reports for the United States Supreme Court and for the state in which your law school is located, you may not see a recent official report during your law school career, because law libraries may not collect official reports of opinions appearing in the National Reporter system. Still, you should always write down parallel citations to official state reports for three reasons: (1) The official citation is a necessary part of the citation (usually serving to identify the source state). (2) The official citation may alert you that you are relying on an opinion handed down by a court other than the highest court in a state. Since at least the late nineteenth century, official reports of the highest state courts have been identified by the abbreviations of the state names (for example, 274 N.Y. 666); citations to the official reports of lower court opinions add something extra (for example, 274 Cal.App. 666) or omit the state name abbreviation (for example, New York's official lower court reports are simply 274 Misc. 666 or 274 App.Div. 666). (3) At a later point you may wish to use a state Shepard's citator rather than a regional-Reporter Shepard's citator, and you will then need the official citation.

3. The official citation may be given at the beginning of an opinion in a National Reporter volume and *vice versa*. Several varieties of parallel reference tables are also available to permit conversion of a case citation in one source to a citation in another source. The most convenient source will frequently be a Shepard's case edition, described in Chapter 7, *infra*. If a Shepard's citator is not available, however, or if available citators do not provide a desired conversion, other possible sources will frequently be available. *First*, all but the most recent state report citations can be converted to the National Reporter citations from tables in the *National Reporter Blue Book*, consisting of a large permanent volume with several bound and paperback supplements. For at least case citations for the state in which a law library is located, all but the most recent National Reporter citations can be converted to the state report citation (if there is one) in the *Blue and White Book* for the state of location; *Blue and White* books are published for about half the states. *Second*, tables of cases provided for most of the comprehensive research sources generally include parallel citations for cases listed therein, for example, the tables provided for the various units of the American Digest System, described in Section 7E, *infra*. *Third*, parallel citations for the most recently published opinions may be available only through National Reporter advance sheets, which provide conversion tables for recent citations to both official reports and National Reporters on pink pages in the front of each advance sheet.

4. Even if the official report is available, you may wish to use the National Reporter volume because it supplies key numbers for easy entry to the American Digest System. On the other hand, offi-

cial state reports may contain some research aids not present in the National Reporter volumes, for example, cross-references to pertinent *American Law Report* annotations or to one of the encyclopedias.

5. Federal court opinions are customarily cited before state court opinions in legal publications. Do not permit this mechanical order of citation to lead you to overvalue the federal court opinions for common law problem areas. In state digests, for example, you will frequently find federal court opinions cited before the state court opinions. These are citations to federal opinions in cases that initially arose in the particular state. Frequently they are opinions in diversity cases, in which the federal court is merely attempting to interpret the particular state law. Such opinions are not mandatory within the state court system on the same state question; they are merely persuasive—and perhaps not very persuasive if they are in conflict with decisions of the controlling courts in the state.

Chapter 6

PRELIMINARY PROBLEM ANALYSIS

SECTION 6A. INTRODUCTION

The first step in working with a problem will frequently be to gather the facts out of which the problem arises. This step may consist of getting information from participants in and observers of events preceding or creating the problem. For example, it may begin with a client interview, the client reporting his view of the problem (why does he believe that he needs an attorney's advice?) and of the events that created the problem. Through questions, the attorney must draw out details of the events that the client otherwise might not report, perhaps because the client does not appreciate their possible significance or even, perhaps, because he regards them as damaging to his position. If other persons have observed events relating to the problem, the attorney may interview them, too, to hear their version of the incidents. Beyond interviewing persons, gathering the "facts" may require viewing the scene of important incidents and may even require that the attorney educate himself or herself about practices and procedures followed in an institution, profession, or employment with which he or she is not familiar.

Note that the foregoing description appears to assume that the attorney knows what information is significant—that is, "significant" both in the sense that a court might be influenced by the information in reaching its decision and in the broader sense that it might influence the attorney's analysis of the problem. In many cases, an attorney may already have such knowledge.[1] Unfortunately, no attorney

---

1. How that knowledge will influence the fact-gathering process has been described as follows:

"As he gathers the facts and reflects upon them almost certainly he is going through a sorting or pigeon-holing process: in what area of the law does this question lie—contracts, torts, property, etc., and, more specifi-

cally, in what particular corner thereof? Very rarely will a client, unless he is another lawyer, open the conversation by saying, for example, 'I have a nice question in contracts for you— a third party beneficiary problem.'
* * *

"Unless a lawyer can do a good job in this pigeon-holing process, law

knows all the law in the sense of knowing what facts may be significant, or even remembers all that he or she might once have known. Hence, the fact-gathering phase may be interspersed with research to aid in identifying the general issues and, thus, in identifying what information must be obtained before effective in-depth research can be begun. In this text, this preliminary research with the accompanying issue and fact analysis is called preliminary analysis.

On the other hand, a researcher may not participate in the fact-gathering phase at all. Rather, he or she may be presented with information gathered by another and asked to answer some general or specific questions about the legal consequences. For example, the information may consist only of a file containing a senior attorney's cryptic notes on a client interview or a file containing such notes, plus pleadings, depositions, responses to interrogatories, and other discovery documents. Or a senior attorney may orally report such information as is available for a particular problem and generally identify questions to be researched. Or, on particularly important or complex problems, a senior attorney may provide a detailed memo presenting the information already gathered and identifying, perhaps with some specificity, the questions to be researched. Under any of these circumstances, unless the researcher has prior knowledge of the legal area in which the questions to be researched may be categorized, some preliminary analysis will probably be necessary to give the researcher sufficient background to identify or understand the questions to be researched.

For preliminary analysis, the secondary-search materials are the most useful starting points, with emphasis on the *secondary*, summarizing function of this class of research books. Legal dictionaries may also be useful as a starting point. The remainder of this chapter is devoted to a description of the books that will be most useful to you as a beginning researcher. Recognize, however, that the secondary-search books will not always be your starting point in legal research. Given background knowledge in the subject area of a problem, you may immediately use search materials to find primary authority in the controlling jurisdiction. This latter possibility will be discussed in the following chapter.

SECTION 6B. GETTING STARTED: DEFINITIONAL PROBLEMS

Part of your preliminary analysis or actual research may require you to ascertain the meaning of technical words or phrases either

books, even thousands of them, will be of little use to him. Only once perhaps in a lifetime will he be helped by such an aid as was said to have been furnished by the Index of a massive work on Corporations. The entry was, 'Spitoon, one director hits another with.' Even in that situation the lawyer would have to realize that he ought to look under 'corporations.' "

Aigler, *Stare Decisis and Legal Education*, 4 Ariz.L.Rev. 39 n. 2 (1962).

that you do not understand or that are an integral part of your problem, requiring that you ultimately obtain authority for the meanings that you decide may be attached. For the first purpose—aiding your own understanding—one of the law dictionaries, such as *Black's* or *Ballentine's* will frequently be sufficient. These dictionaries are unsupplemented, however. If you intend to rely on a definition in your analysis of a problem, you will want a source that will give you current information about definitions and meanings used by courts. One possible source is *Words and Phrases*, an elaborate form of dictionary published by West Publishing Company, supplemented with annual pocket parts. It collects definitions from all reported opinions, usually in the court's language. State editions of *Words and Phrases* have also been published, which collect definitions from the opinions of the courts of that state and of federal courts in cases arising in that state.

Special treatment is also sometimes given to words and phrases in other publications. For example, they may be treated as separate topics or under a "Definitions" sub-entry under the pertinent topic entry.

SECTION 6C.   GETTING STARTED: TWO BASIC RESEARCH APPROACHES

Usually more than definitions will be needed to identify or understand issues, however, requiring use of more elaborate legal research sources than dictionaries. Two basic research approaches are available in most legal research sources.

The basic research approach best suited to preliminary analysis of a problem, is the index approach. This approach requires use of the general index to a publication. If the publication is multivolume, with volume indexes more detailed than the general index, this approach may ultimately require use of the volume indexes. The general index will usually cross-reference to the volume (or title or topic) index if the latter is more detailed.

Words indexed may be legal or fact or mixed. Approach through fact words (key words or phrases) is easiest, because it requires no knowledge of the category or principle of law under which a problem may be treated. This approach has been variously described, but the most useful variant seems to be the TAPP rule.[2]

---

2. Variant approaches usually merge the fact and legal word approaches. See, *e. g.*, How to Find the Law 63–66 (M. Cohen ed. 7th ed. 1976) (uses five elements common to most problems—parties, places and things, cause of action or issue, defense, and relief sought); J. Jacobstein & R. Mersky, Fundamentals of Legal Research 10–11 (1977) (uses TARP rule—Thing or subject matter, cause of Action or ground of defense, Relief sought, and Persons or parties involved).

Simply stated, this rule requires that you search indexes for key words or phrases selected from the distinctive facts of your problem:

> The *Thing involved*: Does the problem revolve around some particular object, such as an automobile, a baseball bat, termites? or some characteristic of a thing involved, such as the quantity of land conveyed?

> The *Act or Activity that created the problem*: Do difficulties stem from a misstatement? golfing? horseplay? an error or mistake?

> The *Persons involved*: Are they of a special class, such as minors? Do they have a particular occupation, such as teacher? Do they have a particular relationship, such as parent and child, attorney and client, vendor and purchaser?

> The *Place to which the problem is related:* Did an incident occur in a park? a school? a bank?

Obviously, there is much room for abstraction in identifying the fact words that you will want to check. For example, an automobile may be more generally classified as a motor vehicle, golfing may be more generally classified as a sport, and so on.

In using this fact word approach, you are gambling on the possibility that one or more of the factual aspects of your problem identified through the TAPP rule have been treated as significant by courts in deciding cases. If so, then a comprehensive index will usually index the fact (or some synonym or classification for the word label you have chosen). Even though a fact has not been treated as significant, the more comprehensive indexes may list it so that you can find discussions of cases having similar facts or a cross-reference to a relevant legal concept. The ideal index entry to find would be one that incorporates your words for each part of the TAPP rule, perhaps indicating that you had found something directly in point for your problem. Do not be misled into believing that research on problems is always so direct, however, because the fact approach has limitations. The facts of your problem may never have been treated as significant in the particular context of your problem or in an analogous context. Further, you must operate within the limits of the whims of indexers (or of your own whims, taking a different view) as to the appropriate labels (key words or phrases) for your particular facts. You will find that certain "facts" are regularly indexed under what are almost, but not quite, technical labels. For example, a person who contracts to transfer real property is indexed as a "vendor," while a person who contracts to transfer personal property may be indexed as a "seller." "Mistake" may be indexed under "malpractice." "Misstatements" may be indexed as "misrepresentations" or, more obscurely,

under "fraud." "Employer" and "employee" may be indexed under the archaic "master and servant." Nevertheless, the index approach using fact words may be productive even though you know nothing about the legal concepts or customary labels that may be relevant to a particular problem.

If you are aware of some legal aspect of a problem, however, a legal-word approach through indexes may lead more quickly to relevant material. To use this approach, check index entries for a legal concept that appears to be relevant (for example, negligence, malpractice, contract offer), a defense you expect to assert or to be asserted (for example, statute of limitations, laches), or the remedy or relief to be sought (for example, rescission, damages). Under these index entries you should then look for your TAPP fact words or for more specific concept, defense, or remedy words.

A second basic approach, called the topic approach, begins with the Summary of Contents (or Analysis) rather than with the general index to a publication. A cautious procedure to follow in using this approach is as follows:

(1) Select what appears to be the appropriate fact, legal, or institutional topic. In your early research experiences, and particularly in doing preliminary analysis, this may be a difficult decision. In fact, you may have to use the index approach—fact and legal—to identify possibly relevant topics, or you may have to scan an outline of available topics if the publication with which you are working has one.

(2) Having chosen an apparently appropriate topic, select the volume that includes coverage of that topic and turn to the beginning of the topic. Ascertain whether there is a scope note or other introductory summary of coverage. If so, read the note or introduction to determine whether the topic is, in fact, relevant.

(3) Once you have assured yourself that the selected topic is probably relevant, run through the Summary of Contents (or Analysis) to identify apparently relevant subtopics. Then, turn to the Table of Contents (or Sub-Analysis) for the coverage outline of such subtopics and attempt to identify the section or sections (or other subdivisions) that appear to deal with your problem area.

If this approach is not immediately productive, you may wish to turn to the individual index for the selected topic in the back of the volume and use the fact-legal index approach (if the publication with which you are working has volume indexes).

SECTION 6D.   SECONDARY SOURCES USEFUL FOR PRELIMINARY ANALYSIS

Three secondary sources are the most useful to beginning researchers for preliminary analysis, that is, encyclopedias, treatises and texts, and Restatements.

After you become experienced in research, you will often find the annotated reports and legal periodicals to be most useful for the preliminary analysis phase, particularly for problem areas for which the law is currently challenged or changing. In your early research, you will be cited to relevant annotations in the annotated reports if you use the *American Jurisprudence 2d* encyclopedia for preliminary analysis. Legal periodicals are not suggested for preliminary analysis in beginning research because the major index to the periodicals is difficult to use if one does not have a clear understanding of the relevant legal concepts.[3] Other sources may cite you to periodical material, however, and thus you may find relevant material without using that index in your beginning research.

Encyclopedias

The competing national legal encyclopedias are *Corpus Juris Secundum* (C.J.S.), published by the West Publishing Company, and *American Jurisprudence 2d* (Am.Jur.2d), published by The Lawyers Co-Operative Publishing Co./Bancroft-Whitney Co.

Both encyclopedias have the basic common research features. Each has a multivolume general index and title indexes. All titles in C.J.S. are listed at the front of each C.J.S. volume and all titles in Am.Jur.2d are listed at the front of general index volumes. Both encyclopedias have scope notes and analyses and sub-analyses at the beginning of each title. Additionally, Am.Jr.2d carries cross references to related titles at the beginning of each title. Each encyclopedia routinely cross references to other basic publications of the respective publishers. Thus, C.J.S. carries cross-references to relevant key numbers (sections) in the American Digest System, under the boldface caption "Library References" (at the beginning of most sections in recently republished volumes or in the pocket supplements in older volumes). In Am.Jur.2d the most important cross-references are to annotations in the annotated reports published by the same publisher. Both encyclopedias are supplemented with annual cumulative pocket parts, and the supplements for both are keyed to the basic volume coverage by page numbers, section numbers, and footnote numbers. A looseleaf *New Topic Service* also supplements Am.Jur.2d, providing coverage of significant new areas of legislation. Neither encyclopedia has a table of cases, but Am.Jur.2d does have, at the front of each volume, tables of statutes cited and discussed, cumulated in a companion volume, *Am.Jur.2d Table of Statutes and Rules Cited*. For an illustrative page from C.J.S., see Illustration 9, following. For illustrative pages from Am.Jur.2d, see Illustrations 3 through 8, *supra*, Section 4D.

---

3. Indexes to legal periodicals are described in Section 7F, *infra*. The in-   dependent indexes for annotated reports are described in Section 7E.

7 C.J.S. ***ATTORNEY AND CLIENT*** **§ 142**

whom and the attorney the contract of employment and service existed, and not to third parties.[52]

§ 141. —— Care and Skill Required

An attorney is required, as respects his client, to exercise such skill, care, and diligence as are common in such matters of professional employment, but by some authority is liable only for gross negligence.

§ 141 ATTORNEY & CLIENT

Pages 979–982

54.5 Ill.—Holmes v. Williamson, 178 N.E.2d 700, 33 Ill.App.2d 458.

§ 142. —— Ignorance of Law

55. Cal.—Wright v. Williams, 121 Cal. Rptr. 194, 47 C.A.3d 802—Smith v. Lewis, 118 Cal.Rptr. 621, 530 P.2d 589, 13 C.3d 349.

Ind.—Mims v. Commercial Credit Corp., 307 N.E.2d 867, 261 Ind. 591.

La.—Ramp v. St. Paul Fire & Marine Ins. Co., 254 So.2d 79, am. on oth. grds. 269 So.2d 239, 263 La. 774.

Mo.—In re Kaemmerer, App., 178 S.W. 2d 474.

Knowledge of laws of foreign state

(1) Held liable.

U.S.—Rekeweg v. Federal Mut. Ins. Co., D.C.Ind., 27 F.R.D. 431.

N.Y.—In re Roel, 165 N.Y.S.2d 31, 3 N.Y.2d 224, 144 N.E.2d 24.

(2) Held not liable.

6 C.J. p 698 note 43 [e].

Not bound to know all law

N.Y.—People v. Vasquez, 189 N.Y.S.2d 955, 18 Misc.2d 614.

56. Cal.—Smith v. Lewis, 118 Cal.Rptr. 621, 530 P.2d 589, 13 C.3d 349.

La.—Ramp v. St. Paul Fire & Marine Ins. Co., 254 So.2d 79, am. on oth. grds. 269 So.2d 239, 263 La. 774.

N.Y.—Gimbel v. Waldman, supra, n. 53.

Degree of knowledge as to well settled rules

(2) Other matters.

Wash.—Hansen v. Wightman, 538 P.2d 1238, 14 Wash.App. 78.

page 980

58. U.S.—Smith v. St. Paul Fire & Marine Ins. Co., D.C.La., 366 F.Supp. 1283, affd., C.A., 500 F.2d 1131.

59. Ariz.—Martin v. Burns, 429 P.2d 660, 102 Ariz. 341—Talbot v. Schroeder, 475 P.2d 520, 13 Ariz.App. 230.

Cal.—Silver v. Shemanski, 201 P.2d 418, 89 Cal.App.2d 520—Lucas v. Hamm, 15 Cal.Rptr. 821, 364 P.2d 685, 56 C.2d 583, cert. den. 82 S.Ct. 603, 368 U.S. 987, 7 L.Ed.2d 525—Smith v. Lewis, 118 Cal.Rptr. 621, 530 P.2d 589, 13 C.3d 349.

Minn.—**C.J.S. cited in** Meagher v. Kavli, 97 N.W.2d 370, 375, 256 Minn. 54.

N.Y.—Gimbel v. Waldman, supra, n. 53.

N.C.—**C.J.S. cited in** Hodges v. Carter, 80 S.E.2d 144, 146, 239 N.C. 517, 45 A.L.R.2d 1.

Okl.—**C.J.S. cited in** Collins v. Wanner, 382 P.2d 105, 109.

Tex.—Cook v. Irion, Civ.App., 409 S.W.2d 475.

Wis.—Denzer v. Rouse, 180 N.W.2d 521, 48 Wis.2d 528.

Good appellate advocacy demands the regular reading of the Advance Sheets of the West Publishing Company for knowledge of pertinent cases decided while the appeal is pending.[59.5]

59.5 Ind.—Boss-Harrison Hotel Co. v. Barnard, 266 N.E.2d 810, 148 Ind. App. 406.

s required,
skill, care,
ssion com-
ers of pro-
nounced in

many of the cases, however, is that an attorney is liable only on proof of "gross negligence."[54]

§ 142. —— Ignorance of Law

An attorney is required to have such knowledge of law as is ordinarily possessed by other attorneys, and is liable for loss resulting from ignorance thereof.

In addition to the care and skill which an attorney is required to exercise on behalf of his client (see supra § 141), an attorney is required to possess such a reasonable knowledge of the law as is ordinarily possessed by other attorneys.[55] Accordingly, an attorney must be acquainted with the statutes and the settled rules of law and practice prevailing in the courts in the locality wherein he practices, and is responsible for loss to his client resulting from ignorance thereof;[56] but he is not to be charged with

ence toward their clients in the manner as physicians and surare liable to their patients (see § 140), attorneys are required ercise that degree of skill and nce in their profession which cians and surgeons are required rcise in theirs.—Olson v. North, Il.App. 457—6 C.J. p 696 note .

Requirements of skill and care ysicians and surgeons see Phys and Surgeons §§ 41–47 [48 1113 note 46–p 1121 note 18].

nable or ordinary care and ill

The true measure of an attorduty and liability to his client een held to turn on the question er the attorney used reasonable and skill.—Good v. Walker, 30 482, 68 Am.D. 134—Evans v. ous, 2 Port.(Ala.) 205.

Similarly it has been held that orney is liable only for want of ry care and skill.—Holmes v. 1 R.I. 242.

aranty of infallibility

torneys do not guaranty that judgment is infallible."—Mey v. Wallace, 214 Ill.App. 618,

ng client's money

It has been held that an attorin whose hands money of a was left to be loaned, although isurer of such funds, had the to exercise the care of a realy prudent person in dealing trust property.—Shockney v. , 147 N.E. 292, 83 Ind.App. 407.

Similarly, where an attorney authorized to lend a clients' on a mortgage, it was held uch attorney was not liable as surer, but only for using due and average skill.—Weinberg v. eman, 234 N.Y.S. 49, 226 App. Div. 3, affirmed 170 N.E. 167, 252 N.Y. 622.

54. Pennington v. Yell, 11 Ark. 212, 52 Am.D. 262—6 C.J. p 698 note 40.

As want of ordinary or reasonable care and skill

(1) Want of ordinary care and skill in an attorney has been held to amount to "gross negligence."—Holmes v. Peck, 1 R.I. 242, 245.

(2) In another case where it was stated that an attorney was liable only for "gross negligence," these words were shown by other language in the opinion to be equivalent to want of "reasonable care and skill."—Evans v. Watrous, 2 Port.(Ala.) 205.

(3) Thus explained, the phrase "gross negligence" has been held to indicate the true measure of the attorney's duty and liability.—Goodman v. Walker, 30 Ala. 482, 68 Am.D. 134—Evans v. Watrous, 2 Port.(Ala.) 205.

Degrees of negligence generally see Bailments §§ 26–29 [6 C.J. p 1118 note 37–p 1128 note 32]; Negligence §§ 8, 9 [45 C.J. p 664 note 64–p 680 note 11].

55. Morris v. Muller, 172 A. 63, 113 N.J.Law 46, reversing 168 A. 772, 11 N.J.Misc. 866.

56. In re Woods, 13 S.W.(2d) 800, 158 Tenn. 383, 62 A.L.R. 904—6 C.J. p 698 note 43.

Degree of knowledge as to well settled rules

"While an attorney does not guarantee the accuracy of all he does, he is bound to exercise reasonable skill and diligence in attending to business intrusted to his care, and he is bound to possess such reasonable knowledge of well-settled rules of law as will enable him to perform the duties he undertakes."—In re Woods, 13 S.W.(2d) 800, 803, 158 Tenn. 383, 62 A.L.R. 904.

979

ILLUSTRATION 9.

Page from *Attorney and Client* topic, *Corpus Juris Secundum*, with excerpt from supplement superimposed

A significant difference between the two encyclopedias is in the extent of citation of court opinions. C.J.S., with its predecessor, *Corpus Juris* (C.J.), is designed to cite all decisions reported in the United States. C.J.S. cites decisions handed down since the early 1930's, with footnote cross-references to C.J. for any earlier decisions. Citations in Am.Jur.2d are selective, that is, the publishers cite representative decisions only. By footnote cross-references to the same publisher's annotated report series (for example, the various A.L.R. series), supporting citations for Am.Jur.2d text statements are substantially broadened. Because the cited annotated report series also supplement the Am.Jur.2d text, any relevant annotations cited therein should be read along with the encyclopedia text at the time you use the encyclopedia.

Some practicing attorneys use the encyclopedias as more than search and preliminary survey books, citing them to courts as authority. Consider the following passage, however:

> Most critical discussions of law books as authority distinguish the two major functions of encyclopedias—as digests and as authoritative texts—and assess their value separately with relation to each function. The general opinion is that these works are useful as digests, [Footnote omitted.] but that the text and documentation are frequently of such uncertain quality as to make reliance on them without prior consultation of the cases and other more reliable authorities a questionable practice.[a]

> No attempt will be made here to evaluate encyclopedias as digests or search books. Their value as authoritative texts depends, in the final analysis, on whether the courts do in fact cite and rely on them, not whether they should do so, and the answer seems to be that they do. However it is possible to raise valid questions concerning the desirability of this practice, if only because the narrow conception of the legal process on which these works are based so obviously assumes a mechanical jurisprudence in which the finest art is that of matching or distinguishing objectively similar or different decisions in order to put them in the proper slots, push a button, and read the answer on the slip of paper which

a. * * * Headnotes arranged vertically make a digest. Headnotes arranged horizontally make a textbook. Textbooks arranged alphabetically make an encyclopedia. * * *" Chafee, Book Review, 30 Harv.L.Rev. 300 (1917). "But none of these speaks authoritatively. They are but search-books—sign-boards, as it were, along the road to the real and only exponents of legal truth, namely the decided cases. And he who is content to rely on these or other similar works as real authority, has misconceived the function of such volumes." Lile, *The Exaltation of Secondary Authority*, 14 Bench and Bar 53, 55 (1919). * * *

comes out of the machine.[b] This conception, even though apparent in every aspect of some of these works, does no great harm to the legal order so long as the work is used solely as a research tool—a guide to the cases, statutes and other appropriate authorities. But anyone who feels that the judicial process involves more than this matching of colors, that, as Cardozo has said,[c] the man who has the best card index is not therefore the wisest judge, must recognize the stultifying effect on law of reliance on such text as authority.[4]

Treatises and Texts

Scholarly syntheses of and commentaries on English law date back to at least the twelfth century, when the *Tractatus* attributed to Glanvil was written. An early publication of this character, Blackstone's *Commentaries on the Law of England* (1765–69), greatly influenced the development of law in the United States, because of the coincidence of its early availability with the separation of this country from English rule. Substantial reliance was placed on Blackstone's *Commentaries* by judges, attorneys, and embryo law schools in our country. This reliance continued, although lessening with passing time, until almost the beginning of the twentieth century. What Blackstone attempted, a scholarly restatement of all the law of England (primarily for the benefit of students, incidentally), or what Kent similarly attempted in his *Commentaries on American Law* (1826–30), soon was beyond the efforts of a single American scholar because of the great extent of case and statutory law and the complexities created by the several state and federal jurisdictional sources of law. Scholarly efforts continued with respect to lesser portions of the law—such as the law of evidence, of contracts, of real property—with substantial multivolume treatises as the result. More recently, scholars have usually surveyed even lesser portions of the law, so that we have many one-volume works dealing with narrow problem areas, such as

b. Thus all of them purport to set out "the law," which consists of the "rules laid down in the reported cases," together with "all exceptions, qualifications, extensions, and limitations." * * * [T]he repeated emphasis on reporting statements of legal rules by courts, usually in the language of the court, the emphasis on reconciling decisions, on dividing rules into minority, majority, etc., rules, on rationalizing conflicts, * * * the obvious intent to simplify that which can never be simple, the determination to rationalize "apparently" inconsistent ideas, the promise of certainty with reference to matters that can never be certain, all of these and many other aspects of the encyclopedias discussed indicate an approach to the judicial process which is mechanical and superficial.

c. Cardozo, The Nature of the Judicial Process * * *

4. From Merryman, *The Authority of Authority*, 6 Stan.L.Rev. 613, 645–46 (1954), copyright 1954 by the Board of Trustees of the Leland Stanford Junior University. Reproduced with permission of the copyright owner and the author.

products liability and comparative negligence. Student texts, on the other hand, frequently attempt to cover substantial segments of the law in a single volume.

The wide range of materials available in this category makes it necessary for you early to develop a critical attitude in selection and use of them. Even at the beginning of your career, it is possible for you to be selective. The following suggested guides to evaluation of materials in this category should aid you in reaching this objective.

First, you will find that some of your instructors will identify reliable treatise sources for your use. Similarly, your course books and the opinions reproduced therein may cite repeatedly to a limited number of these sources. Thus, through each course you study you may expect to become acquainted with the most highly regarded treatises and texts in the subject area. Guided by your own experience in using these recommended sources, you will be able to make your own evaluation of their quality and utility.

Second, as Professor Gallagher points out in Section 4B, most-used treatises and texts will probably be kept on reserve in your law school library. If so, there may be a listing of the reserve books from which you can select books on a particular subject. If no such listing is available, you can survey what is available in a given subject area through the card catalog, assuming that you can classify your area of interest within a broad legal category, such as Contracts. You may find many cards for such a broad topic, but you can evaluate the sources from information given on the catalog cards: (1) When was the work published? Generally, the more recent publications are more useful than older ones, though this is not necessarily true if a publication is currently supplemented or if you are looking for historical or background material. (2) How comprehensive is it? Whether a publication is multivolume is indicated on book cards in the catalog. The larger the work, the more probable it is that it will contain more comprehensive coverage than shorter works. (3) Is it supplemented? This information, too, will be included on the book card. Given this information, you will find that you can identify perhaps not more than a half dozen general sources that are of current interest.

Once you have made a tentative selection of a treatise or text and have an actual volume in hand, you can ask additional questions to evaluate the one you have chosen: (1) Does it have features that make it useful as a research tool: a detailed index? the summary-of-contents and table-of-contents combination? tables of cases and statutes cited? other research aids? (2) How extensive is the documentation? Does it appear to cite only selected cases, or does it cite extended lists of cases? Does it cite other reliable forms of secondary authorities? (3) Is the author's purpose stated in a preface or introduction? Does he or she purport to present a comprehensive analysis

of an area of law or only a basic survey? A student text, for example, may present a basic survey that is useful for preliminary analysis of a problem but not for carrying research forward into detailed consideration of a narrow point of law. A comprehensive treatise, on the other hand, may be useful for both purposes.

Restatements

The Restatements are produced by the American Law Institute, organized in 1923. Composed of judges, lawyers, and law teachers, the institute was organized with the high expectation that its publications would contribute to simplifying the law, making it more certain, and promoting "those changes which will tend better to adapt the laws to the needs of life." [5]

The third purpose—promotion of change—was abandoned before production of the institute's first Restatement, the *Restatement of Contracts*, in 1932.[6] Abandoned also were the plans to include a full explanation of underlying theories and reasoning and a complete citation of authorities upon which all restated rules were based. The early Restatements consist only of a classification and arrangement of the concepts involved in each area, stated and explained in three parts: black letter statements of definitions and rules (only occasionally of broad principles), comments (explanations of the limits and application of the black-letter statements), and illustrations (factual patterns to which the black-letter statements could or could not be applied, frequently drawn from decided cases from which the black-letter statement was derived). The rules stated were usually those traditionally or overwhelmingly accepted by the courts, even though these rules were sometimes clearly inconsistent with the original intent to "adapt the laws to the needs of life."

The general procedure followed in the preparation of each Restatement was similar to that summarized in the introduction to the *Restatement of Contracts*.[7] A reporter, a leading authority in the subject area being restated, was selected by the council, the executive body of the institute. The reporter (sometimes with associate reporters) was primarily responsible for the preparation of preliminary drafts of proposed chapters. After criticism of these drafts by advis-

5. Report of the Committee on the Establishment of a Permanent Organization for the Improvement of the Law Proposing the Establishment of an American Law Institute (1923), as reprinted in American Law Institute, The American Law Institute 50th Anniversary 25 (1973). Subsequent statements about early institute purposes are from the same source, particularly pages 20–33, and from *History of The American Law Institute and The First Restatement of The Law*, Restatement in the Courts 1–23 (perm. ed. 1945).

6. The focus for change shifted over the years from the courts to the legislatures, as increased emphasis has been placed by the institute on the development of model codes and other forms that can be submitted to state legislatures for adoption. See Wechsler, *The Course of the Restatements*, 55 A.B.A.J. 147, 148 (1969).

7. Restatement of Contracts vii–xv (1932).

ers and by the council, the drafts were revised and submitted to the institute membership and to bar associations as tentative drafts. After criticism by these bodies and sometimes further revision, a preliminary (or proposed) official draft of all chapters was published. After a final round of discussion, criticism, and revision, the Restatement was finally published.

Some of the original Restatements are still in use today, those covering Contracts (2 volumes, 1932), Restitution (1937), Property (5 volumes, 1936–40), Security (1941), and Judgments (1942). A 1965 addition was the *Restatement of the Foreign Relations Law of the United States*. Revision of the early works began in 1953. Restatement (Second) volumes have been completed for Agency (1958), Trusts (1959), Conflicts (1971), and Torts (2 volumes, 1965; 2 volumes, 1977–78). See Illustration 10. A substantial portion of the Contracts and Judgment revisions are in approved tentative draft form. The first installment of a new Property Restatement was completed in 1976, covering Landlord and Tenant, a branch of property law not covered in the original *Restatement of Property*.

For the revised editions, the American Law Institute adopted an enlarged format.

> Many additions have been made * * * both to the statements of law because of the development since the first edition and to the explanation of the rules and principles laid down. The effort is being made in the new editions of the various subjects of the Restatement to give the reader * * * more of the background of the development of a rule and an explanation for conclusions reached.
>
> In addition to the revised and enlarged text there is included as part of an Appendix a set of Reporter's notes * * * supplied to the reader from the pen of an accepted and well-known authority in this field. Included also in the Appendix are the citations to the Restatement which courts have made since the first work in the subject of Agency was published.[8]

Although the institute chose to expand its publication format, it did not adopt a firm policy of stating rules contrary to those overwhelmingly accepted by the courts, even where changed social conditions call for contrary rules. Thus, as late as 1966 the director of the institute reported to the members:

> Does not the statement of a rule involve * * * something more than the conclusion that it is supported by

8. As described in *Introduction*, Restatement (Second) of Agency vii, Copyright © 1954. Reprinted with the permission of The American Law Institute. The Appendix referred to is a separate volume or set of volumes for early Restatement (Second) subjects. Appendix volumes are described in detail in Section 7E, *infra*.

Ch. 12   STANDARD OF CONDUCT   § 299 A

special knowledge of other pertinent matters which, separately or together, may enable him to realize the necessity of using his highly competent technique which a person of lesser competence would not realize.

§ 299 A. Undertaking in Profession or Trade

Unless he represents that he has greater or less skill or knowledge, one who undertakes to render services in the practice of a profession or trade is required to exercise the skill and knowledge normally possessed by members of that profession or trade in good standing in similar communities.

See Reporter's Notes.

Comment:

a. Skill, as the word is used in this Section, is something more than the mere minimum competence required of any person who does an act, under the rule stated in § 299. It is that special form of competence which is not part of the ordinary equipment of the reasonable man, but which is the result of acquired learning, and aptitude developed by special training and experience. All professions, and most trades, are necessarily skilled, and the word is used to refer to the special competence which they require.

b. Profession or trade. This Section is thus a special application of the rule stated in § 299. It applies to any person who undertakes to render services to another in the practice of a profession, such as that of physician or surgeon, dentist, pharmacist, oculist, attorney, accountant, or engineer. It applies also to any person who undertakes to render services to others in the practice of a skilled trade, such as that of airplane pilot, precision machinist, electrician, carpenter, blacksmith, or plumber. This Section states the minimum skill and knowledge which the actor undertakes to exercise, and therefore to have. If he has in fact greater skill than that common to the profession or trade, he is required to exercise that skill, as stated in § 299, Comment *e.*

c. Undertaking. In the ordinary case, the undertaking of one who renders services in the practice of a profession or trade is a matter of contract between the parties, and the terms of the undertaking are either stated expressly, or implied as a matter

See Appendix for Reporter's Notes, Court Citations, and Cross References

73

ILLUSTRATION 10.*

Page from *Restatement (Second) of Torts*

the past decisions? * * * [I]f we ask ourselves what courts will do in fact within this area, can we divorce our answer wholly from our view of what they ought to do, given the factors that appropriately influence their judgments, under the prevailing view of the judicial function?

The Institute has been responsive to such questions in situations where the books reveal "opposing lines of authority" * * * In "cases of division of opinion a choice had to be made and naturally we chose the view we thought was right." * * * In judging what was "right," a preponderating balance of authority would normally be given weight, as it no doubt would generally weigh with courts, but it has not been thought to be conclusive. * * *

* * *

What of the case, however, where no substantial cleavage has as yet appeared in the decisions? Here, so far as I can gather from the record, the practice on the whole has been to state the rule of such decisions as there are, without attempting to assess the influence that they would or ought to have on a contemporary court, even if the case should be of first impression in a given jurisdiction.

* * * [T]he Reporter may express in the *Reporter's Notes* such doubts as he may have respecting the continuing vitality of the decisions. Whether the Commentary also may elaborate such doubts, and thus accord the Institute the freedom that it grants to its Reporters, probably is still an open question.[9]

In 1968 the Council of the American Law Institute unanimously approved the 1966 statements of the Director with respect to freedom to predict as well as to restate the law,[10] although the freedom has apparently not been consistently exercised[11] and has not gone unchallenged.[12]

The Restatements have had varying degrees of influence on development of the common law.[13] Court acceptance of the Restate-

9. 1966 ALI Proceedings 546–47. Copyright © 1966. Reprinted with the permission of The American Law Institute.

10. Wechsler, *The Course of the Restatements*, 55 A.B.A.J. 147, 150 (1969).

11. *Id.* at 151.

12. Helms, *The Restatements: Existing Law or Prophecy*, 56 A.B.A.J. 152 (1970) (suggesting that institute indul-

gence in prediction of change misleads courts on what is the existing law).

13. The American Law Institute has regularly kept a count of citations to and discussions of the Restatements. As of April 1, 1976, it reported that Restatements had been cited by the state and federal courts a total of 56,517 times, with a tabulation of how many times each jurisdiction had cited each Restatement subject. 1976 ALI Proceedings 714. It also collects and classifies legal periodical discus-

ments as persuasive authorities, according them an authority value at least equal to that of reputable treatises, makes them a worthwhile beginning point for preliminary analysis of any problem falling within their areas of coverage.

Both the index and the topic approaches can be used with Restatements. A detailed index has been provided for each Restatement subject in both the original and the second series. A detailed listing of chapter and section titles has also been provided in a table of contents in the first volume of a Restatement or at the beginning of each volume of a Restatement (Second), so that the topic approach can be used. One must first be able to classify a problem within a Restatement subject, however. Although a general index was published for the original Restatements in 1946, its usefulness in aiding classification of a problem in a particular Restatement subject area is limited by its age and by its lack of coverage of the second series.

Relevant sections found in those Restatements that are being revised must be cross-checked for possible changes in the latest revision draft for the second series. When a revision is in the tentative-draft stage, this cross-checking may require leafing through a number of tentative draft pamphlets. One such pamphlet is issued each year for each revision project. Thus, for example, by 1977 there were twelve tentative drafts for the *Restatement (Second) of Contracts*. Each tentative draft pamphlet discusses a limited number of sections. For example, Tentative Draft No. 1 of the Contracts revisions, issued in 1964, covers sections 1–74, while Tentative Draft No. 12, issued in 1977, covers sections 314–42, 492–499, and 512–609. To the extent that a revision has proceeded in numerical order of the sections, cross-checking for revision of a particular section requires only trial and error looks at section listings in the table of contents of a few tentative draft pamphlets to find the pamphlet that covers the particular section. Unfortunately, such a simple check will not suffice for a revision that has not proceeded numerically from one group of sections to the directly following group and so on. Thus, for example, note that Tentative Draft No. 12 of the Contracts revision skipped over a substantial block of sections, which were to be covered in later drafts. Note also, for example, that revisions of sections 301–13 were originally presented in Tentative Draft No. 11, but changes approved at the annual meeting where that draft was considered were incorporated in the sections and reproduced in Tentative Draft No. 12.

sions of institute publications annually. See, for example, *Id.* at 716–42. Ready access to court and other citations is provided by the *Restatement in the Courts,* described in detail in Chapter 7, *infra.* For a discussion of one court's reliance on the Restatements and of their general precedential authority, see Byrne, Jr., *Reevaluation of the Restatement as a Source of Law in Arizona,* 15 Ariz.L.Rev. 1021 (1973).

The tentative drafts will not only alert you to changes in the law that the Restatement drafters believe have occurred or will or should occur, but the Reporter's explanations therein may also provide an excellent discussion of specific problem areas.   Further, a foreword in each tentative draft includes general comments about the contents of the draft, and a section entitled "Questions [on the draft] Suggested for Discussion at the Annual Meeting" identifies the most controversial features of proposed revisions.   At a later point in your research you may want to consult reported discussions of the suggested questions.   Discussions of the drafts and proposed revisions are reproduced verbatim in ALI Proceedings volumes, issued annually with an appendix that indexes to the page numbers wherein each draft section was discussed.

SECTION 6E.   TENTATIVE FORMULATION OF QUESTIONS TO BE RESEARCHED

The functions of preliminary analysis are only to orient the researcher to an unfamiliar problem area or to identify the questions to be researched.   Therefore you should limit the time that you spend on this getting-started phase.   Similarly, you need not take extended notes on your findings.   Rather, keep a record of the source or sources checked, with relevant page and section numbers.   If you find in-point discussion that may provide leads to primary authority, you may also wish to summarize the discussion briefly for guidance in returning to it at a later stage in your research.

Unless you are working with a novel problem or one of unusual complexity or obscurity, preliminary research in one or two of the suggested sources—legal dictionary, *Words and Phrases*, encyclopedia, treatise or text, or Restatement—should enable you to phrase specific questions for which you will want to develop answers supported by evaluated authority.   These questions may or may not identify *issues*, in the sense that alternative possible answers are arguable or that the one reasonable answer is statable only after careful analysis, evaluation, and synthesis of available materials.   They may merely identify *analytical points*, that is, questions for which there is only one reasonable, easily found answer, but an answer that you do not know so that you have to educate yourself.

Regardless of the ultimate character of your questions, you will benefit from writing them out in a logical outline form.   The efficiency of your subsequent research efforts will depend directly on how clearly you have in mind the questions for which you are seeking answers.   As your research progresses, your view of the questions may change.   If so, rewrite them (or the whole outline, if necessary) to reflect your advancing view, thus forcing yourself to keep in mind a precise view of what you are searching for—and why.

It is always possible that from your preliminary analysis of a given set of facts, you will conclude that there is no possible basis for recovery or for defense. Be cautious about reaching this conclusion on the basis of secondary authorities, however. Confirmation of such a conclusion in mandatory precedents or legislation should usually be sought. Another possibility is that from your preliminary analysis you may conclude that you need additional facts. Be cautious in reaching this conclusion, too. You will soon find that secondary sources detail many possible bases for recovery, defenses, points of dispute, and so on. Each one tends to call for unique facts. It is easy to be tempted to imagine that all sorts of exotic theories are open to you "if only the facts are ————." Do not be led astray by such speculation. Usually it will be most efficient to go to at least the first phase of your in-depth research—the search for mandatory authority—before you begin asking for additional facts. Given some knowledge of what mandatory authority is available, you will be in a better position to know what additional information you need or whether you really need it at all.

NOTES

1. In Section 6A it is suggested that an attorney may be required to educate himself or herself about practices or procedures followed in an institution, profession, or employment with which he or she is not familiar. How could you "research" such questions, for example, about procedures followed by a local bank in transmitting credit for a depositor to a foreign bank? about accepted practices among social workers in encouraging welfare recipients to seek employment? about how applications for unemployment compensation are processed? about the sequence of operations performed by employees engaged in painting large truck bodies in a truck assembly plant?

2. Recall the discussions in Sections 3C and 3D about limitations on the authority value of statutory-construction precedents. Do the same limitations inhere in precedents that define words? For what purposes do courts define words? For example, in Section 6A "preliminary analysis" is defined for purposes of discussion in this text. Courts usually do not define words with the same kind of "private truth" objective. What purposes do they have for defining words, then? Does the purpose limit the extent to which a definition can be moved from one context to another?

3. Why is Professor Merryman critical of the use by courts of encyclopedias as authority? Does the same objection suggest that you should not cite an encyclopedia as an authority in legal writing prepared for a court? for a senior attorney in a law firm? for publication in a law review? Consider the different purposes for citing

authority: as *support* for a statement—legal, factual, historical, analytical, or policy; as a *source* of such a statement, or as *background* for such a statement. Should the purpose of the citation be considered in answering this question? (For an interesting tabulation of secondary sources cited by the United States Supreme Court and of the purposes for such citations, see Bernstein, *The Supreme Court and Secondary Source Material: 1965 Term*, 57 Georgetown L.J. 55 (1968).)

4. A good treatise, assuming one is available for your problem area, will always be more useful than an encyclopedia, because its opinion analysis and synthesis will be less mechanical and it will contain critical and predictive commentary. Assuming this statement to be true, why might you nevertheless want to start preliminary analysis with an encyclopedia?

5. In the front of each Am.Jur.2d volume is a parallel reference table that translates Am.Jur. section citations for the topics in that volume to Am.Jur.2d citations. These tables are good examples of a similar useful feature of other new editions of legal publications. An earlier edition of a multivolume treatise, for example, may have been frequently cited by courts and other authorities. If the treatise is revised with changes in the section numbering, the value of these citations may be lost if there is no quick way for researchers to convert them to citations for the new edition.

6. Getting started on research problems has human-relations elements too. A law professor with a practice background that includes private practice with a New York firm and service as Assistant General Counsel and Senior Appellate Attorney with federal administrative bodies has given the following advice in *Legal Writing: A Guide for Law Students* (1976), by Peter W. Gross:

> Most of what remains to be said about law office memoranda arises from the fact that memoranda are written in a teamwork setting. A few large law firms may seem to expect you to function as research machines— to prepare legal memoranda as though the assignments had been received in the mail from an anonymous source. You should not accept such a working relationship—or rather, such an absence of a realistic working relationship —lightly.
>
> This section considers law office memoranda as vehicles for an effective working partnership between you and your supervisor. As will be seen, it stresses the fact that—to an extraordinary degree—it is up to *you* to create this relationship.
>
> We begin, then, with the supervisor assigning to you the task of preparing a law office memorandum.
>
> Typically, your supervisor will be overworked—juggling an extraordinary number and variety of problems. Now the supervisor wishes to involve you in one. "Involving" you can include anything from "farming out" a very narrow legal question, to requesting a basic appraisal of the client's

problem and actions which should be taken. Whether the task is defined in broad or narrow terms, you are likely to have a major role to play in coherently formulating the assignment.

While rarely recognized in these terms, the practice is that supervisors may sometimes expect you to undertake formulation of the assignment on the basis of relatively meager directions. Too often, you may fail to recognize this and make the basic mistake of responding to vague directions with an equally vague memorandum. This sequence of "vague direction—vague response" is unfortunately very common in large law firms.

The antidote is simply to put yourself in the place of the supervisor. A moment's reflection should tell you that the supervisor may not have the time to define your task in detail. From the viewpoint of your own development and advancement, you have an obvious interest in taking the initiative and making your contribution to the supervisor's work as much as possible.

If the supervisor indicates to you that s/he is giving you a narrow or limited responsibility—either in general or on a particular assignment— perhaps you must accept this. Begin with a contrary assumption, however. Begin with the assumption that your "assignment" is an invitation to exercise initiative, and to enter into a working partnership with the supervisor on whatever problem you have been given. With this general setting in mind, the following are the principal concerns you should have in embarking upon the assignment to prepare a law office memorandum on some aspect of a client's problem: (a) to gather whatever relevant information is available on the client's problem and (b) to get a clear set of directions—or mandate—from the supervisor.

With respect to the problem facts, you should be concerned with finding out: (a) what the supervisor knows; (b) what additional sources, if any, are available to use; and (c) what the ground rules are for your access to those sources. Here again, the thing to remember is that the supervisor is unlikely to volunteer this information. The burden normally will fall upon you to ask the right questions—with persistence, where necessary. You must expect to exercise initiative here. Especially in a litigation context, you should try to glean as much as you can from the supervisor regarding the position the other side is likely to take regarding facts and law which govern the situation. To your supervisor, as an experienced attorney, it may be fairly obvious what the other side is likely to do, or what position it is likely to take on a certain matter. It may be less obvious to you. A question you often may want to ask is, "Do we have any indication what the other side will do (what the other side's position will be) on this?" It may take persistence and diplomacy, but it is up to you to get the information you need.

The second major concern you should have is the "action context" of your memorandum. On occasion, it will be perfectly obvious to you why the supervisor needs your memorandum, and what use s/he intends to make of it. On other occasions, however, you may need to take steps to get this information. The point of concern to you is that your legal memorandum— however its subject may be couched—is being written to help the supervisor prepare to make some decision, or to equip him/her to take some actions. The supervisor may not realize—but you should—that for you to do an ex-

cellent job, you need to know what those decisions or tasks are. Moreover, this knowledge will help you view the present assignment in light of later research work you may do on the same problem. For example, is the principal function of this memorandum to be to enable the supervisor to decide whether or not the client should file a civil action? If so, is the same research also to form the basis for your drafting of the complaint? In other words, consider the probable staging of your research work on the problem. Is the supervisor about to undertake discovery on the matter? Is s/he about to enter into negotiations? Is s/he about to meet again with the client to explain the client's legal position and get more facts? Is s/he about to advise the client on what course of action to take immediately? Is s/he about to prepare an opinion letter to the client? The answers to such questions constitute the "action context" of the assignment.

In some situations, it may be up to you to consider all these possible action options, and to make appropriate recommendations thereon. More often, however, there probably will be a specific "action context" which the supervisor has in mind, and about which you should inform yourself.

On occasion, your supervisor will intend for a memorandum to be passed on to the client or to other lawyers within the firm. The intended audience for your memorandum is something you should know as well.

One rule of thumb with respect to gathering information about the facts, and the "action context" of your problem, is as follows. It is very difficult, if not impossible, for you to predict exactly what information will and will not prove relevant to your analysis. Therefore, make it a habit to cast your net widely when, at the outset of your assignment, you marshal basic information about facts of the problem and its "action context."

Getting a Clear Mandate

For obvious reasons, it is very much to your interest to be absolutely clear on what the supervisor expects of you. There are three principal areas in which you need to make this inquiry: (a) substance of the memorandum; (b) form of the memorandum; and (c) work schedule.

Substance. Great emphasis should be placed upon the initial stage of research/analysis in which you seek to identify the primary rules and issues applicable to your assignment. In order to get your mandate clear, you should make this preliminary analysis, within the perimeters of your assignment, in order to verify whether all the issues thus identified are to be covered in the memorandum. This preliminary analysis and verification of scope of the memorandum is important in direct proportion to the vagueness with which your initial assignment may have been couched.

In general, the golden rule in this initial inventory of issues, is a *presumption of inclusion.* That is, if the issue *could* be construed as within the initial mandate, you should begin with the presumption that you *are* to treat it. On the other hand, do not forget that you have a basic responsibility in helping to formulate the most reasonable assignment possible.

Thus, if it appears that certain issues are best left for later, or the number and complexity of issues you have identified suggests that priorities ought to be drawn if the given deadline is to be met, you should then

raise these questions with the supervisor—presenting appropriate recommendations.

*   *   *

Some assignments will be "open-ended" in the sense that the supervisor simply tosses the client's problem in your lap, and asks you to advise him/her on what should be done. Your responsibility in spotting rules and issues, in such an assignment, is of course at its greatest. Thus, for example, in a litigation situation, do not look merely to basic questions of liability. Never overlook such threshold questions as choice of laws, statute of limitations, capacity to sue, burden of proof and the like. Further, range broadly over all things that may affect the client. For example, in an open-ended assignment, your research should be directed so as to include questions such as, are there any steps the client should take *now* in order to lessen liability; are there any steps the client should take in order to lessen exposure to similar liability *in the future*; if settlement is at issue, are there tax considerations of major significance in how this is handled? Consider also remedies issues—the measure and extent of damages recoverable. Even where your assignment is narrower, you may wish to make suggestions of relevant rules and issues—perhaps outside the confines of the memorandum itself. This is appropriate, at least, wherever it appears that you will be working with the supervisor on other, successive stages of this same client's problem situation.

With experience, you will learn to explore rules and issues with this degree of comprehensiveness. You can readily see the value to a supervisor of work which shows this kind of imagination and initiative on your part.

Form. *   *   * [At this point you may find it useful to look ahead to Section 10C, *infra,* to read about the general purposes and content of legal memoranda so as to orient yourself to the most common end product of early research assignments for students and for new associates and attorneys in law firms and government offices.]

Work schedule. Most important, of course, is your deadline for submission of the final product. Also included in "work schedule," however, is the question of whether outlines or drafts are to be submitted, and—if so —the expected timetable. Where, as normally will be the case, you will have a variety of other responsibilities as well, it is very much to your advantage to discuss the work schedule in the context of your own work situation. Thus, if the schedule given you does not seem realistic, say so and explain why. This may precipitate judgments about priorities, and work staging, such as discussed in connection with the substance of the memorandum above.

With respect, then, to substance, form, and work schedule, you should get as clear a mandate as you can at the outset. On the other hand, it is not always possible, or desirable to answer all these questions at the outset. For example, with respect to the substance of the memorandum, basic questions of scope may not become apparent until you have gotten well into your overview research or even later. With respect to form, you may prefer— rather than discussing detailed questions of form in the abstract—to work out your own resolution, and then solicit the supervisor's reactions after the job has been done. Finally, it may be to the advantage of both you and

your supervisor to leave your work schedule flexible—leaving the deadline to be set later on the basis of your initial research findings, events surrounding the client's problem, and the like. You can safely leave questions such as these for later determination to the extent that you and the supervisor will be in communication about the problem—functioning as a working partnership on the task. Then, discussion of, and feedback on your research work in progress becomes a substitute for getting all your directions clear at the outset.

Chapter 7

RESEARCH ON QUESTIONS GOVERNED BY
THE COMMON LAW

SECTION 7A. INTRODUCTION

Sources and methods for researching common law problems are discussed in detail in this chapter. Discussion of Step 1 of the general search plan outlined in Chapter 5, the search for written law, is deferred to the following chapter by assuming that you are researching a problem for which there is no controlling written law. Then, when you have tentatively identified questions presented through preliminary analysis, Step 2 requires search for mandatory precedents. If you do not find directly-in-point precedents, you must look for analogous cases or even for cases that are only tangentially similar in an attempt to find some clue to the controlling court's (or courts') possible attitude toward the problem area. If you find no helpful mandatory precedents, or sometimes even if you do, you will want to go on to Step 3, the search for persuasive precedents.

In either the mandatory or the persuasive branch of your search, or both, if you find only a few possibly relevant opinions, you will have no selection problem. You will read all of them. But if you are confronted with a mass of possibly relevant citations, choose a sample of opinions by date—one or two early opinions and two or three of the most recent opinions. (If your source does not include dates with citations, review suggestions in the notes at the end of Chapter 1 about how to identify early and recent opinions.) Sample unfavorable as well as favorable opinions. This type of sampling should get you focused on an appropriate direction for further search and on choice of opinions for careful analysis. For a difficult problem you may ultimately have to scan and analyze many opinions before finding a few on which you want to rely.

For both Step 2 and Step 3, avoid accumulating lists of citations and extensive notes on precedents drawn from secondary and search sources without any sampling of the opinions cited and discussed.

Secondary discussions of precedents often make them seem more clearly in point than careful analysis reveals them to be. So, save yourself misdirected analysis or, at the least, needless note-taking by immediately scanning the most promising opinions cited and getting to careful analysis of apparently relevant opinions before accumulating a string of citations that can overwhelm you. Step 4 will ultimately bring you back to secondary authorities.

SECTION 7B. STEP 2: THE SEARCH FOR MANDATORY STATE PRECEDENTS

STEP 2. The Search for Mandatory Precedents: Assuming no controlling legislation, a search for mandatory precedents will require:

Preliminary search for opinions in the controlling state digest, state encyclopedia, Restatement annotations, local practice text, local periodical, or other local source.

A double-check search in a second of the above-listed sources if more than one is available.

Bringing the search down to date by:

(a) Checking relevant advance sheets, and

(b) Shepardizing relevant opinions in the appropriate Shepard's citator unit.

Following are descriptions of the research sources referred to in the preceding summary.

State Digests

West Publishing Company, the publisher of the National Reporter system and of the C.J.S. encyclopedia, publishes digests for all but three states.[1] These state units are part of West's Key Number System. The parent system, the American Digest, indexes all reported opinions handed down in the United States since 1658. All these digests are constructed on the same basic scheme: Headnotes for the opinions to be indexed are classified according to subjects and points covered. All the headnotes relating to a single subject are collected and printed together under an appropriate topic name, with subtopics and sub-subtopics. See excerpt from topic outline in Illustration 11. With the subjects alphabetized, the headnotes make up a multivolume index to case law. The numbers assigned to the subtopics (for example, **Attorney and Client** ☞**107**) are called "key numbers." As previously noted, these key numbers also appear as part of the headings for headnotes in modern National Reporter volumes.

---

1. Units are not published for Delaware, Nevada, and Utah.

2A Wash D—586

ATTORNEY AND CLIENT

Scope-Note.

INCLUDES the practice of law in any rank or branch of the profession; admission to practice, and privileges, disabilities, and liabilities incident to the office conferred; licenses and license fees and privilege and occupation taxes; regulation of professional conduct; and the relation between attorney and client, and their mutual rights, duties, and liabilities.

Matters not in this topic, treated elsewhere, see Descriptive-Word Index.

Analysis.

I. THE OFFICE OF ATTORNEY, ☞1–61.

    A. ADMISSION TO PRACTICE, ☞1–11.
    B. PRIVILEGES, DISABILITIES, AND LIABILITIES, ☞14–33.
    C. SUSPENSION AND DISBARMENT, ☞34–61.

II. RETAINER AND AUTHORITY, ☞62–104.

III. DUTIES AND LIABILITIES OF ATTORNEY TO CLIENT, ☞105–129.

IV. COMPENSATION AND LIEN OF ATTORNEY, ☞130–192.

    A. FEES AND OTHER REMUNERATION, ☞130–169.
    B. LIEN, ☞171–192.

2A Wash D—589   **ATTORNEY AND CLIENT**

III. DUTIES AND LIABILITIES OF ATTORNEY TO CLIENT.

☞105. Negligence or malpractice.
   106. —— Nature of attorney's duty.
   107. —— Skill and care required.
   108. —— Instructions of client.
   109. —— Acts and omissions of attorney in general.
   110. —— Collection of demands.
   111. —— Unauthorized appearance.
   112. —— Conduct of litigation.
   113. —— Acting for party adversely interested.
   114. —— Fraud.
   115. —— Acts and omissions of partners and associates.
   116. Accounting and payment to client.
   117. —— Liabilities in general.
   118. —— Individual interest of attorney.
   119. —— Acts or defaults of partners and associates.
   120. —— Liability for interest.
   121. —— Persons entitled.
   122. Dealings between attorney
   123. —— In

ILLUSTRATION II.

Analysis and excerpt from Sub-Analysis, *Attorney and Client* topic, *Washington Digest*

Both the index and the topic research approaches can be used with all these digests. Since C.J.S. cross-references to relevant key numbers in the digest, preliminary research in that encyclopedia may supply you with a starting point for your digest search. Or, if a preliminary analysis source provided a citation to a directly-in-point case, the opinion in the National Reporter may provide a relevant key number. In either event, use the descriptive word index for the digest nevertheless to be certain that you have identified all the most relevant key numbers.

The state digests are supplemented by annual cumulative pocket parts and by intervening pamphlets. Very current supplementation is provided by the supplement for the American Digest System, described in Section 7E, and by advance sheets for the appropriate National Reporter unit and for the relevant official reports, both described *infra* in this section. A "closing with" summary of coverage that appears as one of the first pages of both the pocket and pamphlet supplements to state digests identifies the necessary starting point for this final supplementation search. See insert, Illustration 12.

Key number digests are published also for the Atlantic, North Western, Pacific, South Eastern, and Southern regional units of the National Reporter System. When available, a state-regional digest unit may be useful if you want to find decisions of a particular state court for which your library does not have a state digest, because a complete search of one of these units will usually be simpler than a search through the units and supplements of the American Digest System. The state-regional digests may also be useful for research in those states for which key number digests are not published.

The key number digest system is the most comprehensive index to American case law. Comprehensive though the system is it is not without limitations. First, the system is based on the assumption that court opinions can be broken into a determinable number of precise points that can be stated in conventional headnote sentences and classified within a classification outline imposed from outside the common law process. The fallacy in this assumption should be apparent: the common law does not lend itself to such precision. Second, the classification outline was shaped at a time—the late 19th century—when the common law process was simplistically viewed. Third, opinions contain dicta that are incorporated in the headnote-digest sentences without warning.

Recognize that because of these limitations (1) you must use an imaginative approach to be certain that you examine all possibly relevant topics within the system and (2) you will frequently be misled by digest sentences, which may result in your reading or scanning

2A Wash D—217   **ATTORNEY & CLIENT** ☞107

the settlement, even if the statute had not been satisfied prior to that time, in that plaintiff's attorney had not appeared in open court and dictated the terms of the settlement into the record or in the presence of the clerk. RCWA

Closing with Cases Reported in

Washington Reports, Second Series	87 Wash.2d
Washington Appellate Reports	16 Wash.App. (part)
Pacific Reporter, Second Series	553 P.2d
Supreme Court Reporter	96 S.Ct.
United States Reports	424 U.S. (part)
Lawyers' Edition, Second Series	47 L.Ed.2d (part)
Federal Reporter, Second Series	539 F.2d 1304
Federal Supplement	417 F.Supp. 1046
Federal Rules Decisions	71 F.R.D. 234

---

believed he was properly authorized to do so, and where the settlement stipulation entered in that suit contained neither wife's signature nor the signature of the attorney on her behalf, wife was not bound by the settlement; furthermore even had the attorney purported to sign the stipulation on her behalf, he would have exceeded his authority since, absent an emergency otherwise requiring, an attorney does not have implied authority to compromise and settle client's rights. —Grossman v. Will, 516 P.2d 1063, 10 Wash. App. 141.

An attorney, even with authority to appear for a client, absent an emergency otherwise requiring, does not have implied authority to compromise and settle his client's rights; express authority is required.—Id.

Even assuming that statute, requiring written notice to the adverse party of a change of attorney, applies when there is in fact no attorney-client relationship between the first appearing attorney and his purported client, the statute nevertheless was of no help to plaintiff in respect to settlement agreement signed by first appearing attorney on behalf of his purported client, where that attorney did not have express authority to settle. RCWA 2.44.040, 2.44.050.—Id.

Statute relating to the power of an attorney to bind his client does not purport to change the common-law rule that an attorney does not have implied authority to waive the substantive rights of his client by a compromise settlement agreement; furthermore, it applies only when there is in fact an attorney-client relationship. RCWA 2.44.010.—Id.

Wash.App. 1972. An attorney is impliedly authorized to enter into stipulations and waivers concerning procedural matters to facilitate hearing, but had no authority to waive any substantial right of his client, and such waiver must be specially authorized by client.—In re Houts, 499 P.2d 1276, 7 Wash.App. 476.

III. DUTIES AND LIABILITIES OF ATTORNEY TO CLIENT.

Research Notes

Corbin on Contracts.
Library references
    C.J.S. Attorney and Client § 125 et seq.
    2A Wash.Dig.—14½
      1977 P.P.

☞106. —— **Nature of attorney's duty.**
Library references
    ABA Standards for Criminal Justice
     The Defense Function 7.2

dards of conduct imposed
 excuse negligence in con-
rs, even though ho material
 may result.—In re Fraser,
sh.2d 884.
 endeavor to spare client
 anxiety which must be felt
 not pursued with reasona-
mptness.—Id.
ty to the ward, as well as to
 his services.—Id.
lards of legal profession re-
lity of lawyer to his client
n be tolerated.—Van Dyke
0, 55 Wash.2d 601.
 Elements of legal mal-
xistence of attorney-client
e of duty on part of attor-
erform the duty, and the
torney must have been a
mage to the client or other
ansen v. Wightman, 538 P.2d
238, 14 Wash.App. 78.

☞107. —— **Skill and care required.**
Wash. 1968. An attorney is not liable for mere error of judgment if he acts in good faith and in an honest belief that his acts and advice are well-founded and in the best interest of his client, but such an error in judgment must itself fall short of negligence if the lawyer is to be protected from liability.—Cook, Flanagan and Berst v. Clausing, 438 P.2d 865, 73 Wash.2d 393.

The standards for practice of law are the same throughout the state, and do not differ in its various communities.—Id.

The correct standard to which an attorney is held in performance of his professional services is that degree of care, skill, diligence and knowledge commonly possessed and exercised by a reasonable, careful and prudent lawyer in practice of law in Washington.—Id.

Wash. 1960. When a broker undertakes to practice law, he is liable for negligence.—Mattieligh v. Poe, 356 P.2d 328, 57 Wash.2d 203, 94 A.L.R.2d 464.

Wash.App. 1975. Standard of care for lawyers is statewide standard, and is that degree of care, skill, diligence and knowledge commonly possessed and exercised by reasonable, careful and prudent lawyer in practice of law in the jurisdiction.—Hansen v. Wightman, 538 P.2d 1238, 14 Wash.App. 78.

Standard of care required of attorneys does not involve special or different attention to duty because relationship between attorney and client is a fiduciary one; care exercised must still be reasonable, and skill with which legal task is performed must be skill, prudence and diligence that would be exercised by lawyers of ordinary skill and capacity.—Id.

Exercise of trust responsibility by attorney is a part of his work which makes diligence and constancy in handling of a client's concerns an element to be reasonably expected of ordinary lawyers as matter of course.—Id.

Wash.App. 1973. Fiduciary such as an attorney must exercise reasonable care and must protect his client's interest out of a sense of loyalty, good faith and duty to exercise reasonable care; such protection may well involve the duty to investigate the law and facts applicable to the transaction and to disclose the results to his clients, a duty similar to duty to disclose imposed upon a trustee who must disclose all material facts concerning the transaction which the trus-

---

ILLUSTRATION 12.

Pages from pocket supplement to *Attorney and Client* topic, *Washington Digest*

Insert is from page 2 of the supplement

opinions not relevant to your area of interest and, perhaps, in your missing others of direct significance.

Your imagination may have freer scope in using the system if you are aware of the theory underlying the key number classification scheme.   The starting point is a definition of "law":

> "Law is the effort of society to protect PERSONS including CORPORATIONS, in their rights and relations, to guard them in their PROPERTY, enforce their CONVEYANCES and CONTRACTS, and redress or punish their WRONGS or CRIMES, by means of judicial REMEDIES, founded upon EVIDENCE, and administered by the civil arm of GOVERNMENT."

> For the purpose of the American Digest Classification PERSONS is made to include CORPORATIONS, PROPERTY to include CONVEYANCES which are necessarily incidental to property, and REMEDIES to include EVIDENCE, and the theorem is thus modified to read as follows:

> "Law is the effort of society to protect PERSONS in their rights and relations, to guard them in their PROPERTY, enforce their CONTRACTS, hold them to their liability for their TORTS, punish them for their CRIMES by means of REMEDIES administered by the GOVERNMENT." [2]

The categories thus identified by the capitalized words in the foregoing definition are the basis of the classification system.

The order in which these basic categories are stated in the definition is assumed to establish a natural order of precedence.   Thus, if a subject area relates to more than one of these basic categories, it will be classified under the first relevant category that appears in the theorem.   The application of this rule of precedence is illustrated in the following example:

> Negligence, as a tort, is included in category 4.   The liability * * * of a master for negligence as to his servant, involving as it does the personal relation between them, * * * [is assigned to a topic under category 1, namely,] *Master and Servant*.   The liability for negligence as to the condition of premises occupied by a tenant, involving as it does duties relative to an estate in property, goes to the topic including that estate, falling under category 2, namely, *Landlord and Tenant*.   The liability for negligence of a bailee in connection with the bailed property, involving as it does a contract relation, goes to the topic denoting that par-

---

2. As described in Letter to the Editor, 22 Albany L.J. 179 (1880), and explained in Brief Making and the Use of Law Books 166–67 (R. Cooley ed., 5th ed. 1926).

ticular contract relation, namely, *Bailment*, which, of course, is included in category 3. The same may be said as to all other cases of negligence involving any obligation dependent on personal, property, or contract relations. As the result of this distribution of specific propositions, there remains to be placed under the main head *Negligence* only cases arising between strangers, independent of rules of law peculiar to classes of persons, species of property, or rights and obligations incident to either, or to contracts relating thereto. General principles of negligence, contributory negligence, and comparative and imputed negligence are included in the topic *Negligence.* The topic *Negligence* includes also, by reason of its precedence over subsequent categories, matters which might otherwise be placed under heads included in those categories; for example, the general principles of actions for negligence, which might be placed under some remedy head in category 6, and criminal responsibility for negligence, which might be placed under some criminal head in category 5, were it not for the rule of precedence.[3]

For a listing of the topics in each category, see the Law Chart in the front of an index volume for a state Key Number Digest or on the yellow pages in the front of the first C.J.S. index volume. An alphabetical list of all current topics appears in the front of each of the volumes of the most recent decennial digest, discussed in Section 4E, *infra.*

Given the complexity of this classification system, you may understand better the reason for insistence that you always use an index in searching the digest system rather than relying on a cross-reference from another source or consulting only topics you assume to be relevant. The exhortation may well be followed in using all comprehensively indexed sources, since the underlying classification scheme may be as complex as that just described.

Other Local Sources

State digests are not infallible; therefore, you should use another source for a double-check search for mandatory state precedents if another source is available. Two types of sources that focus on the law of individual states are so generally available as to warrant discussion here.

First, almost every state has at least one law school publishing a law review that regularly reports important developments in, and critiques of, the laws of that state. A cumulative index for such a review, if available, will provide the easiest entry to the material pub-

---

3. Brief Making and the Use of Law
Books, *supra* n. 2, at 170–71.

lished therein. If a cumulative index is not available for such a review, then the Step 4 search of the national *Index to Legal Periodicals*, described in Section 7F, *infra*, may lead to such locally focused review coverage.[4]

Second, annotation and citation services for the Restatements are useful double-check search sources if the subject of a problem falls within a Restatement subject area. In many states, pre-Restatement annotations provide background for some Restatements. These annotation volumes cite and briefly discuss pre-Restatement opinions of the state's courts for each Restatement section, indicating whether the decisions were contrary to or agreed with the Restatement rules. You can usually ascertain whether any such annotation volumes have been produced for the state in which your library is located by checking the library catalog under "American Law Institute" and secondarily under "Annotations."

For post-Restatement opinions that cite, discuss, adopt, or reject particular Restatement sections, a citator called *Shepard's Restatement of the Law Citations* collects citations to court opinions and selected law reviews that have, in turn, cited Restatement sections, comments, or illustrations. The service is supplemented with a paperbound cumulative supplement. The publisher's explanation of the service, reproduced in Illustration 13, provides details about its use. At the time of this writing, the service does not report citations to tentative drafts for Restatements being revised, but these citations may be located through a Step 3 search of the *Restatement in the Courts*, described in Section 7E, *infra*.

Other possible local sources include local encyclopedias, practice texts, and continuing legal education materials prepared for lawyers. Local encyclopedias are available for some states, for example, California and Texas. Legal research guides describing local materials are available for California, Florida, Illinois, Louisiana, Michigan, New Mexico, North Carolina, Pennsylvania, South Carolina, Texas, and Wisconsin.[5] In other states, information about commonly used

---

4. Use of the local index, at least initially, will be more efficient, even if it is somewhat dated, if the particular law review has been published for any length of time. A search in the national index proceeds backwards through three-year volumes, a trip backwards in time that is not always justified for Step 4 purposes, so that early local material may be overlooked. Additionally, the national index does not cite very short articles that will be indexed in a local index. The case unit of the state edition of Shepard's Citations, discussed *infra* in this section, may also lead to local review material, but only if you find and Shepardize an opinion that is cited in the review material.

5. Citations to these guides are collected in How to Find the Law 519 (M. Cohen ed. 7th ed. 1976). The *Handbook* cited therein for California is now in a new edition, D. Henke, California Law Guide (2d ed. 1976).

TORTS							**§ 242**

§ 164 349F2d691	§ 167 et seq. Fla 319So2d104	§ 182 269Ap510 NY 56S2d306	§ 200 215Ark526 Ark 221SW428	493P2d1081 Okla 500P2d581 Ore 487P2d1159	42CLQ45 42CLQ173	Ore 141P2d841 17NYL236	§ 234 172F2d466 339F2d298 208FS198 223FS286
§ 165 Scope Note 59CR474	§ 167 341US626 95LE1239 71SC924 262Md273 Fla 180So555 319So2d108	§ 183 168Or230 Ore 122P2d441 § 188 Comment c	§ 201 et seq. 275Ap134 NY 89S2d12 § 201	SD 186NW557 § 209 262NY166 NY 186NE430	§ 220 139F2d41 283Ap701 ND 86NW647 NY 127S2d887 § 221	§ 224 117FS19 172Or279 124Vt454 Ore 141P2d841 Vt 207A2d243	330FS307 59CR448 Comments a to d 21Ap2d469 NY 251S2d86 Comment b
§ 165 127FS467 135FS447 160Me16 227Or246 256Or565 258Or513 Me 196A2d825 Ore 362P2d315 466P2d615 474P2d740 59CR465 Comment c 127FS467 32Msc2d959 NY 223S2d696 Illustra- tion 8 127FS467 32Msc2d959 NY 223S2d696							

ILLUSTRATION

Restate- ment of the Law of Torts		
§ 166 135 FS447 165 FS734	1
24 Ap2d621 160 Me16 55 Msc2d288 255 NC691 267 NC558 307 NY331	2
Me 196 A2d825 NC 122 SE517 148 SE629 NY 121 NE251 262 S2d249 285 S2d124	3
43 CLQ249 59 CR465	4
Comment a 165 FS738 Comment b 165 FS738 Illustra- tions 1 to 5 165 FS738 Illustra- tion 2 160 Me17 Me 196 A2d825 Illustra- tion 3 165 FS738 Illustra- tion 4 17 NYL3 Comment c 165 FS738	6

Citations to section "§"166 of the American Law Institute's Restatement of the Law of Torts are shown in the left margin of this page in the same form in which they appear in the division for that topic in this volume.

Citations to each cited provision are grouped as follows:

1. citations by the United States Supreme Court and lower federal courts;

2. citations by state courts arranged alphabetically by the abbreviations used in this volume for the various state courts;

3. citations in the National Reporter System arranged alphabetically by the abbreviation for the state to which they pertain;

4. citations in articles in selected law reviews and in the American Bar Association Journal;

5. citations in annotations in Lawyers'Edition,United States Supreme Court and in the American Law Reports; and

6. citations to Comments and Illustrations.

For purposes of illustration only, this grouping has been indicated by bracketing the citations accordingly. It will be noted that as yet there are no citations in group five.

The first citations shown indicate that §166 has been cited in two instances by United States District Courts in a case reported in Volume 135 Federal Supplement "FS" 447 and in a case reported in 165 FS 734.

The second grouping shows §166 to have been cited by various state courts, the first of which is a citation in 24 Appellate Division Reports, Second Series, New York Supreme Court "Ap2d" 621, followed by citations in various other state court reports.

The third grouping indicates the same citations referred to in group two as they are reported in the various reporters of the National Reporter System. Each citation in this grouping is headed by the abbreviation of the state to which it relates.

Citations in the fourth group are from law reviews as illustrated by the citation 43 Cornell Law Quarterly "CLQ" 249 and 59 Columbia Law Review "CR" 465.

Citations to Comments and Illustrations are shown in the sixth group. Illustrations follow the Comment to which they relate. Thus, the citation 165 FS 738 following Illustrations 1 to 5 indicates that the citation refers to Illustrations 1 to 5 which relate to Comment b. A cited Illustration not preceded by a Comment would indicate that the Illustration relates to the section and not to a Comment.

197

ILLUSTRATION 13.

Page from *Shepard's Restatement of the Law Citations*
Insert: Publisher's Explanation.

local materials [6] may best be obtained by talking with local law librarians and practitioners. Continuing legal education materials can be found through the library catalog by checking relevant subject entries.

Advance Sheets

In your search for mandatory precedents, you will always search the supplements to the state digest and other sources that you use. Even supplements run somewhat behind in current material, however. You must therefore supplement the supplements through available advance sheets for any official reports,[7] or through the advance sheets for the National Reporter unit that reports opinions of the controlling courts. For example, if you use a state digest with a quarterly supplement dated August of the current year, you must check advance sheets reporting opinions handed down by the controlling state court or courts from at least August and thereafter. Or if you use a digest with only an annual pocket supplement dated "For use during 1978", you must check advance sheets reporting opinions handed down from at least the beginning of the year 1978. Determining how many advance sheets must be checked is quite simple if the supplement to the digest or other source includes a precise statement of coverage such as the explanation used for Key Number digest units. See Illustration 12, *supra*.

Each official advance sheet will usually include a general subject index; a cumulative index may be provided periodically. National Reporter advance sheets, on the other hand, do not have subject indexes. Rather, a miniature key number digest is included at the front of each issue. In each relevant Reporter advance sheet you must check the miniature digest for possible new case citations under the relevant topics and digest key numbers. See Illustration 14.

6. For example, West Publishing Company publishes for the state of Washington a Washington Practice series that currently includes volumes covering Methods of Practice with Forms, Trial Practice, Rules Practice, Evidence, Pattern Jury Instructions, Washington U.C.C. Forms, and Civil Procedure Forms with Practice Comments; the Washington Bar Association has begun publication of a series of Deskbooks on Washington law, beginning with Washington Community Property law.

The publisher of Shepard's citators also publishes *Law Locators* for Illinois, Texas, and New York. These publications combine the features of an encyclopedia and a digest. They consist of several volumes of text with a subject index and several volumes of a comprehensive index. The text volumes summarize the law on selected subject areas, for example, the family, business and labor, personal injuries and tortious conduct, civil rights and civil liberties, governmental assistance programs, and environment. Citation of authorities is selective, including federal statutes and cases that substantially affect state law. The *Law Locators* are designed to be used with a Shepard's citator unit.

7. Official state reports discontinued include those for Alaska, Delaware, Florida, Iowa, Kentucky, Louisiana, Maine, Mississippi, Missouri, North Dakota, Oklahoma, Tennessee, Texas, Utah, and Wyoming.

KEY NUMBER DIGEST

ABATEMENT AND REVIVAL

⚖70. Necessity and mode of suggesting death as cause of abatement.

Ga.App. 1977. Attorney retained by deceased litigant had duty to report death of litigant to court and there was no requirement that suggestion of death be filed by another party to the suit or successor or representative of deceased. Code, § 81A–125(a)(1).—Mullis v. Bone, 238 S.E.2d 748.

⚖74(1). In general.

Ga.App. 1977. Statement of fact of death which included name of deceased and date of death was sufficient suggestion of death to trigger 180-day period allowed by statute for filing motion for substitution. Code, § 81A–125(a)(1). —Mullis v. Bone, 238 S.E.2d 748.

ACCORD AND SATISFACTION

⚖1. Nature and requisites in general.

Ga.App. 1977. Accord and satisfaction is itself a contract and requires a meeting of the minds in order to render it valid and binding.—Warner Robins Supply Co. v. Malone, 238 S.E.2d 709.

⚖11(1). In general.

Ga.App. 1977. Where creditor, without practice of any fraud upon it, accepts, in full satisfaction of debt owed it, a lesser amount than that which it claims was due, it will operate as an accord and satisfaction.—Warner Robins Supply Co. v. Malone, 238 S.E.2d 709.

⚖11(2). Remittances on condition.

Ga.App. 1977. When party makes offer of certain sum to settle a claim, amount of which is in bona fide dispute, with condition that sum offered, if taken at all, must be received in full satisfaction of claim, and party receives the money, he takes it subject to condition attached to it, and it will operate as an accord and satisfaction. —Warner Robins Supply Co. v. Malone, 238 S.E.2d 709.

ACTION

⚖27(1). In general.

Va. 1977. Landowners' action against county board of supervisors to recover for damage to their property as result of discharge of great quantities of water onto their land by storm sewer system used and maintained by board, which had accepted dedication of same from private landowner who built it, was not a tort action, but rather a contract action under provision of State Constitution prohibiting General Assembly from passing any law whereby private property shall be taken or damaged for public uses without just compensation. Const.1971, art. 1, § 11.—Burns v. Board of Sup'rs of Fairfax County, 238 S.E.2d 823.

APPEAL AND ERROR

⚖215(1). Necessity of objection in general.

Ga.App. 1977. Plaintiff appellant's failure to object to charge given on accident in suit to recover for injuries sustained in car-truck accident precluded consideration of charge on appeal. Code, § 70–207(a).—Williams v. Atlanta Gas Light Co., 238 S.E.2d 756.

⚖232(3). Instructions.

Ga.App. 1977. Where plaintiff appellant failed to properly object to language of charge on sudden emergency in suit to recover for injuries sustained in car-truck accident, wherein sole objection raised was that "there is no evidence of sudden emergency," enumeration of error complaining of language used in charge presented nothing for consideration on appeal.—Williams v. Atlanta Gas Light Co., 238 S.E.2d 756.

⚖366. Certificate as to grounds.

Ga.App. 1977. Where order in multiparty action did not settle all issues as to all parties, it was not appealable, absent express determination that there was no just reason for delay and express direction for entry of judgment. Code, § 81A–154(b).—Mullis v. Bone, 238 S.E.2d 748.

⚖662(1). In general.

Ga.App. 1977. Although there was some confusion as to accuracy of transcript of trial proceedings in suit to recover for injuries sustained in car-truck accident, plaintiff appellant failed to show where final transcript, as certified by trial judge as full, complete and correct transcript, was incorrect, or how he was harmed, and there was accordingly no error.—Williams v. Atlanta Gas Light Co., 238 S.E.2d 756.

⚖895(1). In general.

Ga.App. 1977. Trial de novo brings up entire record, and all competent evidence material and relevant to issues, even though once heard, are admissible on trial in the de novo hearing.—In Interest of Smith, 238 S.E.2d 725.

It is not province of de novo court to review and affirm or reverse ruling of original court but to try issues anew and pass original judgments on questions involved as if there had been no previous trial; this does not preclude trial court from examining earlier rulings, judgments, evidence or issues raised thereby, but simply precludes trial court from being bound by those earlier decisions.—Id.

⚖895(2). Effect of findings below.

Ga.App. 1977. It is not province of de novo court to review and affirm or reverse ruling of original court but to try issues anew and pass original judgments on questions involved as if there had been no previous trial; this does not preclude trial court from examining earlier rulings, judgments, evidence or issues raised thereby, but simply precludes trial court from being

For Earlier Cases, See Same Topic and Key Number in Any West Key Number Digest

ILLUSTRATION 14.

Page from Miniature Digest, National Reporter Advance Sheet

If the supplement to be supplemented is quite dated (more than a few months old) the advance-sheet search may actually extend into bound volumes of a report or reporter. The key number digest for a National Reporter volume appears in the back of the bound volumes. If such an extended search is required, however, a shift to the monthly supplement to the American Digest System, discussed in Section 7E, *infra,* will usually result in time saving.

Official advance sheets, when available, can usually be more quickly checked than can Reporter advance sheets. The latter, on the other hand, may alert you to recent persuasive opinions as well as to mandatory precedents. Furthermore, publication of advance sheets for some state courts tends to run behind publication of their opinions in the National Reporter advance sheets, so that use of the Reporter advance sheets may be justified by their greater currency.

Shepard's Citations—State Editions

The basic purpose of a citator is to permit a researcher to ascertain whether an authority in which he or she is interested has been cited. Expanding on this basic purpose, the publishers of *Shepard's Citations* have produced comprehensive citators that also give information about treatment of cited authorities by citing courts. A Shepard's case edition is available for each of the states for which court opinions are officially reported, for each of the regional units of the National Reporter System, for the California Reporter and New York Supplement National Reporter units, for federal courts, and for certain federal administrative tribunals.

A Shepard's state edition *may* consist of one or more red bound volumes (permanent case and statute units), a red bound supplement volume, possibly an ivory or gold paperback supplement, a red paperback supplement, and a current white paper supplement called an "advance sheet." On the cover page of the current supplement is printed a statement about "What Your Library Should Contain" for the particular edition. Always check this description to assure that you use all the supplements.

You can forget about "common research features" when you use Shepard's citators; the citators are unique. Fortunately, help is never far away when you use a citator, because in the front of each bound volume and paperback supplement, a preface explains the contents and use of the particular citator, and tables of abbreviations translate the cryptic symbols used within.

The citators will seem less overwhelming at this point if you take a very narrow view of their function, using them only to ascertain how subsequent courts have treated an opinion in which you are interested, that is, to answer the question, "Has the deciding court, or another court, said something with reference to your selected opin-

ion that adds to, weakens, or destroys its authority value?" That you may find additional recent authorities in point should be regarded as a by-product of this primary function.

To use a Shepard's state case edition, you must have an official citation to a state court opinion. For a reason that will be explained later, you must also have the headnote numbers from the official report for the portions of the opinion in which you are interested. You may also find it helpful to memorize the following mechanical approach to use of any Shepard's citator:

Select the appropriate edition: State or appropriate regional-Reporter edition? *United States Citations* (for Supreme Court opinions) or *Federal Citations* (for lower federal courts)?

Select the appropriate volume: Case, not Statute volume? The volume that first picks up the citation for the opinion that you are Shepardizing? (To select this volume, check the citations or dates on the spines of volumes and on the covering page of supplements.)

Select the appropriate section: The section devoted to the reports of the court that handed down the opinion that you are Shepardizing? 1st series, 2d series, 3d series?

Find the citation for the opinion that you are Shepardizing: Find the volume number in large boldface type; find the page number for your citation in smaller boldface type. Verify your understanding of this step by finding the citation for Smith v. Lewis, 13 Cal.3d 349, 118 Cal. Rptr. 621, 530 P.2d 589 (1975), Appendix B, in the page reproduced from the relevant supplement to *Shepard's California Citations* in Illustration 15. (Citations appearing under the boldface page number are to citing opinions. You should need no explanation of the citations, though you may have to look at the table of "Abbreviations—Reports" that appears in the front of every Shepard's volume in order to decipher some of the citation symbols. In at least the first Shepard's volume in which a citation for a state court opinion appears, any parallel citations—for example, to the National Reporter—will be given immediately following the boldface page number, usually in parentheses but sometimes in boldface.)

Choose citations for citing opinions that you will want to scan or read. This may be the difficult part when you first use a Shepard's citator, so the next three full paragraphs will be devoted to describing selection methods.

CALIFORNIA SUPREME COURT REPORTS, 3d SERIES **Vol. 13**

– 731 –
(528P2d1)
(117CaR393)
s32A3d18
15C3d[10]401
15C3d[21]734
16C3d[21]223
16C3d[21]251
16C3d[21]354
j16C3d[21]359
16C3d[8]563
16C3d[8]570
16C3d[8]571
16C3d760
43A3d[5]1004
44A3d[3]212
f44A3d[8]214
d46A3d[10]265
47A3d[13]32
48A3d[9]772
48A3d[13]773
49A3d[12]79
49A3d[11]80
f49A3d588
51A3d[13]814
f51A3d[13]816
52A3d[13]525
52A3d[2]878
53A3d[11]46
53A3d[8]255
54A3d585a
f54A3d[8]871
55A3d[17]793
56A3d[21]884
56A3d[19]885
58A3d[6]985
64CaL648

– 772 –
(528P2d56)
(117CaR448)
s36A3d825
46A3d861
e56A3d[2]753
e56A3d[3]753
59AG281
64CaL657

– 790 –
(527P2d1153)
(117CaR305)
f47A3d[2]249
L49A3d[5]785
f49A3d[2]786

– 805 –
(528P2d31)
(117CaR423)

– 813 –
(528P2d745)
(117CaR657)
s33A3d339
f46A3d[1]604
53A3d[1]85
53A3d[2]85
58AG855

– 824 –
(528P2d35)
(117CaR427)
13C3d[1]454
13C3d494
13C3d[1]498
13C3d[2]578
14C3d[2]500
14C3d[2]523
15C3d[2]381
15C3d[2]804
15C3d[2]903
16C3d[1]581
17C3d[2]6
17C3d568

– 834 –
(528P2d45)
(117CaR437)
13C3d[1]881
d15C3d[1]281
f51A3d[1]379
52A3d[2]732
52A3d[1]733
e52A3d[3]735
j52A3d736
52A3d[1]923
c52A3d[1]924
54A3d[1]422
j54A3d[2]433
64CaL509
9LoyL392
16SAC54

– 851 –
(528P2d353)
(117CaR537)
13C3d[2]92ŀ

– 858 –
(528P2d41)
(117CaR433)
44A3d[1]1032
49A3d[1]520
j521F2d[1]270
13SDL819

– 865 –
(528P2d372)
(117CaR556)
d58A3d[2]128
59A3d[1]934

– 875 –
(528P2d760)
(117CaR672)
s34A3d1010
14C3d[6]195
14C3d[7]195
15C3d[3]159
15C3d[3]960
15C3d[6]963
46A3d[7]191
46A3d[5]192
d51A3d[5]956
f56A3d[6]132

– 884 –
(528P2d771)
(117CaR683)
f12C3d902
j12C3d902
d15C3d[1]174
e46A3d731
47A3d768
48A3d[2]449
f48A3d[1]450
52A3d[1]107
57A3d[2]434
57A3d[1]435
d59A3d[1]525
40CC334
40CC382
40CC397
40CC606
40CC733
27HLJ637

– 899 –
(528P2d782)
(117CaR694)
f48A3d450
52A3d107
59A3d525
40CC398
40CC734

– 903 –
(528P2d365)
(117CaR549)
s67C2d365
s1C3d486
d14C3d[1]131
55A3d[1]29

– 912 –
(528P2d378)
(117CaR562)
s9C3d199
s418US24
s41LE551
s94SC2655

– 915 –
(528P2d357)
(117CaR541)
f55A3d[1]344
f55A3d[4]344
532F2d92
533F2d[3]504
386FS[2]792
58AG496
6Pcf476
60Cor560

Vol. 13

– 1 –
(529P2d53)
(118CaR21)
s37A3d1058
14C3d732
14C3d[1]735
d48A3d[1]127
53A3d[7]342
54A3d[1]1017
54A3d[5]1017
59A3d[5]617
64CaL655

– 20 –
(528P2d766)
(117CaR678)
53A3d[1]824
40CC796

– 29 –
(528P2d756)
(117CaR668)
55A3d[1]177
56A3d[1]200
64CaL654

– 35 –
(528P2d752)
(117CaR664)
d44A3d[1]384

– 43 –
(529P2d608)
(118CaR184)
(65A3878)
s31A3d500
cc216A2d213
cc254A2d126
44A3d[10]364
44A3d[14]937
46A3d[1]682
48A3d[12]950
49A3d[14]30
51A3d762
56A3d[14]984
58A3d[10]643
59A3d[12]17
59A3d[13]17
j59A3d[12]21
j59A3d[13]21
60A3d[1]81
60A3d[4]84
d60A3d[14]84
60A3d[10]605
50A3dS[6]31

– 68 –
(529P2d66)
(118CaR34)
s36A3d149
cc13C3d486
cc50A3d8
j13C3d[5]293
44A3d[1]165
e44A3d[4]167
44A3d[3]822
e44A3d[4]823
f44A3d[5]824
44A3d[4]838
45A3d188
45A3d[3]192
45A3d[4]194
45A3d[5]194
47A3d[1]513
47A3d[5]515
47A3d[4]518
47A3d[9]528
48A3d[1]546
48A3d[3]547
48A3d[4]547
48A3d[5]590
51A3d404
f51A3d[4]413
f51A3d[5]413
d51A3d[6]416
51A3d[7]416
51A3d[8]416
51A3d[9]416
51A3d[6]667
53A3d[7]1013
58A3d[3]421
58A3d428
f58A3d[4]430
59A3d[8]890
59A3d[5]966
521F2d[1]674
521F2d[7]676
58AG441
58AG615
58AG712
59AG174
59AG305

– 95 –
(529P2d33)
(118CaR1)
13C3d[3]109
f47A3d[3]877
49A3d[2]641

– 107 –
(529P2d42)
(118CaR10)
13C3d[1]104
56A3d[2]709

– 113 –
(528P2d1148)
(117CaR812)
s10C3d337
47A3d[1]834
51A3d[1]113
529F2d804
69FRD[1]316
64CaL634
13SDL208
1975LF288

– 129 –
(528P2d1145)
(117CaR809)
US cert den
in421US976
64CaL305
11CFW260
9SFR648

– 134 –
(528P2d1157)
(117CaR821)
14C3d[10]432
15C3d[8]899
15C3d[9]904
15C3d[10]904
16C3d[10]709
17C3d[4]552
17C3d[6]558

– 149 –
(529P2d46)
(118CaR14)
s37A3d449
45A3d[4]93
46A3d[9]629
f47A3d[9]493
f47A3d[2]494
47A3d[6]690
47A3d[7]690
48A3d[1]198
f49A3d[5]422
53A3d636
d53A3d[2]637
d53A3d[4]637
d53A3d[5]637
d53A3d[9]637
53A3d[6]641
53A3d[7]642
64CaL644

– 162 –
(529P2d599)
(118CaR175)
15C3d[2]621
15C3d771
17C3d[1]573

– 177* –
(529P2d553)
(118CaR129)
v17C3d425
s33A3d275
44A3d[5]674
511F2d[14]416
12SDL770

– 205 –
(529P2d570)
(118CaR146)
D96SC3184
s35A3d384
f13C3d[4]228
j13C3d234
14C3d773
17C3d[3]137
17C3d[5]144
58AG337
8LoyL290

– 225 –
(529P2d582)
(118CaR158)
D96SC3184
17C3d[5]144
64CaL637
8LoyL290

– 238 –
(529P2d590)
(118CaR166)
15C3d[2]656
15C3d[3]656
f47A3d[8]718
f47A3d[2]719
f47A3d[3]719
51A3d[2]491
51A3d[3]491
51A3d[7]491
52A3d[5]520
e53A3d[2]396
e53A3d[3]396
h55A3d[5]379
55A3d769
f55A3d[2]770
55A3d[3]770
58A3d[4]18
f58A3d[2]20
58A3d[5]20
59A3d[8]341
e59A3d[8]781
60A3d[5]263
e60A3d[2]265
e60A3d[8]265
d48LE80
j48LE[2]82
d96SC1625
j96SC[2]1626
d526F2d[3]916
390FS835
64CaL470
51JBC238

– 253 –
(530P2d168)
(118CaR480)
15C3d381
15C3d[5]802
15C3d[4]978
17C3d[5]422

– 263 –
(529P2d1017)
(118CaR249)
s37A3d842
cc13C3d483
f13C3d486
44A3d[8]823
f44A3d[9]824
45A3d188
45A3d[9]192
47A3d[4]515
47A3d[2]525
50A3d[2]24
d51A3d[4]663
d51A3d[13]664
d51A3d[9]665
j51A3d[8]825
53A3d[5]1013
53A3d[5]1060
521F2d[2]672
f521F2d[8]677
58AG441
58AG615
58AG711
59AG130
59AG307
64CaL532
16SAC403

– 297 –
(530P2d175)
(118CaR487)
s37A3d256
f50A3d[1]229

– 303 –
(530P2d161)
(118CaR473)
17C3d[1]92

– 315 –
(530P2d605)
(118CaR637)
13C3d[3]930
17C3d[3]153
17C3d292
17C3d[2]293
17C3d[1]301
17C3d[2]326
50A3d[2]696
50A3d[1]699
50A3d[3]700
408FS[2]510

– 349 –
(530P2d589)
(118CaR621)
s31A3d677
15C3d[1]844
o15C3d[1]851
47A3d[1]205
47A3d[2]205
47A3d[6]808
47A3d[4]809
50A3d[1]152
57A3d[1]310
58A3d[11]643
50JBC363
51JBC207
75WLR933

– 374 –
(530P2d1084)
(118CaR772)
s37A3d486

– 406 –
(530P2d585)
(118CaR617)
s35A3d242
d16C3d[1]700
d16C3d[2]700
d45A3d[1]210
48A3d[3]886
f51A3d[3]348
51A3d[2]612
51A3d[3]612
55A3d[3]361
j57A3d[3]533
59A3d340
59A3d[1]342
e59A3d[2]781
e52A3dS[3]4

– 413 –
(530P2d1073)
(118CaR761)
48A3d[5]764
48A3d[6]764
48A3d[7]764
48A3d[1]988
49A3d[4]860
49A3d[3]861
50A3d[3]604
50A3d[4]604
50A3d[5]604
50A3d[6]605
50A3d[7]605
d54A3d[4]876
f55A3d[3]188
f55A3d[4]188
f55A3d[5]188
f55A3d[6]188
f55A3d[7]188
f55A3d[8]190
57A3d[10]942
64CaL286

– 430 –
(531P2d761)
(119CaR193)
s32A3d637
15C3d256
58AG843
64CaL297

– 448 –
(530P2d1381)
(119CaR5)
14C3d[2]532
14C3d[3]532
15C3d[1]326
15C3d[2]326
15C3d[1]532
15C3d[2]539
16C3d581
16C3d[1]582
17C3d[2]568

– 457 –
(531P2d420)
(119CaR108)
s39A3d526
f13C3d[1]466
15C3d[3]844
o15C3d[3]851
e48A3d[1]192
48A3d[4]194
50A3d[3]153
f52A3d[1]511
f52A3d[4]511
f54A3d[4]684
59A3d[1]291
40CC939
40CC1030
64CaL305
11CFW260
51JBC208
51JBC211

*Rehearing granted

105

ILLUSTRATION 15

Page from state Shepard's Citator

Check through all later supplements. (Note that the supplements may run several months behind publication of opinions. The cut-off points in the report and reporter sources are listed on the second page of each supplement.)

To choose the citing opinions that you will want to read or scan: If the opinion that you are Shepardizing has been cited only a few times, you will want to check all the citing opinions. If it has been cited many times, however, you will have to be selective. To be selective, you must look to three factors: the citing courts' treatment of the opinion that you are Shepardizing, the points for which that opinion is being cited, and the recency of the citing opinions. Picking out the recent citing opinions is easy, because larger volume numbers identify more recent citing opinions. The other two factors require some explanation, however.

Take a look at Illustration 15, *supra*, the sample page from *Shepard's California Citations*. First, you will occasionally find letters in front of some of the listed citations. These are symbols that give information about the history of the case on which you are checking (for example, was the decision therein reversed?) or about the treatment of the opinion by the citing courts (for example, was it overruled, criticized, distinguished?). You will have to look at the abbreviations table in front of the Shepard's volume to find out what these symbols mean. See Illustration 16 for the abbreviation table from the California citator. Second, you will find small superior numbers in the middle of many of the citations, for example 15 C3d [1] 851. The "1" is a headnote number, indicating that in volume 15 of the third series of California Reports at page 851, the court cites the opinion that you are Shepardizing (*Smith*) with reference to the subject matter of headnote [1] *in the official report of the opinion that you are Shepardizing (Smith).* (Different headnotes—different both in content and in number—are used for a National Reporter report and an official report of an opinion.)

Now, you can select citing opinions that you will want to read or scan in this fashion: Run your finger down the column of citations looking for the headnote number(s) for the relevant section(s) of the opinion that you are Shepardizing. At a minimum, you will want to check those citing opinions for which there are both some history or treatment symbol and a superior number identifying the relevant headnote(s) in the opinion that you are Shepardizing. If this seems too selective, select all the official citations that carry your headnote number(s). If no history or treatment symbol appears, select the most recent citations that carry your headnote number(s). Note that if an "r" or an "o" appears in front of a citation, you *may* have to check only that citing opinion, because "r" means "reversed" and "o"

means "overruled." On the other hand, the absence of an "o" does not mean that your decision has not been overruled, because a decision may have been overruled implicitly rather than explicitly, and Shepard's symbol system is based on direct statements by the deciding court. Note further that a misleading statement by a court may result in an erroneous symbol being attached, because the Shepard's symbol system is not backed by analysis of opinions to verify a court's statements about prior decisions. Such an error appears in Illustration 15, for the *Smith v. Lewis* opinion, because no part of the *decision* in *Smith* was overruled in 15 Cal.3d at page 851 contrary to what the "o" appearing in front of that citation would suggest. Rather, decisions cited in *Smith* were overruled.[8]

Finally, a note about the by-products of Shepardizing: You may find relevant precedents that your search in other sources has not uncovered. Citing authorities other than court opinions are also included in Shepard's citators. Thus, for example, all editions pick up citing annotations in the annotated reports series. (An "n" following such a citation indicates a citation in the annotation itself; an "s" indicates a citation in a supplement to the annotation.) Citing attorney general's opinions are included in some of the state editions as well as in the United States edition. (See the AG citations in Illustration 15, *supra*, near the bottom of the fourth column.) Some citing periodical material is included. In older state editions, only local periodicals (bar association publications and reviews published by law schools within the state) were included, but the more recently published volumes and supplements include recent (post-1957) articles from several other nationally recognized law reviews as well. (See Illustration 15, *supra*, last citation for page 349, the *Smith v. Lewis* opinion, citing to the *Washington Law Review*. The preceding two citations are to the *Journal of State Bar of California*.) Shepardizing California and New York cases in the Shepard's units for, respectively, the California Reporter and the New York Supplement will lead to similar citing sources.

Recently published volumes of state case citators also include a section that permits Shepardizing the opinions for the particular state under the parallel National Reporter citations. The only additional information provided by such Shepardizing is the parallel National Reporter citations for citing opinions; the by-products summa-

---

8. You may wish to test the validity of the conclusion stated in the text. In *In re* Marriage of Brown, 15 Cal.3d 838, 126 Cal.Rptr. 633, 544 P.2d 561 (1976), the court overruled French v. French, cited and discussed in Smith v. Lewis, Appendix B, and then observed, note 14, 15 Cal.3d at 851, 126 Cal.Rptr. at 641, 544 P.2d at 569:

"Relying on the *French* rule, numerous decisions of this court and the Court of Appeal have stated that nonvested pension rights are not community property. (See * * * *Smith v. Lewis* * * *) Language in such decisions contrary to the views expressed in this opinion must be disapproved."

ABBREVIATIONS—ANALYSIS

History of Case

a	(affirmed)	Same case affirmed on appeal.
cc	(connected case)	Different case from case cited but arising out of same subject matter or intimately connected therewith.
D	(dismissed)	Appeal from same case dismissed.
m	(modified)	Same case modified on appeal.
r	(reversed)	Same case reversed on appeal.
s	(same case)	Same case as case cited.
S	(superseded)	Substitution for former opinion.
v	(vacated)	Same case vacated.
US cert den		Certiorari denied by U. S. Supreme Court.
US cert dis		Certiorari dismissed by U. S. Supreme Court.
US reh den		Rehearing denied by U. S. Supreme Court.
US reh dis		Rehearing dismissed by U. S. Supreme Court.

Treatment of Case

c	(criticised)	Soundness of decision or reasoning in cited case criticised for reasons given.
d	(distinguished)	Case at bar different either in law or fact from case cited for reasons given.
e	(explained)	Statement of import of decision in cited case. Not merely a restatement of the facts.
f	(followed)	Cited as controlling.
h	(harmonized)	Apparent inconsistency explained and shown not to exist.
j	(dissenting opinion)	Citation in dissenting opinion.
L	(limited)	Refusal to extend decision of cited case beyond precise issues involved.
o	(overruled)	Ruling in cited case expressly overruled.
p	(parallel)	Citing case substantially alike or on all fours with cited case in its law or facts.
q	(questioned)	Soundness of decision or reasoning in cited case questioned.

Operation of Order

A	(amended)	Order amended.
E	(extended)	Provisions of an existing order extended or amplified in scope.
L	(limited)	Provisions of an order declared not to be extended.
m	(modified)	Order modified.
R	(revoked or rescinded)	Existing order abrogated.
Rein	(reinstated)	Order reinstated.
Rp	(revoked or re-scinded in part)	Existing order abrogated in part.
Rs	(repealed and superseded)	Abrogation of existing order and substitution of a new order therefor.
Rv	(revised)	Order revised.
S	(superseded)	New order substituted for an existing one.
Sd	(suspended)	Order suspended.
Sdp	(suspended in part)	Order suspended in part.
Sg	(supplementing)	New matter added to an existing order.
Sp	(superseded in part)	New matter substituted for part of an existing order.

14

ILLUSTRATION 16.

Key to abbreviations
Shepard's case citator for California

rized in the preceding paragraph are not included. The additional benefits to be gained by Shepardizing in a National Reporter regional unit of Shepard's are discussed in Section 7E.

Shepard's editions vary from state to state in some minor ways. Therefore, you may save time or avoid frustration by reading the introductory explanation for a particular edition when you first use it.

SECTION 7C. THE SEARCH FOR MANDATORY FEDERAL PRECEDENTS

Research on a problem governed by federal law will usually begin with a search for some type of federal written law. Whether it is appropriate to say that there is a "federal common law," has, indeed, been the subject of some discussion.[9] Hence, the research materials and suggestions discussed in the following chapter on legislation research are of primary importance if you are working with a problem governed by federal law. You may, nevertheless, sometime be faced with beginning research in the nebulous federal common law area, and you will often supplement a search in legislative materials with a search in research sources of the type discussed in this chapter. Therefore, this section is included to identify the federal materials that parallel the state materials discussed in the preceding section.

Four key number digests are devoted to federal law. Three units constitute an index for the opinions of federal courts:

The *Federal Digest* indexes pre-1939 federal court opinions.

The *Modern Federal Practice Digest* indexes 1939 to 1961 federal court opinions.

West's Federal Practice Digest 2d indexes subsequent federal court opinions.[10] It is supplemented with annual cumulative pocket parts and quarterly noncumulative pamphlets.

The fourth, the *Supreme Court Digest*, is limited to indexing the opinions of the United States Supreme Court. All units have the same classification and key numbering systems and substantially the same features as the state key number digests.

A competitive digest devoted to Supreme Court opinions, *U. S. Supreme Court Digest, Lawyers' Edition*, provides useful information not included in the key number digests. Most notably, it incorporates an unusual citator feature. Whenever a point stated in a digest squib has been expressly overruled, distinguished, limited, or questioned by

9. See generally C. Wright, Law of Federal Courts § 60 (3d ed. 1976).

10. Although this digest cites cases decided from 1960 forward, publication thereof was not begun until 1976.

The basic volumes incorporate material from former supplements to the *Modern Federal Practice Digest*, publication of which began in 1960.

the Supreme Court in a later opinion, that fact is noted in an immediately following small-type squib or in an appropriate place in a supplement. Additionally, this digest provides cross-reference citations to the annotated reports, the *United States Supreme Court Reports, Lawyers' Edition* and *American Law Reports* series, described in Section 7E, *infra*, and to *American Jurisprudence 2d*. See Illustration 17. The Lawyers' Edition digest has all the common features, including a table of cases that identifies sections under which each case has been classified. The digest is supplemented with annual cumulative pocket parts. Current supplementation is provided by *Lawyers Edition 2d* advance sheets, described *infra* in this section.

The availability of two Supreme Court digests permits a double-check of a search in one by a search in the other. So many secondary-search sources deal with federal law in detail that sources for double-checking any federal search are always available. In fact, the double-check search for mandatory federal precedents from the court of appeals tends to merge with the search for persuasive precedents, because discussions are rarely limited to the court decisions from one circuit. Therefore, some of the sources discussed in the following section, particularly the annotated reports dealing with federal law, will also be useful for finding mandatory precedents.

A search for lower federal court opinions can be updated through the advance sheets of the *Federal Reporter* and *Federal Supplement,* the lower federal court units of the National Reporter system. These advance sheets contain the same kind of miniature key number digest as do state-regional National Reporter advance sheets, so that the updating procedure is the same. A key number search for Supreme Court opinions can be updated through the *Supreme Court Reporter* advance sheets, and the key number digest included in these National Reporter advance sheets is cumulative so that only the last issue of a volume need be checked.

Another set of unofficial advance sheets is available to bring a search for Supreme Court opinions down to date. The Court's opinions are reprinted in the *United States Supreme Court Reports, Lawyers' Edition* (L.Ed.) series as well as in the National Reporter series. (The *Lawyers' Edition* reports all Supreme Court opinions, including early opinions not included in the *Supreme Court Reporter* series.) Each *Lawyers' Edition 2d* advance sheet has a subject index at the back that is cumulative for each prospective bound volume. A search in the Lawyers' Edition digest may be most easily supplemented through these advance sheets.

Looseleaf reporters, which may permit a more complete and efficient updating search on many federal problems, are discussed in the following section and in Section 8D, *infra*.

Attorneys   § 19

the honest belief that his advice, in the ordinary case of advice to clients, is well founded and in the just interests of his client, he cannot be held liable for error in judgment. Re Watts, 190 US 1, 23 S Ct 718,

47 L Ed 933

b. An attorney is not liable to his client for every mistake that may occur in practice nor for every error in judgment in the conduct of the client's cause, but is only bound to act with a proper degree of skill and with reasonable care and to the best of his knowledge. National Sav. Bank v Ward, 100 US 195,

25 L Ed 621

c. The ground of an action against an attorney for negligence in the conduct of a case whereby a recovery has been barred by the statute of limitations is the breach of his implied contract to act diligently and skilfully, and not the resulting damage to his client, which dates from the expiration of the period of limitation. Wilcox v Plummer, 4 Pet 172

7 L Ed 821

d. An attorney is liable to his client for the consequences of his want of reasonable care or skill in the conduct of legal controversies or matters not in litigation. National Sav. Bank v Ward, 100 US 195,

25 L Ed 621

e. An attorney cannot be charged with negligence when he accepts, as correct law, a decision of the supreme court of the state in regard to the liability of stockholders of a corporation. Marsh v Whitmore, 21 Wall 178,

(Annotated) **22 L Ed 482**

f. An attorney employed to investigate the title to real property impliedly contracts to exercise reasonable care and skill in so doing, and is responsible to his client for loss arising from failure to do so. National Sav. Bank v Ward, 100 US 195,

25 L Ed 621

g. An attorney who gave a certificate that B's title to a lot (describing it) is good, and the property is unencumbered, there being neither fraud, collusion, nor falsehood on his part, nor privity of contract between him and C who loaned money relying upon the certificate, is not liable to the latter for any loss sustained by reason of the certificate. National Sav. Bank v Ward, 100 US 195,

25 L Ed 621

Distinguished in Waters-Pierce Oil Co. v Deselms, 212 US 178, 53 L Ed 463, 29 S Ct 270, holding oil company liable to subsequent purchaser for damage caused by mixture sold by it as coal oil but which contained gasoline.

(B) AUTHORITY

§ 19 Generally.
(In Am Jur 2d, see Attorneys at Law §§ 100–106.)

Annotation—
Admissions and statements of attorney or his clerk as binding on client, 14 L Ed 824.
Authority of attorney, 8 L Ed 60.

Estoppel by acts of attorney, see ESTOPPEL AND WAIVER, § 112.

a. No man has a right to appear as the attorney of another without the authority of such other. Osborn v Bank of United States, 9 Wheat 738,

6 L Ed 204

b. The attorney is the agent of his client to conduct his suit to judgment and to superintend the execution of final process. United States use of Rogers v Conklin (Rogers v Marshal) 1 Wall 644,

17 L Ed 714

c. The instructions of an attorney to an officer will bind his client and protect the officer. United States use of Rogers v Conklin (Rogers v Marshal) 1 Wall 644,

17 L Ed 714

d. Where notes are left with attorneys for collection, their proceeds to be paid by them to creditors of the depositor, the attorneys become trustees of such creditors, and are authorized to pay such proceeds to them. Hinkle v Wanzer, 17 How 353,

15 L Ed 173

e. On a bill of review filed by a defendant to set aside a decree, he is bound by the answer filed on his behalf by his solicitors, although he did not himself read it, unless he can show mistake or fraud in filing it. The answers of other defendants cannot be read in his favor. Putnam v Day, 22 Wall 60,

22 L Ed 764

f. An attorney virtute officii has no authority to purchase property in the name of his client, even at a sale upon the foreclosure of the mortgage in which he is the attorney of record. Savery v Sypher, 6 Wall 157,

18 L Ed 822

g. The attorney of the city and county of San Francisco had no authority, by disclaimer and consent to a decree against the city in a suit to quiet title, to relinquish rights reserved for the benefit of the public by the Van Ness ordinance, by which the city relinquished its pueblo land within its corporate limits as defined by its charter of 1851, with certain exceptions, and reserved from the grant all the lots which it then occupied or

185

ILLUSTRATION 17.

Page from *U. S. Supreme Court Digest, Lawyers' Edition*

Two Shepard's case editions are published for the federal courts.

Shepard's United States Citations provides citation service for Supreme Court opinions. Use of the large permanent volume, called the 1943 Case Edition, requires that you have the official citation for an opinion to be Shepardized, that is, a citation to the *United States Reports* (U.S.). Two slim sections in the back of the volume list citations for the two unofficial reporters already described, the *Supreme Court Reporter* and the *Lawyers' Edition*, but only to provide the parallel citations in the official reports. With one exception, the method of Shepardizing for an official citation in the main part of the volume is the same as has been described for the state Shepard's case editions. The exception is that this 1943 Case Edition does not use the headnote number system described in the preceding section (the small superior numbers, as in 15 C3d [1] 851) to identify the subject matter portion of an opinion to which a citing court refers. Rather, brief phrase descriptions are inserted before groups of citations to identify the subject matter discussed in the citing opinions, thus:

—145—	21 NE 792	**—158—**	IRA1915A	34 FS 295
(25 LE590)	191 Ill 374	(25 LE632)	[1145n	215 Ala 372
s FC7430	61 NE 77	**App. & E.**	AC'17C 13n	110 So 807
App. & E.	198 Ill 427	Division of	AC'17C 15n	217 Ala 500
Defective	64 NE1007	Opinion—	**—195—**	117 So 48
Title—	225 Ill 184	Certified	(25 LE621)	236 Ala351
Amend-	80 NE 104	Question	9 F2d 470	182 So 476
ment	128 Mas 480	116 US 700	**Atty. & C.**	21 AlA 399
128 US 229	122 Ten 676	29 LE 772	Officers of	108 So 628
32 LE 438	126 SW1087	6 SC 622	Court	61 Ark280
9 SC 59	72 AR 195n	127 US 402	101 F2d 680	32 SW1074
157 US 347	**—149—**	32 LE 197	**Contracts**	43 Az 230
39 LE 727	(25 LE573)	8 SC1201	Liability to	29 P2d1069
15 SC 628	cc127 US494	136 US 229	Third	110 Cal 343
27 F 310	cc 32 LE163	34 LE 343	Party—	42 P 900
51 F 800	cc 8 SC1250	10 SC1015	Privity—	57 CaA 65
74 F 916	**Trusts**	137 US 3	Usage	206 P 768
106 F 489	Public Sale	34 LE 587	55 US 468	9 CoA 27
(5 AB690)	—Price—	11 SC 30	123 US 222	47 P 410
250 F 12	Adequacy	163 US 137	31 LE 127	111 Ct 541
Shipping	29 F 809	41 LE 103	8 SC 101	150 At 510
Mortgage—	68 F 682	16 SC 985	d212 US 178	176 Ga 94
	82 F2d 980			

Supplements to the 1943 Case Edition volume (currently, three bound volumes and varying numbers of paperbacks), use the headnote number system, however.

Another basic difference between the 1943 Case Edition and the supplements thereto is the more comprehensive citation service provided in the supplements for *Lawyers' Edition* and *Supreme Court Reporter* citations. Shepardizing under these unofficial citations will lead to citing federal court opinions and citing annotations in the *Lawyers' Edition* and *American Law Report* series. Shepardizing un-

der the official citations may still yield more, however, because for the U.S. section of the supplement volumes, citing sources also include federal administrative reports, United States Attorney General opinions, state court opinions (with citations for both the official and National Reporter volumes), and articles appearing in the *American Bar Association Journal*.   (When would you ever want to Shepardize under the unofficial citation, then?   When you have only an unofficial citation *and* only the headnote numbers from an unofficial report of the opinion, because each of the three sources uses a different set of headnotes for each case.   Avoid the possibility of missing a significant citation, however, by Shepardizing under the official citation and headnotes whenever possible.)

Shepard's Federal Citations provides citation service for lower federal court opinions.   It includes two separate units.   One unit covers the *Federal Reporter* series, and the other unit covers the *Federal Supplement* and *Federal Rules Decisions* units of the National Reporter System.[11]   These units are slightly less complicated than the Supreme Court citator, there being no official reports for the federal courts of appeal and district courts to require parallel sections.   Citing sources appearing in both units are the same as those identified for the official Supreme Court citations in the preceding paragraph. The procedure for using these units is generally the same as for using the state case editions.

If you are looking only for recent opinions of a particular lower federal court (for example, for opinions of the Court of Appeals for the Second Circuit or for opinions of federal district courts sitting in a particular state), you may use an extra step to eliminate citing opinions of courts in which you are not interested.   *Shepard's Federal Circuit Table* (1960–1971), a slim red volume with a paperback supplement, may be used to identify the citing circuit (for recent F. 2d citations) or the state in which a citing district court sits (for recent F.Supp. and F.R.D. citations).   This extra step is necessary because the United States and Federal citators do not identify the particular citing courts.

To assure that you use all parts of the United States or Federal citators, begin your use of either by checking the "What Your Library Should Contain" explanation on the front of the currently dated paperback supplement.   This explanatory statement is a useful be-

---

11.   The first volume of the *Federal Reporter* Shepard's unit also covers the nineteenth century lower federal court opinions collected in the *Federal Cases* unit of the National Reporter System.   The second unit (F.Supp., F.R. D.) also covers the official Court of Claims reports.   Separate subject matter units are also published, *Shep-* ard's *United States Patents and Trademarks* (including copyright) *Citations* and *Shepard's Federal Labor Law Citations*.   Their coverage and use are explained in introductory pages therein.   Shepard's citators for written laws are described generally in Chapter 8, *infra*.

ginning point for use of any Shepard's unit, but it is particularly important for these citators because of the number of volumes and supplements they comprise. Note particularly the occasional use of ivory-colored paperback supplements in addition to the more commonly used red and white paperback supplements.

A recently added Shepard's unit, *Federal Law Citations in Selected Law Reviews*, permits Shepardizing of citations to the U.S. reports, lower federal court units of the National Reporter System, and certain federal written law, to find post-1971 citations in nineteen nationally recognized law reviews.

SECTION 7D. WHAT TO DO WITH MANDATORY PRECEDENTS: A REVIEW

Whether relevant mandatory precedents that you find are favorable or unfavorable, you should compare, analyze, evaluate, and synthesize them as though the problem on which you are working will ultimately be resolved through the courts. You should compare the facts of your problem with the facts of relevant precedent cases. Your analysis of opinions in similar or analogous cases should be directed toward identifying the narrowest possible view of each decision that a court could validly take as well as the broadest possible view and, hence, toward identifying the narrowest and broadest rules that might be said to underlie the decisions. You should evaluate each opinion, using the two-pronged approach discussed in Section 2E, *supra*. You should synthesize the opinions. On the basis of your factual comparisons, analyses, evaluations, and synthesis, you should attempt to predict whether the courts will distinguish, apply, extend, limit, or overrule relevant precedents.[12] If you have been conscientiously tending to class preparation and discussions, you will probably find that you need not consciously direct your thinking toward these intellectual tasks; you will do them instinctively as you read and analyze the opinions.

SECTION 7E. STEP 3: THE SEARCH FOR PERSUASIVE PRECEDENTS—WHY AND WHERE

STEP 3. The Search for Persuasive Precedents. If mandatory precedents do not supply a clear answer, a search for persuasive precedents will require:

> **Preliminary search through one of the sources used for preliminary analysis (encyclopedia, treatise, Restatement, or legal periodicals), the American Digest System, the annotated reports, or a Shepard's regional-Reporter citator unit.**

> **A double-check search in a second of the above-listed sources.**

---

12. See, Section 2D, *supra*. For a more extended description of predictive analysis of this character, see Aigler, *Stare Decisis and Legal Education*, 4 Ariz.L.Rev. 39 (1962).

Bringing the search down to date by:

(a) checking relevant advance sheets and, perhaps, the supplement to the American Digest System, and

(b) Shepardizing relevant persuasive opinions in the appropriate Shepard's unit.

If you find mandatory precedents directly in point and are able to predict confidently what the controlling courts would do with them in relation to your problem, your research may be ended. If you do not reach this state of confidence, however, you will want to look to the decisions of courts of other jurisdictions. Perhaps you will need to fill in gaps, that is, to find precedents on points for which there is no authority in the controlling jurisdiction. Or you may wish to test the validity of the reasoning and rules applied by the court(s) of the controlling jurisdiction by examining the approaches taken by other courts. Thus, you may find either support for or ammunition against the approach previously taken in the controlling jurisdiction. Your comparison, analysis, evaluation, and synthesis of representative persuasive opinions will be as rigorous as your treatment of mandatory precedents.

Four basic alternatives are available to you for preliminary and double-check searches for persuasive precedents on state law questions. The four alternatives will be described in the remainder of this section. When a source is also useful for research on federal questions, that fact will be mentioned.

Alternative (1)—Returning to a Preliminary Analysis Source

This alternative is most useful if you found directly relevant material in one of the sources suggested for preliminary analysis research. Citations to supporting primary authority, both federal and state, are readily available in treatises and encyclopedias, for example. For definitional questions, a preliminary search of *Words and Phrases* can be brought down to date through words and phrases tables appearing in the front of National Reporter volumes and advance sheets published subsequent to the coverage of the *Words and Phrases* pocket supplement.

As noted earlier, when you become more experienced as a researcher, you will frequently find legal periodicals and annotated reports to be useful sources for preliminary analysis, particularly for changing or developing areas of law. The periodicals will supply selected citations to relevant precedents; the annotated reports, with their supplements (described in Alternative (3), *infra*) will provide exhaustive citations.

Unless your research problem is novel, you should find at least one similar or analogous case through Step 2. Given one opinion, a

new research approach is open to you, the case approach. You can check for the name of the case in tables of cases. (Treatises usually have such tables, but encyclopedias do not.) Further, you can identify the relevant digest key number(s) from the National Reporter reprint of the opinion (if it appears in one of the National Reporter units) and thus have easy entry to the key number digests.

For relevant Restatement sections, comments, or illustrations, citing court opinions and secondary material may be found through *Shepard's Restatement of the Law Citations*, described in the preceding section, or through the *Restatement in the Courts* or Restatement (Second) Appendix volumes, described in the following paragraphs.

The first volume called *Restatement in the Courts* (permanent edition) was published in 1945. It collected, section by section for each of the Restatement subjects, headnote squibs on all 1932–1944 federal and state court opinions wherein the Restatements had been cited or discussed. The *Restatement in the Courts* is supplemented in:

Restatement of the Law, 1948 Supplement

Restatement in the Courts, thus:

　　1954 Supplement in 2 volumes

　　1965 Supplement in 3 volumes

　　1967 Supplement in 1 volume

　　Thereafter, annual paperback supplements with biennial bound volumes or, more recently, annual bound volumes.

Appendix volumes have been published for completed Restatement (Second) subjects. In addition to Reporter's Notes (see Illustration 18), and court citations to the predecessor Restatement, each Appendix also includes cross-references to the American Digest System and to annotations in the annotated reports series. In the recently published volumes of the *Restatement of the Law (Second) of Property*, the Reporter's Notes are included in the Restatement text volumes. Court citations to tentative drafts for the Restatement (Second) subjects are collected in the supplements to the *Restatement in the Courts*.

Alternative (2)—Using the American Digest System

The American Digest System and its smaller units, previously discussed, are all constructed on the same basic scheme described in Section 7B. The American Digest System is said to index all the reported opinions handed down in the United States since 1658. It is the most comprehensive index to our case law. In addition, the descriptive word indexes prepared for use with the system constitute the most comprehensive word index available.

§ 299A   74   Torts

§ 299A. <u>UNDERTAKING IN PROFESSION OR TRADE</u>

UNLESS HE REPRESENTS THAT HE HAS GREATER OR LESS SKILL OR KNOWLEDGE,
ONE WHO UNDERTAKES TO RENDER SERVICES IN THE PRACTICE OF A PROFESSION OR
TRADE IS REQUIRED TO HAVE AND EXERCISE THE SKILL AND KNOWLEDGE NORMALLY
POSSESSED BY MEMBERS OF THAT PROFESSION OR TRADE IN GOOD STANDING IN
SIMILAR COMMUNITIES.

<u>Note to Institute</u>:   This Section is new. It supplements the general
rule as to the requirement of competence, stated in § 299, with a special
rule as to skilled professions or trades.

<u>Comment</u>:

a. <u>Skill</u>. Skill, as the word is used in this Section, is something
more than the mere minimum competence required of any person who does an
act, under the rule stated in § 299. It is that special form of competence which is not part of the ordinary equipment of the reasonable man,
but which is the result of acquired learning, and aptitude developed by
special training and experience. All professions, and most trades, are
 ssari skilled, and th   used   the   ial compe-

Note: This Section has been added to the first Restatement.

Comment b: In addition to physicians and surgeons, the rule stated
has been applied to other professions. United Dentists v. Bryan, (1932)
198 Va. 880, 164 S.E. 554 (dentist); McCullough v. Sullivan, (1926) 102
N.J.L. 381, 132 A. 102 (attorney); Humboldt Bldg. Ass'n v. Ducker's Ex'r,
(1901) 111 Ky. 759, 64 S.W. 671 (same); Citizens' Loan Fund & Sav. Ass'n
v. Friedley, (1890) 123 Ind. 143, 23 N.E. 1075 (same); Cowles v. City of
Minneapolis, (1915) 128 Minn. 452, 151 N.W. 184 (engineer); Louisville &
N. R. Co. v. Perry's Adm'r, (1917) 173 Ky. 213, 190 S.W. 1064 (engineer);
Smith v. London Assur. Corp., (1905) 109 App. Div. 882, 96 N.Y.S. 820
(accountant); L.B. Laboratories v. Mitchell, (1952) 39 Cal. 2d 56, 237 P.
2d 84 (same); City of East Grand Forks v. Steele, (1913) 121 Minn. 296,
141 N.W. 181 (same); Stern v. Langg, (1901) 106 La. 738, 31 So. 303
(oculist); Kahn v. Shaw, (1941) 63 Ga. App. 563, 16 S.E. 2d 99 (optome-
trist); Allan v. State S.S. Co., (1892) 132 N.Y. 91, 30 N.E. 482 (pharmacist); Ballance v. Dennington, (1928) 241 Mich. 383, 217 N.W. 329
(X-ray operator); The Tom Lisle, (D. Pa. 1892) 48 F. 690 (ship pilot).

ILLUSTRATION 18 *.

Excerpts from Reporter's Notes for Section 299A,
Restatement (Second) of Torts
Tentative Draft No. 4 (April 15, 1959)

The American Digest System is divided into nine multivolume units. Except for the first, each unit indexes the opinions handed down during a ten-year period; hence, these units are called decennial units. The *Decennial Digest* covers the period from 1897 to 1906, the *Second Decennial Digest* covers the period from 1906 to 1916, and so on through the new *Eighth Decennial Digest*, covering the period from 1966 to 1976. The true "first" unit of the system is the *Century Digest*, which indexes opinions from 1658 to 1897.

Each of these units is essentially independent of the others. Each has all the common research features, including its own table of cases and descriptive word index, covering only cases decided during the time period covered by that unit. (Hence, if you fail to find a key word in the index to the most recent decennial digest, you might want to check the index to the preceding unit and so on backwards if you are having great difficulty finding a case or key number in point.) The basic research approaches can be used with all units.

The system is supplemented by the General Digest. The current supplement is the *General Digest, Fifth Series*. This supplement is not difficult to use if you understand the publication sequence. First, as you already know, the headnotes for all the opinions appearing in a National Reporter advance sheet are reprinted in the miniature digest appearing in the front of each advance sheet. At the end of a month, all these miniature digests are cumulated into a larger digest and republished in a light blue paperback General Digest pamphlet. The pamphlet digests are then cumulated and republished in dark blue bound volumes, four or five times each year. In 1986 all the material in the bound volumes (by then, perhaps forty to fifty volumes) will be cumulated to produce the Ninth Decennial Digest.

A Descriptive-Word Index pamphlet for the *General Digest* is published monthly (also a light blue paperback). The index and other research aids in the monthly pamphlets are in turn cumulated in a bound index volume for every ten bound volumes of the *General Digest*. Use of these subject indexes is most significant for currently developing problems, for example, problem areas that have not previously been indexed in a decennial unit. Of more frequent importance for efficient use of the supplement system is the cumulative Table of Key Numbers that appears first in the monthly index pamphlets. If you have found a specific and in-point key number in the digest classification scheme, you need only check that key number in the Table of Key Numbers in the most recent monthly index pamphlet and in the back of any bound index volumes (one is prepared for each ten bound General Digest volumes) to determine in which volumes of the current General Digest one or more headnotes are indexed under that key number. See Illustration 19. Even the Table of Key Numbers cannot make an independent search of a General Digest supplement efficient by about midpoint of a decennial time period and thereafter

TABLE OF KEY NUMBERS

GENERAL DIGEST, VOLUMES 1–5 5th SERIES

A Time Saver for Locating The Latest Cases

Example: Having found a proposition of law under the topic Licenses ☞24, refer to the same topic and Key in this table which will show that other cases appear in the General Digest, Fifth Series, Volume 1. Search is therefore unnecessary in Volume 2 of the General Digest, Fifth Series.

ABANDONMENT

☞

2—1, 2, 3, 5
3—1, 2, 3, 5
4—1
5—1, 3
7—5

**ABATEMENT AND RE-
  VIVAL**

4—1, 2, 3, 4, 5
5—4
7—1, 2
8(1)—1, 2, 3, 4
8(2)—1, 2, 3, 4
8(4)—4
8(5)—4
8(8)—1, 2
9—1, 2, 3, 4
10—3
11—5
12—5
13—3
14—1
15—1, 2
16—1, 2, 5
17—1, 2, 3
27—1

ABSENTEES

☞

5—1, 3

ABSTRACTS OF TITLE

3—1, 2, 3
2—3

**ACCORD AND SATIS-
  FACTION**

1—1, 2, 3, 4, 5
2(2)—3
3—5
4—2, 5
5—2, 3
6—3
7(1)—5
8(1)—3
9—1, 5
10(1)—1, 2, 4, 5
11(1)—4
11(2)—1, 2
11(3)—1, 3
12(1)—2
13—2, 5
15—3
16—2
17—5

**ACCOUNT ACTION ON—
  Cont'd**

☞

7—1, 2, 3, 4, 5
8—2, 3, 4
9—2
10—1, 5
11—2
12—2, 3, 5
13—2
14—2, 3, 4
15—3, 4

ACCOUNT STATED

1—3, 4, 5
3—4
4—3, 4, 5
5—3, 4
6(1)—4
6(2)—4
7—5
15—5
19(3)—1

ACKNOWLEDGMENT

1—2, 5
4—1
5—1, 3
38—4

ACTION—Cont'd

☞

27(5)—5
34—2
35—1, 2, 3, 4
36—2, 3, 4, 5
38(1)—1, 2, 5
38(3)—1
38(4)—1, 3, 5
38(6)—2
40—1, 2
43—5
45(2)—5
45(4)—1
48(1)—2
48(2)—5
50(4)—1, 3, 4, 5
52—4
53(1)—1, 2, 3, 4
53(2)—3, 4, 5
53(3)—4
55—2, 3
56—2, 4, 5
57(1)—4, 5
57(2)—5
57(3)—1, 2, 3, 4, 5
57(4)—5
57(5)—5
57(6)—2, 5

ILLUSTRATION 19.
Page from Table of Key Numbers
General Digest, Fifth Series

if the table indicates that you must check your key number in a substantial number of bound volumes. For all but the most novel problems, however, you will then be justified in relying on an alternative source to find persuasive opinions during the early years of the decennial time period, using the General Digest volumes and pamphlets for the current and preceding year.[13] The modern alternative to supplement a Key Number search is WESTLAW, a computer-assisted research system described in Section 9B, *infra.*

Although the basic classification scheme of the key number digest system is fixed, it is not closed-end. When a new area of law

---

13. The difficulties of using the General Digest supplement late in a decennial time period will be apparent to those who use this text during 1978, before publication of the Eighth Decennial unit. The *General Digest, Fourth Series,* which supplemented the Seventh Decennial unit and provides the material for the eighth unit, reached forty-two volumes. The Table of Key Numbers service was not provided for the *General Digest, Fourth Series,* so use of it became difficult rather early in the decennial period.

has developed to the point that a special topic for it seems justified, the publishers assign a topic title, create a subclassification outline, assign key number classification headings, and publish all relevant headnotes for all existing opinions or for relevant recent opinions in the new topic classification. The new topic will appear in the General Digest. Thus, for example, in the *General Digest, Fourth Series* (now the Eighth Decennial Unit), new topics were added for Drugs and Narcotics, Securities Regulation, Products Liability, Public Contracts, Federal Courts, and Military Justice. Existing topics may also be revised and published with expanded key lines in the supplement and then in the next decennial unit. Thus, in the Eighth Decennial Unit will appear revised classification schemes for Arbitration, Civil Rights, Commerce, and Taxation. A table appearing at the beginning of a new or revised topic converts former key numbers to the new classification numbers.

The key number classification system was not created until publication of the first *Decennial Digest*. Therefore, if you want to work backwards through the decennial units into the *Century Digest*, watch for the cross references to the *Century Digest* numbering system that appear at the beginning of the key number subtopics in the *Second Decennial Digest*. Or if you start with the *Century Digest*, you can convert the Century section numbers to the key numbers through a table printed on pink pages in volume 21 of the first *Decennial Digest*.

The American Digest System is an excellent search tool if you have found a specific and in-point key number subtopic (through C. J.S., a National Reporter report of an opinion, a state or federal key number digest, or some other source) or can find such a subtopic. When you are doing original research, that is, research on a point for which relevant state precedents have not previously been collected, you must use the American Digest System. Since you can collect all relevant federal precedents through the federal key number digests, you will not usually use the American Digest units in researching problems governed by federal law.

Alternative (3)—Annotated Reports

Annotated reports were originally published on two premises: that only a small percentage of published opinions really contribute anything to the development of our law and, therefore, that it would be useful for attorneys to have in one convenient series those opinions selected by the editors as making some substantial contribution to the law. Brief annotations (comments regarding other opinions dealing with a point or points raised in the selected opinions) were appended. The afterthought annotations soon outgrew the selected-opinion parent, however, and the selective reports have now become valuable primarily for the annotations.

The annotated reports having the greatest scope are three of the *American Law Reports* series, A.L.R., A.L.R.2d, and A.L.R.3d.[14]

Many of the annotations in the first series, A.L.R., have now been superseded (updated, rewritten, and republished) by annotations in A.L.R.2d and A.L.R.3d.   Enough useful material that cannot be found elsewhere still appears in A.L.R. to justify your knowing that annotations therein can be found through the black *A.L.R. 1st Quick Index* volume or through the four red A.L.R. Word Index volumes (note that the first three volumes have pocket parts).   Unfortunately, the service supplementing the first series is of limited value if a substantial number of opinions have been handed down in the subject area of an A.L.R. annotation.   This service, the *A.L.R. Blue Book of Supplemental Decisions*, consists of five blue permanent volumes, each one citing opinions handed down during a different period of time, and an annual cumulative blue pamphlet supplement.   If you

---

14.   You should also be aware of A.L.R. predecessors, however, at least to the extent that you recognize citations to them.   Because of their age, they will frequently not be of great assistance to you; more recent material will usually be available.   Occasionally, however (if, for example, you are in-terested in early history of a rule or principle or type of reasoning), you may find these early annotated re-ports useful.   The following chart showing period of opinions reported, not necessarily publication dates, is adapted from R. Notz, Legal Research 122 (1952).

American Decisions (Am.Dec.) 1760–1868		
American Reports (Am.Rep.) 1868–1887		
American State Reports (Am.St.Rep.) 1887–1911	American and English Annotated Cases (Am. & Eng.Ann.Cas.) 1906–1911	Lawyers Reports Annotated (L.R.A.) 1888–1906
	American Annotated Cases (Am.Ann.Cas.) 1912–1918	Lawyers Reports Annotated (New Series) L.R.A. (n.s.) 1906–1915
		Lawyers Reports Annotated (Third Series) 1915–1918 (This series is cited by year with capital letters identify-ing the different volumes published within a given year. Thus, the first and last volumes published in 1918 are designated L.R.A. 1918A and 1918F.)

In 1919 the publishers of the *Annotat-ed Cases* and *Lawyers Reports Anno-tated* series consolidated their efforts to produce *American Law Reports*.

look at Illustration 20, you will find that the contents somewhat resemble Shepard's citators: columns of opinion citations without text, collected under the volume and page numbers of annotations in A.L.R. If an A.L.R. annotation is relevant, however, the most recent citations from the supplement can be checked. Note that jurisdictions are identified in citations therein, permitting you to select recent decisions from the controlling jurisdiction for a particular problem or from jurisdictions having early precedents that are most significant for a particular problem.

The second series, A.L.R.2d, also has a black Quick Index volume (currently indexing both 2d and 3d series) and red word-index volumes (but only three.) [15] Its supplement, the *Recent Case Service* (dark blue volumes), is more useful and efficient than the parallel A.L.R. Service. You need check only one volume of the service to supplement an A.L.R.2d annotation (find the volume and page number of the annotation in the appropriate blue volume) and the pocket part supplement in that volume. Rather than bare citations under page numbers, you will find headnote squibs collected under the section headings of the annotation.

The A.L.R.3d series provides the most efficient system. Annotations are indexed in the *A.L.R.2d and 3d Quick Index* volume (supplemented in a *front* pocket part) and the annotations are supplemented by pocket parts in the back of the A.L.R.3d volumes. Like the A.L.R.2d supplement, these supplements also collect headnotes under section headings.

The existence of superseding annotations has already been mentioned. Annotations may also be textually supplemented, that is, an annotation discussing opinions handed down subsequent to the original annotation will be printed. Thus, for example, an A.L.R. annotation may be textually supplemented or superseded in A.L.R., in A.L.R.2d, or in A.L.R.3d; an A.L.R.2d annotation may be textually supplemented or superseded in A.L.R.2d or in A.L.R.3d. To locate superseding and supplementing annotations that appear in A.L.R.2d or 3d, consult the "Annotation Historical Table" at the back of the *A.L.R.2d & 3d Quick Index* volume, supplemented in the *front* pocket part. See Illustration 21. To determine whether an A.L.R. annotation has been superseded or supplemented in the A.L.R. series, you must also check the current pamphlet for the A.L.R. supplemental service, because the "Annotation Historical Table" cites only to superseding and supplemental annotations appearing in A.L.R.2d or 3d.

---

15. The publishers also provided substantial digest systems as finding aids for the first two A.L.R. series, but the Quick Index volumes now provide the advantages of the digest-style topical outline organization without the bulk of the digests created by inclusion of headnote squibs from the selectively reported cases.

118 ALR   SUPPLEMENTAL DECISIONS   402

Ga.—Fidelity & Deposit Co. v G. I. W., Inc. 125 Ga App 829, 189 SE2d 130
Hawaii—Honolulu Roofing Co. v F. 426 P2d 298
Ill.—Chicago Bridge & Iron Co. v R. Ins. Co. (App) 245 NE2d 127
Chicago Bridge & Iron Co. v R. I. Co. 264 NE2d 134
La.—Bailey v R. E. H. Const. Co. (App) 205 So 2d 503
Levingston Supply Co. v D & M M. C. Inc. (App) 211 So 2d 414
Fireman's Fund Am. Ins. Companies v M. (App) 253 So 2d 571
Md.—Montgomery Co. Bd. of Ed. to Use of Carrier Corp. v G. C. Co. 225 A2d 448
Peerless Ins. Co. v B. of C. C. for P. G 237 A2d 15
Mass.—J. P. Smith Co. v W. C. Co. 233 NE2d 723
American Air Filter Co. v I. B., Inc. 260 NE2d 718
Minn.—Hedberg & Sons Co. v N. A. C. Co. 144 NW2d 263 (citing anno)
Grazzini Bros. & Co. v B. C., Inc. 160 NW2d 259
Miss.—National Sur. Corp. v J. R.-M. C. 222 So 2d 119
Frazier v O S., Inc. 223 So 2d 661 (citing anno)
Mo.—La Salle Iron Works Inc. v L. 410 SW2d 87 (citing anno)
Mont.—Treasure State Industries. Inc. v L. 443 P2d 22
Carl Weissman & Sons, Inc. v S. P. F. 448 P2d 740
C. E. Mitchell and Sons v D. 511 P2d 316
Neb.—Ritzau v W. C. Co. 214 NW2d 244
Nev.—Capriotti L. & A. Inc. v J. S. Co 440 P2d 386 (citing anno)
N. M.—S. ex rel. State Elec. Supply Co v M. 444 P2d 978
Employment Security Comm. v C. R D. C. Co., Inc. 462 P2d 608 (citing anno)
N. Y.—Scales-Douwes Corp. v P. R. Corp. 30 App Div 2d 682, 292 NYS2d 210
Bogner-Seitel Lumber Co. v I. Co. of N. A. 31 App Div 2d 575, 294 NYS2d 931
Frontier Excavating, Inc. v S. C. Co. 30 App Div 2d 487, 294 NYS2d 994
United States Steel Corp. (Certified Industries Div.) v C. C. Corp. 55 Misc 2d 946, 286 NYS 2d 743
Honeywell, Inc. v T. S. M., Inc. 60 Misc 2d 1049, 304 NYS2d 330
N. C.—West Durham Lumber Co. v A. C. & Sur. Co. 184 SE2d 399 (citing anno)
N. D.—Kinney Elec. Mfg. Co. v M. E. Co. 149 NW2d 69
Or.—S. ex rel. Virginia Glass Products Corp. v G. F. Ins. Co. 460 P2d 858
Pa.—County Comrs. of Tioga Cty. v C. D. Inc. 266 A2d 749 (citing anno)
S. D.—State for Use and Benefit of J. D. Evans Equipment Co. v J. 160 NW2d 637
Tenn.—J. A. Jones Const. Co. v L. B. Inc. (App) 419 SW2d 186
Air Temperature, Inc. v M. (App) 469 SW2d 495

Heglar v M. C., Inc. (App) 487 SW2d 312
Tex.—Graham v S. A. M. & S. Corp. (Civ App) 418 SW2d 303
Trinity Universal Ins. Co. v B., Inc. 435 SW2d 849
American Indem. Co. v D.-C. P. M. Co. (Civ App) 508 SW2d 944
Va.—Contee Sand & Gravel Co. v R. Ins. Co. 166 SE2d 290
Joseph F. Hughes & Co. v G. H. R. Corp. 175 SE2d 413
Wash.—Beardmore Heavy Hauling & Crane Service v M. 71 Wash 2d 273, 127 P2d 975

---

118 ALR 106–120
Supplemented 61 ALR2d 1445✦

---

118 ALR 124–132
Ark.—North Little Rock Urban Renewal Agency v V. B., 483 SW2d 223
Cal.—Karbelnig v B. 244 Cal App 2d 333, 53 Cal Rptr 335
La.—Blanchard v S. B. of L. Inc. (App) 305 So 2d 748

---

118 ALR 138–148
U. S.—U. S v McCorkle (CA7 Ill) 511 F2d 477
Ark.—Stout v S. 244 Ark 676, 426 SW2d 800
Colo.—Mathis v P. 448 P2d 633
Conn.—S. v Savage, 290 A2d 221 (citing anno)
Ill.—Johnson v Cunningham (App) 244 NE2d 205
N. J.—S. v Wade, 99 NJ Super 550, 240 A2d 689
Or.—S. v Kessler, 458 P2d 432
S. C.—S. v Bailey, 170 SE2d 376
Tex.—Day v S. (Crim) 451 SW 2d 508

---

118 ALR 155–166
Superseded 41 ALR2d 1263✦

---

118 ALR 170–177
Conn.—Chambers v N. H. 31 Conn Supp 362, 331 A2d 347
Ind.—Re Terry, 323 NE2d 192
Iowa—S. v Bartz, 224 NW2d 632

---

118 ALR 215–232
Superseded 18 ALR3d 978✦

---

118 ALR 242–259
Superseded 63 ALR2d 5, 63 ALR 2d 108 and 63 ALR2d 184✦

---

118 ALR 269–274
N. Y.—Re Kaufman's Will, 46 App Div 2d 857, 361 NYS2d 179
Re Center's Will, 61 Misc 2d 193, 304 NYS2d 944
Pa.—Re Estate of Rosenblum, 328 A2d 158 (citing anno)

---

118 ALR 283–297
U. S.—F & D Property Co. v A. (CA Colo) 385 F2d 97
N. Y.—Nathan's Famous, Inc. v F. Inc. 70 Misc 2d 452, 333 NYS2d 708

---

118 ALR 302–313
Supplemented 149 ALR 1150✦

---

118 ALR 324–331
Superseded, in so far as it discusses state taxes, in 73 ALR 2d 157✦
Supplemented 150 ALR 1268✦

---

118 ALR 334–338
Superseded 39 ALR3d 1311✦

---

118 ALR 386–387
N. Y.—Miles v B. of C. 76 Misc 2d 623, 351 NYS2d 513

---

118 ALR 393–397
Supplemented 147 ALR 632✦

---

118 ALR 401–411
U. S.—Hunt v Y. (DC Pa) 264 F Supp 490
U. S. v Noble (DC NY) 269 F Supp 814
Tex.—Gallegos v C. (Civ App) 417 SW2d 347
Davis v D. (Civ App) 507 SW2d 841
Utah—Whitney v W. 25 Utah 2d 202, 479 P2d 469

---

118 ALR 425–458
For annotations on various specific aspects of the problem treated, see ALR Digests Negligence §§ 62–90.

---

118 ALR 462–474
U. S.—Mirro-Dynamics Corp. v U. S. (CA Cal) 374 F2d 14
Stephens, Inc. v U. S. (CA Ark) 464 F2d 53
Stephens, Inc. v U. S. (DC Ark) 321 F Supp 1159
Midland-Ross Corp. v U. S. (DC Ohio) 352 F Supp 1287

---

118 ALR 481–485
Superseded 32 ALR2d 1270✦

---

118 ALR 506–521
Supplemented 128 ALR 1126✦

---

118 ALR 530–533
U. S.—Traynor v W. (DC Pa) 342 F Supp 455
Colo.—Stroth v A. R. & M. H. Corp. of C. (App) 530 P2d 989
La.—Universal C. I. T. Corp. v F. (App) 201 So 2d 12
Md.—Lazorcak v F. 327 A2d 477

---

118 ALR 543–554
Ga.—Smith v B. 231 Ga 39, 200 SE2d 95
Idaho—Mattson v B. 448 P2d 201 (citing anno)
Ill.—Felton v C. (App) 238 NE2d 191
Gillson v G. M. & O. R. Co. 246 NE2d 269
Mo.—Houlihan v S. F. M. A. Ins. Co. (App) 441 SW2d 58
Okla.—Oller v H., 441 P2d 356
Wash.—Bombardi v P. A. & TV C. 9 Wash App 797, 515 P2d 540

✦**When Supplemented see later Note and Blue Book under caption of later Note**
[Supp Dec]

ILLUSTRATION 20.

Page from *A.L.R. Blue Book of Supplemental Decisions*

ANNOTATION HISTORY TABLE

ANNOTATIONS FROM AMERICAN LAW REPORTS
(1st or 2d Series) SUPPLEMENTED OR
SUPERSEDED IN ALR2d, ALR3d OR ALR FEDERAL
[For ALR 1st Series annotations supplemented or superseded in ALR Volumes 1–175 (First Series) consult the latest issue of the ALR Blue Book]

1 ALR 148–149 Superseded 74 ALR2d 828	**2 ALR 6–36** Supplemented 49 ALR2d 982	**3 ALR 312–323** Superseded 24 ALR2d 194
1 ALR 222–264 Subdiv VIII superseded 71 ALR2d 1140	**2 ALR 61–67** Superseded 14 ALR3d 783	**3 ALR 610–612** Superseded 12 ALR2d 611
1 ALR 329–331 Superseded 36 ALR2d 861	**2 ALR 225–236** Supplemented 41 ALR2d 1263	**3 ALR 824–829** Superseded 13 ALR3d 848
1 ALR 343–349 Superseded 51 ALR2d 1404	**2 ALR 345–347** Superseded 44 ALR2d 1242	**3 ALR 833–844** Superseded 22 ALR3d 1346

ILLUSTRATION 21.

Excerpt from Annotation History Table
A.L.R. Series
A.L.R.2d and 3d Quick Index

The existence of a superseding or supplementing annotation may be discovered as part of the initial search of the annotation system (for example, through checking both Quick Index volumes for the A. L.R. series). An independent check then becomes a double-check step. The independent check is even more important when you find a citation to an annotation through another source (for example, in a treatise), particularly to an annotation in the first series.

Because Am.Jur.2d cross-references to the A.L.R. series, use of that encyclopedia in the preliminary analysis phase may alert you to the existence of a relevant annotation. Even if you used Am.Jur.2d and failed to find an annotation cited, a check of the Quick Indexes is wise, because you could have missed an annotation citation. An in-point annotation, particularly one of the more recent ones in A.L.R. 2d or 3d, may substantially shorten a search for relevant precedents.

The publishers of the American Law Reports also publish two other annotated reports that are of great value for research on a question governed by federal law, *A.L.R. Federal* and *Lawyers' Edition*. Until 1969 the various A.L.R. series already described covered both state and federal law. In that year, however, *A.L.R. Federal* (A.L.R.Fed.) was initiated to cover federal law development exclusively. It has a Quick Index volume (supplemented by a front pocket

part) that is especially useful because it also indexes material in the A.L.R. and *Lawyers' Edition* series and in Am.Jur.2d. Its annotations will be supplemented through back pocket parts in the volumes in which the annotations appear. *Lawyers' Edition*, on the other hand, is a long-established series. It is one of the unofficial reporters of United States Supreme Court opinions, discussed *supra* in Section 7C. In the first series (L.Ed.), short notes were appended to the reprinted opinions; these annotations became longer and longer. In the second series (L.Ed.2d) these now comprehensive annotations collecting federal court opinions, together with summaries of counsel's briefs in the reported cases, appear at the back of each volume. Annotations in both series can be found most easily through the *Federal Quick Index* volume. Annotations in the first thirty-one volumes of the second series are supplemented in *L.Ed.2d Later Case Service*, a blue volume with a pocket part supplement. Annotations in volume 32 of the second series and thereafter are supplemented in pocket parts in the backs of the volumes in which the annotations appear. The pocket-part supplements also incorporate a useful citator service, described in the foreword to each pocket supplement. The usefulness of the annotations in the first series is impaired by lack of a regular supplementation service, although supplementing annotations have been published for some of them. Any supplementing annotation can be found by checking an L.Ed. annotation citation in the "Annotation History Table" in the dark red *Lawyers Edition Index to Annotations* volume.

Alternative (4)—Using a Shepard's Citator

State court opinions reported in the National Reporter System can be Shepardized in the appropriate Shepard's regional-Reporter edition as well as in a state edition, permitting you to ascertain whether courts of other jurisdictions have cited relevant mandatory state precedents. Note that before you can Shepardize in a regional-Reporter edition, you must have the Reporter citations for the state opinions that you wish to Shepardize *and* you must have the relevant headnote numbers from the Reporter reprints of the opinions. (The headnote numbers in the Reporter volumes will differ from those in the official report of the opinions.)

The by-products of Shepardizing in a regional-Reporter edition are more limited than the by-products of a state Shepard's search. In addition to finding citing opinions, you can find citations only to the annotated reports and the *American Bar Association Journal*. See Illustration 22.

Double-Check Search. Unless you find a large number of in-point persuasive precedents by using one of the alternative sources just described, you should do a double-check search in at least one other source to be certain that you have not overlooked relevant

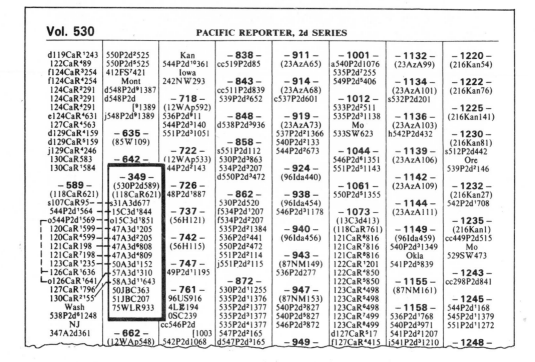

ILLUSTRATION 22.

Page from *Shepard's Pacific Reporter Citations*

Citations under page 589 are for opinions wherein *Smith v. Lewis* is cited. Superimposed alongside for comparison are the citations for the same opinion from *Shepard's California Citator*. Parallel or other citations to the same cases are connected with dotted lines.

precedents. For this double-check search, do not use a source produced by the same publisher that produced the alternative source that you first used. If you find few or no in-point precedents, you may have to work your way through each of the alternatives.

Bring Your Search Down To Date. Your search for persuasive precedents should be brought down to date through the General Digest pamphlets (described *supra* in this section) that post-date the most recent supplement you have used (assuming you have not already used the General Digest) and through advance sheets published after the last General Digest pamphlet. Thus, if you wish to do a complete search on a question of state law, you must check post-General Digest advance sheets for each Reporter unit [16]—a minimum of one-half hour of flipping through pages of the miniature digests ap-

16. To limit the number of advance sheets through which you must search, check the first page of the latest General Digest pamphlet for the table headed, "DIGESTING THE DECISIONS of the following volumes of reporters." From that table you can identify for each of the National Reporter units the last volume and page covered by that General Digest pamphlet.

pearing in the Reporter advance sheets. Such a search will be necessary when you are working, for example, with a problem in a new or rapidly changing subject area or on a scholarly project. (On a federal question, a search of the advance sheets reporting federal court opinions will not be necessary for this step of your research if you have already conducted such a search in looking for mandatory precedents.)

If you are researching a problem involving an important federal question, you may wish to carry your search into a looseleaf reporter, *CCH United States Supreme Court Bulletin*, in which recent opinions of the United States Supreme Court may appear earlier than in advance sheets. A unique periodical, *United States Law Week* (U.S.L. W.), "Supreme Court section," also distributes recent opinions of the Supreme Court earlier than do publishers of advance sheets, though not as quickly as the CCH reporter. In addition, each of these looseleaf publications has an index of cases filed on the docket of the Supreme Court and continues to give information about each case until it is disposed of, for example, whether certiorari is granted or denied and whether a case has been argued orally. Each case index must be used in connection with another index. The case index gives the docket number for each case, and the Docket Number Table in U.S. L.W. or the Status Table in the CCH reporter shows the page or pages whereon the case is mentioned.

Finally, persuasive precedents on which you intend to rely must be Shepardized to determine whether subsequent treatment by the deciding court has destroyed, weakened, or enhanced them.

SECTION 7F. STEP 4: THE SEARCH FOR REFINEMENTS OF YOUR ANALYSIS

STEP 4. The Search for Refinements of Your Analysis. The fourth step should take you into materials that will support or show the errors of the doctrinal approach or approaches of courts. As a minimum, it should include a search of the Index to Legal Periodicals. **The library catalog may help you to identify additional sources. For many problems, a search of nonlegal materials will be justified. Government documents, federal or state, may provide statistical and other data.**

By the time you reach this phase of your search, you should have at least a reasonably sound doctrinal basis for an answer to your question. By "doctrinal" basis is meant an understanding of how courts have dealt with your problem area and an evaluation of an appropriate selection of court opinions at least in terms of the consistency of the courts' reasoning and the validity of their discussion of precedents. Of course, a secondary-search source for one of the preceding research steps, enlightened court opinions, or your own imagination may have suggested criticisms of and approaches at variance with existing precedents. Whether or not this is your experi-

ence, the final step in your search and analysis should focus on a search for such criticisms and possible variant approaches or for non-doctrinal support in secondary sources. In actual practice, you will frequently look for such refinements concurrently with your search for persuasive precedents. Available to you as a starting point of search for these types of refinements of your analysis are many legal periodicals dealing with almost every conceivable aspect of law, its development, its applications, its shortcomings, and its future. Through preceding research steps, you may have found citations to relevant periodical material. If not, or even if you have, you can search for relevant material in periodicals through one of the indexes to legal periodicals.

A large number of the legal periodicals referred to are produced through the law schools in the form of law reviews (or law journals). A law review is a periodical produced by law students, frequently with only minimal assistance from faculty members. A typical review includes four basic types of materials, which are also representative of the types of materials found in most other legal periodicals:

> Leading articles—signed articles written by legal educators, practitioners, judges, or scholars of other disciplines (the author's name and background are usually indicated at the beginning of an article).
>
> Comments or Notes—student-written articles.
>
> Recent developments—variously titled Recent Developments, Recent Cases, Casenotes, or Case Comments—shorter student articles discussing recently decided cases or recent legislation.
>
> Book reviews.

These materials usually appear in the individual issues of the reviews in the order in which they are described above. (Note, however, that the issues for a one or two year period will then be bound together in a hardback volume.)

The student (and other) material appearing in reviews is frequently of very high quality. In large part, this is a result of the production process. Although the initial preparation of a student work may be the primary responsibility of a single student, on the better reviews the final product is the result of intensive editing and criticism and searching review by one or more revisers or editors, assuring that every possible aspect of the subject area has been considered and researched and that the writing is precise and concise. Unfortunately, this process is not followed on all reviews, and this process sometimes functions poorly for even the best of the reviews. Thus, the skepticism about accuracy of secondary materials that you should by now have developed must extend to the review materials as well as to other legal materials.

There are many types of periodicals other than reviews. One large category is bar association material, ranging from superficial and provincial small newspapers to the sleek *American Bar Association Journal.* Many commercial and scholarly periodicals deal with specialized areas of the law.

Indexes to legal periodicals

The most frequently used index is the *Index to Legal Periodicals.* Begun in 1908, and then indexing a modest seventeen periodicals, it now indexes in excess of four hundred titles. Most of the indexed periodicals are published in the United States, but also included are some published in the English language in other countries. Unless you are searching for local precedent, the non-United States publications are as valuable a source of ideas and information as are those published in this country. (A complementary index, the *Index to Foreign Legal Periodicals,* was begun in 1960 to index selected foreign periodicals, including many that are not printed in the English language.)

Another index to English-language periodicals of value if you are interested in the historical aspects of a problem is the *Jones-Chipman Index.* The first two volumes index selected materials appearing in legal, political, economics, and sociology periodicals—the first volume covering 1786 to 1886 and the second, 1887 through 1899. Thereafter, four more volumes were published to cover only legal periodicals for the periods 1898–1907, 1908–1922, 1923–1932, and 1933–1937.

Finally, note that individual periodicals have indexes. A search of the cumulative index to a review produced locally, to a local bar association publication, or to a specialized publication in the subject area of your interest will be simpler than a search of one of the comprehensive indexes and may identify short articles or notes that are not indexed in the comprehensive indexes.

The first-mentioned *Index to Legal Periodicals* is the one most regularly used, and it is therefore the one with which you must be most familiar. This index originally appeared in semiannual pamphlets, then one-year pamphlets, and finally, since 1926, in the currently maintained three-year volumes. Brown paperback supplements are now published monthly, and cumulated into quarterly paperback supplements. These are then cumulated into annual volumes until a three-year sequence is completed and a three-year volume can be published. A mimeographed supplement for the period between monthly supplements is also available in many law libraries.

Subject approach to the index: Because you will usually be interested in the most recent periodical material available, you should start your search for periodical material with the most recent three-year volume, then work forward through all available supplements. You can then search backwards through prior three-year volumes if

this seems appropriate. Essentially, you will be using a "topic" approach. The topics that you may wish to check can be identified from the "List of Subject Headings" appearing in the front of the one-year and three-year volumes.

Two shortcomings of the index should be noted. Articles and other materials are indexed under only one or two general topics, requiring that you select your topics with care. Additionally, titles of articles frequently do not adequately describe content, requiring that you scan articles with titles even remotely suggestive of your problem area.

Case approach to the index: You will be searching for recent development material when you use the case approach to the index, that is, a casenote or case comment focused on a relevant opinion. Since recent development material is usually published within a year of the date of the opinion discussed, you need check the table of cases sections of only the index volume or volumes covering the year of decision and the immediately following year. (Cases were not indexed prior to the 1917 volume, but volume 3 of the *Jones-Chipman Index,* discussed earlier in this section, does include a case table for the period from 1898 through 1907.)

Prior to 1963, recent development material was also indexed by title in the subject index of the *Index to Legal Periodicals;* thus, in the earlier volumes one may discover citations to all relevant casenotes through the subject index even without prior knowledge of the existence or relevance of the noted cases. Currently, however, for very short notes or comments, only the names of the cases noted are listed at the end of each appropriate subject listing.[17] Therefore, in recent volumes it is necessary to use the table of cases section for all possibly noteworthy cases or else to scan the case names collected at the end of each relevant subject listing in addition to using the subject approach if one wishes to collect all notes and comments on a given case.

Author approach to the index: The author approach will be appropriate if, for example, you are interested in the writings of a particular person because you have found that he or she takes a distinctive approach in your general problem area. Prior to volume 13 of the index, authors of articles were listed in a separate section, but they are now indexed with the subject headings. The complete titles of published articles and the citations are not listed under the authors' names, however—only the subject heading whereunder the title

17. For a statement of limitations on material indexed, see the "Prefatory Note" in any recent volume of the index.

is indexed and the initial letter in the title to facilitate finding the title when you turn to the indicated subject heading, thus:

Hardman, D. Juvenile Delin (D)

Book reviews: A book review of a secondary authority may be of assistance in evaluating that authority or in furnishing additional ideas in the subject area. To find book reviews, you need check only the volume or volumes of the index covering a one- or two-year period following publication of the book in which you are interested. Book reviews are indexed by the name of the book author—until 1940 under the subject entry "Book Reviews" and since 1940 in a separate section appearing at the back of volumes and pamphlets.

Shepardizing periodical material

Material appearing in many of the major reviews, the *American Bar Association Journal,* and a few other scholarly and commercial periodicals may be Shepardized in *Shepard's Law Review Citations.* Through this unit you can find post-1957 court opinions and other periodicals that cite, for example, a particularly helpful article, if the article was published subsequent to 1947.

Other legal materials

No detailed listing for this category can be suggested. What will be useful will depend upon the nature of your problem. The law library catalog will be your point of entry.

Nonlegal materials

Some of the most useful nonlegal periodicals (that is, those not written predominantly by and for law-trained persons) are indexed in the *Index to Periodical Articles Related to Law,* consisting of bound volumes covering 1958–68 and 1969–73, with quarterly supplements. It indexes articles from political science, economics, medical, sociology, and other periodicals.

You are not limited to indexes and periodicals available through the law library. The materials from which you can build acceptable analyses and arguments are limited only by your imagination in seeking them out and your own realistic evaluation of their persuasiveness. This view has been succinctly stated by Professor Karl Llewellyn:

> But surely, in regard to description of fact, or of economic or social conditions or events, or of historical matters, or of the state of current opinion or current use of language at any time, or of business practice, or the like, the literature of the social disciplines is materially more likely to be both pertinent, accurate and relatively complete than is that

to be derived from the "law" books. The same university library offers all. How can one justify, in sense, consulting Webster or Fowler or Oxford about current or older usage in regard to the meaning of a word, and barring out a monograph on the practice or history of the clearinghouse or of marine insurance?

But the matter goes much further. Any effort at limitation to "legal" literature has for now some forty years been growing into something so arbitrary and inept as to verge on farce. Look at today's "legal" literature, the law review especially, but the modern good text as well, and you find the footnotes and the argument shot through with social discipline material like double-colored silk. No workable rule can keep such material out of the brief.[18]

Professor Llewellyn was discussing use of nonlegal materials at the appellate level of argument. Such materials may be of equal value at every stage of analysis of a problem, however. For example, is there no clearly controlling mandatory precedent and only confusion in the opinions of other courts? Perhaps relevant social, economic, or other data will persuade the trial judge to accept one approach rather than another. Or, is there a clearly controlling mandatory precedent that is inconsistent with such relevant data? Perhaps you can conclude that though you will inevitably lose in the trial court, the controlling appellate court might be persuaded to overrule the precedent on appeal.[19]

Survey, statistical, and other informational data are often collected for congressional and state legislative committees and for and by both federal and state commissions, task forces, and other groups specially appointed to study and make recommendations regarding identified problem areas. When published as government documents, these studies can be found through sources discussed in Section 8F, *infra,* particularly the *Monthly Catalog of United States Government Publications* and the *Legislative Research Checklist.*

18. The Common Law Tradition: Deciding Appeals 234 (1960), published by Little, Brown and Company, Copyright 1960 by Karl N. Llewellyn. Reproduced with permission of the copyright holder.

19. For an example of such use of nonlegal material, *see e. g.,* the reprint of a statement by social scientists that was attached as an Appendix to Appellants' Briefs filed with the United States Supreme Court in the School Segregation Cases, *The Effects of Segregation and the Consequences of Desegregation: A Social Science Statement,* 37 Minn.L.Rev. 427 (1953). For a discussion of the origin of this type of use of nonlegal materials before appellate courts in what is now called a "Brandeis Brief" and practical suggested limitations on use of nonlegal materials, see F. Wiener, Briefing and Arguing Federal Appeals 187–196 (1967). For expressed reservations about the future of such briefs, see Cahn, *Jurisprudence,* 30 N.Y.L.Rev. 150, 153–54 (1955). The remainder of the Cahn article discusses the shortcomings of the social science evidence in the School Segregation Cases.

NOTES

1. For a description of useful general (nonlegal) reference materials, see How to Find the Law, ch. 12 (M. Cohen ed. 7th ed. 1970).

2. If you Shepardize every mandatory opinion on which you intend to rely in a state Shepard's edition, you may identify some very recent mandatory opinions. Why must you nevertheless search recent advance sheets?

3. State and United States Shepard's case editions list citing Attorney General's opinions. What is an Attorney General's opinion? What is its authority value within the author's jurisdiction, mandatory or persuasive?

4. The suggestion has been made that for a double-check search for persuasive precedents, you should not use a source produced by the same publisher that published the source you initially used to search for persuasive precedents. What justification can you advance for this suggestion? Can you think of any other guidelines for choice of source for a double-check search?

5. It is sometimes suggested that lacking mandatory precedents, state courts find the opinions of neighboring-state courts more persuasive than those of other state courts. In an interesting analysis of authority cited by the California Supreme Court in opinions handed down during 1950, it was found that the other state courts most frequently cited by the California court were: New York, 127 (Court of Appeals, 57; lower courts, 70); Massachusetts, 36; Illinois, 28; Missouri, 25; Texas, 23; Minnesota, 21; Pennsylvania, 21; Washington, 21. Merryman, *The Authority of Authority,* 6 Stan.L.Rev. 613, 668–669 (1954). Since this listing does not suggest a preference for neighboring-state courts, what other factors may influence what courts will be cited? Perhaps the answer is, persuasiveness of particular opinions—not of particular courts. However, another researcher analyzed court opinions cited with approval during a period from June 1955 to April 1959 and concluded that the important factors leading to reliance on another court's opinions were the per capita income within the jurisdiction whose court's opinions were cited (jurisdictions having a high per capita income tend to spend more money on judicial personnel and institutions); the number of cases decided (the more cases a court decides, the more likely it is to cover a situation that comes before another court), and closeness of cultural contacts and common sectional problems. S. Nagel, The Legal Process from a Behavioral Perspective 61–62 (1969). If the courts in the state in which you ultimately practice appear to have geographical or other preferences, you will of course take account of them. For present purposes, guessing at possible preferences in choosing opinions to read may only lead you to ignore some relevant opinion.

Chapter 8

RESEARCH ON QUESTIONS GOVERNED BY STATUTES AND OTHER FORMS OF WRITTEN LAW

SECTION 8A. INTRODUCTION

STEP 1. The Search for Statutes or Other Written Law. The first step is always to determine whether there is any controlling or relevant written law. This step is usually directed toward finding statutes, and may require search for four basic types of material:

Statutes, in the controlling code or other available source.

Court opinions construing the relevant statutes, in an annotated code or other available source.

Secondary commentary, in periodicals, annotated reports, treatises or encyclopedias, or for court opinions construing similar legislation.

Legislative history materials.

The searches for both controlling statutes and construing opinions should be double-checked and brought down to date.

To simplify your introduction to legal research, discussion of the use of legislative materials has been deferred to this point. As already noted, however, the first rule of research is: Never assume the absence of relevant legislation.

Secondary sources used for preliminary analysis will often alert you when a problem area may present federal constitutional questions and will sometimes alert you when a problem area is affected by legislation. The encyclopedias and treatises discuss relevant federal legislation and uniform and other statutes generally in force throughout the states. Statutory problems are frequently covered in the annotation series that supplement *American Jurisprudence 2d,*

particularly *A.L.R. Federal*.   If a preliminary analysis source does not alert you to the existence of relevant legislation, you should, at a minimum check the controlling code or other commonly used statutory compilation for the controlling jurisdiction or problem area.   In your early problem research, until you gain familiarity with the scope of the federal legislative power, you may find it necessary to check both federal and state statutory sources.

Step 1 may require a search for forms of written law other than statutes, for example, constitutional requirements, court rules, or local legislation such as city or county ordinances.   In this chapter, however, Step 1 and its subsidiary steps will be described in detail with respect to a statutory search.   Basic statutory materials will also be described in detail.   The other types of searches and materials will then be dealt with more summarily in the concluding section.

A statutory search may have sub-branches.   Questions about what construction rules may be applied or about the authority value of some types of extrinsic legislative history material may lead you into an essentially common law search, following Step 2 and perhaps even Steps 3 and 4.   Should relevant statutes include a delegation of rulemaking authority, adjudicatory power, or licensing or other regulatory functions to an administrative agency or other executive body, relevant agency sources will have to be consulted.

SECTION 8B.   THE SEARCH FOR CONTROLLING OR RELEVANT STATUTES: CODES AND RELATED MATERIALS

The starting point for your search for controlling statutes may be the official *United States Code* or official compilation of statutes for the controlling state jurisdiction.[1]

The first official publication of statutes in collected form will usually be a volume or volumes commonly called "session laws," variously titled for the states (for example, "Public Laws," "Public Acts") and for the United States, in *Statutes at Large* (Stat.). These publications collect, chronologically, statutes enacted during a session of a state legislature or Congress.   Publication of this collec-

---

1.   If the official compilation of statutes is not current to within about a year, use of a more up-to-date annotated code or other unofficial source, discussed in the following Section 8D, may be more efficient.   For many areas of statutory law, the most efficient starting point will be a looseleaf service that collects relevant statutes, administrative rules and regulations, court opinions, and other sources for a subject area such as tax or labor law.   Looseleaf services are also de-scribed *infra* in Section 8D.   You may form some idea of the range of subject matters covered by the most commonly available services by checking the list thereof in the citation *Blue Book* at 95–99.   Some background knowledge of the statutory area is necessary for effective use of some of these services, because indexing tends to be based more on commonly used technical terms rather than on fact words.

tion of federal legislation is preceded by official slip laws (prints of the individual statutes as enacted and approved by the President). The slip laws are distributed within four to six weeks of enactment, for use until a new *Statutes at Large* volume is published. A state may have slip laws and preliminary pamphlet editions of its new laws, or a privately maintained legislative service may make legislation available in collected form shortly after enactment.

Until they expire or are repealed, superseded by new legislation, or declared ineffective by a court, the *Statutes at Large* and the state session laws are "the law" (more properly, "best evidence of the law" —the enacted, signed, and enrolled acts are "the law"). The volumes in which they are printed contain subject indexes and other search aids. (For example, the most recent *Statutes at Large* volumes contain a subject index, a list of bills enacted into law by bill number, a listing of the new laws by public law number, and numerous tables, including a guide to the legislative history of bills enacted and tables of prior laws directly affected or referred to by the new laws contained therein.) Nevertheless, use of session law or *Statutes at Large* volumes as a starting point for a search for possibly relevant statutes still in force would require a search of the index and tables of each volume, with a danger that an act, a repeal, or an amendment might be overlooked despite a conscientious search.

The unwieldiness of the *Statutes at Large* and session law publications as research sources demonstrated the necessity for some convenient reorganization and republication of laws currently in force in more orderly and readily findable form. This form is the compilation commonly known as a "code" or some variant form such as "Revised Statutes," "Compiled Laws" or "Consolidated Laws," all hereinafter called "codes."

The first such official compilation of United States statutes was the *Revised Statutes of the United States.* The compilers of this code (like codifiers generally) analyzed statutes appearing in the *Statutes at Large*, identified those of general application, ascertained which had been repealed or amended, and then grouped those still in force under 74 subject matters called Titles. (Sections were numbered section 1, title 1, through section 5601, title 74; hence, in citing these *Revised Statutes*, you need only cite to a section, thus: Rev.Stat. § 10 (1875).) Congress then enacted this entire code into law, repealing the prior legislation that had been incorporated into the code.[2] Despite careful and conscientious work by the compilers, however, the *Revised Statutes* contained many errors. Congress immediately enacted a new law correcting a long list of errors, then found it neces-

---

2. Rev.Stat. § 5596 (1875): "All acts of Congress passed prior to said first day of December one thousand eight hundred and seventy-three, any portion of which is embraced in any sec- tion of said revision, are hereby repealed, and the section applicable thereto shall be in force in lieu thereof * * * "

sary to enact another law correcting another long list of errors.   In 1877, Congress authorized a new edition of *Revised Statutes*, to incorporate the correctional and other legislation adopted subsequent to the coverage of the first edition.   The following year it adopted an act providing that the new edition should not "preclude reference to, nor control, in case of any discrepancy, the effect of any original act as passed by Congress since the first day of December, eighteen hundred and seventy-three." [3]   Therefore, this second edition, the 1878 edition, never became "law" in the sense that the first edition did.

In 1926 Congress approved a new official code, the *United States Code*.   Again, however, Congress did not enact the code into law and repeal the prior legislation from which it was drawn.   Rather, it provided:

> In all courts, tribunals, and public offices of the United States * * * (a) The matter set forth in the Code * * * shall establish prima facie the laws of the United States, general and permanent in their nature, in force on the 7th day of December, 1925; but nothing in this Act shall be constructed as repealing or amending any such law, or as enacting as new law any matter contained in the Code. In case of any inconsistency arising through omission or otherwise between the provisions of any section of this Code and the corresponding portion of legislation heretofore enacted effect shall be given for all purposes whatsoever to such enactments.[4]

Congress has since enacted some of the titles into law, however, and will continue to enact other titles from time to time.   Thus, today, Titles 1, 3, 4, 5, 6, 9, 10, 13, 14, 17, 18, 23, 28, 32, 35, 37, 38, 39, and 44 are "law" [5] in the sense that they supersede the *Statutes at*

---

3.   20 Stat. 27 (1878).

4.   44 Stat. 1 (Part 1, 1926).   See also 1 U.S.C. § 204(a) (1976).

5.   These titles cover the following subjects: General Provisions; The President; Flag and Seal, Seat of Government, and The States; Government Organization and Employees; Official and Penal Bonds; Arbitration; Armed Forces; Census; Coast Guard; Copyrights; Crimes and Criminal Procedure; Highways; Judiciary and Judicial Procedure; National Guard; Patents; Pay and Allowances of the Uniformed Services; Veterans' Benefits; Postal Service; and Public Printing and Documents.   Title 34 (Navy) was eliminated by enactment of Title 10 (Armed Forces).   The Internal Revenue Code of 1954, appearing as Title 26 of the *United States Code*, has also been enacted in the form of a separate code.   Congress has provided, " * * * [T]hat whenever titles of [U.S.C.] shall have been enacted into positive law the text thereof shall be legal evidence of the laws therein contained, in all the courts of the United States, the several States, and the Territories and insular possessions of the United States." 1 U.S.C. § 204(a) (1970).   The distinction between the unenacted prima facie titles of the code and the enacted titles has not always been appreciated.   *See* Abell v. United States, 207 Ct.Cl. 207, 518 F.2d 1369, 1376 n. 4 (1975).   *But see* United States v. Welden, 377 U.S. 95, 98 n. 4 (1964).

Large and *Revised Statutes* sections from which they were drawn. The titles enacted into positive law are identified in the Preface to Code and Code supplement volumes.[6]

State code histories are similarly, and sometimes more frequently, checkered with adopted and authorized-but-not-adopted versions. Adding to the confusion is another variety—the unadopted, unauthorized commercial or private compilation. Thus, for example, the Washington reports are sprinkled with citations to the *Code of 1881, Ballinger's Code, Hill's Statutes and Codes, Remington & Ballinger's Code, Remington's Code, Remington's Compiled Statutes, Pierce's Code,* and *Remington's Revised Statutes.* Only the *Code of 1881* was enacted into law, however. The subsequent compilations were at first privately produced, though some were ultimately approved by the legislature. In 1950, the legislature adopted the *Revised Code of Washington* as a prima facie statement of the law, but also stated: "In case of any omissions, or any inconsistency between any of the provisions of said code and the laws existing immediately preceding this enactment, the previously existing laws shall control."[7] The subsequent history of the code resembles that of both the *Revised Statutes* of the United States and the *United States Code.* There was immediate and substantial dissatisfaction with the code because of errors and because of liberties taken by the codifiers in changing language and punctuation. Therefore, the legislature in 1951 provided for a permanent Statute Law Committee to revise the Code. Many of the titles have now been enacted by the legislature as corrected. The remaining titles have been restored to the session law language by the Statute Law Committee.

From the foregoing description of two representative code histories, the importance of ascertaining the status of a state code or other compilation when you first use it should be apparent. A preface or other introduction will often describe the status and history of the code. If it has not been enacted into law but has been legislatively approved as only a prima facie statement of the law, the language of the underlying law—the session law—may control if, for example, code language does not accord with the original language of an act. If a code or other form of compilation has not been legislatively approved as a prima facie statement of the law of a jurisdiction, then even citation of it to the courts may be inappropriate. Nevertheless, you may begin your search for controlling statutes in whatever code

6. Until the 93rd Congress, detailed information about the titles enacted into positive law was also provided in Table 5(a) of the *Statutes at Large* volumes 71 through 86. Beginning with volume 87 of the *Statutes at Large,* however, that table and several other informational tables were discontinued because they were thought to be of limited usefulness and because other research aids existed for some of the materials. 87 Stat. B1 (1973).

7. Wash.Rev.Code § 1.04.021 (1956).

or other compilation of statutes is available for the governing jurisdiction.

Statutory compilations may be divided into titles or articles (subjects), with further subdivisions into chapters and sections. Thus, for example, the *United States Code* (U.S.C.) consists of 50 titles, each subdivided into chapters and then into sections.[8]

Codes and other compilations are indexed so that the index research approach can be used to find relevant or controlling provisions. Analyses and subanalyses—that is, listings of title, chapter, and section headings—are also commonly included. The topic research approach may then be used. Thus, in U.S.C., listings of titles and then of titles with chapter headings appear at the beginning of each code volume. Chapter headings are listed again at the beginning of each title, and section headings are listed at the beginning of each chapter. Both the index and topic approaches should be used, if available, to avoid missing relevant provisions. This double approach is particularly important for statutory research because statutes are generally indexed by *their* subject matter and language, not by the fact words that describe situations to which the statutes may be or have been applied. Thus, use of the TAPP (key facts) approach in an index to statutes may not be effective.

Specialized finding aids are also commonly provided. For example, the first volume of the U.S.C. general index contains a Table of Statutes by Popular Names, which sometimes permits quick finding of the code citation for statutes having a commonly used title, such as the Civil Rights Act of 1964 or the Consumer Credit Protection Act. Compilers of codes also usually prepare comprehensive parallel reference tables, providing convenient cross citations to and from prior forms of each section of the code. Thus, volume 11 of the U.S. C. contains tables, the most important one being Table III, which cross cites from *Statutes at Large* citations to U.S.C. citations. Such parallel reference tables have greater importance in states for which there have been numerous successive compilations, because citations in old court opinions must more frequently be traced to current citations.

Historical information about sources may be given at the beginnings of titles or other subdivisions or at the ends of sections. These historical notes may be meager for state statutes, but much significant information is provided in these notes in the federal code. Thus, concluding each U.S.C. section are citations to the source or sources of the section in the *Statutes at Large* (or *Revised Statutes*) and to any amending acts adopted subsequent thereto. Changes effected by

---

8. A citation of a U.S.C. section requires only the title and section subdivisions, *e. g.*, 5 U.S.C. § 10, with the date of the code edition in parentheses. Citation practice for the states varies. Basic statutory citation forms for all states are collected in the citation *Blue Book*, pages 104–42.

the cited amendments are briefly described in following fine print "Amendments" notes, with "Effective Dates" listed thereafter. Notes on "Savings Provisions" or "Repeals," may provide information about uncodified provisions that preserve pending governmental actions or preamendment or prerepeal rights, benefits, or responsibilities of individuals.   Changes in language and other codification history will be given in "Codification" notes.   Reviser's Notes may provide excellent legislative history.[9]   Cross references to related sections in the code may be listed.   Information about enforcement or administrative responsibilities may be provided in other notes headed "Enforcement," "Transfer of Functions" (under governmental reorganization plans), or "Delegation of Functions" (by the President). The variety of sometimes crucial information that may be provided in these fine-print notes following U.S.C. sections is such that you should always scan all the notes to consider possible relevance to your problem.

Methods of keeping codes current vary.   A new edition of U.S.C. is published every six years in order to incorporate newly enacted material into the appropriate titles in the basic code volumes.   The most recent edition, the 1976 edition, consists of several basic volumes and four general index volumes.   A new cumulative supplement volume is published annually.   Thus, during 1978, a search of the code will require use of the basic 1976 volumes and of Supplement I, cumulating and indexing changes from January 1977 to January 1978. Supplement II will include changes effected by 1978 legislation, and so on until the new 1982 edition is published, with all the changes of the prior six years incorporated into the basic code volumes. Amendatory legislation adopted beyond the date of the most recent code supplement must be found through the supplement to the *United States Code Annotated* or the *United States Code Service*, described in Section 8D, *infra*.

Some state codes are supplemented in separate volumes.   Others are supplemented by pocket parts.   Some are published in looseleaf form, permitting insertion of supplementing sheets at the beginning or end of each title and, ultimately, replacement of affected pages by reprinting.   Paperback editions permit frequent republication.   Supplementations may tend to run behind enactment of new and amendatory statutes so that it may be necessary to use pamphlet editions of session laws or private legislative services to find very recent changes and additions.   In some states, Shepard's statute citator, discussed in Section 8E, *infra*, may identify amending legislation before that legislation is otherwise generally published.

---

9. On the authority value of such notes, see United States v. National City Lines, Inc., 337 U.S. 78, 81 (1949).

SECTION 8C. ANALYSIS OF THE LANGUAGE OF RELEVANT STATUTES

Having found a possibly relevant statute and verified the accuracy of the language in the *Statutes at Large* or session laws if this seems necessary, you should analyze the language of the statute. This analysis will require, at a minimum:

Careful reading to ascertain whether the statute contains any ambiguous, inconsistent, or vague language, particularly in relation to your problem.

Checking any internal or external cross-reference citations to other statutory sections.

Examining the total act of which the statute is (or was) a part to ascertain whether the overall act contains a statement of purpose, construction guidelines, a definition section, or anything else that may shed light on the meaning of the section or sections in which you are interested.

The third part of the analysis of the statutory language may require further recourse to the *Statutes at Large* or session law source of a section or sections. Codifiers sometimes split up a single act—particularly older acts—and codify the individual sections in different titles or chapters of a code. The historical notes for a section in which you are interested and for preceding and following sections will reveal whether they all come from the same act or are drawn from diverse sources.

At some point in your analysis of the language of the relevant statute(s), you will want to identify the elements or conclusions that must be established to justify application of the statute to the problem you are researching—in written outline form if the statute is at all complex. You can then consider whether the facts of your problem satisfy these requirements. After this analysis you should be able to write tentative questions for further research if you conclude that your problem cannot be solved with certainty on the basis of the statutory language alone.

SECTION 8D. THE SEARCH FOR CONSTRUING OPINIONS AND SECONDARY COMMENTARY: ANNOTATED CODES AND LOOSELEAF SERVICES

Having completed your analysis of the language of relevant statutory sections and identified tentative questions for further research, you can then use the appropriate annotated code or other statutory annotations to find citations to relevant construing court opinions. Some annotated codes also provide citations to relevant secondary

discussions. If the source that you use does not provide such citations, or perhaps even if it does, you may wish to conduct an independent search for relevant secondary discussion in a looseleaf service, a treatise, the annotated reports, or legal periodicals. For federal statutes, you may consult the *Am.Jur.2d Table of Statutes and Rules* to find possible relevant discussions in that encyclopedia. For problems governed by state statutes, you may find opinions construing the same or similar statutes of other states through the American Digest System. For uniform statutes, *Uniform Laws Annotated*, discussed *infra* in this section, will be useful.

Should you have questions about construction rules or guidelines, the key number digest for the controlling jurisdiction will be a useful search tool. A good general starting point is J. Sutherland, Statutes and Statutory Construction (4th ed., C. Sands. ed., 1972), a four-volume currently supplemented treatise.

The most useful type of annotated code prints the code of a particular jurisdiction, together with the same section-by-section historical information and other research aids provided by the separately printed code. Headnote squibs for construing court opinions are collected following each section. If the opinions in which a section has been construed are numerous, the headnotes may be presented in a classification outline of descriptive headings, all preceded by a miniature index. Citations to relevant discussions in secondary sources may also be included. Index volumes and listings of title, chapter, and section headings in the annotation volumes permit use of the index and topic research approaches. Other forms of annotated codes vary primarily in providing only opinion citations, without headnote squibs, or providing varying historical and secondary citations.

If an annotated code is available, you may wonder why you should bother using an unannotated official code for the initial search for controlling statutes. It is wise procedure to begin your search and analysis of statutory language with the official code if one is available, because annotated codes are usually unofficial and statutory language may not be accurately reprinted therein. Additionally, when searching for statutory sections initially, you will find it easier to skim through the code sections, interrupted only by historical notes, than to skim through an annotated code with sections widely separated by extended opinion annotations. Even these advantages may not justify use of an official code, however, if it is substantially out of date.

United States Code Annotated

The *United States Code Annotated* (U.S.C.A.), published by West Publishing Company, is the classic form of annotated code. See Illustration 23. A similar form has been used for nineteen state statutory

Ch. 7 AID TO NEEDY FAMILIES 42 § 601

Library References

Social Security and Public Welfare
ℝ721.

C.J.S. Social Security and Public Welfare §§ 238, 239.

West's Federal Forms

Enforcement and review of decisions and orders of administrative agencies, see § 851 et seq.

Stays, see § 445 Comment.

Supreme Court,
    Jurisdiction on certificate, see § 321 et seq.
    Jurisdiction on writ of certiorari, see § 221 et seq.

SUBCHAPTER IV.—GRANTS TO STATES FOR AID AND SERVICES TO NEEDY FAMILIES WITH CHILDREN AND FOR CHILD-WELFARE SERVICES

Historical Note

1968 Amendment. Pub.L. 90–248, Title II, § 240(a), Jan. 2, 1968, 81 Stat. 911, provided for grants for child-welfare services in the heading of this subchapter.

1962 Amendment. Pub.L. 87–543, Title I, § 104(a)(1), July 25, 1962, 76 Stat. 185, substituted "Aid and Services to Needy Families with Children" for "Aid to Dependent Children" in the heading of this subchapter.

PART A.—AID TO FAMILIES WITH DEPENDENT CHILDREN

Historical Note

1968 Amendment. Pub.L. 90–248, Title II, § 240(b), Jan. 2, 1968, 81 Stat. 911, added part A heading.

Library References

Social Security and Public Welfare
ℝ191 et seq.
United States ℝ82.

C.J.S. Social Security and Public Welfare ℝ56 et seq.
C.J.S. United States § 122.

§ 601. Authorization of appropriations

For the purpose of encouraging the care of dependent children in their own homes or in the homes of relatives by enabling each State to furnish financial assistance and rehabilitation and other services, as far as practicable under the conditions in such State, to needy dependent children and the parents or relatives with whom they are living to help maintain and strengthen family life and to help such parents or relatives to attain or retain capability for the maximum self-support and personal independence consistent with the maintenance of continuing parental care and protection, there is authorized to be appropriated for each fiscal year a sum sufficient to carry out the purposes of this part. The sums made available under this section shall be used for making payments to States which have

39

ILLUSTRATION 23.

Pages from *United States Code Annotated*
(continued on following page)

42 § 601   PUBLIC HEALTH AND WELFARE   Ch. 7

submitted, and had approved by the Secretary, State plans for aid and services to needy families with children.

Aug. 14, 1935, c. 531, Title IV, § 401, 49 Stat. 627; 1946 Reorg.Plan No. 2, § 4, eff. July 16, 1946, 11 F.R. 7873, 60 Stat. 1095; 1953 Reorg.Plan No. 1, §§ 5, 8, eff. Apr. 11, 1953, 18 F.R. 2053, 67 Stat. 631; Aug. 1, 1956, c. 836, Title III, § 312(a), 70 Stat. 848; July 25, 1962, Pub.L. 87–543, Title I, § 104(a)(4), (c)(2), 76 Stat. 185, 186; Jan. 2, 1968, Pub.L. 90–248, Title II, § 241(b)(1), 81 Stat. 916.

Historical Note

1968 Amendment. Pub.L. 90–248, § 24(b)(1), substituted in first sentence "part" for "subchapter".

1962 Amendment. Pub.L. 87–543 substituted in the second sentence "aid and services to needy families with children" for "aid to dependent children", and inserted in the first sentence "and rehabilitation" following "financial assistance" and "or retain capability for" following "attain".

1956 Amendment. Act Aug. 1, 1956 restated the purpose to include encouragement of care of dependent children in their own homes or in the homes of relatives, and authorized services to needy dependent children and the parents or relatives to help maintain and strengthen family life and to help such parents or relatives to attain the maximum self-support and personal independence consistent with the maintenance of continuing parental care and protection.

Transfer of Functions. All functions of the Federal Security Administrator were transferred to the Secretary of Health, Education, and Welfare and all agencies of the Federal Security Agency were transferred to the Department of Health, Education, and Welfare by section 5 of 1953 Reorg.Plan No. 1, set out in the Appendix to Title 5, Government Organization and Employees. The Federal Security Agency and the office of Administrator were abolished by section 8 of 1953 Reorg.Plan No. 1.

"Administrator" was substituted for "Board" by 1946 Reorg.Plan No. 2. See note under section 902 of this title.

State Plans in Effect Jan. 1, 1968: Automatic Conformity to Amendments. Section 240(h) of Pub.L. 90–248 provided that: "Each State plan approved under title IV of the Social Security Act [this subchapter] as in effect on the day preceding the date of the enactment of this Act [Jan. 2, 1968] shall be deemed, without the necessity of any change in such plan, to have been conformed with the amendments made by subsections (a) and (b) of this section [amending heading of this subchapter and enacting heading of this part]."

State Plans in Effect July 25, 1962: Automatic Conformity to Amendments. Section 104(b) of Pub.L. 87–543 provided that: "Each State plan approved under title IV of the Social Security Act [this subchapter] and in effect on the date of the enactment of this Act [July 25, 1962] shall be deemed for purposes of such title [this subchapter], without the necessity of any change in such plan, to have been conformed with the amendments made by subsection (a) of this section [to sections 601 604, 606 608, 1202 and 1352 of this title]."

Legislative History. For legislative history and purpose of Act Aug. 1, 1956, see 1956 U.S.Code Cong. and Adm.News, p. 3877. See, also, Pub.L. 87–543, 1962 U.S.Code Cong. and Adm.News, p. 1943; Pub.L. 90–248, 1967 U.S.Code Cong. and Adm.News. p. 2834.

Library References

United States ⊜85.

C.J.S. United States § 123.

Code of Federal Regulations

Research, information and advisory service, see 42 CFR 206.1 et seq.

40

ILLUSTRATION 23.
(continuation)

(The statutory language and historical notes, excepting the last note on legislative history, are reprinted from the *United States Code*. Notes on decisions appear on pages not reproduced here.)

annotations.[10]   The form includes all the material described earlier in this section.   It reprints the U.S.C. sections with the same historical information as appears in the U.S.C.   In addition, U.S.C.A. includes citations to Attorney Generals' opinions; to legislative history, discussed in Section 8F, *infra*; and to administrative sources, discussed in Section 8G, *infra*.   Citations to secondary discussions are listed under a "Library References" heading, appearing in the basic volume in recently republished volumes and in the pocket-part supplements in the older volumes.   These references are to the key number digests and C.J.S. and occasionally to leading treatises.

The U.S.C.A. is supplemented annually with pocket parts and with intervening noncumulative paperback pamphlets.   Pending republication of a volume with a thick pocket part, the publishers will also occasionally issue a white "Supplementary Pamphlet" for that volume, including the supplementing material from the thick pocket part, and thereafter issue an annual pocket part cumulating material becoming available subsequent to the date of the "Supplementary Pamphlet."   The cover page of the pocket part then identifies the limits of its coverage.[11]   All the U.S.C.A. supplements include the text of new and amendatory legislation and headnote squibs on recent construing opinions.

Finding legislation enacted and opinions handed down after publication of the latest paperback supplement is a two-pronged search. First, the text of new legislation is printed in the paperback publication, *U.S.Code, Congressional and Administrative News* (U.S.Code Cong. & Ad.News), published monthly while Congress is in session. It has a cumulative subject index and a cumulative table of U.S.C. sections amended, repealed, and added.   Thus, you must check the cumulative subject index in the latest issue for entirely new legislation, and you can check the citations for the existing code sections in which you are interested in the cumulative table of affected U.S.C. sections for possible amendatory legislation.[12]   Second, possible recent

10. Arizona, California, Connecticut, Florida, Illinois, Iowa, Louisiana, Maine, Massachusetts, Michigan, Minnesota, Missouri, New Jersey, New York, Oklahoma, Pennsylvania, Texas, Washington, and Wisconsin.   The same form is used for the *District of Columbia Code Encyclopedia*, with encyclopedia-type commentary added.

11. For example, at this writing, such a supplementary pamphlet has been issued for the fourth volume of Title 29 (Labor Law), which was last republished in 1965.   The pamphlet carries supplementing material for the years 1965–75, and the annual pocket part issued for the volume will collect

material subsequent to 1975 until the volume is republished.   The coverage page of the pocket part carries the prominent message:

CONNECTS WITH
SUPPLEMENTARY PAMPHLET 1965
to 1975

12. Even the U.S.Code Cong. & Ad. News pamphlets do not always include the most recent acts of Congress.   Occasionally, the text of significant new legislation may appear earlier in *United States Law Week* (General Law Volume), described in Section 7E, *supra*.   The *CCH Congressional Index*, a looseleaf service, can

construing opinions must be found through Cumulative Statutes Construed tables that appear in the front of National Reporter advance sheets. As a minimum, you must check these tables in the last issue of each F.2d and F.Supp. advance-sheet volume issued subsequent to the advance sheets covered by the most recent supplement to U.S.C. A.,[13] and the cumulative table in the latest *Supreme Court Reporter* advance sheet.

United States Code Service

The *United States Code Service* (U.S.C.S.) is the annotated code for federal statutes published by The Lawyers Co-Operative Publishing Co./Bancroft-Whitney Co. It is a republication of an earlier service called the *Federal Code Annotated*, with ongoing revision and addition of new research features. Some of the volumes are updated republications of the earlier service. These volumes carry red name labels on the spine and front cover with a *Federal Code Annotated* subtitle. Other volumes have been revised and republished with new research features. The revised volumes carry blue name labels on the spine and front cover with a *Lawyers Edition* subtitle. Volumes for a dozen titles of the United States Code have been revised and republished as of the date of this writing, and revision and republication will continue until the complete service has been revised.

The U.S.C.S. contains most of the common and useful research features. It reprints all sections of the *United States Code* with section-by-section historical information and cross-references, but it also uses *Statutes at Large* language if the codifiers have changed that language in any respect (for example, to change a section number from the original act to the section number assigned for the code). It provides a headnote digest of construing court opinions for each section, but citations in revised volumes are selective, that is, the digests include headnotes for only those opinions that the editors believe provide meaningful construction of the statutes. The revised volumes provide citations to administrative sources, discussed in Section 8G, *infra*. Citations to secondary sources in the revised volumes are extensive, including Am.Jr.2d, the annotated reports, and law review articles. One volume, the *United States Code Guide*, collects these citations to secondary sources by code title and section citation.

be used to obtain information about very recent congressional action, but it does not contain the text of new legislation. Through weekly reports, issued while Congress is in session, action on all bills and resolutions is traced from introduction to final disposition. The *Index* consists of two volumes with indexing by topic, bill number, and author.

13. Use of the tables is similar to use of the miniature Key Number Digests in the front of National Reporter advance sheets to supplement a search for recent opinions on a common law problem. See Section 7B, *supra*. The statutory search is somewhat simpler, however, because the statutes construed tables are cumulated through the three to five issues of advance sheets for each hardbound volume of F.2d and F.Supp., so that only the last issue of each prospective hardbound volume need be checked.

The U.S.C.S. is supplemented with annual pocket parts, an intervening *Later Case Service* pamphlet, and monthly paperback *Advance* pamphlets containing the text of new and amendatory legislation, a cumulative table of U.S.C. sections affected by new legislation, news about proposed legislation and current and proposed administrative regulations, citations to recent annotations in the A.L.R. and L.Ed. series, and a cumulative subject index.

Looseleaf Services

The three major publishers of topical looseleaf services are Bureau of National Affairs (BNA), Commerce Clearing House (CCH), and Prentice-Hall, Inc. (P–H). The names of services in common use as of 1976 are collected in the citation *Blue Book*, but new services continued to be introduced as the scope of governmental regulatory activity expands.

The looseleaf services that are the easiest to use are the information services published by BNA in the form of biweekly or weekly reports. These services review developments in an area of law, with limited reporting of the full text of court opinions. The periodic reports and opinions are filed chronologically in gray looseleaf binders under a limited number of tab-indexed sections. The *Criminal Law Reporter* is of this variety, as is the *United States Law Week*, discussed *supra* in Section 7E. Reading the introductory explanation of the service and the explanations at the beginnings of indexes should suffice to permit effective use of these services.

The more comprehensive services provide full-text reporting of more sources of law, however, including court and administrative opinions, statutes, administrative regulations, and other primary material, along with editorial comments and explanations. The greater the quantity and variety of material reported in a service, the more complex the indexing and supplementation, and therefore the use thereof, must be. A common feature of these complex services (primarily, those published by CCH and P–H) is a detailed explanation of the contents and use in a how-to-use section appearing at the front of the first volume of the service, usually with a prominent cardboard tab projecting above the top of the other pages. Because features of the services vary from topic to topic and from publisher to publisher, reading that section is a necessary starting point each time you use a new service. A preliminary perusal of the general contents of the volumes through the descriptive material on the spines of volumes, the tab indexes along the sides of the volumes, or the general and tabbed-section tables of contents will usually make the how-to-use explanation more readily understandable. Awareness of certain features of the services that differ from the common features of other legal materials, however, may help you to avoid unproductive self-education.

First, like other research materials, the comprehensive services have multiple indexing systems—for example, a topic or subject index, a case table, and a statute index, plus a current-material index —and each index is supplemented. Because of the looseleaf system, however, supplements for any index will appear in the same volume and section as the index itself. For example, a CCH subject index may actually consist of three sub-indexes, a "Topical Index," a "Current Topical Index," and "Latest Additions to Current Topical Index." How many sub-indexes must be consulted for a complete search must be determined by checking the introductory page for the particular index or any cross-referencing reminders at the top of the index pages.

Second, the indexes generally cite to paragraph numbers rather than to page numbers.

Third, bringing a search down to date through looseleaf materials differs in requiring that another index be used to find current material. For example, given the location, through a subject index, of a paragraph number covering relevant material, more recent material is found by checking that paragraph number in the current-material index, that is, in a "Cumulative Index" or a "Cumulative Cross-Reference Table". The new developments or current matter, to which you will be cited by new paragraph numbers, will appear in a chronological order rather than a logical topic order.

Finally, many of the services have one or more "permanent" (looseleaf or bound) volumes or sections that contain the basic texts and explanatory material, with one or more "current" sections or volumes, the contents of which are replaced periodically. The pages of current material that are removed (for example, yearly) will usually be retained in some other form to which citations may continue to appear in the service. Thus, for example, texts of court opinions or of arbitrators' awards reported in prior years may be collected in a set of hardbound reports that may contain opinions not published elsewhere. Other types of current material may be collected in separate "transfer binders" by year or years, but citations to the paragraph numbers thus removed from the service may remain in material left in the regular looseleaf binders. Transfer binders are usually shelved with the services, but the hardbound sets of reporters may be shelved in a different part of the library.

Illustrations 24(1)–24(5) on following pages collect some of the features just described from the *CCH Poverty Law Reports,* published and copyrighted by Commerce Clearing House, Inc., Chicago, Illinois. (Reproduced with permission).

ILLUSTRATION 24(I).

Poverty Law Reports (CCH)
Page from topical index

46 2-6-74

2145

DEPENDENT CHILDREN—ELIGIBILITY

>>>→ *The special requirements of the Supplemental Security Income program that became effective January 1, 1974 are summarized at ¶ 1015.*

¶ 1200   Requirements in General

Needy children, according to the HEW regulations, may be eligible for AFDC if they are (1) under the age of 18, or under 21 if regularly attending a school, college, or university, or regularly attending a course of vocational or technical training; (2) deprived of parental support or care by reason of the death, continued absence from the home or physical or mental incapacity of a parent, or unemployment of a father; and (3) living in the home of a parent or of certain specified relatives or in foster care under certain conditions (45 CFR 233.10(b)(2)). Also eligible for AFDC may be the parent or other caretaker relative of a dependent child and, in certain situations the parent's spouse (45 CFR 233.10(b)(2)). In addition, all individuals under 21 who are, or would be, except for age of school attendance requirements, dependent children under a state's approved AFDC plan are eligible for medical assistance under Title XIX of the Social Security Act (45 CFR 248.10 (b)(1)(ii)). Also eligible for medical assistance under Title XIX are the caretaker relatives of such dependent children (45 CFR 246.10(b)(2)(v)).

The specific factors that may be considered for eligibility under the AFDC program are detailed in the following paragraphs. For example, age requirements for, and the school status of, applicants or recipients are discussed at ¶ 1205. The persons with whom a child may live are discussed at ¶ 1210. The suitability of the home of the child is treated at ¶ 1215. The circumstances that may constitute deprivation of parental support or care, such as death, continued absence from home, the physical or mental incapacity of a parent, or the unemployment of a father, are described at ¶ 1220, 1225. In addition, the requirements pertaining to foster care in connection with an AFDC program are detailed at ¶ 1230.

For HEW requirements that the states must meet to reduce errors in determining eligibility, see ¶ 1860.

Federal Financial Participation

The federal regulations provide for the availability of federal financial participation for assistance payments for the entire month if for any portion of the month the individual met all of the eligibility conditions imposed by federal requirements (45 CFR 233.10(b)(3)). Also, the availability is continued in accordance with a state plan for a temporary period during which the effects of an eligibility condition are being overcome, such as the continued absence of a parent or unemployment of a father (45 CFR 233.10(b)(4)).

Annotations to ¶ 1200 Appear Topically Below, as Follows:

Adopted child	.07	Legitimate v. illegitimate childre.	.35
Dependent child—meaning	.14	Unborn child	.82
Expectant mother applying for private adoption services	.20		

¶ 1200

ILLUSTRATION 24(2).

Poverty Law Reports (CCH)
Page from permanent text section

---

38   10-16-73   **Dependent Children**   **2147**

or adoptive was not in violation of the Fourteenth Amendment to the U. S. Constitution on the ground that it discriminated between legitimate and illegitimate children. Also, it was not in violation of the Social Security Act, making it ineligible for federal funding, inasmuch as no federal funds were involved. The alleged constitutional violation was rejected on the ground that the U. S. Supreme Court upheld the distinction between legitimate and illegitimate children so long as a rational basis for the classification existed (citing *Levy v. Louisiana*, 391 U. S. 68; *Glona v. American Guarantee Co.*, 391 U. S. 73). Since no constitutional question was presented, a petition to convene a three-judge court was denied and a motion to dismiss the complaint was granted. *New Jersey Welfare Rights Organization v. Cahill* (DC N. J. 1971); reversed on ground that substantial constitutional questions were requiring resolution by a three-judge court (CA-3 1971).

.351 Illegitimate children may maintain an action for the wrongful death of their mother. Illegitimate children "are clearly 'persons' within the meaning of the Equal Protection Clause of the Fourteenth Amendment." Discrimination against illegitimates in such a wrongful death action was "invidious." *Levy v. Louisiana* (U. S. Sup. Ct. 1968) 391 U. S. 68, 88 S. Ct. 1509.

.82 **Unborn child.**—In South Dakota, a pregnant woman is not eligible for assistance from ADC funds, because the definition of a dependent child (SDCL, Sec. 28-7-1(2)) obviously does not refer to an unborn child and it is impossible to put that interpretation on such a definition. The reference to eligibility requirements for dependent children (SDCL, 1967, Sec. 26-1-2) in a former attorney general's opinion, which reached the same conclusion (1945-1946 AGR 338), was unnecessary and was surplusage to the present conclusion. *South Dakota Attorney General's Opinion*, No. 69-77 (8-28-69).

¶ 1205   Age—School Status

The federal regulations provide that federal financial participation is available in financial assistance provided to persons otherwise eligible who were, for any portion of the month for which assistance is paid in AFDC under 18 years of age or under 21 years of age if a student regularly attending a school, college, or university, or regularly attending a course of vocational or technical training designed to fit him for gainful employment (45 CFR 233.30(a)(1)(ii)). This provision, however, has been interpreted by federal district courts to mean only that Congress has made matching funds available to states that wish to extend welfare benefits to needy children between 16 and 18 who are not attending school without precluding the denial of benefits to children in that age group (.10, .20). In other words, a state may limit eligibility to children under 18 years of age (.75) or deny benefits to children between the ages of 16 and 18 (.10) or between 16 and 21 (.15) who are not regularly attending school. Moreover, a state may remove from AFDC eligibility children who reach the age of 19 and are not in full-time attendance in a secondary school during a school year (.20).

Furthermore, some states may require that the application for AFDC benefits must be made by an adult person (eighteen years or older) who lives with the dependent child (.53).

School Status

The U. S. Supreme Court, however, has held that, under the federal requirements, a state may not deny AFDC benefits to needy dependent children between the ages of 18 to 20 who attend a college or a university while permitting such benefits to such children who attend high school or vocational training school (.69). The provisions in the Social Security Act that make dependent 18 to 21-year-olds eligible for benefits whether attending a college or university or attending a course of vocational or technical training are mandatory. Consequently, the U. S. Supreme Court ruled, state requirements that limit AFDC eligibility to students attending high school or vocational training school are invalid under the Supremacy Clause. Congress left

---

ILLUSTRATION 24(3).

Poverty Law Reports (CCH)
Page from permanent text section showing case squib
(A comprehensive reporter also provides the text
of statutes and regulations.)

15,646   **Latest Additions to Cumulative Index**   141   9-77
See also Cumulative Index.

From Compilation   **To New Development**
Paragraph No.   **Paragraph No.**

Sufficiency of medical evidence of total and permanent disability (Wis Cir Ct)	20,091
Sufficient evidence of permanent disability to be entitled to ATD benefits (Cal Sup Ct)	23,208
Temporary disability period for eligibility not to be limited to six months of year (NM Ct App ¶ 21,402). Rev'd (NM Sup Ct)	22,305
Totally and permanently disabled petitioner entitled to assistance (Vt Sup Ct)	22,142
Welfare financial and custodial responsibility for emotionally disturbed and mentally retarded children (Nev Atty Gen)	23,518
.07 Alcoholism with schizophrenia constituted disability entitling person to welfare (Ore Ct App)	19,495
.67 Eligibility not precluded by possibility of rehabilitation (Ind Super Ct ¶ 17,767). Aff'd in part and rev'd in part on other grounds (Ind Ct App)	19,660
.67 Regulations covering the newly authorized provisions under Title I of the Rehabilitation Act Amendments of 1974 adopted (HEW Regs)	21,843

► 1200

AFDC mother not entitled to Internal Revenue Code dependency exemption (CA-7)	20,929
Aid for unborn children sought (DC Ill ¶ 15,956). Aid granted (DC Ill ¶ 16,540). Aid extended to class members (DC Ill ¶ 17,115). Injunctive relief and retroactive benefits ordered (DC Ill ¶ 17,116). Aff'd in part and rev'd in part (CA-7 ¶ 18,961). Vac'd and rem'd (US Sup Ct)	20,668
Aid for unborn children sought (DC Ill ¶ 15,956). Aid granted (DC Ill ¶ 16,540). Aid extended to class members (DC Ill ¶ 17,115). Injunctive relief and retroactive benefits ordered (DC Ill ¶ 17,116). Aff'd in part and rev'd in part (CA-7 ¶ 18,961). Vac'd and rem'd (US Sup Ct)	21,008
Child's social security number not required for AFDC eligibility (DC Vt)	24,262
Cultural, equitable or *in loco parentis* adoption not legal adoption for AFDC eligibility (Colo Sup Ct)	19,887
Divorced minor daughter no justification for denial of aid (Cal Super Ct ¶ 19,723). Aff'd (Cal Ct App)	21,193
Duty of HEW to oversee state AFDC programs (DC DofC)	22,130
HEW regulation rendering aid to unborn optional unauthorized (DC Va ¶ 17,831). Aff'd (CA-4 ¶ 18,569). Vac'd and rem'd (US Sup Ct)	20,666
Legal marriage requirement denies equal protection of law (Wash Super Ct)	19,356
Refusal to supply welfare agency with social security numbers due to religious beliefs was proper (DC NY)	24,240
Statutory presumption that employment is terminated in order to obtain aid unconstitutional (DC NY ¶ 19,961). Rev'd and rem'd (US Sup Ct ¶ 22,232). Action returned to single-judge court (DC NY)	23,214
Unborn child entitled to AFDC grant (NY Sup Ct ¶ 16,424). Aff'd (NY Sup Ct, App Div)	19,491
Unborn child not mandatory recipient (DC Ga ¶ 16,852). Motion for reconsideration denied (DC Ga ¶ 17,503). Rev'd (CA-5 ¶ 20,099). Vac'd and rem'd (US Sup Ct ¶ 20,790). Vac'd and rem'd (CA-5)	21,368
► Unborn children entitled to aid under the Social Security Act (DC Iowa ¶ 17,606). Judgment stayed (US Sup Ct ¶ 17,755). Judgment aff'd (CA-8 ¶ 18,777). Rev'd and rem'd (US Sup Ct ¶ 20,548). Rem'd (CA-8 ¶ 20,823). Aff'd (DC Iowa)	23,120 ◄
Verification of ages and relationships of children for AFDC eligibility required (DC Mass)	22,270
.14 Class composed of persons eligible as AFDC caretaker relatives proper (DC Ill)	22,123
.82 AFDC mother entitled to grant for both of her unborn twins (NY Sup Ct)	24,088
.82 Denial of AFDC benefits to or for unborn children upheld (DC Iowa ¶ 23,120). Aff'd (CA-8)	23,569
.82 Denial of aid to pregnant women otherwise childless invalid (DC NH ¶ 18,271). Aff'd (CA-1 ¶ 19,453). Vac'd and rem'd (US Sup Ct)	20,667
.82 Denial of aid to unborn children contrary to federal law (DC Mich)	19,945
.82 Girl who failed to show that needs occasioned by her pregnancy were not being met ineligible for AFDC (NY Sup Ct)	23,467
.82 Indigents pregnant with first child ineligible for AFDC (DC NC)	23,016
.82 Indigents pregnant with first child ineligible for AFDC (DC NC ¶ 23,016). Aff'd (US Sup Ct)	24,537
.82 Medical verification after birth of child sufficient (NY Sup Ct)	21,168
.82 No congressional authority for exclusion of unborn children from AFDC (DC Miss ¶ 18,466). Aff'd (CA-5 ¶ 20,099). Vac'd and rem'd (CA-5)	21,368
.82 Non-needy unwed pregnant minor girl ineligible for AFDC (DC Idaho)	24,310
.82 Pregnant applicant supported by parents entitled to AFDC benefits on behalf of unborn child (NY Sup Ct, App Div)	24,401
.82 Pregnant woman's right to benefits (NY Sup Ct)	20,884
.82 Retroactive benefits granted as of fourth month of pregnancy (NY Sup Ct)	21,168
.82 Stay of order denying benefits denied (CA-1)	21,358
.82 Stay of order denying benefits denied (CA-1 ¶ 21,358). Benefits properly denied (CA-1)	21,700
.82 Unborn child entitled to AFDC (NY Sup Ct, App Div)	19,491
.82 Unborn child entitled to AFDC—emancipated minor may be entitled to AFDC (NY Sup Ct)	22,698
.82 Unborn child entitled to AFDC grant (NY Sup Ct, App Div)	22,362
.82 Unborn child entitled to AFDC grant (NY Sup Ct, App Div ¶ 22,362). Aff'd (NY Ct App)	24,346
.82 Unborn child not entitled to AFDC (DC NJ)	22,014
.82 Unborn child of unemancipated pregnant minor entitled to AFDC (NY Sup Ct)	23,231
.82 Unborn children are part of an AFDC family unit (DC Pa)	19,681
.82 Unborn children no basis for denial of AFDC benefits (DC Conn ¶ 19,064). Rev'd (CA-2 ¶ 19,871). Rehearing den'd (CA-2)	21,357
.82 Unwed pregnant female entitled to medical assistance and AFDC for unborn child (NY Sup Ct)	20,462
.82 Unwed pregnant female entitled to medical assistance and AFDC for unborn child (NY Sup Ct ¶ 20,462). Aff'd (NY Sup Ct, App Div)	22,153
.82 Welfare sought on behalf of unborn children (NY Sup Ct)	22,945

©1977, Commerce Clearing House, Inc.

ILLUSTRATION 24(4).

Poverty Law Reports (CCH)
Page from current-material index
(Latest Additions to Cumulative Index)

113   8-76   **New Developments**   **19,501**

Rules. New York Supreme Court, Appellate Division, First Department. No. 2660. Opinion dated July 20, 1976. Kupferman, J.P.

Juvenile Delinquents—Detention—Separate from Adults.—In the maintenance of separate detention facilities for youths and adults at the New York City Criminal Court, the dividing line between youths and adults was deemed to be between those under nineteen years of age and those nineteen years of age and over. **Back reference:** ¶ 4125.77. *Available from National Clearinghouse for Legal Services.*

[¶ 23,118] *New York Laws of 1976,* Chapter 828, Assembly Bill No. 272-A, approved July 26, 1976; adding Section 235-c to the New York Real Property Law; effective immediately.

Landlord and Tenant—Unconscionable Lease or Clause.—New York has added a new section to its real property law. The section provides that if a court as a matter of law finds a lease or any clause of a lease to have been unconscionable when made, then the court may refuse to enforce the lease, or may enforce the remainder of the lease without the unconscionable clause, or may so limit application of the clause as to avoid any unconscionable result. When it is claimed or appears to the court that a lease or any clause thereof· may be unconscionable, the parties shall be afforded a reasonable opportunity to present evidence as to its setting, purpose, and effect to aid the court in making the determination. The act applies to all leases regardless of when executed. **Back references:** ¶ 2025, 3330.

[¶ 23,119] *In the Matter of St. Lawrence County Department of Social Services v. Charles Menard, et al.* New York Family Court, St. Lawrence County. Opinion dated August 8, 1975. Follett, J.

Welfare—Parents' Obligation to Children—Reimbursement of Support Funds.—Where a 20-year-old young woman chose to live away from her father's home and deliberately flouted her parents' directions, her father could not be required to reimburse a New York county welfare department for support of his daughter. The young woman had borne the illegitimate child of a convicted criminal, was therefore unable to work, and preferred to maintain a separate residence with the help of public assistance rather than return to her family home with her child as requested. It was incomprehensible that a parent should be required to contribute toward the support of a child where the child committed acts in total derogation of the relationship of parent and child, regardless of whether the proceeding was commenced by a social service official or the errant child. **Back reference:** ¶ 1330.

[¶ 23,120] *Linda Alcala, et al. v. Kevin J. Burns.* U.S. District Court, Southern District of Iowa, Central Division. Civ. Nos. 76-86-2 and 72-110-2. Order on Cross-Motions for Summary Judgment dated March 8, 1976. Hanson, Ch.J.

A F D C — E l i g i b i l i t y — U n b o r n Children.—The constitutionality of the Iowa welfare officials' denial of AFDC benefits to pregnant women for and on behalf of their unborn children was upheld by a federal district court. The pregnant women's due process and equal protection rights were not violated by this policy. The court further determined that the pregnant women had standing to assert their claim for declaratory relief in this matter since they were asserting their entitlement, and not their unborn children's entitlement, to AFDC benefits and therefore had a sufficient personal stake in the lawsuit to assert their constitutional claims. **Back reference:** ¶ 1200.82.

[¶ 23,121] *Raymond Baiza v. Southgate Recreation and Park District.* California Court of Appeal, Third District. No. Civ. 15085. Opinion dated June 29, 1976. Regan, Acting P.J.

Appeal from Superior Court, Sacramento County.

Urban Renewal and Redevelopment—Relocation Benefits—Exhaustion of Administrative Remedies—Displaced Person.—A tenant in property which had been acquired by a park district was not entitled to a writ of mandamus seeking to command the park district to provide him with statutory relocation benefits because such tenant failed to exhaust his administrative remedies. The petition for writ of mandate clearly was a claim for money and thus within the mandatory requirements of formal filing with the park district as a prerequisite to any court proceedings as provided by statute. Thus, there was no lack of administrative remedy available. In

ILLUSTRATION 24(5).

Poverty Law Reports (CCH)
Page from New Developments section

State Annotated Statutes

State annotated statutes not published by the publishers of [14] U. S.C.A. are in various forms. They may be supplemented by pocket parts, separate volumes, or looseleaf insertions. To find very recent state legislation, you may have to use a pamphlet edition of session laws or a private legislative service. Recent construing opinions may be found through the Cumulative [State] Statutes Construed tables in the appropriate National Reporter advance sheets or through the appropriate state edition of Shepard's statute citator, described in the following section.

Uniform Laws Annotated

For uniform statutes, an additional useful search tool is available. Numerous laws have been drafted by committees appointed by and reporting to the National Conference of Commissioners on Uniform State Laws, with commissioners appointed by the governors of the fifty states. The laws so drafted and approved have been recommended to all the state legislatures for adoption, and much significant state legislation has been the result. The *Uniform Laws Annotated, Master Edition,* reports the text of the recommended uniform laws and of model acts; the drafters' comments and explanations; variations in text adopted by the various state legislatures; tables showing adopting states; annotations of court opinions that cite, discuss, or construe the laws; citations to legal periodical commentaries, and citations to relevant digest key numbers and C.J.S. sections. It is supplemented with occasional pamphlet supplements for individual volumes and annual pocket supplements. Recent citing court opinions are collected in the Cumulative Statutes Construed tables of National Reporter advance sheets, just preceding the citations for state codes.

SECTION 8E. USE OF SHEPARD'S CITATORS IN CONNECTION WITH STATUTORY RESEARCH

Construing opinions on which you intend to rely should be Shepardized in the case citator of the appropriate Shepard's edition; that is, the state or regional edition or one of the federal editions.

Statute citators are available for states, as part of the state editions, and for the United States, as part of the *United States Citations* edition. A statute citator may identify citing court opinions handed down subsequent to the most recent supplement for an annotated code. It will provide citations to opinions construing session laws not included in a current code. Additionally, you may wish to use a state statute citator for double-check purposes if the only avail-

---

14. For a list of states for which annotated codes in U.S.C.A. form are available, see *supra,* note 10.

able annotated code or annotation service is not reliable. Use of statute citators is sufficiently similar to the use of case citators that explanation is not included in this text. You will, however, have to acquaint yourself with a new set of alphabetical symbols that appear in front of citations to identify court and legislative treatment of statutory sections.

A separate unit, *Shepard's Acts and Cases by Popular Names,* supplemented annually, is of value for collecting citations from several states for a particular type of statute. For example, if you want to check antidiscrimination statutes in force in several or all states, you can quickly obtain citations to them through this unit.

SECTION 8F. THE SEARCH FOR LEGISLATIVE HISTORY MATERIALS

Reports, documents and other materials generated during the enactment process may be useful in identifying the reasons for adoption of particular legislation (the problem to be solved); the reasons for the particular approach, form, or language of the legislation; purposes not expected to be served by the legislation; difficulties in application or construction predicted or considered; amendments made or rejected; and so on. Much of this kind of background material is readily available for federal legislation, particularly for legislation adopted in the last three decades. Unfortunately, such information is not usually available for state legislation.

Legislative history materials are classified as government documents, a class consisting of all publications of governments and governmental agencies. Government documents that embody "law"— primary authority (for example, the *United States Code* and official reports)—are frequently treated like other materials in law library collections, that is, they are cataloged in card catalogs and may be shelved in the most accessible areas of the library. Other government documents, however, are frequently traceable only through the indexes prepared by the government printer, the issuing agency, or a library staff. Original legislative history materials fall in this latter category. For this reason, they have acquired a reputation as rather exotic, hard-to-find source materials—a reputation that is not always justified.

Since 1941, much significant federal legislative history material has been reprinted in the publication that supplements the *United States Code Annotated.* Beginning in 1941 as the *U. S. Code Congressional Service,* this service first reprinted a limited number of excerpts from congressional committee reports. In 1948, the service was extended to include, for each new statute, citations to reports and a full reprint of either the House or Senate committee report and of any conference report. In 1951 the name was changed to that

with which you are already familiar—*U. S. Code Congressional and Administrative News*. At the present time, it also cites the volume of the *Congressional Record* in which congressional debate on each new statute may be found. Appearing first as monthly paperback pamphlets, these legislative history materials are republished in annual bound volumes following each session of Congress. Citations to legislative history in the service appear in the U.S.C.A. as the last item of historical notes. See Illustration 23, *supra*.

Your search may be easily extended beyond the *U. S. Code Congressional and Administrative News* to the Senate or House committee report that is not reprinted therein, because the number of the omitted report will be given in the *News* at the beginning of the legislative history for the particular statute. With this number and the number and session of the enacting Congress, you may obtain a copy of the omitted report through your librarian if a copy is available in the documents collection of your library.

Then you may wish to extend your search to the *Congressional Record,* which is, in current form, a daily publication (Monday through Friday during sessions of Congress) reporting debate and actions of Congress. It is bound into permanent hardback volumes at the end of each session. The permanent form has a cumulated index, but the daily editions are indexed only fortnightly, and not cumulatively. The indexes are in two parts, first a listing of subjects and Congressmen, then a "History of Bills and Resolutions" section. The latter section indexes by bill number and lists each action taken with reference to a bill, citing to the page in the *Record* where the action is reported. Thus, given the bill number (which, again, you will find cited in the *News* at the beginning of the legislative history for the statute), you may find that number in the history of bills and resolutions for the year of enactment and thus find citations to relevant actions and debate reported in the *Congressional Record*. Although much debate may be useful only for background information, statements of a reporting committee chairman or member or of others having some special relationship to an act may be authoritative.

Note that the sources just described may be consulted simply on the basis of information reported in recent *U. S. Code Congressional and Administrative News* volumes. The same sources may be found easily even though that service is not available, because you may obtain the same information for all bills introduced in a session of Congress by checking the subject and history indexes of the *Congressional Record* for the year of enactment of the statute in whose history you are interested.[15] Thus, basic legislative history research is not

---

15. Other sources of information include:

    (1) Beginning with 1963, a guide to legislative history of bills *enacted* into law is printed at the end of each slip law and is included in the *Statutes at Large*.

    (2) A looseleaf service, *CCH Congressional Index*, described *supra*, note 12, includes excellent status tables,

unduly complex. It may be complex for early federal legislation, however, and it may be complex if you attempt to extend your search beyond the basic sources discussed thus far. Apparent complexity may also be introduced by nonavailability of desired materials in the library on whose resources you must rely.

If you wish to undertake a complex search, you will have to engage in a little self-education, aided by what you now know about the *Congressional Record,* by information to be found in L. Schmeckebier & R. Eastin, *Government Publications and Their Use* (2d rev. ed. 1969) (hereafter referred to as Schmeckebier), and by members of your library staff. Familiarity with the *Monthly Catalog of United States Government Publications* (called the *Monthly Catalog United States Public Documents* from 1907 to 1939) will also be useful. The *Monthly Catalog* is the equivalent of a card catalog for government publications, though not as efficient. It is issued monthly with a non-cumulative subject index and bound annually with (since 1939) an annual cumulative subject index. Decennial cumulative indexes are also provided. The *Monthly Catalog* is now also indexed in the 14-volume *Cumulative Subject Index to the Monthly Catalog of U.S. Government Publications—1900–1970* (1972). *The Congressional Information Service Annual* provides a detailed index of all congressional publications since 1970 except the *Congressional Record.* Some of the basic types of materials for which you will search have already been identified. Other possible historical materials are identified in Table II, *infra,* which should suffice to get you started on finding historical materials for much twentieth century federal legislation.

As previously indicated, legislative history materials for state legislation may be very limited. For example, legislative hearings, reports, and debates are not generally reported. Nevertheless, historical and background material may sometimes be developed.

Among official materials may be House and Senate Journals. These state legislative journals tend to be skeletal reports of proceedings, but they may occasionally supply information about votes on proposed amendments, substitution of one bill for another, or other procedural moves that may suggest legislative approval or rejection of a particular approach to a problem related to a statute. Copies of bills introduced in a legislative session may be made available to law libraries within the state. An explanation by an official drafting body may be printed at the end of a bill. Varying bills introduced for an area of legislation, combined with information gleaned from the journals, may occasionally give valuable clues. In recent years, the coverage of state legislative journals has been expanding. They

kept up to date weekly in the current volume, but bills are not listed in the tables until *reported out of committee.* Publication of this service was begun in 1941.

(3) U.S.Code Cong. & Ad. News, in its Table 4, carries histories of the most important bills *enacted* into law since 1964.

TABLE II

Federal Legislation: Possible Route to Adoption and Possible History Materials

1. Identification of problem.

   (a) Hearings conducted by Senate or House Committee.

   A hearing transcript may be available. See Schmeckebier at 166–67, 180–82.

   (b) Study conducted for Senate or House Committee.

   See Schmeckebier at 150–57.

   (c) Administrative request.

   May be reported in publication of administrative body, such as an Annual Report.

   (d) Presidential message.

   Printed in Cong.Rec.; most important ones printed in U.S.C.C.A.N.

   (e) Agitation by private groups; current events.

   Newspapers and periodicals may record unauthoritative background material.

2. Drafting of bill.

   If drafted by official body, explanations may be published.

3. Introduction of bill. (A bill may be introduced in House (cited as H.R. 4) or in Senate (cited as S. 4). Variant forms of bills on same subject may be introduced in both branches.

   Congressional Digest, 1921 to date, carries features about bills pending in Congress. The Digest has a cumulated index to 1968 in vol. 47.

4. Assignment to committee.

   (a) Hearing.

   Possible official print. See 1(a) above.

   (b) Report. (Usually contains description of bill and purposes, reasons for recommendation to pass or not pass.)

   Official print. Committee reports reported selectively in U.S.C.A.N. Others: see Schmeckebier at 179 *et seq.*

5. Action on bill.

   Debate reported in Cong.Rec.

6. If passed by one branch, sent to other branch as an "Act."

   See 4 and 5 above.

7. If Act is amended or enacted in different form in second branch, conference committee appointed.

   See Cong.Rec. for possible re-debate.

   (a) Conference report.

   Official print. Usually printed in U.S.C.C.A.N

   (b) Conference bill.

   Printed in Cong.Rec.

8. If passed in one form by both branches, sent to President.

   (a) May be approved.

   Slip law.

   (b) May be vetoed, with possible veto message. (May still be passed by ⅔ vote.)

   Cong.Rec.; messages reported selectively in U.S.C.C.A.N.

may ultimately be a source of more substantial legislative history, including brief committee or conference reports, excerpts from debate, or statements of sponsors. Finally, the official publication of legislation adopted in a legislative session may incorporate more than the text of enactments; for example, the Governor's message explaining the veto of a portion of an enactment or the explanation provided by an official drafting body may be appended to the text of an act.

A sometimes fertile source of information may be the reports of committees or commissions charged with overseeing the continuing validity of a state's laws. The broadest type of such body is a law revision or law reform commission. A notable example is the New York Law Revision Commission, which, since the 1930's, has successfully proposed many statutory changes, the proposals being reported with supporting explanations. Many states have other bodies charged with overseeing less extensive areas of law. For example, a statute law or code committee may be charged with bringing to the attention of the legislature obsolete or inconsistent material in a code. An interim legislative committee or council may conduct hearings and propose legislation. A judicial committee or council may be charged with maintaining a continuous review of court systems and procedures, proposing changes that will improve the administration of justice. Reports of these legislative service agencies, task forces, commissions, and of other study committees in the states are indexed in the *Legislative Research Checklist,* published three times yearly by the Council of State Governments. Although the *Checklist* is not indexed cumulatively, your library may provide a legislative reference index, a card file indexing state reports and studies by subject, made up from the *Checklist.* If not, the *Checklist* can be conveniently used only to find reports for a known, short period of time.

Interpretation of statutes by an administrator charged with enforcement, as reflected in the practices of the particular administrator or administrative agency, may assume particular importance. An Attorney General's opinion can be quite persuasive, particularly if government officials have conducted operations in accordance with such an opinion.

Unauthoritative material may be available in the form of newspaper or trade or labor newsletter reports of proceedings at legislative sessions. Local law journals or reviews may provide preenactment information in the form of studies or proposed legislative changes. Post-enactment articles therein may report valuable contemporary background material. A local or state bar association may engage in law reform activities. For example, a committee may actually draft proposed legislation and prepare an explanatory report for association members, copies of which will be supplied to legislators. Such activities may be reported in the bar association journal or other publication. Even though unauthoritative, these kinds of

materials may furnish background that will at least aid your own understanding of a statute.

To find what types of legislative historical material may be available where you ultimately practice will be a matter of self-education once you form an attachment to a particular state. You may find a few sources to be productive with sufficient frequency to justify their regular use in the course of state statutory research. For the most part, however, extensive searches for state legislative history materials will be reserved for problems justifying unusually comprehensive research.

SECTION 8G.   THE SEARCH FOR ADMINISTRATIVE MATERIALS

Already noted is the possible branching-off of your research if you discover that Congress or a state legislature has delegated law-making, adjudicatory, or regulatory authority to an independent agency or other executive office. Having identified the grant of authority in the controlling statutes, you would direct your search toward finding basic materials similar to the object of statutory research: (1) opinions construing the delegating statute; (2) "legislation," such as rules, regulations, and guidelines [16] adopted by the administering body; (3) either judicial or administrative opinions construing any such legislation; (4) materials detailing the history of any such legislation (for example, information about hearings held in connection with its adoption or about changes in form between proposal and adoption or after adoption), and (5) possible secondary commentary. As is the case with state statutory research, the research trail for administrative materials may be thin at the history and commentary stages of search and for state administrative materials may be obscure even at the starting point.

Two problems peculiar to administrative law may lead into additional branches of search: whether a particular agency rule is within the scope of the delegation of authority or whether the agency followed required procedures in its adoption of a rule. Distinctive procedures in agency adjudications and other matters may also require research with respect to appropriate procedures.

Federal Rules and Regulations

All generally applicable rules proposed or adopted by federal agencies are now published chronologically, as they are proposed and

16. Rules and regulations are forms of administrative legislation adopted pursuant to authority expressly conferred by Congress. Guidelines are written interpretations adopted by an administrative body outside such express authority. For a recent discussion of the comparative authority value of the two types of administrative "legislation," see General Elec. Co. v. Gilbert, 429 U.S. 125, 97 S.Ct. 401, 410–11, 50 L.Ed.2d 343 (1976). *See generally* K. Davis, Administrative Law Text §§ 5.03, 5.04 (1972).

adopted, in the *Federal Register,* an official publication somewhat akin to the *Statutes at Large.* It is the chronological order of publication and the all-inclusiveness of the *Register* (rules subsequently superseded, amended, or abandoned remain therein) that make it similar to the *Statutes at Large.* There the similarity ends. The *Register* is a daily publication (except Sunday, Monday, and days following official holidays) that includes not only general "legislation" adopted, but also rules that are proposed, together with notices and other informative current material. See Illustration 25. The daily issues ultimately may be bound into more convenient hard cover volumes by the collecting library. (Cited: 20 Fed.Reg. 10789 (1962)— the numbers being the volume and page numbers).

The *Register* has subject indexes—daily, cumulated monthly, quarterly and annually—and cumulative codification guides described hereafter.

Akin to the *United States Code* is the *Code of Federal Regulations* (C.F.R.), an official codification of generally applicable rules and regulations in force as of the date of the codification, as revised and supplemented. The current edition of C.F.R. consists of 50 subject titles, which, except for the first three (General Provisions, The Congress, The President) are alphabetically arranged (Accounts through Wildlife and Fisheries). The titles, in turn, are usually divided into chapters (identified by roman numerals) for each of the departments and agencies having authority to issue rules and regulations with respect to the title subject matter. Chapters are subdivided into subchapters (identified by capital letters), and the subchapters are divided into parts and, finally, sections (both arabic numerals). (Cited: 16 C.F.R. § 162.11 (1949)—the first number identifying the title and the second number identifying both the part and the section.)

The slim *CFR Index,* revised as of July 1 each year, contains a general explanation of C.F.R.; a subject index; a "List of Titles, Chapters, and Subchapters, and Parts;" an "Alphabetical List of Agencies," and other useful information. A *Finding Aids* volume provides other research aids.

The C.F.R. volumes are paperbound, and most are reissued annually on roughly the following schedule: Titles 1–16, as of January 1; Titles 17–27, as of April 1; Titles 28–41, as of July 1, and Titles 42–50, as of October 1. Material in current issues of the *Federal Register* supplements material in C.F.R. Citations to supplementing material in the *Register* are found through cumulative codification guides described hereafter. A minimum search for possible rules and regulations currently in effect in a particular subject area includes both C.F.R. and the *Federal Register.* Cross-references to C.F.R. in a looseleaf service or in one of the annotated codes, U.S.C.A. or U.S.

RULES AND REGULATIONS   18513

ices Corporation Act of 1974, Pub. L. 93–355, 88 Stat. 376, 42 U.S.C. 2996–2996*l* ("the Act"). Section 1007(a)(7) of the Act requires recipients to establish guidelines, consistent with regulations promulgated by the Corporation, for review of appeals taken on behalf of clients.

A proposed regulation was issued on March 12, 1976 (41 FR 10629), and interested persons were given until April 11, 1976 to submit comments on the proposed regulation. All comments received by the Corporation with respect to appeals were given full consideration and the following issues were taken into account in redrafting the regulation:

Coverage of Part 1605. Section 1007(a)(7) of the Act requires all recipients to establish guidelines, consistent with Corporation Regulations, for review of appeals. Since the purpose is to insure efficient utilization of Corporation resources, this Part does not apply to any part of a recipient's practice that is undertaken with other than Corporation funds. (Comments received noted that the published draft did not address the problem of mixed practices.) The Part requires a recipient to establish a policy and procedure for review of every appeal, as defined by local usage, taken to an appellate court from the decision of any court or tribunal.

Standards for Review. Aside from that clarifying change, the only other changes are the addition of some relevant statutory language omitted from the published draft, and a fuller, but substantively unchanged, statement of the standards for review. A recipient is required to adopt a review policy that discourages frivolous appeals and gives appropriate weight to priorities in resource allocation required by the Act, the Corporation, or its own governing body, but does not interfere with an attorney's professional responsibilities to a client.

Accordingly, the Board of Directors of the Legal Services Corporation adopts the final regulation, as set forth below, to become effective on June 3, 1976, pursuant to section 1008(e) of the Act.

Sec.
1605.1.   Purpose.
1605.2   Definition.
1605.3   Review of appeals.

AUTHORITY: Sec. 1007(a)(7), 1008(e), 42 U.S.C. 2996*l*(a)(7), 2996g(e).

§ 1605.1   Purpose.

This Part is intended to promote efficient and effective use of Corporation funds. It does not apply to any case or matter in which assistance is not being rendered with funds provided under the Act.

§ 1605.2   Definition.

"Appeal" means any appellate proceeding in a civil action as defined by law or usage in the jurisdiction in which the action is filed.

§ 1605.3   Review of Appeals.

The governing body of a recipient shall adopt a policy and procedure for review of every appeal to an appellate court taken from a decision of any court or tribunal. The policy adopted shall

(a) Discourage frivolous appeals, and
(b) Give appropriate consideration to priorities in resource allocation adopted by the governing body, or required by the Act, or Regulations of the Corporation; but
(c) Shall not interfere with the professional responsibilities of an attorney to a client.

THOMAS EHRLICH,
President,
Legal Services Corporation.

[FR Doc.76–12953 Filed 5–4–76; 8:45 am]

PART 1612—RESTRICTIONS ON CERTAIN ACTIVITIES [1]

Picketing, Boycotts, Strikes, Illegal Activities; Legislative and Administrative Representation

The Legal Services Corporation was established pursuant to the Legal Services Corporation Act of 1974, Pub. L. 93–355, 88 Stat. 378, 42 U.S.C. 2996–2996*l* ("The Act"). Section 1006(b)(5) of the Act requires the Corporation to issue regulations implementing the Act's restrictions on picketing, boycotts, strikes and illegal activities by employees of the Corporation and of recipients, as well as restrictions on legislative and administrative representation using Corporation funds.

Temporary regulations were published on September 12, 1975 (40 FR 42362) and became effective on October 14, 1975. Proposed final regulations were published on March 5, 1976 (41 FR 9571), and interested persons were given until April 5, 1976 to submit comments on the proposed final regulations. All comments received by the Corporation with respect to the proposed final regulations were given consideration and the regulations were reorganized and revised substantially in light of those comments. In addition, Part 1600 was renumbered and now appears as Part 1612. This change was made to permit the inclusion of a general "Definitions" section (now Part 1601), and to establish a more logical order for future regulations.

The following considerations were taken into account in redrafting the proposed final regulations:

Prohibition Against Encouraging Action by Other People. The Act contains a number of provisions designed to prevent legal services attorneys from engaging in activities unrelated to the provision of legal assistance to eligible clients. The prohibitions against direct participation by attorneys presented no difficult issues of interpretation; but the prohibition against encouraging others to engage in lawful activities such as public demonstrations and picketing presented the major policy issue in this Part. In construing the prohibition we tried to reconcile demands presented by the Code of Professional Responsibility, the Constitution, and the intent of Congress.

We believe a lawyer is obligated to advise a client about lawful alternatives to litigation [2] and we do not think Con-

gress intended to prevent such advice.[3] An appropriate construction of the term "encourage" would permit such advice, and at the same time, would satisfy the restriction against vagueness and overbreadth in the First Amendment area, and the parallel ethical constraint against external interference with a lawyer's professional judgment.[4]

The legislative history of the Act suggests that the intention of Congress was to prevent lawyers from deliberately propelling others toward activities they otherwise might not engage in; so from the many possible meanings of "encourage" we chose those that seemed best suited to convey that intention, and replaced "encourage" with the words "exhort, direct, or coerce others to engage in such activities, or otherwise usurp or invade the rightful authority of a client to determine what course of action to follow." The definition of "encouraging" that appeared in Sections 1600.3(a)(2) and 1600.3(a)(3), as published, is now superfluous, and has been omitted.

Men's Rea Requirement. The final regulations modify the prohibitions of Section 1600.2 by the addition of mens rea requirements. To invoke Corporation sanctions, an employee's direct participation in prohibited activities must be undertaken "knowingly", and action leading another to engage in such activities must be taken "intentionally". These requirements were added in the belief that there is no place for absolute liability in the First Amendment area, and that Congress did not intend to impose it.

Other Illegal Activity. As published, the proposed regulations did not interpret the Act's prohibition against "other illegal activity". Section 1612.2(b)(1)(C), as here presented, bars illegal activity that is inconsistent with an employee's responsibilities under the Act, Corporation Regulations, or the Code of Professional Responsibility. These categories seem sufficient to cover the situations when the Corporation should add its sanctions to those imposed by the law.

Legal Assistance Activities. The definition of "carrying out legal assistance activities" that appeared in the published version of Section 1600.3(a)(1) included any time during which an attorney "could reasonably be expected to provide legal advice or representation." That phrase has been dropped because it introduced unnecessary uncertainty into a reasonably clear provision. The definition of "legal assistance activities" now appears in Section 1612.1.

Attorney-Client Relationship. A single provision, Section 1612.3, replaces the repetitive disclaimers and exception found in the published version of Section 1600.3(a)(2) and its terminal proviso.

---

[1] See FR Doc. 76–12951 supra.

[2] See Ethical Considerations 7–7 and 7–8 of the ABA Code of Professional Responsibility.

[3] See Section 1006(b)(3) of the Act; Conference Report p. 21–22; House Report p. 7.

[4] See, e.g., ABA Committee on Ethics and Professional Responsibility, Formal Opinion 334 (1974), p. 7.

ILLUSTRATION 25.

Page from *Federal Register*

C.S., may give you an immediate citation to C.F.R. If not, several methods are available for finding materials in C.F.R.:

Assuming that you have found a statute delegating authority to a particular agency, you might use the Parallel Table of Statutory Authority and Rules that appears in

the Finding Aids volume as Table 1.   (Thus, if the delegating statute is 42 U.S.C. § 601, the parallel table shows that rules adopted under authority of that statute appear in 42 C.F.R., Part 206.) [17]   This approach is not always productive, or it may lead to so many citations as not to be efficient.

Assuming that you know the name of the agency whose rules you want to check, you could search under that name in the subject index or in the "Alphabetical List of Agencies" in the *CFR Index* volume.   (More specific entries will be found through the subject index.)

Assuming that you know only the subject area that you believe may be covered by some federal agency rules, you can check for that subject in the subject index.

Use of the subject indexes for the *Federal Register* may be necessary for recently enacted statutes.   Regardless of which of these methods you use to search for material in C.F.R., you will also want to use the topic approach: At the beginning of each chapter, the headings for the parts are listed; at the beginning of each part, the section headings are listed.

Like the U.S.C., C.F.R. provides citations to the original and amending adoption forms at the beginning of a part or at the end of a section (but citing to pages in the *Federal Register* rather than to the *Statutes at Large,* of course).   See Illustration 26.   Because an adopting agency may explain new regulations at the time of adoption or original proposal, these historical citations to pages in the *Register,* particularly in recent years, are worth checking for possible historical background.   See Illustration 25, *supra.*

If you find relevant material in C.F.R., you must bring your search down to date by checking the C.F.R. citations in the cumulative codification guides that supplement C.F.R.:

(1) First check your C.F.R. citation in the most recent C.F.R. supplement, the pamphlet called *LSA—List of C.F.R. Sections Affected.*   Occasionally you will have to check your citations in a second of these pamphlets, because receipt of revised C.F.R. volumes tends to be delayed.   Thus, if the revision date has passed for the C.F.R. title in which you are interested, but the revised volumes have not yet been received, you may also have to check the prior *LSA* pamphlet that

---

17.   There is no necessary relationship between title numbers in the *United States Code* and title numbers in C.F. R., though occasionally they coincide. Thus, for example, regulations under the Consumer Protection Act, codified in title 15 of U.S.C., appear in title 12 of C.F.R.; by coincidence, however, regulations relating to the Childrens' Bureau, created by statutes appearing in title 42 of U.S.C., also appear in title 42 of C.F.R.

Chapter XVI—Legal Services Corporation   § 1612.4

with the purposes for which they were provided.

§ 1610.4   Accounting.

Funds received by a recipient from a source other than the Corporation shall be accounted for as separate and distinct receipts and disbursements, in the manner lirected by the Corporation.

§ 1610.5   Waiver.

Any provision of this Part may be waived by the President when necessary to permit the Corporation to make a contract or other arrangement for the provision of legal assistance with any private attorney, law firm, state or local entity of attorneys, or a legal aid organization that has a separate public defender program.

PART 1612—RESTRICTIONS ON CERTAIN ACTIVITIES

Sec.
1612.1   Definition.
1612.2   Public demonstrations and other activities.
1612.3   Attorney-client relationship.
1612.4   Legislative and administrative representation.
1612.5   Enforcement.

AUTHORITY: Secs. 1006(b)(5), 1007(a)(5), 1011, 1008(e), P.L. 93–355, 88 Stat. 378 (42 U.S.C. 2996e(b)(5), 2996f(a)(5), 2996j, 2996g (e)).

SOURCE: 41 FR 18514, May 5, 1976, unless otherwise noted.

§ 1612.1   Definition.

"Legal assistance activities", as used in this Part, means any activity

(a) Carried out during an employee's working hours;

(b) Using resources provided by the Corporation or by a recipient; or

(c) That, in fact, provides legal advice, or representation to an eligible client.

§ 1612.2   Public demonstrations and other activities.

(a) While carrying out legal assistance activities under the Act no employee shall

(1) Knowingly participate in any public demonstration, picketing, boycott, or strike, except as permitted by law in connection with the employee's own employment situation; or

(2) Intentionally exhort, direct, or coerce others to engage in such activities, or otherwise usurp or invade the rightful

authority of a client to determine what course of action to follow.

(b) While employed under the Act, no employee shall, at any time,

(1) Knowingly participate in any

(i) Rioting or civil disturbance;

(ii) Activity in violation of an outstanding injunction of any court of competent jurisdiction; or

(iii) Any other illegal activity that is inconsistent with an employee's responsibilities under the Act, Corporation Regulations, or the Code of Professional Responsibility; or

(2) Intentionally exhort, direct, or coerce others to engage in such activities, or otherwise usurp or invade the rightful authority of a client to determine what course of action to follow.

§ 1612.3   Attorney-client relationship.

Nothing in this Part shall prohibit an attorney from

(a) Informing and advising a client about legal alternatives to litigation or the lawful conduct thereof;

(b) Attending a public demonstration, picketing, boycott, or strike for the purpose of providing legal assistance to a client; or

(c) Fulfilling the professional responsibilities of an attorney to a client.

§ 1612.4   Legislative and administrative representation.

(a) No funds made available to a recipient by the Corporation shall be used, directly or indirectly, to support activities intended to influence the issuance, amendment, or revocation of any executive or administrative order or regulation of a Federal, State or local agency, or to influence the passage or defeat of any legislation by the Congress of the United States or by any State or local legislative body; except that

(1) An employee may engage in such activities in response to a request from a governmental agency or a legislative body, committee, or member made to the employee or to a recipient; and

(2) An employee may engage in such activities on behalf of an eligible client of a recipient, if the client may be affected by a particular legislative or administrative measure; but no employee shall

(i) Solicit a client for the purpose of making such representation possible, or

(ii) Solicit a group of clients for the purpose of representing it with respect to matters of general concern to a broad

741

ILLUSTRATION 26.

Page from *Code of Federal Regulations*

carries on its cover the notation, "SAVE THIS ISSUE for Annual Cumulation of Titles [span of numbers including the number of the C.F.R. title in which you are interested]" (assuming there is a more recent pamphlet). That prior pamphlet will cumulate the changes for the preceding year that will ultimately be incorporated in the revised volume.

> *Example*: Suppose that you want to determine whether any changes have been made or proposed in 45 C.F.R. § 1612.2. You must check for that title and section citation in the most recent *LSA* pamphlet. If the revision date for the year for C.F.R. Title 45 (October 1st) has passed, but the revised volumes are not yet in your library, then you may also have to check the citation in the *LSA* pamphlet marked "SAVE THIS ISSUE for Annual Cumulation of Titles 42–50." If any change in section 1612.2 has been *adopted* since the last revision of Title 45, a citation to the page or pages in the *Federal Register* on which the change is reported would be provided. See Illustration 27. If any change in any section in part 1612 has been *proposed*, that fact would be noted at the end of the listings for the title.

(2) Finally, you must check issues of the *Federal Register* itself, the last issue for each month subsequent to the date of the latest *LSA* pamphlet. You must check your C.F.R. citation in the "CUMULATIVE LIST OF PARTS AFFECTED" appearing at the front of the daily issues of the *Federal Register*. See Illustration 28. (Be sure to check the monthly cumulative list, not the list on the preceding page, titled less boldly, "cumulative list of parts affected," which covers only changes in that daily issue.) For the example previously given, if on October 15th the latest *LSA* pamphlet was dated July of the current year, you would have to check the cumulative list in the last *Federal Register* issues for each of three months, August, September, and October, to bring your search down to date.

Portions of the rules, regulations, procedures, and guidelines that are codified in the official C.F.R. may also be reproduced in unofficial publications. For example, a useful feature of many looseleaf services is the collection of administrative material related to the subject of the service. Selected administrative material is also reproduced in the *United States Code Annotated*. See, for example the U.S.C.A. regulations volume for Title 42 (reproducing regulations for the Federal Old-Age, Survivors and Disability Insurance provisions of the Social Security Act) and the Truth-In-Lending regulations reproduced

78   **LSA—LIST OF CFR SECTIONS AFFECTED**

CHANGES OCTOBER 1, 1976 THROUGH AUGUST 31, 1977

Title 45, Chapter X—Continued

Page

1042   Removed _____ 44860
1050   Removed _____ 44860
   Added _____ *3272
   Revised _____ *18034
1050.80–1—1050.80–3   (Subpart)
   Added _____ *43843
1060   Heading revised_____ 44860
1060.2–1   Revised _____ *21108
1060.2–2   Revised _____ *21108
   Undesignated table heading
   added _____ *23151
1061   Heading revised_____ 44860
1061.20–1—1061.20–10 (Subpart)
   Revised _____ *13292
1061.30–14   Appendix A added__ *37208
1061.31–1—1061.31–6   (Subpart)
   Added _____ 52876
1061.50–1—1061.50–14   (Subpart)
   Added _____ *12047
1061.50–15   Added _____ *27593
1062   Heading revised_____ 44860
1067   Heading revised_____ 44860
1067.1–1—1067.1–11   (Subpart)
   Removed _____ *18047
1067.10   Suspended in part_____ *29873
1067.30–1—1067.30–5   (Subpart
   1067.30)   Added _____ 56197
1067.40–1—1067.40–5 (Subpart)
   Added _____ *10689
1067.40–3   (f) and (g) revised__ *18402
   (f) table corrected_____ *21292
   (f) table revised_____ *22365
1068   Heading revised_____ 44860
   Effective date corrected_____ *22145
1068.6   Authority citation revised _____ *3165
1068.9–1—1068.9–5   (Subpart)
   Removed _____ *18038
1068.10–1—1068.10–9   (Subpart)
   Removed _____ *18038
1068.22–1—1068.22–3   (Subpart)
   Revised _____ *21485
1068.23–1—1068.23–4 (Subpart)
   Added _____ *3165
1068.24–1—1068.24–3   (Subpart
   Added _____ *20469
1069   Heading revised_____ 44860
1069.3–4   (a)(2) revised_____ 50825
1069.4–1—1069.4–5   (Subpart
   1069.4)   Revised_____ 50825
1070   Heading revised_____ 44860
1071   Heading revised_____ 44860

Page

1071.30   Suspended indefinitely_ *15704
   Suspension removed; eff. 6–1–
   77 _____ *25734
1075   Heading revised_____ 44860
1076   Heading revised_____ 44860
1078   Heading revised_____ 44860

Chapter XII—ACTION

1209   Added; redesignated and
   revised from Part 1221_____ 53483
1221   Removed; redesignated and
   revised as Part 1209_____ 53483

Chapter XIII—Office of Human Development, Department of Health, Education, and Welfare

1326   Redesignated and revised
   from 911_____ *34282, 34432
1336   Added _____ *3785
1340   Heading and authority citation revised_____ 53663
1340.1–2   (h) revised_____ 53663
1340.1–3   (a) revised_____ 53663
1340.2–2   Revised _____ 53663
1340.2–3   Revised _____ 53663
1340.4–1—1340.4–4   (Subpart D)
   Added _____ 54763
1351   Added _____ 54297
1369   Added _____ *15810
1385   Added _____ *5276
1386   Added _____ *5279
1386.61   (b)   corrected_____ *34282
1387   Added _____ *5287

Chapter XIV—National Institute of Education, Department of Health, Education, and Welfare

1440   Added _____ *14721

Chapter XVI—Legal Services Corporation

1611   Added _____ 51606
   Appendix A revised_____ *24271
   Appendix A corrected_____ *25734
1617   Added _____ 51608
1618   Added _____ 51609
1619   Added _____ *4848
1620   Added _____ 51610
1621   Added _____ 37551

Chapter XVII—National Commission on Libraries and Information Science

1703   Added _____ *13553

Note: Symbol (*) refers to 1977 page numbers

ILLUSTRATION 27.

Page from *LSA—List of CFR Sections Affected*

CUMULATIVE LIST OF PARTS AFFECTED DURING OCTOBER

The following numerical guide is a list of parts of each title of the Code of Federal Regulations affected by documents published to date during October.

1 CFR

Ch. I _____ 53593, 53627
305 _____ 54251

3 CFR

PROCLAMATIONS:

4528 _____ 53591
4529 _____ 53893
4530 _____ 53895
4531 _____ 53897
4532 _____ 55443

EXECUTIVE ORDERS:

10033 (Amended by EO 12013) __ 54931
10252 (Amended by EO 12013) __ 54931
11541 (Amended by EO 12013) __ 54931
11951 (Amended by EO 12013) __ 54931
11183 (Amended by EO 12012) ____ 54249
12011 _____ 53899
12012 _____ 54249
12013 _____ 54931

MEMORANDUMS:

September 20, 1977 _____ 55081

4 CFR

331 _____ 54254

PROPOSED RULES:

416 _____ 54296

5 CFR

213 _____ 53901,
   53902, 54295, 54554, 55189, 55595,
   55596
591 _____ 54554

7 CFR

2 _____ 55083

7 CFR—Continued

PROPOSED RULES—Continued

982 _____ 55245
989 _____ 54423
999 _____ 54950
1049 _____ 54831
1425 _____ 54566
1427 _____ 54660
1464 _____ 54951
1701 _____ 55622
1487 _____ 53628
2852 _____ 54952

8 CFR

316a _____ 55445

PROPOSED RULES:

242 _____ 54423

9 CFR

73 _____ 53947
97 _____ 55598
350 _____ 54829
351 _____ 54829
354 _____ 54829
362 _____ 54829

PROPOSED RULES:

1 _____ 53968
3 _____ 53968, 55221
92 _____ 54834
114 _____ 53968
317 _____ 54437, 55221
319 _____ 54437, 55226

10 CFR

10 _____ 54402
Ch. II _____ 54...

14 CFR—Continued

73 _____ _____ 53598, 54797
75 _____ 54796, 55448
97 _____ 54414, 55448
385 _____ 53599, 54798

PROPOSED RULES:

21 _____ 55176
23 _____ 55427, 55474
25 _____ 54427, 55474
27 _____ 55474
29 _____ 55474
33 _____ 55474
36 _____ 55176
39 _____ 53631,
   54428, 54429, 55102, 55475, 55476
71 _____ 53632,
   54430, 54836, 55103, 55104, 55477–
   55480
75 _____ 54430
91 _____ 53632, 54427, 55176, 55480
121 _____ 54427
135 _____ 54427
234 _____ 54303
241 _____ 55226
399 _____ 54431, 55226

15 CFR

17 _____ 54415
387 _____ 54529
388 _____ 54529
390 _____ 54530
2002 _____ 55611
2006 _____ 55611

16 CFR

1009 _____ 53950
1505 _____ 54273

ILLUSTRATION 28.

Page from *Federal Register*—Cumulative List

following the Consumer Credit Protection Act, 15 U.S.C.A. §§ 1601–1700. Changes in the regulations so reproduced are covered in the U.S.C.A. supplements, but use of the official C.F.R. volumes and supplementing services is recommended because of their consistently greater currency. Nevertheless, appearance of administrative regulations and procedures in U.S.C.A. provides a handy entry to C.F.R. and is the basis for a useful citator service (described hereafter), which is not otherwise available.

Agency and Court Opinions Construing Regulations

Agency rules and regulations may be construed or applied by courts or by agencies having adjudicatory powers. The opinions of federal adjudicatory agencies [18] are reported in sets of volumes comparable in bulk to a substantial portion of the National Reporter System. For the search for applying and construing opinions, however, the general research-book publishers have failed us: there is no Code of Federal Regulations Annotated; there is no Shepard's Citator for the codified regulations. There are, however, looseleaf services for many of the administrative areas of greatest activity, wherein are collected relevant opinions, digests, commentary, or other helpful research aids. Absent a looseleaf service or a treatise in the area of in-

18. See the listing of official administrative publications in the citation *Blue Book* at 101–03.

terest, or periodical coverage thereof, however, you may find no easy entry to agency opinions, because few of the published reports of the agencies have cumulative digests or other cumulative indexes. The kind of index available for an agency's opinions can be determined by examining available volumes and noting research features.

Relatively simple finding of *recent* court opinions construing some regulations is possible. National Reporter volumes and their advance sheets cite, in the Cumulative Statutes Construed tables, opinions reported therein that cite any federal agency regulation reprinted in U.S.C.A. See Illustration 29.

<table>
<tr><td colspan="2" align="center">CUMULATIVE STATUTES CONSTRUED</td></tr>
<tr><td align="center">UNITED STATES CODE ANNOTATED
—Cont'd</td><td>Sec.
1462—556 F.2d 978</td></tr>
<tr><td>15 U.S.C.A.—Commerce and Trade—Cont'd</td><td>1511—556 F.2d 799
1706—556 F.2d 948</td></tr>
<tr><td>Sec.
1638(a)(10)—552 S.W.2d 490
1639(a)(8)—552 S.W.2d 490
1640(a)—553 S.W.2d 174
1640(e)—347 So.2d 853
1644(b)—556 F.2d 278
1681h(e)—236 S.E.2d 154</td><td>1952—556 F.2d 1209
1952(a)(3)—556 F.2d 799
1953—556 F.2d 799
1955—556 F.2d 450
1955—556 F.2d 709
1955—556 F.2d 799
1955—556 F.2d 811
1955—556 F.2d 1209
1961—556 F.2d 855</td></tr>
<tr><td>Following § 1700. Truth in Lending Regulations

Regulation
Z, § 226.1 et seq.—347 So.2d 853
Z, § 226.4(a)(5)—553 S.W.2d 174
Z, § 226.6(a)—553 S.W.2d 174
Z, § 226.8(b)(4)—553 S.W.2d 174
Z, § 226.8(b)(5)—556 F.2d 772
Z, § 226.8(j)—556 F.2d 772</td><td>1961(1)(C)—556 F.2d 855
1961(5)—556 F.2d 855
1962(c)—556 F.2d 855
2031—556 F.2d 1177
2113(a)—556 F.2d 366
2114—556 F.2d 948
2312—556 F.2d 752
2313—556 F.2d 752</td></tr>
<tr><td>Sec.
2051 et seq.—556 F.2d 242
2052—556 F.2d 242
2301 et seq.—7 Ill.Dec. 113, 364 N.E.2d 100</td><td>2510–2520—552 S.W.2d 418
2511(1)(b)—556 F.2d 257
2511(2)(c)—552 S.W.2d 418
2511(2)(d)—552 S.W.2d 418
2515—556 F.2d 709</td></tr>
<tr><td align="center">16 U.S.C.A.—Conservation

577g—556 F.2d 1096
577g-1—556 F.2d 1096</td><td>2515—364 N.E.2d 815
2516—556 F.2d 709</td></tr>
</table>

ILLUSTRATION 29.

Excerpt from National Reporter Advance Sheet table
showing recent court citations to Truth-in-Lending
regulations reproduced in U.S.C.A.

If the regulations are reprinted in U.S.C.A. in a separate regulations volume (as for the Social Security regulations mentioned in a preceding paragraph), the citations appear in the advance sheet table at the end of the citation listing for the title. Annotations on these recent court opinions are now being appended to the sections of the regulations as reproduced in U.S.C.A.[19]

A Shepard's citator unit, *Shepard's United States Administrative Citations,* is useful if you find relevant opinions or decisions of cer-

19. Administrative opinions regarding veterans' benefits, are digested along with court opinions in U.S.C.A. anno-tations for Title 38 of the *United States Code.*

tain federal departments, boards, and commissions.   This citator unit identifies federal and state court opinions that cite such administrative opinions or decisions.   Thus, for example, you can Shepardize the opinions and decisions of Attorneys General, the Department of the Interior, several customs and tax tribunals and departments, the Interstate Commerce Commission, the Federal Communications Commission, the Federal Power Commission, the Federal Trade Commission, and the Securities and Exchange Commission.

State Agency Materials

Given continuing expansion of state regulatory activities, states are being forced to provide state equivalents of the *Federal Register* for the publication of proposed state regulations for the information of affected persons and companies.   Many states have already published or are in the process of publishing codes that collect their state agency rules and regulations already in force.   Other states will undoubtedly do the same eventually.   If a state has no such code, then some state agencies publish their rules, regulations, and procedures in agency pamphlets, distributed to persons and companies directly affected by their activities and made available to others on request.

SECTION 8H.   RESEARCH AIDS FOR OTHER FORMS OF WRITTEN LAW

Constitutions

Annotated codes usually include annotations for constitutions. Thus, both U.S.C.A. and U.S.C.S. print the Federal Constitution with section-by-section and sometimes clause-by-clause annotations.   State annotated codes usually include similar annotations for the governing state constitution and sometimes annotations to state opinions for the Federal Constitution as well.   Hence, an annotated code may be an effective starting point for research on constitutional provisions. The digest for the controlling jurisdiction will also be useful for research on constitutional points.

For the Federal Constitution you should note the annotated *Constitution of the United States: Analysis and Interpretation* (1972 ed.), with biennial cumulative pocket supplements.   It is particularly useful for background research by persons who have not taken a course in Constitutional Law.   Prepared by the Congressional Research Service of the Library of Congress, its preparation and publication were authorized by joint resolution of Congress.   *A.L.R. Federal* and recent *Lawyers Edition 2d* annotations will sometimes be useful.   The most effective source for detailed analysis of federal constitutional law problems will frequently be periodicals.   Legal periodicals and periodicals published in related disciplines contain exhaustive

discussions of past and current problems and, frequently, of problems that may be anticipated for the future.

Executive Orders

Executive orders promulgated by the President may sometimes be a significant source of federal law. These orders generally deal with the organization of the executive department and the conduct of government business, but some may have widespread influence. For example, an executive order establishes equal opportunity in federal employment (Exec. Order No. 11478, superseding on this subject Exec. Order No. 11246). Executive orders are initially published in the *Federal Register*. They are then compiled annually and reprinted in numerical order in Title 3 of C.F.R. Title 3 consists of several permanent compilation volumes, a cumulative index, and annual supplementing paperbacks with noncumulative subject indexes. Orders issued since 1965 are also published in the *Weekly Compilation of Presidential Documents*. Executive orders having general effect may be reprinted in U.S.C. volumes following related code sections. Thus, Exec. Order No. 11478, mentioned above, was reprinted in the code following 42 U.S.C. § 2000e, which prohibits discrimination in private and state government employment. Orders reprinted in the code will also be reprinted in U.S.C.A. and U.S.C.S. Court opinions that cite executive orders reprinted in U.S.C.A. are included in annotations for the related statute under a note entitled Executive Orders. Recent citing court opinions are cited at the end of the United States listings for the Cumulative Statutes Construed tables in National Reporter advance sheets. Implementing regulations, if any are authorized by an executive order, and citations to executive orders in C.F.R. may be found through Table II, List B, in the C.F.R. *Findings Aid* volume.

Court Rules

Either through inherent power or express legislative grant of power, courts are empowered to promulgate rules governing pleading, practice, and procedure. Thus, appellate courts prescribe procedures governing appeal and review; trial courts adopt particular rules governing procedures within their courts. In addition, the highest appellate courts within a jurisdiction may have power to prescribe general rules relating to pleading, practice, and procedure in the courts within that jurisdiction. For example, the United States Supreme Court was expressly empowered to prepare a unified system of general rules for the federal trial courts for both civil and criminal proceedings. State courts may exercise similar power. The general and particular rules adopted by the Supreme Court or by state appellate courts are annotated in the pertinent annotated codes and may be Shepardized in the pertinent Shepard's Statute edition. Annotated compilations of general rules for a particular state may be published as well. The

federal rules—those prepared and adopted by the United States Supreme Court and subsequently adopted in several states—are the subject of comprehensive treatises. The possible existence of local trial court rules, describing local practice, should not be forgotten.

Local Government Legislation

Ordinances of cities and legislation of other local government units are sometimes codified. The status of these local codes—enacted, prima facie, or unofficial—may be significant in determining whether they may be cited to courts and how the local legislation must be pleaded. Annotated versions of these codes are not generally available. Thus, Shepard's citations (the state statute editions) are commonly the most convenient source for finding mandatory construing court opinions. Another Shepard's publication, *Shepard's Ordinance Law Annotations*, in six volumes, may be useful for finding nonlocal opinions that construe analogous provisions.

NOTES

1. The enactment process for federal statutes is detailed in Zinn, How Our Laws are Made, as revised and updated by E. Willett, Jr., H.R.Doc.No.93–377, 93rd Cong., 2d Sess. (1974). For a livelier account of the process as it worked with reference to one act, see E. Redman, The Dance of Legislation (1973).

2. A detailed description of historical materials for the Federal Constitution and statutes is provided in G. Folsom, Legislative History: Research for the Interpretation of Laws (1972). For general discussions of interpretation of statutes, see in this text, *supra*, Section 3B and text note 7 following chapter 3, and see the numerous articles reprinted in the Legal Commentary section of 3 Sutherland, Statutes and Statutory Construction 409 *et seq.* (4th ed. C. Sands. ed. 1972). For discussion of the value of various forms of legislative history, see Wasby, *Legislative Materials as an Aid to Statutory Interpretation: A Caveat*, 12 J.Pub. 262 (1963); R. Dickerson, The Interpretation and Application of Statutes 154–64 (1975). See also, Walgren, *A Lawmaker's Point of View*, 30 Wash.St.Bar News, October 1976 at 12 (use of planned colloquy to effect recording of understanding of meaning in state legislative journals). Perhaps the most realistic view of the value of legislative history materials will be derived from reading E. Redman, *supra* note 1. He discusses, for example, the planning of questions and answers for committee hearings (at 47–48, 125); the practice of providing introductory speeches for bills for printing in the *Congressional Record* even though they are seldom read (at 95); creating the appearance of administrative support that was lacking in fact (at 120); drafting a committee report to reflect legislative intent and to persuade Senators to vote for a bill (at 140); intentionally writing an ambiguity into a bill to avoid making a diffi-

cult legislative choice (at 144); drafting a committee report to announce legislative intent as encompassing provisions removed from a
bill by committee amendment (at 152, 157–58); inserting statements
in support of a bill in the *Congressional Record* though not read (at
157) and without indication whether they were or were not read (at
250); and correcting remarks made on the floor before printing in
the *Congressional Record* (at 206).

3. On executive orders and executive power in the legislative
setting, see Comment, *Presidential Legislation By Executive Order,* 37
U.Colo.L.Rev. 105 (1964).

4. The *United States Government Manual,* an annual government publication, provides useful background information about the
organization, statutory origin, authority, purpose, functions, and
informational sources of federal courts, departments, agencies,
boards, commissions, and committees. Annual reports and other publications of such governmental bodies may provide background information about policies and legislative proposals. Materials prepared
for internal agency use (for example, claims manuals) are now available to researchers under the Freedom of Information Act. See K.
Davis, Administrative Law Text § 3A.12 (1972). See generally *Id.* at
ch. 3A (1972). Reports of Presidential advisory commissions may
furnish excellent background for legislation proposed as a result of
such a report. For a discussion of the functions and effectiveness of
such commissions, see T. Wolanin, Presidential Advisory Commissions (1975) (listing commissions and reports to 1973 at 205–215).

5. A paragraph in Section 8B is devoted to describing the history of the Washington state code. Can you find or prepare a similar
description of the code or other compilation for the state in which
you expect to practice or in which your law school is located?

Chapter 9

A LOOK BACKWARD AND A LOOK FORWARD: COMPUTER–ASSISTED LEGAL RESEARCH

Section
9A. Using What You Have Learned.
9B. Computer-Assisted Legal Research.
    Notes

SECTION 9A. USING WHAT YOU HAVE LEARNED

This text has described only the basic traditional legal research sources. The descriptions of even these basic sources have not been exhaustive. Hence, an important thing for you to remember in the future is that legal research is not limited to the materials and approaches discussed in this text to this point. Nevertheless, what you have learned about research sources and techniques will suffice for most problem-related research and will provide the basis for identifying other sources and learning to use them effectively.

In your future research, should you find yourself at a dead end or unable to get started toward finding anything of direct or analogous interest, ask yourself three questions:

1. *Does the fault lie in your analysis?* Have you failed to identify a sufficiently precise area of inquiry? If this fault is creating the difficulty, return to a basic source such as a treatise or a periodical article. Or are you directing your search toward answering too narrow a question? If direct answer to your narrow question is not available, a broader formulation of the question may lead you to useful analogous materials.

2. *Does the fault lie in your inefficient use of a source?* Are you using a nonproductive approach or failing to take advantage of special finding aids? If faulty use of a source appears to be creating the difficulty, review use of the source in this text, read the preface or how-to-use explanation in the source itself, or use a detailed legal bibliography text to determine whether it will identify other approaches to use of the source.

3. *Is there a more useful source with which you are not familiar?* This question will identify the obvious difficulty if you are, for example, researching an international law problem for the first time. A legal bibliography

219

text may help you if you have such an obvious difficulty. But do not consider this question as a possible lead only in such obvious situations. Always keep in mind the possibility that a source with which you are not familiar will furnish the authority or information for which you are searching. Use the library catalog. Once you find the area of the library in which materials on the subject matter of your interest are shelved, browse through the section to learn what is available. Remember that library personnel are pleased to be of assistance to you.

If the solution to your difficulty lies in using materials with which you are not familiar, you will usually find that the common features and the research approaches about which you have learned in this text are equally "common" and effective in the new materials. If new materials do baffle you, however, remember to look for a preface or other introductory material that explains the particular publication. If such explanatory material is lacking, turn to one of the legal bibliography texts or a member of the library staff for explanation.

Some of your research difficulties may seem to result from nothing more than the sheer bulk of the sources that you feel compelled to examine. Given the latent deficiencies in our indexing and digesting systems, how can an individual researcher with limited time for research expect consistently to discover the available relevant material for each problem researched—or even the most significant material? The research steps and methods suggested in this text are intended to provide the basis for a research system that will permit use of a realistically limited number of sources while yielding, in the shortest possible time, the highest probability that clearly significant materials have not been missed. Whether the system consistently yields that result for you will depend on your readiness to modify and refine it as the peculiarities of particular problems seem to require.

Remember also that, like the law itself, legal research materials are constantly changing. It is predictable that within a short time after publication of this book, descriptions of some research sources will be inaccurate because of changes. Therefore, try to remember what you have learned in terms of the functions served by research features and types of publications rather than in terms of particular features of particular research sources. Then, too, new research materials are continually being published. Do not permit habit and the comfort of using familiar sources to keep you from benefitting from advances in legal publishing. One comparatively recent development in research methodology—computer-assisted research—is discussed in the following section. A few other modern developments are men-

tioned in the text notes at the end of this chapter. Continuing self-education will keep you aware of future significant developments.

SECTION 9B. COMPUTER–ASSISTED LEGAL RESEARCH

Approximately thirty years ago, the development of high-speed binary digital computers first became known to the general public in the United States.[1] Approximately twenty years ago, computerized legal information retrieval was first demonstrated to lawyers.[2] Approximately five years ago, the first commercially available computer-assisted case law research service was offered nationally.[3] Today, several different types of legal information retrieval systems are commercially available, and departments of the federal government, state and local governments, and legislative bodies have available retrieval systems of varying degrees of sophistication.

Published information about computer-assisted legal research and related developments is extensive. New developments occur so rapidly that published descriptions rapidly become dated. Therefore, only the fundamental features of the two most comprehensive commercial services, LEXIS and WESTLAW, will be described in the following paragraphs, followed by one researcher's description of the research tasks best performed by such systems. Text notes at the end of this chapter provide citations to discussions of major computer applications in the law setting.

LEXIS and WESTLAW each provide access, via telephone lines, to legal documents stored in the data banks of their respective central computer systems. A search request is typed on the keyboard of a terminal provided for subscribers. The terminal is also equipped with both a television display panel and a printer that can provide copies of retrieved and displayed documents on command.

LEXIS was developed by Mead Data Central, Inc., in collaboration with the Ohio and New York Bar Associations. Its services were made available nationally in 1973. Documents stored in its data bank include the full texts of recent opinions of the federal courts and, currently, the courts of eleven states and of the *United States Code.*[4] A

1. Lawlor, *Historical Perspective and Future Prospects*, in Standing Committee on Law and Technology, American Bar Association, Sense & Systems in Automated Law Research 12 (1975).

2. *Id.* at 16.

3. Rubin, *LEXIS: An Automated Research System*, in Standing Committee on Law and Technology, American Bar Association, Automated Law Research 35 (1973).

4. The LEXIS data base is being expanded every year. The states represented currently are California, Florida, Illinois, Kansas, Kentucky, Massachusetts, Missouri, New York, Ohio, Pennsylvania, and Texas. The time span covered for court opinions varies from state to state and from court to court, ranging for the state courts from the 1940's (California Supreme Court; Illinois Supreme Court; Missouri appellate courts; New York Court of Appeals; and Ohio Supreme Court, courts of appeal, and county

search request may be a single word, a phrase, a number, or a combination thereof in a prescribed logical form. Responses to the request (full opinions or statutes or segments thereof) may be called up for display on the display panel.[5]

The second commercially available case-law retrieval system, WESTLAW, was created by West Publishing Company. Its data bank includes headnotes from the National Reporter System, including the topic and key number identifications, for federal court opinions from 1961 forward and for reported state court opinions from 1967 forward. Thus, for federal court opinions it parallels the *West's Federal Practice Digest 2d,* supplementing the earlier federal Key Number digests. For state court opinions, it parallels the *Eighth Decennial Digest* (in the form of almost forty *General Digest 4th* volumes at the time the service was introduced in 1975) and the current supplement thereto, the *General Digest 5th*. As of January 1978, the full text of federal court opinions from the National Reporter System from 1961 forward have been added to the data bank, and the full text of current appellate court cases from all the states are being added.

A search request may be addressed to WESTLAW in a question in natural language, in key words, in a prescribed logical form, or in a combination of natural and logical language. The documents retrieved in response to such a request are ranked by the computer on the basis of the frequency of occurrence of the search terms in each document. The retrieved documents are then displayed in the sequence of their apparent relevance thus determined. A search request may also be given by digest topic and Key Number.[6]

Legal document retrieval systems were recently studied by a research attorney of the American Bar Foundation, James A. Sprowl. Among his general conclusions about the usefulness of computer-assisted legal research after studying full-text retrieval systems were the following:

> Computerized document retrieval systems are now a commercial reality; they enable attorneys and other re-

and municipal courts) to the 1970's (Kansas Civil and Criminal Courts of Appeal added most recently, in 1977). Opinions of the federal courts currently include those of the Supreme Court from 1938, the court of appeals from 1945, the district courts from 1960, and the court of claims beginning in 1977. The text of the *United States Code* is kept up to date by regular additions of Public Laws as enacted. LEXIS also has topical data files for federal tax law; federal securities law; federal trade regulation; and federal patent, trademark, and copyright law. These topical files include court and administrative court opinions, relevant statutes and regulations, and a variety of other materials, including legislative history materials, interpretive releases, and proposed regulations. The one topical file for state law is Delaware corporation law.

5. For a fuller description of the LEXIS system, see Sprowl, A Manual for Computer-Assisted Legal Research ch. II (1976).

6. For a fuller description of the WESTLAW system, see *Id.* at ch. III.

searchers to search quickly through large collections of judicial decisions and statutes for those containing words pertinent to their inquiries. While these systems can free the researcher from the constraints of formal indexing, they leave him enslaved to a different master—word usage in the documents through which he is searching. With these new systems, the retrievability of a document is determined by its word content, and that in turn is determined by the vocabulary and stylistic habits of the document's author. Thus, judges and other document authors unwittingly serve as the indexers of these systems.

The motivation for the development of these systems has come primarily from researchers who are dissatisfied with conventional case-law searching tools such as digests and annotations. Computerized retrieval systems do represent relatively good, albeit expensive, alternatives to such conventional tools, and most subscribers to computerized systems use them primarily for conventional research. But computerized systems also have a number of special capabilities that enable them to carry out certain research tasks so quickly, accurately, and economically that their use is justifiable even on a one-time-only basis by nonsubscribers.

*   *   *

These new systems differ so drastically from manual research systems that no general conclusions can be reached on the relative merits of computerized versus manual research. Research needs vary, and some researchers will undoubtedly find these new systems invaluable while others will find them of little value and, perhaps, too costly. Every researcher should therefore learn as much as he can about these new systems and then judge their merits in the light of his own needs. *   *   *

A researcher who does not learn what computerized retrieval systems are capable of doing for him will be unable to recognize when they can save him time, trouble, and money. These systems can carry out some research tasks so well that their use seems almost mandatory. This section briefly lists and discusses the various types of tasks that these systems can perform.

The tasks computerized systems perform best are those that involve assembling collections of documents related to each other in a simple, well-defined way. For example, such systems can collect the decisions handed down by a particular judge or court over a specified period, or statutes or judicial opinions containing specific phrases or bits of statutory language, more quickly and accurately than a researcher

could collect them by hand. Many legislatures use them in the latter way as an aid to the drafting of statutes. They may even be used to collect the decisions in which a particular attorney is named as counsel, provided the stored documents contain that information. As citators, these systems can not only collect all the judicial decisions that have cited a particular decision or statute, but they can also collect all the decisions that have cited a specified combination of two or more earlier decisions or statutes, even limiting such collections to the decisions of a particular court or judge or to a particular area of law. And to the extent that these systems contain slip opinions that have not been formally published and assigned volume and page numbers, they can be more current than a published citator service. A researcher faced with a retrieval task like any of those just described should use a computerized retrieval system even if he has to lease a library or bar association system temporarily.

These systems can also help a researcher find an individual document if he knows its title. If he is familiar with the contents of a document but cannot recall its title, he can supply samples of language that he knows appear within the document and instruct the system to retrieve all documents containing the language. The system will quickly retrieve a small collection of documents, including the one he is seeking.

Computerized systems are very good at retrieving documents relating to specific factual situations (for example, all decisions that mention Cadillac Eldorados or condominiums or poisons). The researcher formulates a document search request with a list of the words one would normally use in describing the factual situation and then submits the request to the retrieval system, which retrieves all of the documents that contain the listed words. The documents can be displayed individually on a television-like display, or the computer system can print out the full text of the collected documents.

The above tasks all involve the retrieval of documents that are readily identifiable through certain words, phrases, numbers, or combinations of them. In every case, the researcher knew exactly what he wanted retrieved.

Even when the researcher is unfamiliar with the documents he wants, a computerized document retrieval system can be helpful. The researcher supplies the system with words and phrases he believes will appear in the documents he wishes to see. To the extent those words and phrases do

correspond to the wording of the desired documents, the computer system finds and retrieves the documents. However, some such documents may be missed because their wording is not as predicted, while others the researcher does not wish to see may be retrieved because by mischance they contain the words and phrases designated. A search through unfamiliar documents typically requires a series of document retrievals. After each such retrieval, the researcher can evaluate the retrieved documents and revise the selection of words and phrases in an effort to capture more wheat and less chaff the next time. Once a few documents of interest have been found, they will suggest additional words and phrases that the researcher may use in later searches. The less the researcher knows about the documents he is searching, the less successful he will be in finding the documents he needs.

When a researcher knows little or nothing about an area of law, he may do himself a disservice by relying solely upon a computerized system. These systems presently require one to know in advance what words and phrases are likely to be in the documents to be retrieved, and they do not stimulate the thinking of the researcher by suggesting possible alternative words and phrases other than those he may encounter while browsing. If the researcher is unaware of the existence of a particular issue or doctrine, a computerized system will not necessarily draw it to his attention. A researcher unfamiliar with an area of law is better served by treatises, articles, loose-leaf services, and other more traditional tools of legal research that can stimulate his thinking by suggesting to him a variety of possible solutions to his problem.[7]

The addition of full texts of opinions to the WESTLAW system followed completion of Mr. Sprowl's studies, but he reached the following conclusions about the WESTLAW system with its headnote data bank:

The WESTLAW system enables a researcher to browse through headnote summaries more rapidly than he can using the bound volumes of the *General Digest*. In the first place, he does not have to contend with monthly and yearly supplemental volumes (such as the green hard-bound and blue soft-bound supplements to the *General Digest*). The WESTLAW system contains, and can rapidly display, the

7. Sprowl, *Computer-Assisted Legal Research—An Analysis of Full-Text Document Retrieval Systems, Particularly the LEXIS System*, 1 ABF Research J. 175, 175–80 (1976) (footnotes omitted). Reproduced with permission.

headnotes for all cases West has indexed since 1966, the last year covered by West's *Seventh Decennial Digest,* and reference to more recent digest volumes is thus unnecessary. In addition, when one is using the WESTLAW system to search through headnotes indexed under a key number and topic heading that encompasses many hundreds of individual headnotes, one may use the word and phrase searching capability of the WESTLAW system to prevent the retrieval of headnotes that are clearly irrelevant to the researcher's inquiry, thereby reducing substantially the number of headnotes that the researcher has to read individually. Finally, one may search selectively through the headnotes of a particular state or federal case collection using the WESTLAW system in a way that cannot be done otherwise without access to individual published digests for each such collection.[8]

NOTES

1. Both LEXIS and WESTLAW can be used for citator purposes. The Lawyers Co-operative Publishing Company and its affiliate, Bancroft-Whitney Company, have developed an extensive automated citation system called Auto-Cite. It provides citations for the history of a case and citing references that affect the validity of decisions in the case. The data base is much more up-to-date than generally available printed citators. The system is described in Frost, *Verifying Citations by Computer at LCP/BW*, 8 Law & Computer Tech. 58 (1975), and favorably appraised by an attorney, McGonigal, *Report on the Lawyers Co-operative Publishing Company's Automated Citation Testing Service ("Auto-Cite")*, 16 Jurimetrics J. 130 (1975). The publishers of Shepard's Citations services provide for their subscribers a citation update service that includes updates from daily computerized listings of federal citings.

2. Early success in statute-related computer searches led to organization of Aspen Systems, a private corporation offering searches for all state statutes. Difficulties in keeping the data bank current, along with other problems, however, led to abandonment of this ambitious service. Committee on the Office of Attorney General, The National Association of Attorneys General, *Computerized Research in the Law* 12–13 (1976). Aspen Systems then began contracting with private firms to maintain the data bank for every state's law on given subjects, such as insurance regulation. *Id.* at 13.

Of greatest value have been statutory search systems combined with bill-drafting and legislative services, which can combine a search

---

8. J. Sprowl, A Manual for Computer-Assisted Legal Research 57–58 (1976) (footnotes omitted). Copyright ©️ 1976, American Bar Foundation. Reproduced with permission.

of statutes with bill-drafting that progresses through changes during the enactment process, to enactment, codification, and publication, and even later amendment, all with savings in cost, time, and error. *Id.* at 11–12.   See also the description of the Washington legislative service combined with a data base that includes opinions of the attorney general and of the state supreme court as well as the statute and administrative codes.   Standing Committee on Law and Technology, American Bar Association, Automated Law Research 113–17 (1973).

3.   Computerized information systems for some secondary sources are described in J. Jacobstein & R. Mersky, Fundamentals of Legal Research 471–75 (1977) (social science and law review, and *New York Times* data bases) and in How to Find the Law 463 (M. Cohen ed. 7th ed. 1976) (census and medical information data bases and Library of Congress monthly legal bibliography).

4.   For detailed descriptions of history, studies, and other information about computer applications in computer fields, see Standing Committee on Law and Technology, American Bar Association, Sense & Systems in Automated Law Research (1975) and Automated Law Research, *supra*, note 2, collecting papers presented at two national conferences on automated law research.   A continuing source of such information is the quarterly journal published by the ABA committee, *Jurimetrics Journal.*   See also its predecessor, the *M.U.L.L.* newsletter (Modern Uses of Logic in Law).   The *Rutgers Journal of Computers and the Law* provides a regularly updated bibliography.

5.   For descriptions of reduced forms, including microfilm, microcard, microfiche, and ultrafiche, now used for several major legal publications, see How to Find the Law, *supra*, note 3, at 447–56. Each of the 2,300 volumes of the first series of the National Reporter system has now been reproduced on a single 4″ by 6″ ultrafiche card.   The cards for the complete first series fit in nine small filing trays that can be stored in the drawers of a desk or filing cabinet. The cards are read on a 9″ by 12″ illuminated screen.   The *Federal Register* is also published in microforms.   On use of such forms for law library catalogs, see footnote 2, Chapter 4, *supra.*

6.   Two comprehensive bibliography texts have been repeatedly cited in Part II of this text as sources of more detailed information, J. Jacobstein & R. Mersky, *supra*, note 3, and How to Find the Law, *supra*, note 3.   Another excellent comprehensive bibliography text is M. Price and H. Bitner, Effective Legal Research (3d ed. 1969).   Citations to specific discussions therein have not been provided because it is currently being revised.   When the new edition is published late in 1978 it will be a detailed source of the most up-to-date legal bibliography information.

Part III

REPORT AND ARGUMENT

Chapter 10

WRITTEN REPORT OF ANALYSIS AND RESEARCH FINDINGS

SECTION 10A. INTRODUCTION

For most general purposes, forms of legal writing may be roughly divided into two categories: objective and argumentative. Objective writing should be exploratory and unaffected by personal goals or desires, though it will usually lead to a conclusion. Argumentative writing, on the other hand, should be directed toward persuading readers to a predetermined conclusion.

Argumentative writing for courts will be discussed in the following chapter. Two forms of objective writing, office memoranda and Recent Case Notes, will be discussed in this chapter. Some other significant forms of legal writing are briefly discussed in text notes following this chapter.

Some general suggestions about drafting and revising office memoranda, including a few basic legal writing conventions and some common writing errors to be avoided, are also summarized in this chapter. Although they are discussed in relation to office memoranda, most of the suggestions are also relevant to other forms of legal writing. They are here related to office memoranda because that is the form required for much early problem-solving writing of law students and recent law graduates.

SECTION 10B.   RECENT CASE NOTE FORM

One of the forms of legal writing with which you are already familiar is the "Recent Case Note" (or "Case Comment" or "Case Note") such as the sample note reproduced in Appendix C. The subject of a recent case note is a recent opinion that is considered noteworthy because of the aptness or inaptness of the court's approach to, for example, a difficult, changing, or novel problem area. A recent case note builds from a textual report of the selected opinion. Interrupting or following this textual report will be a concise summary of relevant background materials, which will frequently include a synthesis of opinions in similar and analogous cases. The remainder of the note is the author's critical analysis of the noteworthy feature (or features) and an evaluation of the court's decision and reasoning in light of the background materials and the considerations suggested in the critical analysis. Therefore, recent case notes include excellent examples of the kind of textual reports and synthesis that form the nucleus of much legal writing.

Following is a description of one note form.[1] Reading critically the sample note in Appendix C and other published notes with this description in mind may assist you in shifting from writing opinion briefs to this and other kinds of textual reporting of your analysis, evaluation, and synthesis. It may also guide you in making the actual selection of what to include in, for example, case statements, or in determining more generally what should be included in other forms of legal writing. Thus, for example, preparation of an office memorandum on a legal problem requires a statement of the facts, identification of the issue(s) in the problem (akin to the noteworthy feature), selection and evaluation of relevant materials (akin to the background materials), and a critical analysis and evaluation.

The textual report of the opinion in a note is divided into two parts—the "squib" paragraph and the "court's reasoning" paragraph —which may be the first two paragraphs of the note but will more often be separated by the "background" paragraph.

The Squib Paragraph. The squib paragraph states the relevant facts of the case and the decision. As with the entire note, the predetermined noteworthy feature of the case dictates the factual content of the squib. Only those facts relevant to the feature to be developed in the "analysis and evaluation" should be included. The relevant facts are not necessarily limited to the significant facts, because a noteworthy feature may be failure of the court to consider facts that should have been treated as significant. Occasionally the noteworthy

---

1. The description is adapted from instructions prepared by the 1965–66 Editorial Board of the *Washington Law Review*, with permission of the editor of the 1969–70 Board. Some parts are produced verbatim; the major changes are in terminology, in reordering of some explanations, and in omission of many details.

feature of a case will require that the facts be stated in minute detail; more often, only a small portion of the reported facts is required.

The procedural history, when relevant, is also presented in the squib. Relevance is dictated again by the noteworthy feature. A minimum procedural history is always required. The reasoning of the lower court may be treated as relevant procedural history.

The squib is terminated by a statement of both the procedural and the substantive holdings in the case. This statement is preceded by a formal lead-in, which may take any one of several forms, for example:

> On appeal to the Court of Appeals for the Second Circuit, reversed. **Held:** * * *

> Denial of plaintiff's motion was appealed to the Nevada Supreme Court, which affirmed and held: * * *

The Court's Reasoning Paragraph. This paragraph presents a precise exposition of the steps in the court's analysis and resolution of the case. If the court's analysis involves unstated assumptions or conclusions, these assumptions should be pointed out and supplied by the author of the note.

Just as selection of facts for the squib paragraph is directed toward leading the reader down a limited and predetermined path, so must the selection and statement of the court's analysis in the court's reasoning paragraph be guided by relevance to the analytical goal. Thus, this paragraph completes the process of setting the stage for the analysis and evaluation. If the evaluation is to criticize the decision for illogical or imprecise reasoning, those deficiencies must be objectively noted in the court's reasoning paragraph. If a dissenting or concurring opinion is to be discussed in the analysis and evaluation, a very brief statement of that opinion must appear in the court's reasoning paragraph.

The Background Paragraph. The purpose of this paragraph is twofold: to present to the reader the relevant background material and to focus the reader on the noteworthy feature and the theme of the analysis and evaluation. Relevance is dictated again by the predetermined noteworthy feature of the case.

Although the author is limited in the squib and court's reasoning paragraphs by the content of the opinion itself, no such limitation exists for the background paragraph. Instead, the background paragraph should contain the information that the author believes the court should have considered in reaching its decision. This information may include, *e. g.,* a conflicting line of authority, a recent decision of the United States Supreme Court, prior judicial history of the litigation, the views of a noted scholar, an economic policy supporting an opposite result, equitable considerations, or relevant social or sci-

entific data. Judicious selection of background material by the author will direct the reader's attention to the feature or features that are considered by the author to be noteworthy, and why. Occasionally a proper setting of the stage will require that the author state the problem in direct terms, *e. g.*, "The court was faced with a conflict between contract precedents and community property precedents and incorrectly chose to follow the latter."

The Analysis and Evaluation: Here the author discusses the noteworthy feature of the case, according to his or her analysis and evaluation.

SECTION 10C. FORMAT AND SUBSTANTIVE CONTENT OF AN OFFICE MEMORANDUM

An office memorandum critically analyzes and discusses a problem. Acceptable memorandum forum varies from office to office and from problem to problem. In some offices, and particularly for a simple question, a one- or two-page outline of controlling rules with citation of supporting authorities may be all that is required. Other offices require a highly stylized format. Some require that a brief be attached for every cited case.

The comprehensive form described hereafter and illustrated in the sample memorandum reproduced in Appendix D, is recommended for the first few memoranda that you prepare. This comprehensive form is recommended because it will lead you to do the kind of careful and comprehensive analysis that is always necessary, even if a required memorandum is to be only a two-page outline.

TITLE: (Under this heading state the name of the client for whom research is being done or the title of a pending action.)

REQUESTED BY:

SUBMITTED BY:

DATE SUBMITTED:

Question(s) Presented

Under this heading state the legal question or questions presented by the problem to be analyzed. This section serves an analytical purpose by requiring you to formulate the question(s) presented by the problem with great particularity. If the questions are complex, attention to outlining and phrasing them will sharpen your own understanding and simplify your writing of the discussion. This section also serves two practical purposes: it informs readers of the content of the memorandum and facilitates filing and indexing a copy for future office uses.

Recall the suggestion that you outline and revise your tentative questions as your research progresses. From that outline you should select issues (that is, questions for which there is more than one possible answer or for which there is only one reasonable answer requiring careful analysis and evaluation of available materials) for inclusion in the "Question(s) Presented" section. Questions that identify only analytical points (that is, questions for which you can state a short, simple answer) need not, but may be included if, for example, to do so would provide a useful outline of your overall analysis.

Many legal problems do not lend themselves to such simple statements. With complicated fact patterns presenting several or alternative questions, a tendency of students is to present only the ultimate question to be resolved, dressing it up with the significant facts.

Example: Can a broker, licensed in Montana but not in Washington, recover a promised commission for procuring a purchaser for hotel furnishings and a lease on the hotel real property, located in Washington, where:

1. the oral promise to pay a commission was made in Montana,

2. the broker found the purchaser in Montana, and

3. the seller accepted the purchaser's offer, sent from Montana, by telegram sent from Seattle?

Such phrasing of a question may be helpful as a tentative formulation to aid in identifying significant facts, but it does not identify a precise legal question. Compare the following example: does it give you a clear picture of the legal problems even though you have no background in the substantive problem area? Note that it satisfies three basic guides for phrasing questions presented: The whole question incorporates significant facts, each subsidiary question incorporating the facts that are peculiarly significant to that subsidiary issue; the whole question states facts and not legal conclusions; and the subsidiary questions are related to the specific problem, not phrased in the abstract.

Example: 1. Does the lack of a Washington real estate broker's license prevent a Montana-licensed broker from recovering a promised commission for finding a purchaser for Washington property?

  a. Does a person act as a "real estate broker," within the meaning of the Washington licensing act, in finding a purchaser for a real property leasehold interest and personal property used in the conduct of a hotel business?

  b. Does RCW 18.85.100, providing that no action shall be brought by a real estate broker for collection of

compensation without proof that he was a "duly licensed real estate broker" at the time the cause of action arose, close Washington courts to all but Washington-licensed brokers?

2. Is an oral promise to pay a commission for finding a purchaser of a real property leasehold interest enforceable?

   a. Will Montana or Washington law govern the validity of the commission promise where the promise was made in Montana and the broker located the purchaser in Montana, but the property was located in Washington and the promisor-seller accepted the purchaser's offer, sent from Montana, by telegram sent from Seattle?

   b. Assuming that Montana law will govern, does the requirement of the Montana statute of frauds that brokerage contracts for the "sale or purchase of real estate" be in writing prevent recovery under the oral promise?

If many facts are significant, particularly if a marginal law-fact question (such as a question as to sufficiency of evidence) is presented, you may find it necessary to begin a memorandum with the statement of facts or to preface your questions with a brief preliminary fact statement.

Example: Our client was injured in an automobile accident that occurred when she was accompanying a friend who was learning how to drive.

Would recovery be precluded by a finding of assumption of risk as a matter of law?

1. Would the information about the accident justify a conclusion, as a matter of law, that the accident was caused by inexperience?

2. Assuming that the accident was caused by inexperience or lack of skill, would assumption of risk be found as a matter of law?

   a. Should knowledge of risk of inexperience be presumed from knowledge that the driver had a learner's permit?

   b. Would Royce's total knowledge of Beth's past driving experience and permittee status justify the conclusion, as a matter of law, that Royce knowingly assumed the risk of inexperience and lack of skill?

      i. At the time of entering the car?

      ii. If not initially, after exposure to Beth's driving?

Brief Answer

This section should contain a brief, specific answer to the question(s) presented, with a brief, general summary of the grounds upon which the answer is based. The purpose of the brief answer is to give to the person who requested the memorandum and to other readers a quick answer to the question(s) presented. It should summarize only, referring to nothing that is not fully discussed in the discussion.

> *Example:* Smith should be able to sue successfully for his commission in a Washington court. Although it would appear that he acted as a "real estate broker" in finding a purchaser of a "business opportunity" within the meaning of the licensing statute, the Washington court has evidenced a willingness to construe the licensing statutes liberally so as to enforce the claims of brokers properly licensed in other states. Montana law will govern the validity of the commission promise because the promise-offer was made and accepted in Montana (acceptance by performance). The oral promise is enforceable because the Montana court has confined the term "real estate" to estates of freehold in construing statutes analogous to the statute of frauds. A leasehold interest is not a freehold estate and the statute of frauds therefore should not apply to this commission promise.

Statement of Facts

Summarize the material facts as succinctly as possible. Be careful, however, not to omit facts that might in any way influence an analysis of the problem.

This section of a memorandum serves the obvious purpose of identifying the facts that you deem to be significant. It should therefore be included even though the person for whom you prepare a memorandum has the same information about the problem as you have. Additionally, in an office with numerous attorneys, a memorandum may ultimately go to others who do not share that informational background.

Applicable Statutes

If the problem is controlled by a statute or statutes, relevant portions thereof should be quoted in this section. (Or, if statutes are of only analogical or tangential assistance to your analysis, you may omit this section and simply quote the relevant language in your discussion at the point where the significance of the statutes is discussed.) Statutes should be quoted accurately. Portions not relevant to the problem may be omitted, and the omission indicated by three periods, thus: . . . . Be certain that you do not change the

meaning of language by removing it from necessary context, however.

Discussion

In this section you should fully explain your analysis of the problem and the authorities upon which your analysis is based.

If your problem involves a subject area with which not all attorneys can be presumed to be immediately familiar, a general background introduction setting forth a minimum background for quick understanding of the issues that you discuss will be helpful to educate your reader or to refresh his or her recollection. If you are in doubt as to your reader's familiarity with the area, include a general introduction. If your problem involves issues in unrelated subject areas, the issues may be introduced separately.

Examples: (1) In Swanson v. Solomon, 50 Wash.2d 825, 828, 314 P.2d 655, 657 (1957), the Washington court enumerated nine elements that must be established if rescission of a contract is to be granted on the ground of fraud:

(1) a representation of an existing fact; (2) its materiality; (3) its falsity; (4) the speaker's knowledge of its falsity or ignorance of its truth; (5) his intent that it should be acted on by the person to whom it is made; (6) ignorance of its falsity on the part of the person to whom it is made; (7) the latter's reliance on the truth of the representation; (8) his right to rely upon it; (9) his consequent damage.

As will be subsequently discussed, the facts you have given me will support findings as to all elements except (2) and (8). These two elements—materiality and the right to rely—raise some difficult questions; they are therefore separately discussed.

(2) A person assumes the risk of harm when he knows of the risk and voluntarily enters into some relation with another that will necessarily subject him to that risk. See generally W. Prosser, Torts 450–56 (3d ed. 1964). Under decisions of the Vermont Supreme Court, the assumption of risk defense is available "only where the circumstances are such as warrant the inference that the plaintiff encountered the risk freely and voluntarily with full knowledge of the nature and extent thereof." Gover v. Central Vermont Ry., 96 Vt. 208, 118 A. 874, 877 (1922). On facts similar to those presented in our problem, some courts have held that knowledge that the driver was operating under only a learner's permit is sufficient to justify the required inference as a

matter of law. The principal question to be considered, therefore, is whether the Vermont court will accept this line of decisions or will treat the questions of knowledge and acceptance of the risk as fact questions.

(3) The controlling federal statute, applicable portions of which are quoted in the preceding section, is entitled Aid to Families with Dependent Children (AFDC), and appears within Title IV of the Social Security Act (hereinafter, the Act). Within the last two years, many cases have been litigated in the federal courts on the question whether an unborn child is a "dependent child" for the purposes of this program. The majority of the courts have answered in the affirmative, holding that the mother of the fetus is eligible for AFDC benefits on its behalf. Of the six circuit courts that have considered the question, five have so concluded. All the decisions are collected in Wisdom v. Norton, 507 F. 2d 750, 751 n. 2 (2d Cir. 1974), in which the Court of Appeals for the Second Circuit reached the contrary conclusion. Before considering the competing rationales, I will discuss a trilogy of Supreme Court decisions that are interpreted by some courts as establishing a special construction rule for the AFDC statutes.

In a concise concluding paragraph or two, you may also report possible questions that you did not research, questions partially researched that proved to be false leads, significant research steps or sources omitted (for example, if you rely on a section of the *Restatement of Torts* and have not checked the tentative drafts for possible revision), and unproductive research (for example, that you checked the *Restatement (Second) of Torts* tentative drafts and found no change proposed for a section on which you rely).

If the problem on which you are reporting presents more than one or two questions, or even a single but complicated issue, use headings to identify the distinct portions of your discussion. Use of the questions themselves as headings is helpful.

Conclusion

If the problem on which you are reporting presents many seemingly unrelated issues, it may be helpful to tie together the conclusions (already expressed in your discussion) as to each issue in a final summarizing paragraph. You may use a conclusion to relate the specific legal issues discussed to factual or legal issues that you do not believe warrant detailed discussion, or to state your advice as to how the matter should be handled. Do not introduce new authorities in your conclusion. Your conclusion should not repeat your brief answer; even though it closely parallels your brief answer, however, it

serves a summarizing purpose for your reader, who should not have to go back to your brief answer to be reminded of your conclusions.

Signature

A memorandum may be concluded with "Respectfully submitted," and your signature.

SECTION 10D. COMMON ERRORS TO AVOID IN SUBSTANTIVE CONTENT OF YOUR DISCUSSION

1. *Failure to explain conclusions.* A common error is to discuss thoroughly all aspects of a question and then leave the discussion dangling without any indication of how, for example, inconsistent approaches by different courts were resolved to lead to the final conclusion embodied in the conclusion or brief answer.

2. *Excessive use of quotations.* If you draw from an opinion conclusions that might be disputed, you should quote the language on which you rely in reaching your conclusions. Courts' statements of rules should be quoted if paraphrasing may change the meaning. Or, if a court has used particularly apt language on a point important to the solution of your problem, you may wish to quote the language. Frequently, however, you will make your point more clearly by using your own language. You will probably also avoid falling into the error of placing unintended reliance on dictum or too much emphasis on what the courts say rather than on what they do in relation to the facts of the cases before them. Courts do rely on language from prior opinions, sometimes without consideration of the relationship of the language to the decision, but you should not unintentionally suggest conclusions that can be supported only if a court uses this technique.

3. *Excessive use of authorities.* String citations are rarely necessary or effective. If a rule is generally accepted, the most recent opinion from the controlling jurisdiction wherein the rule is applied will usually suffice. Or, if no mandatory authority is available, one or two recent opinions from other jurisdictions wherein the rule is applied and supported by citation of authorities may suffice. Even a reputable secondary authority may suffice for generally accepted rules. If a rule is not generally accepted, then representative opinions pro and con should be fully analyzed and discussed.

4. *Failure to analyze objectively.* The purpose of a memorandum is to explore the strength of your opponent's case as well as the strength of your client's case. You should therefore discuss fully any authorities contrary to your client's position as well as those favoring his or her position. You should, of course, attempt to distinguish, limit, or criticize contrary authorities and to present the best possible arguments that can be made for your client's position, but do not lay

a trap for your reader by failing to point out the weaknesses of the arguments you suggest.

5. *Failure to relate authorities discussed to the facts of the problem.* Students will sometimes collect and concisely abstract a number of opinions without indicating in what manner they may bear upon the problem being discussed. Make clear the relevance of each authority that you discuss.

SECTION 10E. DRAFTING YOUR DISCUSSION

The general suggestion has been made, *supra*, Section 5C, that you rough draft your discussion and conclusion for each tentative question immediately after completing your research on it. (Even though you ignore the suggestion that you draft your discussion in segments as your research progresses, you will probably find it necessary to write your first draft in the suggested segments, particularly if you do not have prior research and writing experience.) For your tentative questions that identified only analytical points, this discussion may be a single sentence expressing a conclusion, supported by authority; it may include an explanation of a reason for a rule or of why a rule affects your particular problem. For the questions presented, the minimum basic content is statement of the question with a summary statement of your conclusion, discussion of relevant authorities, relation of the authorities to your particular problem, and full expression of your conclusion. You should not mechanically follow this presentation outline, but you may avoid omitting some important part of your analysis by reminding yourself of this minimum content as you draft your discussion segments.

When you have completed your research, review your rough drafts. Consider first the substantive content: Have you indulged in any of the common errors described in the preceding section? Have you over-simplified discussion of any question? Or, have you treated a simple analytical point as an issue, reviewing at length authorities on a point that is not open to dispute? (Sometimes an "obvious" answer to a question is found only after extensive research. The temptation then is to include extended discussion of the background and tangential materials over which you earlier labored. The test to be applied in determining whether material should be included in your discussion section is whether it is necessary to understanding of the problem, its analytical difficulties, relevant authorities, or your suggested solution. Do not include extended discussion that you cannot relate to your problem under this test.)

Consider next the order in which you have developed each discussion segment. Have you used a mystery style of development, building toward your conclusion but not letting your reader know where you are headed or why you are headed there? First drafts

tend to be written in mystery style because that is the way we sometimes reason in problem solving. We find relevant material, identify that which appears to be significant, then begin to put the significant pieces together in a logical arrangement, and finally reach a conclusion in which we have confidence. Forced to write while that conclusion is recent, or while it is still jelling (or sometimes, even, while we are still putting the pieces together), we write an explanation that parallels the process of reasoning, producing the conclusion at the end, just as a mystery writer produces a solution at the end of the story. If you have used a mystery style, rewrite. Tell your reader in advance why you discuss what you discuss. If necessary, explain the significance of a question that you intend to discuss and how it relates to the ultimate suggested solution of your problem. Express your conclusions in advance so that your reader can evaluate them as he or she reads your supporting discussion. Lead your reader from one point to the next in logical order.

Consider your paragraphing. Have you used paragraphs that deal with logical divisions of your subject matter? or long, rambling paragraphs without recognizing logical divisions? or short paragraphs that give your discussion a chopped-up effect and conceal relationships among the ideas within them?

If you have followed the suggested procedure to this point, writing the first full draft of your discussion should involve little more than putting in logical order your conclusions on analytical points and discussions of questions, with the addition of a background introduction and transitions. Transition paragraphs and sentences should be added to let your reader know when you have concluded discussion of one point and are beginning discussion of another; if necessary, they should identify the relationship or lack of relationship of the two points. Headings may be used to identify marked changes of subject.

Upon completion of the first full draft of your discussion, your major analytical work should be completed, too; that is, you should have a feeling of confidence that you have considered and discussed all important points and have expressed supported conclusions. Read through your full draft. Do you, at any point, feel doubt about your analysis? about the accuracy of your report of authorities? Pin down the cause of your doubt: can it be removed by rechecking an authority or by searching for additional authority on a point? Is your full analysis presented in a logical, cohesive order that always lets your reader know where you are leading him or her? If you are still left with a feeling of confidence after reading your draft, put it aside for a time. You will be able to revise your memorandum more critically later. No one can revise critically immediately after composing. Even the lapse of a few hours will take the edge off a tendency to read over one's own errors.

CHAPTER 10F. REVISING YOUR DISCUSSION: COMMON WRITING ERRORS TO AVOID

In the immediately preceding discussion, emphasis was placed on your analysis and organized exposition of your analysis and supporting authorities. But saying clearly and precisely what you want your reader to understand requires more than an organized presentation of segments of discussion. Precision, clarity, and conciseness are achieved by choosing precise words; by reporting thoughts in sentences in which logically related words, phrases, and clauses are presented in an order that suggests or demonstrates their relationship and relative importance; and by resisting urges to pad with verbose, trite, or pompous expressions.

Since reading your first court opinion, you may have read thousands of sentences in legal prose. Many of those sentences have been long, rambling, disconnected—enough, perhaps, to lead you to believe that long, complex, even pompous sentences are a hallmark of "legal" writing style. To be sure, some thoughts must be expressed in complex sentences in order to incorporate necessary qualifications and to show significant relationships. The fifty-word headnote-style sentences found in some legal writing, however, are frequently not necessary. In revising your first and future memoranda, therefore, look first at the length of the sentences. Reexamine any sentences that run on for several lines. Can you more clearly express a complex thought by two or three sentences? or by two sentences loosely connected by a semicolon? or by removing unnecessary qualifying words and phrases? Or, is there a liberal sprinkling of deadwood phrases such as "due to the fact that" (rather than "because"), "was in reference to" (rather than "referred to"), or "maintained that there was" (rather than "stated that")? Do you tend to say the same thing twice, such as "sufficient enough"?

Have you produced any convoluted monstrosities because you have used the passive rather than the active voice? (Active: the subject of the verb performs the action. Passive: the subject receives the action described by the verb). Here are some examples from student papers:

> The concept has not been attributed the same meaning by the court in each case.
>
> (Active: The court has not attributed the same meaning to the concept in each case.)
>
> A conclusive presumption was attempted to be created.
>
> (Active: The legislature attempted to create a conclusive presumption.)

Have you used parallel (the same) structure in listing series of points or in making comparisons? Or have you shifted around as the student did in the following sentence:

> Two facts consistently appear in the cases: first, a lease provision whereby * * * ; second, a specific use has been contemplated. (To correct, change the "first" structure to include a verb, "the lease *has contained* a provision," or change the "second" structure to remove the verb, "a contemplated specific use.")

Have you kept logically related parts of your sentence together? Do your modifiers clearly modify some word or phrase? Or have you started out with a phrase intended to modify x and then shifted your discussion to y? Any sentence beginning with an "*-ing*" verbal form is suspect on this point, as the following sentences illustrate:

> Containing no evidence of the time for payment, the court reasoned that they could be only evidence of a sale. (The student started out writing about a credit-sale slip and then shifted to writing about the court. Correction: Containing no evidence of the time for payment, the sales slip was found to be only evidence of a sale.)

> Having assumed the responsibility of vigilance over each state's application of the guarantee against unreasonable searches and seizures, it remains to be seen whether *Sullivan* goes beyond the permitted leeway. (This student shifted his train of thought completely. One can only speculate as to what he originally intended to say.)

> Looking at the legislative history of the Anti-Kickback Act, the primary purpose of the Act is pointed out. (Here, the student was apparently reluctant to inject "I" into the sentence. Correction: Looking at the legislative history of the Anti-Kickback Act, I found the primary purpose of the Act to be * * *) But, sentences of this general type, beginning with "Looking at x" or "Examining x" or "Considering x" can usually be rewritten more concisely, for example: Legislative history suggests that the purpose of the Anti-Kickback Act is * * *

Be certain that you have not included sentence fragments. The fragments that most frequently slip into early legal writing are afterthought explanations that contain a verbal form rather than a verb, such as the following:

> The reason being [is] that early courts were hostile to arbitration.

The result being [is] that the landlord is without a remedy.

The latter [possibility?] depending [depends] on the meaning of such terms as "property," "taking," and "damage."

Another common error, one that can stem from and cause fuzziness in the reasoning process of both author and reader, is the incorrect substitution of "but" (and its synonyms) for "and." In a complex sentence, when you have used, for example, "but" or "however" to begin a clause, consider whether that clause really does contradict, or represent an exception to, the preceding one. For example, in the following sentence, "but" is not necessarily the proper logical connective:

The court considered all of the alternatives, but chose that of the minority rule.

Even though your discussion is logically ordered, and your sentences are logically constructed and concise, you may still fail to communicate if the smallest units of your writing, your words, are not precise. Have you used legal terms that you really don't understand? Use a legal dictionary to ascertain the meaning of any words about which you have doubt. Have you used precise non-legal words?

Use verbs that say what you mean. As you are now aware, the verb "held" has a special meaning among law-trained persons. If one says that a court "held" x, this means that x is the result reached by the court in deciding the specific issue presented to it for decision. Confine your use of "held" to express this meaning so that you do not slip into misleading uses of the word. ("The court held in a dictum" is an extreme example of erroneous use.)

Note that a court "overrules" only its own prior decisions and the decisions of lower courts within its jurisdiction. A decision is "overruled" only when the subsequent decision is directly contrary to the earlier decision. If the later decision is not directly contrary, then the earlier decision may be merely "limited" or "modified." Dictum is "disapproved," not "overruled."

Rules may be "reaffirmed" (if previously applied by the same court), "adopted," "accepted," or "stated," not "laid down," "set down," or "set forth."

Courts do not, "contend " "maintain," or "argue." Counsel "contend" and "argue." Courts "hold," "decide," "reason," "state," "suggest," "imply." And, you cannot accurately state that a court "felt" x. You may conclude that a court appears to have been influenced by a particular bias, or a vague conception, or an emotional persuasion, and if this is what you mean, say so. Search for a verb that expresses what you mean. You should have second thoughts, too, if

you are inclined to write, "I feel * * *." Usually you will realize that you "conclude," "believe," "assume," or "infer."

One word, "this," accounts for more fuzzy writing by law students than any other word. It is used to refer indefinitely to entire paragraphs of preceding discussion. It is used to refer to ideas, arguments, reasoning, or things not previously mentioned. Avoid indefinite reference by following the simple rule never to use "this" without a following word that identifies what is referred to. Some examples: (In the first three sentences, the student writers were referring to preceding discussion that extended from one to three paragraphs. Addition of the bracketed words would have made the apparently intended meaning clear.)

> This [rule] opens the way for indiscriminate seizure.
>
> This [conclusion] is further substantiated in a case decided last year.
>
> This [lack of distinction] is what leads me to conclude that the *Harold* decision will be controlling.
>
> In 1960 the statute was amended. This [amendment] was intended to broaden the statute to cover new types of contracts. (Better: In 1960 the statute was amended to extend its coverage to new types of contracts.)

Use labels (descriptive words) and use them consistently. Once you attach a distinctive label to an idea, a doctrine, a problem area, a section of a statute, a questioned activity, or any other thing to which you must continue to refer, use the same label—even if it results in seemingly inelegant repetition. It is better to be inelegant than to be obscure. Conversely, avoid using the same label for different concepts.

Finally, observing three basic rules will help you to avoid the marks of a nonprofessional in your early legal writing:

Properly identify the decision-maker. A decision may be reached by the single judge of a trial court, all the judges of an appellate court, or less than all, but at least a majority, of the participating judges of an appellate court. The decision-maker may nevertheless be identified as "the court" or, if you are referring to the United States Supreme Court, "the Court." You will report more precisely, however, if you initially refer to "the majority of the court" as the decision-maker in reporting nonunanimous decisions. If you are reporting a particular judge's view (for example, that of a concurring or dissenting judge), use "Judge ———" or, for the United States Supreme Court, "Mr. Justice ———."

Use "the court" when you mean "the court." Do not fall into the habit of substituting the name of the jurisdiction for "the court." For example, rather than, "Oregon has held * * *," use, "The Or-

egon court has held * * *" or, if you are writing about other
than the highest court in a jurisdiction, "An Oregon court has held
* * *." Avoid also the substitution of "case" or "opinion" for
"court" or "judge"; for example: "The *Mabardy* case held
* * *" (rather, "The Massachusetts court held in the *Mabardy*
case * * *") or, "The dissenting opinion discussed * * *"
(rather, "In a dissenting opinion, Judge ——— discussed
* * *").

Use the past tense EXCEPT in stating accepted rules. Events
and procedures in decided cases are past events and therefore should
be reported in the past tense. Consistent use of the past tense for reporting the facts of decided cases will help you to avoid the confusion
that otherwise may result from using the present tense for both your
discussion of decided cases and the facts of the problem that you are
analyzing. The court's decision, its reasoning, and any dicta are also
past "events"; the court "decided" in the past, "reasoned" in the
past, "held" in the past. Therefore, the past tense is also appropriate
for a report of what a court did and said with reference to a case.
An accepted rule, on the other hand, should always be stated in the
present tense: "The court applied the rule that a contracting party is
entitled to rely upon * * *".

SECTION 10G. CITATION FORM AND SPADING

The final step in preparation of legal materials is "spading"—
checking the accuracy and completeness of your citations and the accuracy of your quotations.

The basic purpose of a citation is to enable a reader quickly and
easily to locate the source cited. A secondary purpose is to give a
reader basic information about a cited source. The following rules
describe minimum content to serve these two purposes.

The content of citations tends to be the same for all citation systems, of which there are many. The form of citations (that is, the
abbreviations, order, typeface, and spacing—or lack of spacing),
however, tends to vary from system to system. You should note,
therefore, that excepting only this section, the citation forms used
throughout this text are those of the publisher. In this one section citations are printed in the forms recommended in *A Uniform
System of Citation*, already referred to in this text as the citation
Blue Book.[2] Prepared originally to prescribe content, form, and typeface styles for law review writers, the *Blue Book* rules are now also
used for citations in other forms of legal writing. The typefaces recommended in this section (*e. g.*, italics) are based on special rules
stated in *Blue Book* Rule 1 for material with few or no footnotes.

---

2. See text note 3 following chapter 1.

General Citation Rules

1. A citation form should not be used as the subject of a sentence:

    Not: H. Weihofen, *Legal Writing Style* ch. 3 (1961) discusses conciseness at length.

    Rather: Professor Weihofen discusses conciseness at length in H. Weihofen, *Legal Writing Style* ch. 3 (1961).

2. The year of decision or of publication of any legal authority must be given in parentheses as the last part of a citation unless the year is part of the name of a publication.

3. Periods for citation abbreviations should be retained unless a publisher has adopted an abbreviation without periods as part of the title of a publication, for example, *ALR Federal.*

Citing Court Opinions

4. In nonfootnoted writing, all case names must be italicized (underlined): *Jones v. Allen* or *Jones.*

5. State court citations must include the official state citation (if there is one) and the National Reporter citation (if there is one), including both the regional and state-unit Reporters if an opinion appears in both. The official state citation should appear first. Federal lower court cases are cited to the National Reporter. United States Supreme Court opinions need be cited to the official report only: 332 U.S. 444. (Note, however, that other citation systems, notably those of some courts, require citations to both unofficial citations as well.)

6. The court that rendered a decision must be identified in parentheses, preceding the date, in the following instances:

    Lower federal court decisions: (E.D. Tenn. 1954) or (9th Cir. 1960).

    Decisions of other than the highest appeal court of a state if the citation form does not otherwise identify the court: 23 Misc. 2d 26, 200 N.Y.S.2d 278 (Sup. Ct. 1960).

    Decisions for which no official state reports are available: (Fla. 1958) or (Fla. Ct. App. 1958).

Citing Periodicals

7. Citations of leading articles must include the author's name and the title, italicized (or underlined):

    Blaustein, *Liability of Attorney to Client in New York for Negligence,* 19 Brooklyn L. Rev. 233 (1953).

Student works should be cited as follows:

Long material: Comment, *Modern Approach to the Legal Malpractice Tort,* 52 Ind. L. Rev. 689 (1977). Short material, such as a Recent Case Note: 40 Texas L. Rev. 1046 (1962).

Citing Other Secondary Authorities

8.   A minimum citation to a treatise or text includes author (with initial of first name), title, page or section or paragraph number, and publication date in parentheses (and, if there has been more than one edition, the number of the edition); if the treatise is multivolume, the volume number should appear first:

W. Prosser, *Handbook of the Law of Torts* 144 (4th ed. 1971).

2 R. Patton & C. Patton, *Patton on Land Titles* § 287 (2d ed. 1957).

9.   Restatements are cited thus:

Restatement of Contracts § 559 (1932).

Restatement (Second) of Torts § 299A, Comment c (1965).

Restatement (Second) of Torts § 766, Illustration 2 (Tent. Draft No. 23, 1977).

10.   Textual annotations are cited thus:

Annot., 12 A.L.R.2d 382 (1950); Annot., 12 ALR Fed. 664 (1972).

Quotations

11.   Quotations exceeding five or six lines should be indented and single-spaced. Quotation marks may then be omitted.

12.   Omissions from quoted materials should be indicated with three periods, thus: . . .

13.   Always cite to the exact page of the source where a quotation appears: 110 Minn. 664, 24 N.W.2d 227, 229, or 24 N.W.2d at 229 (the latter form is used if you have already given the full citation). Do not run this citation in with the quotation so that it appears to be part of the quotation.

Use of *supra*

14.   There is no firm rule about use of *supra* in memoranda. Whenever you use it to avoid restating a citation, ask yourself whether your reader will be able to find the citation without difficulty. If the full citation appears more than a page or two earlier or if several other citations intervene, you may assume that your

reader will have difficulty. To avoid such difficulty, give the page number where the citation appears, thus: *supra* at page 6, to enable your reader to find the citation immediately. You need not repeat a citation or use *supra* when you are continuing discussion of a case.

NOTES

1. For additional discussions of memoranda form and content and other sample memoranda, see W. Statsky & R. Wernet, Jr., Case Analysis and Fundamentals of Legal Writing 456–74 (1977); H. Weihofen, Legal Writing Style 148–55 (1961); How to Find the Law ch. 19 (7th ed. M. Cohen ed. 1976); E. Re, Brief Writing and Oral Argument ch. III and 451–52 (4th ed. rev. 1974).

2. Memoranda must be objective in coverage, but they may be somewhat argumentative in style. One attorney has urged that memoranda should be argumentative, that is, written so as to persuade the reader to reach the same conclusions that the researcher has reached. See vom Baur, *How to Look Up Law and Write Legal Memoranda—Revisited*, 11 Prac. Law, May 1965 at 23. Mr. vom Baur also describes an effective way to outline a memorandum in argumentative style.

3. For discussion of basic drafting principles, see R. Dickerson, The Fundamentals of Legal Drafting (1965); F. Cooper, Writing in Law Practice, chs. V, VIII, X (Rev. ed. 1963). Numerous form books are available for various types of legal documents. The forms should be used only as sources for inspiration, not as authoritative sources. Many multivolume, supplemented form books are available. Those covering legal documents generally include *American Jurisprudence Legal Forms 2d*; J. Rabkin & M. Johnson, *Current Legal Forms with Tax Analysis;* and *Modern Legal Forms* (keyed to C.J.S. and Key Number digests). Forms covering all phases of court proceedings are collected in *American Jurisprudence Pleading and Practice Forms* (Revised). Forms for use under the federal rules are provided by several sources, including *Bender's Federal Practice Forms; Federal Procedural Forms, Lawyers' Edition*; and *West's Federal Forms*. Local practice form books are available in many states. On drafting discovery documents, see *Bender's Forms on Discovery* and W. Barthold, Attorney's Guide to Effective Discovery Techniques 170–76 (1975); on drafting responses to interrogatories, see *Id.* at 225–31.

4. Books on usage can provide useful guidance to more precise use of non-legal words. The one most commonly recommended is Fowler's Modern English Usage (2d ed. E. Gowers 1965). Also useful, however, and better related to usage in the United States, are T. Bernstein, The Careful Writer (1965) and W. Follett, Modern American Usage (1966). A small but excellent paperback covering basic composition principles as well as select usage problems is W. Strunk,

Jr., The Elements of Style (2d ed. 1975), revision by E. B. White. For a more comprehensive review of basic writing, including sentence structure and composition techniques in the legal setting, an exceedingly useful book is N. Brand & J. White, Legal Writing: The Strategy of Persuasion (1976). Even though you have a well-developed writing ability and style, you can improve both by becoming well acquainted with H. Weihofen, Legal Writing Style (1961). A reviewer has written about the Weihofen book as follows:

> While it is most difficult to properly assess and evaluate a book on legal writing, there is an apparently definite and proven need for books such as this one. Anyone who has read Professor Weihofen's book, *Legal Writing Style*, should have winced at the preceding sentence; anyone who did not wince, should read the book.
>
> The title of the book, *Legal Writing Style*, is accurate. This is not a book on grammar (although grammatical principles are discussed), on rhetoric (although artistic and elegant language is discussed), on preparation of memoranda, briefs, opinions, and letters (although a chapter is devoted to each), or on drafting of legal documents (although some mention is made of documents). Rather, this book purports to delve into the various factors that make up style and apply these factors to writings produced by lawyers.
>
> What factors comprise the elusive quality called style? Professor Weihofen devotes the first four chapters to precision, conciseness, simplicity, and clarity; in addition, chapters on forcefulness, organization, and eloquence are included. The book does not merely exhort the legal writer to be precise, clear, and concise; the author's treatment of these factors is replete with well-chosen examples.
>
> The examples, in this reviewer's opinion, are the *sine qua non* of the book. Most of them are more than lists of words and phrases the writer should avoid; the majority of examples are comparative—*i. e.*, they demonstrate alternative methods of conveying the same idea. In addition, the author shows why certain expressions or words should be avoided. Besides the obvious advantages of using comparative examples, Professor Weihofen has been perspicacious in choosing for his illustrations words and expressions that are commonplace in lawyers' writings.

Gitelman, Book Review, 14 J. Legal Educ. 535 (1962) (footnotes omitted). Copyright, 1962, Association of American Law Schools. Quoted with permission.

Chapter 11

ARGUMENTS TO COURTS

SECTION 11A.   INTRODUCTION

Forms of written legal argument range from simple letters offering settlement in terms intended to persuade, to formal appellate briefs addressed to the United States Supreme Court.   Both written and oral arguments may be addressed to administrative tribunals, legislative bodies, and trial courts, as well as to appellate courts.   In this Part III, only court-directed arguments and those oral arguments that are supported by written arguments are discussed.   Nevertheless, the basic forms and techniques discussed can be adapted for arguments in other settings as well.

SECTION 11B.   ARGUMENTS ADDRESSED TO TRIAL COURTS

Written and oral arguments may be addressed to trial courts at every stage of litigation.   In the pretrial stage, for example, arguments must support or oppose motions for preliminary injunctions, for summary judgment, for dismissal for failure to state a claim, and for discovery-related orders.   A trial memorandum (or trial brief for the court) [1] is a practical necessity for a trial of any complexity—and

---

1. "Memorandum for the court" is commonly used for written argument at the trial court level rather than "brief," apparently to distinguish arguments filed with the court from the "trial brief" prepared for counsel's own use, as described in Joiner, *The Trial Brief*, in Advocacy and the King's English 45 (1960), a revision of Joiner, *The Trial Brief—The Law-* *yer's Battle Plan and Ammunition*, 1 Prac.Law., Oct. 1965 at 53; E. Re, Brief Writing and Oral Argument 29–44 (4th ed. 1974); M. Pittoni, Brief Writing and Argumentation 3–16 (3d ed. 1967). "Memorandum of Authorities" and "Memorandum of Points and Authorities" are also commonly used titles for all forms of written arguments addressed to trial courts.

a formal necessity under some court rules, or at least under some circumstances.[2] Short memoranda for the court (sometimes called slip memoranda) may be prepared in advance for presentation to the court should anticipated questions actually be raised during trial (for example, on admissibility of particular evidence). A trial judge may request memoranda on questions that arise in the course of a trial. Post-trial motions also require argument.

Much that will be said about appellate briefs in the following sections applies also to written arguments for trial courts. Particularly relevant are Section 11E, describing the use of point headings to structure an argument; Section 11F, describing effective and ethical use of precedents in arguments; and Section 11H, identifying common writing errors. Nevertheless, the setting and stage of litigation influence the form, content, and length of written arguments that may be appropriate. Hence, the primary focus in this section will be on the possible variations.

Some of the suggestions about oral argument discussed in Section 11*I, infra,* are also relevant in the trial court setting, but the time available for argument and the probable level of preparation of the judge (through prior reading of written arguments, for example) can substantially affect the style and content of oral argument.

Rules of procedure for some jurisdictions prescribe content, length, or time for service and filing of some forms of memoranda for lower courts. More often, local court rules will state such prescriptions.[3]

In general, memoranda for lower courts will be prepared within shorter time limits than appellate briefs. They must usually be substantially shorter. They permit—perhaps require—greater emphasis on mandatory precedents; fewer opportunities to argue policy will be presented. More extensive use of quotations from controlling precedents may be justified. With these generalizations as back-

---

2. See, *e. g.*, the pretrial-order form used by a judge of the United States District Court for the District of Columbia, describing required contents of trial brief, in Richey, *A Federal Trial Judge's Reflections on the Preparation for and Trial of Civil Cases,* 52 Ind.L.J. 111, Appendix I at 118 (1976).

3. *E. g.*, Civ.Rule 8(c), U.S.Dist.Ct., Western Wash., provides:

Briefs relating to motions for summary judgment or other dispositive motions shall not exceed twenty 8½ x 13 pages or twenty-four 8½ x 11 pages without prior approval of the Court. Briefs relating to all other

motions shall not exceed ten 8½ x 13 pages or twelve 8½ x 11 pages without prior approval of the Court.

Compare N.J.App.Prac.Rule 2:6–7, S. Pressler, Current N.J. Court Rules (1977):

The initial briefs of parties shall not exceed 50 pages if printed or 65 pages if typed or otherwise reproduced and reply briefs shall not exceed 15 pages if printed or 20 pages if typed or otherwise reproduced. These page limitations shall be exclusive of tables of contents and citations and may be relaxed by leave of court which may be applied for ex parte.

ground, we can now consider characteristics of the general types of written arguments filed with trial courts.

The most distinctive and most comprehensive form of written argument is the trial memorandum, usually served and filed prior to or at the beginning of a trial. It may contain a digest of the pleadings in the case, a statement of the facts as counsel expects to be able to develop them, a synopsis of evidence, and perhaps even requested jury instructions, in addition to argument on the legal issues. The content and form will vary from trial to trial.[4]

Comprehensive memoranda may also be prepared in support of motions and other procedures for which oral argument is set at a specific time. The time permitted for argument may equal the time usually provided for oral arguments before appellate courts. Thus, for example, argument on a pretrial or post-trial motion that presents complex legal issues may be heard at a predetermined time before an identified judge, scheduled far enough in advance to permit the judge carefully to read and consider the written arguments and other material in the case file. Then, comprehensive written argument is appropriate if the issues presented justify it. Excerpts from a typical file (pleadings, interrogatories, motion, and memoranda) on a specially set motion are reproduced as Appendix E, presenting the significant portions of the file that was before the lower court judge in *Peters v. Simmons*, reproduced in text note 6 following Chapter 3.

Comprehensive argument does not require long argument, and rarely should trial court memoranda exceed twenty pages. Excessive length creates the risk that the judge will not read the memorandum; at best, it may be read and summarized by the judge's clerk in a "bench memorandum." A comprehensive memorandum should have an index and point headings if it exceeds more than a few pages.

The shortest and simplest form of memorandum for the court is simply an outline of points of law and conclusions, each followed by a few supporting authorities, perhaps preceded by a short statement of facts or summary of pleadings. The whole may not exceed two or three typewritten legal-size pages. This form of memorandum will be used, for example, for a matter to be heard as one of many on a regular motion calendar, with a time limitation for the oral presentation not exceeding five or ten minutes. The judge often will not have an opportunity to look at the memorandum in advance, and he or she may be expected to render a decision before going on to hear the next matter. Such oral argument as is permitted must quickly inform the judge of the posture of the case, the gist of the motion, and the reasons for granting or denying it. The memorandum, then, serves only to direct the judge's attention to the controlling points.

---

4. For more extended discussions of trial memoranda, see R. Figg, R. McCullough & J. Underwood, Civil Trial Manual 384–88 (1974) (including bibliography at page 459).

If the motion for summary judgment in *Peters v. Simmons* had been heard in such a setting, defendant's supporting memorandum might have consisted of a brief summary of the pleadings and the significant interrogatory response (see the summary in the memorandum actually filed for defendant in Appendix E) and the following statement of points:

> AN ACTION ON A CONTRACT NOT IN WRITING MUST BE COMMENCED WITHIN THREE YEARS
>
> > RCW 4.16.080(3)
>
> THE SUPREME COURT OF WASHINGTON HAS APPLIED THE THREE–YEAR STATUTE OF LIMITATIONS TO ATTORNEY MALPRACTICE CASES, STATING THAT SUCH CASES ARE BASED ON BREACH OF CONTRACT.
>
> > *Cornell v. Edsen,* 78 Wash. 662, 139 P. 602 (1914)
> >
> > *Schirmer v. Nethercutt,* 157 Wash. 172, 288 P. 265 (1930)
> >
> > *Busk v. Flanders,* 2 Wash.App. 526, 468 P.2d 695 (1970)
>
> DEFENDANT'S ALLEGED ACT OF NEGLIGENCE HAVING OCCURRED MORE THAN THREE YEARS PRIOR TO COMMENCEMENT OF THIS ACTION, THE ACTION MUST BE DISMISSED.

This form may be extended to include some textual argument or quotations from mandatory precedents, or both, as circumstances justify.[5]

SECTION 11C.   AFTER A TRIAL

We must now leap over what may be an important segment of legal problem-solving, the trial, to the point at which an appeal is taken from a trial court resolution of the problem.   Nevertheless, before considering work with an appealed case, we must look at some of the consequences of a trial in terms of the posture of the problem on appeal.

You may now have had experience with the type of research and analysis that follows consultation by a client with an attorney, serv-

---

5. For examples of short memoranda and discussions of memoranda for courts generally, see Weihofen, Legal Writing Style 155–60 (1961) (discussion and examples); Re, Brief Writing and Oral Argument 453–60 (1974) (examples); M. Pittoni, Brief Writing and Argumentation 18–19 (1967) (post-trial brief); W. Barthold, Attorney's Guide to Effective Discovery Techniques 216–22 (1975) (memoranda supporting and opposing objections to interrogatories).

A brief but useful discussion of the differing emphasis for briefs prepared for administrative agencies is included in F. Cooper, The Lawyer and Administrative Agencies 265–68 (1957), although the text is otherwise dated in some respects.

ing in the position of researcher only and not in the position of fact-gatherer. You should have developed some awareness, however, of the which-comes-first problem presented by the need for an attorney to serve these different functions. The fact-gathering function requires that an attorney know what general aspects of a dispute might or should be regarded as significant by a court; this is the criterion that initially guides an attorney in approaching a problem that may ultimately have to be resolved by a court. But, unless an attorney has a background of knowledge and experience in the specialized area of a problem, he or she soon reaches a point at which research must be done to identify significant facts and considerations with greater specificity. Preliminary research of this character may point up additional questions to be asked and additional details to be investigated. The additional information thus gained may require more research. Depending upon the attorney's experience background and the complexities of the problem, this back-and-forth attention between "facts" and "law" may continue for a short or extended period.

In the research that you have done thus far, you may have been thrust into problems at some point in this back-and-forth trail. If so, you have worked with what might be called "probable facts"—that is, the facts that investigation suggested would probably be provable should the dispute be resolved through the judicial process, with the open-end possibility that further investigation dictated by your research might change or add to these "facts."

Assuming that a dispute must be resolved by a court, the pretrial research will determine the legal theory or theories to be used, which, in turn, will guide the drafting of pleadings and preparation for trial. Ultimately, the probable facts must be proved in court through testimony of witnesses and tangible evidence. Here, the ever-present human element or evidentiary or other procedural rules may destroy the pretrial view of the dispute: a witness may change his story, a witness may not be believed, proffered testimony or other evidence may be excluded, or the opposition may present totally unanticipated evidence. Ultimately, the "facts" on which the jury or the court bases its decision may be quite different from the probable facts on which counsel based preparation of the case.

Subsequent to trial or hearing, when counsel's attention is directed to review by an appellate court, the "facts" will usually be less tentative than they were before trial. Appellate courts do not receive evidence. (An exception, of course, is in the *de novo* trial accorded by courts of general jurisdiction in matters appealed from inferior courts.) Unless an appellate court resorts to the vague concept of judicial notice of matters of common knowledge, it is expected to base its decision on the information contained in the report of lower court proceedings commonly called the record on appeal. Therefore, the range of probable facts is fixed by evidence received in the lower

court. The range of probable facts may be even further reduced by the reluctance of appellate courts to review factual determinations except within somewhat narrow limitations. Thus, an appellate court may review factual matters in reviewing rulings on motions testing the sufficiency of evidence (for example, motions for directed verdict, for nonsuit, or for judgment n.o.v.), or in passing on whether a particular jury instruction should or should not have been given, or even in ruling on a lower court's findings of fact in a non-jury case. This does not mean, however, that the court will indulge in a freewheeling reexamination of all the evidence to ascertain what factual determination the appellate judges would have made had they been sitting in the place of the trial judge or as members of the jury. Rather, it will affirm unless the ruling in question or the verdict is "clearly erroneous" or "against the clear weight of evidence."

Not only the facts, but the basic legal issues and theories, too, will generally be established in the trial court. As a general rule, a legal theory not presented to the trial court will not be considered by an appellate court as grounds for reversal.[6]

SECTION 11D. A GENERAL OVERVIEW OF
REVIEW PROCEDURES

From a lower court's final decision, order, or judgment, review may be available as a matter of right, simply through the aggrieved party's following the controlling appeal procedures.[7] In many jurisdictions, however, and particularly in jurisdictions having a multilevel appellate court system, review may lie entirely within the discretion of the higher court. Thus, for example, a large number of the cases reviewed by the United States Supreme Court are reviewed only

---

6. Exceptions to this generalization are limited. An argument that a lower court lacked jurisdiction may be heard, and under some circumstances new theories that support affirmance of a lower court may also be heard. See generally E. Re, Brief Writing and Oral Argument 71–77 (4th 1974).

The prevailing party may, of course, assert in a reviewing court any ground in support of his judgment, whether or not that ground was relied upon or even considered by the trial court * * * "[I]t is likewise settled that the appellee may, without taking a cross-appeal, urge in support of a decree any matter appearing in the record, although his argument may involve an attack upon the reasoning of the lower court or an insistence upon

matter overlooked or ignored by it."

Dandrige v. Williams, 397 U.S. 471, 475–76 n. 6, 90 S.Ct. 1153, 1156–57, 25 L.Ed.2d 491, 496 (1970).

7. Lower court orders and rulings short of final adjudications are frequently not reviewable, even though a final decision or order in the same proceeding would be reviewable as a matter of right. Exceptions to this generalization may be spelled out in rules of court describing when an appeal is allowed. The reluctance to review other than final adjudications is the result of a desire to avoid piecemeal review of cases. Intermediate orders and rulings can be reviewed when the final adjudication is reviewed.

because the Court decided to grant an application for a writ of certiorari.[8] Whether review is a matter of right or within the discretion of the court will be established by constitutional or statutory provisions.

Rules adopted for the particular appellate court will establish the steps necessary to obtain review. Regardless of the jurisdiction, these rules will describe common details: what is required to establish jurisdiction of the appellate court over the matter, the record with which the court must be furnished, other required formalities, and the times within which required steps must be taken. Four basic steps are usually described: (1) filing notice of appeal,[9] (2) preparing and transmitting to the appellate court a record on appeal, (3) submitting written arguments (briefs), and (4) presenting oral arguments. The first two steps are generally described in this section, the purpose of the description being to give you sufficient background knowledge to understand a record on appeal. More extended discussion of briefs and oral arguments will follow.

Filing notice of appeal in accordance with the governing rules is a crucial step. Notice must be given within the stated time limits to give the appellate court jurisdiction over the matter. Failure to take other steps in timely fashion may be grounds for dismissal of the appeal, but whether the appeal will be dismissed is usually within the discretion of the court.

A record on appeal is required because an appellate court must have before it some record of the proceedings in the lower court, de-

---

8. This seems an appropriate point to identify the inaccuracy of an assumption frequently made—that denial of certiorari by the United States Supreme Court may be equated to approval of the decision thus denied review. The validity of this assumption cannot be more strongly denied than through the language of Mr. Justice Frankfurter in an opinion written in connection with the denial of the petition for writ of certiorari in Maryland v. Baltimore Radio Show, 338 U. S. 912, 70 S.Ct. 252, 94 L.Ed. 562 (1950). After itemizing some of the many technical reasons and policy considerations that may lead to denial, he states, 338 U.S. at 919:

> Inasmuch, therefore, as all that a denial of a petition for a writ of certiorari means is that fewer than four members of the Court thought it should be granted, this Court has rigorously insisted that such a denial carries with it no implication whatever regarding the Court's

views on the merits of a case which it has declined to review. The Court has said this again and again; again and again the admonition has to be repeated.

Note, however, that opinions written in connection with a denial of a petition for certiorari may be a valuable source of ideas, reasoning, and insights to the views of some of the Justices.

9. If appeal is not available as a matter of right, the notice of appeal will be replaced by the more substantial petition for writ of certiorari or its equivalent, wherein will be urged the reasons justifying review. The types of reasons considered by the Court are suggested in S.Ct.R. 7, and discussed in R. Stern & E. Gressman, Supreme Court Practice §§ 4.2–4.27 (4th ed. 1969). Form and content of petitions for certiorari are discussed *Id.* at §§ 6.25–6.47.

scribing or detailing at least those portions of the proceedings that are relevant to the points on which appeal is based. Less than a full record may be provided. The appellant (or petitioner) will have the moving burden of identifying what material will go into this record, drawing from three basic sources: the documents filed, introduced, or entered in the proceeding (for example, pleadings, written motions, written orders, exhibits), the hearing or trial proceedings (that is, testimony, oral motions, oral rulings, oral decisions), and docket or minute entries (summary notations in the court's daily record of rulings and actions taken or directed). The moving party does not have the exclusive right to designate the contents of the record, however, since opposing counsel may designate excluded matters as relevant to his or her arguments and require their inclusion.

The important point to remember is that a record of the total proceedings may not be transmitted to the appellate court. That counsel may include less than the entire lower court record creates the hazard that some crucial part of the record may be omitted (for example, some ruling of the lower court, some portion of the evidence). Failure to include the bases for points on appeal may preclude appellate consideration of that point.

There are no generally accepted labels for the parts of a record on appeal. Thus, for example, the term "transcript" is commonly used to describe the portion based on the trial or hearing proceedings. This is a particularly appropriate designation, since the report of what happened will frequently be transcribed from the court reporter's notes or a recording of what was said in the course of the proceedings. In some jurisdictions, however, "transcript" is used to describe the total record on appeal, while the portion drawn from the hearing or trial may be called the "statement of facts."

Both a record and printed excerpts from that record, called an "appendix," are required under the Supreme Court rules. Effective July 1, 1970, the Court adopted the appendix system previously used successfully, and still used, in some federal court of appeals circuits. Under this system, the original record, or such portion thereof as is agreed on by the parties, is ultimately transmitted to the clerk of the Supreme Court. Rules 12 and 21(1).[10] In lieu of printed copies of this record, previously required, the moving party must file forty printed copies of an appendix, which may contain substantially less than the record. Rule 36(1). The parties are encouraged to keep the appendix short. Rule 36(2). Omission of material from the appendix does not preclude reference to the record on file with the clerk.

10. Unless otherwise indicated, these and subsequent citations to rules are to the Rules of the Supreme Court of the United States, effective July 1, 1970, as amended to July 11, 1977.

SECTION 11E. FORMAL REQUIREMENTS FOR AN APPEAL BRIEF

Court rules may detail numerous requirements about brief form, ranging from specification of permissible type size to the form in which particular points must be urged if they are to be considered by the court. Although some of these rules may seem to be without rationale, most of them can be justified on the basis of convenience of the court or fairness to opposing parties. Even if picayune requirements seem to lack justification entirely, however, they cannot be ignored. This point is here emphasized because for law school moot court purposes, many of the seemingly picayune requirements are eliminated. For your future reference, however, remember that the starting point for handling appeals and preparing briefs will always be a careful reading of the governing rules, with particular attention to detailed time and form requirements.[11]

The following discussion will describe commonly required parts of briefs. When necessary, the particular requirements of the Supreme Court rule will be identified. The discussion is not intended to be exhaustive, only introductory. Hence, you should not feel relieved of the necessity of reading Supreme Court Rule 40, reproduced in Appendix F, which describes requirements for briefs filed with the Supreme Court, or other governing rule before you prepare your first appellate brief. Many of the examples used are based on *Peters v. Simmons* and *Burns v. Alcala,* the opinions for which are reproduced following Chapter 3, in text notes 6 and 7. "Appellant" will be used throughout as including "Petitioner," and "Respondent" will be used as including "Appellee," unless otherwise indicated.

Cover or Title Page

Subject Index

Index each section of the brief that is required by your governing rule. In addition, index a breakdown of your argument by point headings. (A point heading is a concise argumentative statement of a segment of your overall argument, described in greater detail in Section 11F.) Your index will be the first page to which your judges open your brief. If you have written your point headings with care, your judges will immediately have before them a complete, concise,

---

11. And youth and inexperience will not justify failure to comply with rule requirements. One court has observed:

"The appellant failed to comply with Court of Appeals Rule on Appeals 43 * * * in that he failed to set out verbatim the findings of fact of the trial court in his brief. He has moved for leave to amend his brief on the basis that the error was the result of the youth and inexperience of his counsel. We believe that youth and inexperience of counsel is a reason to read the rules on appeal rather than an excuse for failure to read them." Johnson v. Johnson, 1 Wash.App. 527, 529, 462 P.2d 956, 958 (1969).

logically ordered summary of your argument. Thus, your index will also provide a formally structured introductory summary of argument.

> *Supreme Court:* Under Rule 39(3), briefs "shall, unless they are less than ten pages in length, be preceded by a subject index of the matter contained therein, with page references * * *"

> *Under other rules:* Include an index even though your governing rule does not expressly require one, unless your brief is very short.

Table of Authorities

> *Supreme Court:* Under Rule 39(3), briefs shall contain a "table of cases (alphabetically arranged), text books and statutes cited, with references to the pages where they are cited." You may wish to add an "Other Authorities" category.

Opinion Below

> *Supreme Court:* Rule 40(1)(a) requires that the citation to the lower court opinion or opinions, if reported, be indicated.

Jurisdiction

The requirement that a statement of jurisdiction be included in a brief is imposed in jurisdictions having a multi-level appellate court system or, for some other reason, an appeal court with restricted jurisdiction. The purpose of the statement is to identify the constitutional, statutory, or rule provision or other grounds on which the court's jurisdiction to review is based.

> *Supreme Court:* Rule 40(1)(b) requires a statement re jurisdiction.

Constitutional Provisions (or Statutes) Involved

> *Supreme Court:* Rule 40(1)(c) requires quotations of relevant written law in a preliminary section or in an appendix.

> *Under other rules:* Such a section should be included, when relevant, even though not required by the governing rule.

Questions Presented

You already know something about writing questions presented from your knowledge about memoranda. Recall what you learned. Questions should be phrased with some specificity and should make sense standing alone. (If a number of facts must be incorporated, you may wish to preface a question with a *brief* statement of the sig-

nificant facts.) Note, however, that you must take an additional factor into account in writing questions for a brief: your questions should be phrased with a view toward interesting and persuading to your viewpoint the judges who will read your brief.

> *Examples:* Here are the questions presented included in two *amici curiae* (friend of the court) briefs filed with the Supreme Court in *Burns v. Alcala.* Does the phrasing of the questions suggest to you affirmative or negative answers?

> (1) Whether a fetus is a "child" within the meaning of Section 406(a) of the Social Security Act.[12]

> (2) Whether the Social Security Act, 42 U.S.C. § 601, *et seq.,* mandates payment for unborn children pursuant to the Aid to the Families with Dependent Children program, where such payments have been interpreted for over twenty-five years to be optional by the Department of Health, Education and Welfare, the agency charged with the responsibility for administering the Act, and where Congress has acquiesced in such interpretations? [13]

> *Supreme Court:* Statement of questions is required under Rule 40(1)(d).

> *Under other rules:* In addition to or rather than questions presented, many state court rules require appellants to include "Assignments of Error," discussed *infra.* However, if your assignments do not identify the basic questions to be argued, you may find statement of questions to be an effective technique for focusing the court's attention on your view of your case. Respondents, also, may find statement of questions useful for this purpose.

Statement of the Case

In this section, the procedural history and facts of the case being reviewed should be briefly summarized, including only the information that is relevant to an understanding of the points in dispute and the arguments on those points.

A clear and concise statement of the facts is an exceedingly important part of your brief. If you represent appellant, present the facts fairly but persuasively in an interesting narrative style. Strive to present the strongest view of your case that you believe the oppos-

---

12. Brief for the United States as Amicus Curiae at 2.

13. Brief for William L. Lukhard, Director of the Department of Welfare, Commonwealth of Virginia at 2.

Both questions cite to the same section of the Social Security Act. In the first question, the citation is to the original section numbering of the Act; in the second question, the citation is to the present Code section number.

ing counsel will accept, but avoid an argumentative statement. Never try to mislead the court as to the facts. Never omit a damaging fact. If you do, your opponent will be given an opportunity to place that fact before the court in a manner that may make it even more damaging to your arguments. If the facts are complicated, consider whether a diagram or a chronological listing of events will aid the judges to understand the facts more quickly. If you represent respondent, do not waste your readers' time with trivial corrections, but do not fail to challenge an obviously biased presentation of the facts by the appellant's counsel.

> *Supreme Court:* Note that Rule 40(1)(e) requirement for references to the record on appeal or appendix.

Assignments of Error

The purpose of assignments of error is to apprise the appellate court of errors of the court below on which appellant relies for reversal. They specify the erroneous actions and rulings of the judge, not his or her erroneous reasoning and not necessarily the legal issues raised by your appeal.

> *Example:* Assume a suit for specific performance of a contract for the sale of real property, in which the defendant relies on two defenses: that the description of the property in the written contract is insufficient to comply with description requirements under the Statute of Frauds and that the terms are not sufficiently definite to permit specific performance. Assume that the defendant moves for dismissal for failure to state a claim on the basis of the first defense. Assume that that motion is denied and the suit proceeds through necessary steps to trial and to judgment for the plaintiff. Defendant's Assignments of Error on appeal might be:
>
> 1. The court erred in denying Defendant's Motion to Dismiss the Complaint for Failure to State a Claim.
>
> 2. The court erred in entering Judgment for Plaintiff.

Note that in your assignments it is not necessary to state why the court's actions were erroneous, though you may do so if incorporation of the reasons can be smoothly accomplished. For example, under the foregoing example, the following assignments would be proper:

> 1. The court erred in denying Defendant's Motion to Dismiss the Complaint for Failure to State a Claim, because the copy of the contract attached to Plaintiff's Complaint did not comply with the Statute of Frauds.

> 2. The court erred in entering Judgment for Plaintiff, because the contract enforced does not comply with the Statute of Frauds, and its terms are too indefinite to permit specific performance.

The important point to remember is that you should not assign error to the court's reasoning alone. You must identify the action or ruling that was based on the allegedly erroneous reasoning.

Here is the assignment of error used in the Appellant's brief in *Peters v. Simmons:*

> The court erred in granting respondent's motion for summary judgment and dismissing appellants' complaint on the ground an action against an attorney for malpractice accrues and the statute of limitation begins to run on the date of the attorney's negligent act.[14]

Errors commonly assigned include admitting or excluding particular evidence, granting or denying ι motion, giving or refusing to give a particular jury instruction, finding or refusing to find a particular fact, entering or refusing to enter a conclusion of law, entering or refusing to enter judgment, and granting or denying a motion for a new trial.

> *Supreme Court:* Assignments of error are not required. Note, however, that the concept of error by a lower court is the basis of all appellate review. Therefore, you should at least mentally identify the particular action or ruling challenged by each argument that you intend to present, if you are appellant, or that is presented by your opponent, if you represent respondent. Be certain that the action or ruling was prejudicial (that is, affected the outcome of the case).

Summary of Argument

> *Supreme Court:* A summary of argument is required under the circumstances specified in Rule 40(1)(f). Note that a summary of argument is somewhat similar to a brief answer in a memorandum, with the added ingredient of argumentative form; that is, it should be written in a style calculated to interest and to persuade the judges who will read your brief.

Here is the Summary of Argument from the Government's amicus brief in *Burns v. Alcala:*

> The question presented here is whether a fetus is a "child" within the meaning of Section 406(a) of the Social Security Act. If a fetus is a "child" within the meaning of that statute, payments of aid to families with dependent

---

14. Brief of Appellants at 5.

children must be made on behalf of a fetus, and to the pregnant woman as the adult relative living with and caring for the "child," when the woman otherwise satisfies AFDC eligibility requirements.

The stated purpose of the AFDC title, its various provisions, and the legislative history, all reveal congressional concern only for living dependent children and their families. Section 401 of the Act states that the purpose of the AFDC program is to "encourage the care of dependent children in their own homes or in the homes of relatives * * *." No provision of the AFDC title expressly applies to fetuses or unborn children, whereas many have application only to living children. The legislative history shows a predominant concern with "keep[ing] the young children with their mother in their own home, thus preventing the necessity of placing the children in institutions." S.Rep.No. 628, 74th Cong., 1st Sess. 17.

Accordingly, we believe that Congress intended the word "child" to be given its commonly accepted meaning, i. e., a living child, not a fetus. The Secretary's regulations permitting payments on behalf of fetuses are not to the contrary; they rest upon the assumption that the Secretary may authorize payments on behalf of persons other than "dependent children" in certain limited circumstances.[15]

Argument

Supreme Court: The Rule specifies no required format for the argument.

Conclusion

At a minimum, a conclusion should clearly state the relief requested. Types of relief that may be requested include affirmance, reversal, modification of judgment or order, a new trial, or some other further proceedings.

Supreme Court: Rule 40(1)(h) requires a conclusion "specifying with particularity the relief to which the party believes itself entitled."

Reply Briefs

A reply brief may be filed on behalf of an appellant. If respondent's position has been effectively argued, failure to file a reply brief will leave the court with the more favorable impression of respondent's position. Counsel for appellant may then be forced to devote a

---

15. Brief for the United States as Amicus Curiae at 5.

substantial part of oral argument time to defensive argument that could have been presented more effectively in a reply. A reply brief must respond to arguments raised in the Respondent's brief; it should not be used merely to supplement contentions already advanced in the opening brief.

> *Supreme Court*: Under Rule 40(4) reply briefs are permitted, and "shall conform to such portions of this rule as are applicable to the briefs of an appellee or respondent, but need not contain a summary of argument, regardless of their length, if appropriately divided by topical headings."

Special Moot Court Rules

The type of brief exchange used for law school moot court arguments may change the form of brief to be prepared for respondents. If exchange of briefs by opponents is patterned after procedures used in actual appeals, appellant's brief is submitted first; respondent's brief is then due a short time later, and it directly responds to an opponent's brief. However, simultaneous exchange may be used for moot court, that is, submission of all briefs will be required on the same date. If so, respondent's brief would include a full statement of the case and, under the Supreme Court rule, reference to the opinion below, constitutional and statutory provisions, and questions presented. Only assignments of error, if required, would be omitted. Reply briefs are sometimes not permitted.

SECTION 11F. STRUCTURING YOUR ARGUMENT: POINT HEADINGS

A point heading is a concise, argumentative statement of a conclusion that you want the court to reach with respect to a segment of your overall argument. Effective point headings are a significant part of your argument. They will be effective only if you plan them carefully and labor over them to create an interesting, persuasive, logically ordered capsule summary of your total argument.

Begin drafting your point headings by making a list of the series of specific conclusions that the court must reach if it is to decide your case in your client's favor. Then consider what is the most logical, easily followed integration and order of presentation of these points. Spend some time on this step; the order that you choose will become the outline for your argument. Finally, write the points and sub-points in argumentative form. Choose precise and persuasive words. Arrange the thoughts (clauses and phrases) within each heading in easily followed, persuasive order.

Here are the point headings from the brief filed with the Supreme Court for respondent in *Burns v. Alcala*:

I. **STATES PARTICIPATING IN THE AFDC PROGRAM MAY NOT EXCLUDE INDIVIDUALS ELIGIBLE UNDER FEDERAL STATUTORY STANDARDS IN THE ABSENCE OF CLEAR CONGRESSIONAL AUTHORIZATION FOR SUCH EXCLUSION, H.E.W. REGULATIONS TO THE CONTRARY NOTWITHSTANDING**

    A.   This Case Is Governed By This Court's Holdings In *King v. Smith, Townsend v. Swank,* and *Carleson v. Remillard*

    B.   This Court's Decision In *N.Y. State Department Of Social Services v. Dublino* Did Not Qualify The *King-Townsend-Remillard* Trilogy, And Is Inapplicable To This Case

II. **AN UNBORN CHILD IS A "DEPENDENT CHILD" WITHIN THE MEANING OF TITLE IV OF THE SOCIAL SECURITY ACT**

    A.   The "Common Meaning" Of The Words "Dependent Child" Is Not Sufficiently Clear To Dispose Of This Case

    B.   The Statutory Purposes Of The Social Security Act Show That An Unborn Child Is A "Dependent Child" Within The Meaning Of 42 U.S.C. § 606

        1.   Exclusion of unborn children and their mothers from AFDC eligibility is inconsistent with the purposes of Title IV of the Social Security Act

        2.   Title V of the Social Security Act demonstrates Congressional concern with pre-natal protection and provides pre-natal health services that are complementary to AFDC assistance for the unborn

        3.   The eligibility provisions of Title XIX (Medical Assistance) indicate that unborn children are covered by Title IV

        4.   The Social Security Amendments of 1950 demonstrate Congressional intent to require the inclusion of unborn children in state AFDC programs

        5.   The provisions of the Social Security Act other than 42 U.S.C. § 606(a) are not helpful in resolving the issues in this case

        6.   The existence of other public assistance programs does not imply Congressional intent to exclude unborn children and their mothers from the AFDC program

    C. Long-standing Interpretation Of 42 U.S.C. § 606(a) By The Agencies Charged With The Administration Of The AFDC Program Establishes That Unborn Children Must Be Included In AFDC Coverage [16]

SECTION 11G. USE OF PRECEDENTS IN YOUR ARGUMENT

What you learned about using precedents in a memorandum discussion has relevance in writing an argument for a brief also: String citations are rarely necessary or effective. If a rule is generally accepted, the most recent opinion from the controlling jurisdiction wherein the rule is applied will usually suffice. Or, if no mandatory authority is available, one or two recent opinions from other jurisdictions wherein the rule is applied and supported by citation of authorities may suffice. Of course, if a proposition on which you rely is not generally accepted or has not been accepted by the court to which argument is addressed, representative cases must be discussed. And, for all such cases, you should include, as a minimum, a statement of the nature of the case, the significant facts, and the holding. Detailed discussion of reasoning will frequently be necessary. (But, keep your brief "brief" by using synthesis reporting form whenever possible.)

In writing your argument, you will encounter a presentation problem not encountered in writing a memorandum, however: What should you do about the decisions adverse to your position? In a memorandum, adverse decisions are discussed freely and frankly. They should also be discussed in an argument, but in a framework that highlights your supporting decisions and then permits a subordinated but persuasive showing that adverse decisions are distinguishable, should be limited, or have weaknesses that make them invalid—at least for your particular case.

Both practical and ethical reasons dictate such discussion of adverse decisions. The practical reason: If you have found them, it is highly probable that your opponent will also find them and recognize their significance. Far better that you discuss them in a framework wherein you can dispose of them in the shadow of your affirmative argument than that you give your opponent the opportunity to present them in the most favorable light, forcing you to use precious oral argument time to deal with them as you best can in limited time (or, for appellants, forcing you to deal with them defensively in a reply brief).

The ethical reason stems from your duty as an attorney, governed by the Code of Professional Responsibility. To what extent does your attorney status require that you "reveal" unfavorable au-

---

16. Brief for Respondents at i, ii.

thorities for the court's consideration? This question was addressed to the American Bar Association's Committee on Professional Ethics and Grievances. Their first answer (Opinion 146) was not definitive, and they were asked to clarify it. Here is their response:

Formal Opinion 280

(June 18, 1949)

Opinion 146, rendered July 17, 1935, was in response to a question by a member of the Association as follows:

> Is it the duty of a lawyer appearing in a pending case to advise the court of decisions adverse to his client's contentions that are known to him and unknown to his adversary?

The Opinion, stated by Judge Phillips and concurred in by the other members of the Committee, was as follows: [Case citations omitted.]

> A lawyer is an officer of the court. His obligation to the public is no less significant than his obligation to his client. His oath binds him to the highest fidelity to the court as well as to his client. It is his duty to aid the court in the due administration of justice.
>
> The conduct of the lawyer before the court and with other lawyers should be characterized by candor and fairness. *Canon 22.*
>
> We are of the opinion that this Canon requires the lawyer to disclose such decisions to the court. He may, of course, after doing so, challenge the soundness of the decisions or present reasons which he believes would warrant the court in not following them in the pending case.

It will be noted that in the last paragraph the Committee refers to the right of the lawyer to "challenge the soundness of the decisions or present reasons which he believes would warrant the court in not following them in the pending case," but does not refer to his right to "distinguish" them, thus indicating that the Committee had in mind only decisions which were *directly* adverse.   *   *   *

The lawyer, though an officer of the court and charged with the duty of "candor and fairness," is not an umpire, but an advocate. He is under no duty to refrain from making every proper argument in support of any legal point because he is not convinced of its inherent soundness. Nor is he under any obligation to suggest arguments against his

position. His personal belief in the soundness of his cause or of the authorities supporting it, is irrelevant. See *Canons 5 and 15*.

We would not confine the Opinion to "controlling authorities"—i. e., those decisive of the pending case—but, in accordance with the tests hereafter suggested, would apply it to a decision directly adverse to any proposition of law on which the lawyer expressly relies, which would reasonably be considered important by the judge sitting on the case.
*   *   *

Canon 22 should be interpreted sensibly, to preclude the obvious impropriety at which the Canon is aimed. In a case involving a right angle collision or a vested or contingent remainder, there would seem to be no necessity whatever of citing even all the relevant decisions in the jurisdiction, much less those from other states or by inferior courts. Where the question is a new or novel one, such as the constitutionality or construction of a statute, on which there is a dearth of authority, the lawyer's duty may be broader. The test in every case should be: Is the decision which opposing counsel has overlooked one which the court should clearly consider in deciding the case? Would a reasonable judge properly feel that a lawyer who advanced, as the law, a proposition adverse to the undisclosed decision, was lacking in candor and fairness to him? Might the judge consider himself misled by an implied representation that the lawyer knew of no adverse authority?[17]

The Canons of Professional Ethics cited by the committee in the foregoing opinion have been revised and adopted by the American Bar Association under the new title, Code of Professional Responsibility. Canon 7 now provides: "A lawyer has a duty to represent his client with zeal limited only by his duty to act within the bounds of the law." In material labelled "Ethical Considerations," the committee explains the significance of this Canon 7 to the duty of a lawyer to our adversary system of justice, stating in part:

The complexity of law often makes it difficult for a tribunal to be fully informed unless the pertinent law is presented by the lawyers in the cause. A tribunal that is fully informed on the applicable law is better able to make a fair and accurate determination of the matter before it. The adversary system contemplates that each lawyer will present and argue the existing law in the light most favor-

17. American Bar Association, Opinions of the Committee on Professional Ethics 618 (1967).

able to his client.[a]   Where a lawyer knows of legal authority in the controlling jurisdiction directly adverse to the position of his client, he should inform the tribunal of its existence unless his adversary has done so; but, having made such disclosure, he may challenge its soundness in whole or in part.[b] [18]

The heart of the new Code of Professional Responsibility is a set of disciplinary rules drafted in relation to the new canons and explanatory ethical considerations.   These rules have been widely adopted in the states as the basis for disciplinary action.   Of ultimate significance, then, is the related disciplinary rule:

DR 7–106 Trial Conduct

*   *   *

(B) In presenting a matter to a tribunal, a lawyer shall disclose:

   (1) Legal authority in the controlling jurisdiction known to him to be directly adverse to the position of his client and which is not disclosed by opposing counsel.[19] *   *   *

SECTION 11H.   "SEVEN ABC'S OF APPELLATE ARGUMENT"

Many articles and books have been written about preparation of appeal briefs—by judges, by practitioners, by educators, and by students.   None, however, has stated the essence of appellate argument as effectively as did Professor Karl Llewellyn.   The core of his sum-

a. [footnote 39 in original] "Too many do not understand that accomplishment of the layman's abstract ideas of justice is the function of the judge and jury, and that it is the lawyer's sworn duty to portray his client's case in its most favorable light." Rochelle and Payne, *The Struggle for Public Understanding*, 25 Texas B.J. 109, 159 (1962).

b. [footnote 40 in original] "We are of the opinion that this Canon requires the lawyer to disclose such decisions [that are adverse to his client's contentions] to the court. He may, of course, after doing so, challenge the soundness of the decisions or present reasons which he believes would warrant the court in not following them in the pending case." *ABA Opinion* 146 (1935).

Cf. ABA Opinion 280 (1949) and Thode, *The Ethical Standard for the Advo-*

cate, 39 Texas L.Rev. 575, 585–86 (1961).

18. American Bar Association, Code of Professional Responsibility and Code of Judical Conduct EC 7–23, at 34C (1976).   An earlier version stated, "Where *legal authority that is directly adverse* to the position of his client is known to a lawyer, he should inform the tribunal * * * *" Special Committee on Evaluation of Professional Ethics, American Bar Association, Code of Professional Responsibility 83, ¶ 24 (Preliminary Draft, Jan. 15, 1969) (emphasis added).

19. American Bar Association, Code of Professional Responsibility and Code of Judical Conduct 36C, 37C (1976). In particular states, the rules may have been adopted in modified form.

mary is quoted below, with footnotes omitted.[20] Read it and re-read it several times; you can learn something from every sentence.

First, and negatively, *the Insufficiency of Technical Law: it is plainly not enough to bring in a technically perfect case on "the law"* under the authorities and *some* of the accepted correct techniques for their use and interpretation or "development." Unless the judgment you are appealing from is incompetent, there is an equally perfect technical case to be made on the other side, and if your opponent is any good, he will make it. If you are the appellee, a competently handled appeal confronts you with the same problem. The struggle will then be for *acceptance* by the tribunal of the one technically perfect view of the law as against the other. Acceptance will turn on something beyond "legal correctness." It ought to.

Second, the Trickiness of Classification: a "technically" perfect case is of itself equally unreliable in regard to the interpretation or classification of the facts. For rarely indeed do the raw facts of even a commercial transaction fit cleanly into any legal pattern; or even the "trial facts" as they emerge from conflicting testimony. No matter what the state of the law may be, if the essential pattern of the facts is not seen by the court as fitting *cleanly* under the rule you contend for, your case is still in jeopardy.   *   *   *

Per contra, and *third,* the *Necessity of a Sound Case "in Law": Without a technically perfect case on the law,* under the relevant authorities and some one or more of the thoroughly correct procedures of their use and interpretation, *you have no business to expect to win* your case. Occasionally a court may under the utter need for getting a decent result go into deliberate large-scale creative effort; but few courts like to. Such effort may interfere with the court's sense of duty to the law; such effort requires in any event independent skill and labor from a hard-pressed bench. Sound advocacy therefore calls for providing in the brief a job all done to hand; sound advocacy calls as of course for not stirring up any conflict, *conscious or unconscious,* between the court's two major duties.   *   *   *

All of this serves only to lead up to the crux:

Fourth, the Twofold Sense and Reason: the real and vital central job is to satisfy the court that sense and decency

---

20. Originally summarized in an article which appeared in the *Columbia Law Review,* the ABC's were later paraphrased and shortened in his 1960 book, *The Common Law Tradition:* *Deciding Appeals.* The portion quoted is reprinted from the book at pp. 237–39, 241, copyright 1960 by Karl N. Llewellyn, with permission of the copyright owner.

and justice require (a) the rule which you contend for in this *type* of situation; and (b) the result that you contend for, as between these parties. *You* must make your whole case, on law and facts, make *sense,* appeal as being *obvious* sense, inescapable sense, sense in simple terms of life and justice. If that is done, the technically sound case on the law then gets rid of all further difficulty: it shows the court that its duty to the Law not only does not conflict with its duty to Justice but urges to decision along the exact same line.

* * * It is a question of making the facts talk. For of course it is the facts, not the advocate's expressed opinions, which must do the talking. The court is interested not in listening to any lawyer rant, but in seeing, or better, in discovering, from and in the facts, where sense and justice lie.

This leads to interesting corollaries:

Fifth, the Statement of Facts is the Heart: It is trite that it is in the statement of the facts that the advocate has his first, best, and most precious access to the court's attention. The court does not know the facts, and it wants to. It is trite, among good advocates, that the statement of the facts can, and should, in the very process of statement, frame the legal issue, and can, and should, simultaneously produce the conviction that there is only one sound outcome.

Sixth, Simplicity: It is as yet less generally perceived as a conscious matter that the *pattern of the facts* as stated must be a *simple* pattern, with its lines of simplicity never lost under detail; else attention wanders, or (which is as bad) the effect is drowned in the court's effort to follow the presentation or to organize the material for itself.

Neither is it yet adequately perceived by most that the lines of argument just discussed lead of necessity to *maximum simplicity on the legal side* of a brief, as well. The benighted who, intoning again the pauper's saw about courts and pegs and hats, throw in point after point upon point— such manage only to scatter and waste their fire, to destroy all impact and unity of drive. As with the launching of the foredoomed appeal, this happens because counsel in question have not become clear that it is a vital matter in any normal case to satisfy the court that decision their way is imperative, is at least desirable, as a matter of sense and justice; and they are still thinking and arguing as if "the relevant law"—*before* the decision, were single and clear *and in itself enough.* Whereas in truth three, two, or one good legal points of appeal (i. e., points technically correct and sound)

are all that any court needs—or any lawyer—once the court gets satisfied that *this* is the way the case *ought* to, *must* come out. And each unnecessary point sins severally against:

> *Seventh, The Principle of Concentration of Fire:* Even three points, or two, can prove troublesome as dividers of attention unless a way can be found to make them sub-points of a single simple line of attack which gains reinforcement and cumulative power from each sub-point as the latter is developed.

Professor Llewellyn then states other principles, one of which he calls the "Proffered, Phrased, Opinion-Kernel":

> If a brief has made the case for what is right, and has made clear the reason of the rightness, and has found and tailored and displayed the garment of law to clothe the right decision fittingly, then it is not only unwise but indecent not to furnish also in that brief a page or two of text which gathers this all together, which clears up its relation to the law to date, which puts into clean words the soundly guiding rule to serve the future, and which shows that rule's happy application to the case in hand. What is wanted is a passage which can be quoted verbatim by the court, a passage which so clearly and rightly states and crystallizes the background and the result that it is *recognized* on sight as doing the needed work and as practically demanding to be lifted into the opinion.

> The wisdom, for counsel, of supplying such a passage is obvious. There is the matter of crystallization. An argument can slowly bring a court into a condition like an over-chilled windless fjord; such a passage, *recognized,* can firm and fix the whole with the abruptness of the one thrown stone. When the argument has not got quite so far along— or across—then a clean wording of the whole-in-context is a reinforcing stroke which may drive the spike clean home.

* * *

SECTION 11*l*. WRITING YOUR ARGUMENT: COMMON ERRORS TO AVOID

The most common errors of students in preparing their first argumentative briefs are as follows:

1. *Failure to give the judges adequate background.* Do not be reluctant to lay a foundation for understanding of your issues and your argument by stating basic propositions. Judges do not have miracle minds that can call up for immediate review all the basic law necessary to an understanding of, for example, a constitutional law

problem, when in a given day they have heard oral argument on an eminent domain problem, worked briefly on an opinion in a difficult conflicts of law case, and read a brief on a negligence case just before turning to the brief involving the constitutional law question. Whenever it may seem necessary, summarize basic propositions or explain why an issue is presented before you plunge into the details of your argument. Ideally, this summary should be combined with an introduction that emphasizes the importance of the questions presented. (At least this ideal is appropriate for an appellant's brief. Respondent's counsel will want to suggest, whenever possible, that it is an unexceptional case, properly decided by the lower court.)

Here is the introduction used by counsel for Appellant in *Peters v. Simmons:*

> This case "raises the issue whether members of the legal profession should enjoy a preference as to the date when they may successfully bar adverse claims under the statute of limitations." *Neel v. Magana, Olney, Levy, Cathcart & Gelfand,* 6 Cal.3d 176, 491 P.2d 421, 424, 98 Cal.Rptr. 837 (1971). In an attorney's malpractice action, the Court should adopt the rule that an action accrues and the applicable three year statute of limitation, RCW 4.16.080(3), begins to run only after the plaintiff discovered or should reasonably have discovered the defendant's negligence. The Court should reject the present Washington rule that an action for attorney malpractice accrues and the statute of limitations begins to run on the date of the attorney's breach of duty. *Cornell v. Edsen,* 78 Wash. 662, 664–65, 139 P. 602 (1914); *followed by Busk v. Flanders,* 2 Wash.App. 526, 532–33, 468 P.2d 695 (1970).

> The present rule is an anachronism. Recent Washington malpractice cases involving other professions have adopted the date of discovery rule proposed herein. *See, e. g., Ruth v. Dight,* 75 Wash.2d 660, 453 P.2d 631 (1969) (physician's malpractice action); * * *[21]

2. *Use of a mystery style development of argument.* Remember what you have learned about writing office memoranda: Always let your reader know where you are heading—and why. State the conclusions that you want your judges to reach and then support them. Busy judges may be even less inclined than attorneys to read on if they do not understand why you present the arguments that you do.

3. *Failure to argue as an advocate.* State your arguments affirmatively. For example, if you are aware that your opponent has a

---

21. Brief of Appellants at 5–6.

particularly effective argument and you wish to refute it as best you can, do not do so by stating your opponent's argument first, thus: "Respondent may argue (or appellant has argued) that the statute of limitations is not a defense in this case because the statute did not start running until the alleged fraud was discovered. However, the general rule is that * * *" Rather, state your argument affirmatively first, thus: "The statute of limitations began to run when the alleged fraud should reasonably have been discovered. * * *" Develop your affirmative argument first; then dispose of your opponent's authorities.

4. *Overuse of "we contend," "we submit," "we believe," "we feel," etc.* Be as affirmative as you can be without misleading the court or overstating your authorities. If your proposition is very doubtful, use, "It is submitted," because appellate briefs should be written in an impersonal style.

5. *Excessive use of quotations.* Carefully selected quotations from opinions or from highly regarded secondary authorities can be very effective; a court's statement of a rule should always be quoted, not paraphrased. However, you should never quote that which you can say more concisely or more persuasively in your own language. When you do quote, quote a logical unit of language, omitting that which is not pertinent; but be certain that you do not change the meaning of the language by your omissions. Quote accurately. Always indicate the significance or relevance of a quotation if it is not obvious.

SECTION 11J. ORAL ARGUMENTS

An appellate brief must lay the foundation for oral argument. Never withhold an argument from your brief in order to surprise your opponent in oral argument. If you attempt such a course, the surprise may be yours when the court refuses to hear the argument.

To prepare for an oral argument, examine your entire case from both your view and your adversary's view. Then make a general outline of your argument and revise the outline as many times as necessary to give you confidence that you are prepared to present a logically organized argument. Just how detailed your outline should be is a matter of individual preference, but do not try to write your total argument with the idea of reading it to the court or memorizing it to recite to the court. The United States Supreme Court has stated in its Rule 44(1), "Oral argument should undertake to emphasize and clarify the written argument appearing in the briefs theretofore filed. The court looks with disfavor on any oral argument that is read from a prepared text." Do not plan to repeat the arguments as set out in your brief; plan to restate your crucial arguments simply and concisely.

Do not plan to cover too much material in your argument. You will find that time passes quickly, and the judges may ask questions that require substantial time to answer. In fact, you should plan a "short" argument—one that covers the bare essentials—and a "long" argument—one in which you have an opportunity to develop the points underlying the bare essentials. Then, if the judges ask many questions, you may drop the details of the long argument and concentrate on only the essential points; if they ask few questions, you will be prepared with an adequate argument.

Plan to limit your coverage to two or three major issues or points and plan to cover them as thoroughly as time permits, rather than planning to use a shot-gun approach.

You need not plan to discuss authorities supporting all the points you wish to make. Crucial decisions may be discussed, but in no greater detail then necessary to establish their relevance or lack of relevance. You need not state the citations for decisions that you discuss; merely cite to the page(s) in your brief where they are discussed. For the most part, you can state the propositions established by your authorities and rely on the brief to provide the details.

The traditional procedure is for appellant to argue first, then counsel for respondent, and, finally, counsel for appellant in rebuttal. Court rules usually limit the amount of time for oral argument. Appellant's counsel must indicate the amount of time to be reserved for rebuttal after introducing himself or herself. The traditional opening is, "May it please the court, I am * * * of counsel for * * * " In law school moot court work, the team system is frequently used. Then, the introduction should extend to co-counsel: "My co-counsel is * * * " Opposing counsel should not be introduced.[22]

Following the introduction, a brief statement of the nature of the case and the points to be argued is useful. If a co-counsel will also argue, a brief statement of the points that co-counsel will argue is helpful, although this will not insure that the court will not direct questions concerning the entire argument to each counsel.

Counsel for appellant should state the facts unless the court advises to the contrary. The facts must be presented clearly, yet they must be presented concisely. Usually formalities such as legal descriptions, names, distances, dates, elapsed times, and other similar matters may be omitted. A diagram may be used to present complicated fact patterns. Never present a too-biased picture of the facts.

---

22. For future reference, note that dividing oral argument between two counsel is not advisable unless conflicting interests joined on one side require it. "When two lawyers undertake to share a single presentation, their two arguments at best will be somewhat overlapping, repetitious and incomplete and, at worst, contradictory, inconsistent and confusing." M. Pittoni, Brief Writing and Argumentation 78 (1967) (from suggestions by Hon. Robert H. Jackson). "Divided arguments are not favored by the court." Sup.Ct.R. 44(4).

Nothing could serve your cause worse than to have the court come to the conclusion that you have tried to deceive it as to the facts. Respondent's counsel may use a short counterstatement, or if the statement of facts already presented was basically fair, may omit such a counterstatement; he or she should not go into a lengthy restatement of facts that are undisputed.

Know the contents of your record so that you can respond to any questions about the proceedings or evidence. Take your copy of the record, or the most significant parts of it, to the podium with you so that you will have it immediately available should you need to refer to it. If necessary, prepare an index for the record or tab-index it so that you can quickly find information on particular points beyond your immediate recall.

Speak directly to the judges and maintain eye contact with them so that you can determine whether they are following your argument. Speak slowly and distinctly—and loud enough to be heard easily. Pause occasionally to give the judges time to think about what you have said. Stand erect, with your hands resting lightly on the podium or at your side when you are not using them. Do not handle a pencil, pen, or papers nervously or jingle change in your pocket; repeated nervous actions may distract your judges' attention from what you are saying. Do not read extensively from your brief. Avoid reading extended quotations. If you do want to read something to the court, read to the court and not to the book or paper from which you are quoting.

Welcome questions. Take the attitude that your major reason for appearing before the court is to answer questions. They provide the only opportunity you will have to clarify points that one or more members of the court may have failed to understand from a reading of your brief. Try to answer all questions fully and immediately. Do not go beyond the question asked unless it is defensively necessary to do so. If you do not understand a question, ask for clarification. Never attempt to bluff or evade a question; if you do not know the answer, admit it. When an unexpected question is asked, pause and think carefully before answering to make certain that you do not concede more than is necessary. If you become aware that you have made a mistake in answering a question, it is far better frankly to admit the mistake and restate your answer than to become involved in trying to justify the answer. When answering a question, address the inquiring judge as "Your Honor" rather than "Sir," "Gentlemen," or "Ma'am."

Do not become concerned if questions seem unfavorable to your client's position. The character of questions asked does not necessarily signal a judge's views. In actual practice, questions fall into three general categories—neutral, favorable, and unfavorable. Neu-

tral questions are genuinely directed toward seeking information or clarification. A judge persuaded as to the correctness of your position may ask questions that put your view in the most favorable light. A judge already persuaded to your viewpoint may also ask unfavorable questions, however, in order to: (1) permit you to suggest favorable resolution of points that are bothering him or her, or (2) permit you to suggest favorable resolution of points that he or she knows are bothering a judge who is neutral or opposed to your position. Finally, a judge already persuaded as to the invalidity of your position may ask unfavorable questions that reveal the weaknesses of your position.

Reproduced in Appendix G, is a summary of the oral arguments presented to the Supreme Court in *Burns v. Alcala,* together with quotations of some of the questions addressed to each counsel and their answers. Consider to what extent the questions signalled the Court's decision, reported in its opinion reproduced at the end of Chapter 3, in text note 7.

If you find yourself running short of time, drop your lesser arguments and finish with a strong point. Whatever you may sacrifice in terms of informational content will be outweighed by the psychological impact of a forceful closing argument. When you are advised that your time is up, stop after completing your thought in a sentence or two. If substantially all your time has been consumed by questions and answers, the Chief Justice may permit you to sum up in an additional two or three minutes.

As counsel for appellant, use rebuttal time to correct gross misstatements of respondent's counsel or to attack respondent's strong points. Do not deal with trivial points; you may give the impression that you do not have a strong response. Limit yourself to two or three important, specific points. You should not raise points or issues not covered in your opponent's argument.

NOTES

1. Examine some actual appeal briefs. Briefs that you will find most instructive will be those submitted in cases with which you are familiar. To request or find a specific brief you will need the appeal or docket number (given immediately before or shortly after the case name in all reports and reporters). For briefs filed with the United States Supreme Court, you will also need the term of court (shown prominently at the top of every other page in the official reports). Be very critical of these briefs. Shoddy work has gone into some briefs filed with courts, even with the Supreme Court. See also the sample briefs in M. Pittoni, Brief Writing and Argumentation 93–211 (3d ed. 1967) and in Introduction to Advocacy (2d ed. 1976); J. Searles, Advocacy in the Moot Court Program (3d ed. 1971); M. Josephson, Handbook of Appellate Advocacy (1967), and Moot Court

Handbook: Introduction to Brief Writing and Oral Argument (1968), handbooks for moot court programs at the law schools of, respectively, Harvard, Case Western Reserve University, University of California at Los Angeles, and New York University.

2. Oral arguments are not usually reported in full. You may find interesting excerpts of arguments and questioning by browsing through the "Proceedings" section of the Supreme Court Section of the *United States Law Week,* the source of the summary reproduced in Appendix G. Oral arguments in the *School Desegregation Cases* are collected in Argument (L. Friedman ed. 1969). See also the "Annotated Critique of an Oral Argument" in F. Wiener, Briefing and Arguing Federal Appeals ch. XIV (1967).

3. A significant new source for both briefs and oral arguments is a series entitled Landmark Briefs and Arguments of the Supreme Court of the United States: Constitutional Law, edited by Phillip B. Kurland and Gerhard Casper. Almost 100 volumes have already been published. Included are reproductions of the briefs and transcriptions of some of the oral arguments in significant cases decided by the Court. Oral arguments heard subsequent to 1955 are reported for the included cases decided thereafter, and oral arguments previously heard are reported if transcriptions can be found.

4. Many books and articles have been written about arguments on appeal. The following should supply answers to most questions that you may have.

    E. Re, Brief Writing and Oral Argument (4th ed. 1974): Briefs are discussed in Chapters VI and VII. Chapter VI contains a particularly good description of how to write effective point headings. Oral arguments are discussed in Chapters VIII and IX.

    H. Weihofen, Legal Writing Style (1961): Briefs are discussed in Chapters 9 and 10. Chapter 11 contains excellent suggestions on how to write forcefully.

    F. Cooper, Writing in Law Practice (Student's ed. 1963): Chapter III, "Selecting and Stating the Issue," is useful for its many examples of questions.

    F. Wiener, Briefing and Arguing Federal Appeals (1967): Written for practitioners, this book contains many practical suggestions about brief-writing details not covered in the books cited above.

    R. Stern and E. Gressman, Supreme Court Practice (4th ed. 1969): This book, also written for practitioners, may provide answers to your questions about Supreme Court jurisdiction and procedures as well as about briefs and oral arguments.

Many useful articles on a variety of subjects related to both trial and appellate briefs and arguments are collected in Advocacy and the King's English (1960).

5. A traditional assumption in the United States has been that both written and oral arguments are necessary for appellate review. With overwhelming increases in caseloads in appellate courts throughout the country, this assumption has recently been challenged. By 1976 all but one of the circuits of the federal court of appeals were screening cases to determine whether oral argument should be denied or limited. Only the court for the second circuit did not use a screening procedure, but it affirmed from the bench about 30% of all cases argued orally. Betten, *Institutional Reform in the Federal Courts,* 52 Ind.L.J. 63, 71 (1976). The Commission on Revision of the Federal Court Appellate System, established by Congress to study problems in the federal appellate system, concluded that oral argument should not so generally be denied and therefore recommended in its final report that the following limitation should be added to the Federal Rules of Appellate Procedure:

> 1. In any appeal in a civil or criminal case, the appellant should be entitled as a matter of right to present oral argument, unless:
>
> > (a) the appeal is frivolous;
> >
> > (b) the dispositive issue or set of issues has been recently authoritatively decided; or
> >
> > (c) the facts are simple, the determination of the appeal rests on the application of settled rules of law, and no useful purpose could be served by oral argument.
>
> 2. Oral argument is appropriately shortened in cases in which the dispositive points can be adequately presented in less than the usual time allowable.

Structure and Internal Procedures: Recommendations for Change 48 (1975). The Commission concluded that oral argument contributes to judicial accountability, guards against excessive reliance on staff work, promotes understanding as written communication cannot, and assures litigants that their cases have been given consideration. *Id.*

An even stronger position with respect to oral argument was urged as the result of a more general study of appellate justice. Concluding that measures to promote efficiency are not acceptable if the quality of appellate justice is impaired, three scholars urged: (1) as to first-level review, oral argument should be heard for every appeal to be decided on the merits if requested by any party or any member of the court, and (2) courts should be permitted to limit the length of argument or *invite* waiver of oral argument if appellant's case appears hopeless or unanswerable or if the briefs on both sides are complete and sufficient. P. Carrington, D. Meador, M. Rosenberg, Justice on Appeal 226 (1976) (discussing also the merits and demerits of both written and oral arguments at 16–29).

APPENDICES

APPENDIX A

LUCAS v. HAMM

Supreme Court of California, 1961.
56 Cal.2d 583, 15 Cal.Rptr. 821, 364 P.2d 685.

GIBSON, Chief Justice.

Plaintiffs, who are some of the beneficiaries under the will of Eugene H. Emmick, deceased, brought this action for damages against defendant L. S. Hamm, an attorney at law who had been engaged by the testator to prepare the will. They have appealed from a judgment of dismissal entered after an order sustaining a general demurrer to the second amended complaint without leave to amend.

The allegations of the first and second causes of action are summarized as follows: Defendant agreed with the testator, for a consideration, to prepare a will and codicils thereto for him by which plaintiffs were to be designated as beneficiaries of a trust provided for by paragraph Eighth of the will and were to receive 15% of the residue as specified in that paragraph. Defendant, in violation of instructions and in breach of his contract, negligently prepared testamentary instruments containing phraseology that was invalid by virtue of section 715.2 and former sections 715.1 and 716 of the Civil Code relating to restraints on alienation and the rule against perpetuities.[1] Paragraph Eighth of these instruments "transmitted" the

---

1. Former section 715.1 of the Civil Code, as it read at the times involved here, provided: "The absolute power of alienation cannot be suspended, by any limitation or condition whatever, for a period longer than 21 years after some life in being at the creation of the interest and any period of gestation involved in the situation to which the limitation applies. The lives selected to govern the time of suspension must not be so numerous or so situated that evidence of their deaths is likely to be unreasonably difficult to obtain."

Section 715.2 reads as follows: "No interest in real or personal property shall be good unless it must vest, if at all, not later than 21 years after some life in being at the creation of the interest and any period of gestation involved in the situation to which the limitation applies. The lives selected to govern the time of vesting must

not be so numerous or so situated that evidence of their deaths is likely to be unreasonably difficult to obtain. It is intended by the enactment of this section to make effective in this State the American common-law rule against perpetuities."

Former section 716, as it read at the times involved here, provided: "Every future interest is void in its creation which, by any possibility, may suspend the absolute power of alienation for a longer period than is prescribed in this chapter. Such power of alienation is suspended when there are no persons in being by whom an absolute interest in possession can be conveyed. The period of time during which an interest is destructible pursuant to the uncontrolled volition and for the exclusive personal benefit of the person having such a power of destruction is not to be included in determining the existence of a suspension of

residual estate in trust and provided that the "trust shall cease and terminate at 12 o'clock noon on a day five years after the date upon which the order distributing the trust property to the trustee is made by the Court having jurisdiction over the probation of this will." After the death of the testator the instruments were admitted to probate. Subsequently defendant, as draftsman of the instruments and as counsel of record for the executors, advised plaintiffs in writing that the residual trust provision was invalid and that plaintiffs would be deprived of the entire amount to which they would have been entitled if the provision had been valid unless they made a settlement with the blood relatives of the testator under which plaintiffs would receive a lesser amount than that provided for them by the testator. As the direct and proximate result of the negligence of defendant and his breach of contract in preparing the testamentary instruments and the written advice referred to above, plaintiffs were compelled to enter into a settlement under which they received a share of the estate amounting to $75,000 less than the sum which they would have received pursuant to testamentary instruments drafted in accordance with the directions of the testator.

(The third cause of action will be discussed separately because it concerns matters not involved in the first two counts.)

It was held in Buckley v. Gray, 110 Cal. 339, 42 P. 900, 31 L.R.A. 862, that an attorney who made a mistake in drafting a will was not liable for negligence or breach of contract to a person named in the will who was deprived of benefits as a result of the error. The court stated that an attorney is liable to his client alone with respect to actions based on negligence in the conduct of his professional duties, and it was reasoned that there could be no recovery for mere negligence where there was no privity by contract or otherwise between the defendant and the person injured. 110 Cal. at pages 342–343, 42 P. 900. The court further concluded that there could be no recovery on the theory of a contract for the benefit of a third person, because the contract with the attorney was not expressly for the plaintiff's benefit and the testatrix only remotely intended the plaintiff to be benefited as a result of the contract. 110 Cal. at pages 346–347, 42 P. 900. For the reasons hereinafter stated the case is overruled. [The court concluded that the intended beneficiaries might be entitled to recover as third party beneficiaries.]

* * *

However, an attorney is not liable either to his client or to a beneficiary under a will for errors of the kind alleged in the first and second causes of action.

The general rule with respect to the liability of an attorney for failure to properly perform his duties to his client is that the attorney, by accepting employment to give legal advice or to render other legal services, impliedly agrees to use such skill, prudence, and diligence as lawyers of ordinary skill and capacity commonly possess and exercise in the performance of the tasks which they undertake. Estate of Kruger, 130 Cal. 621, 626, 63 P. 31; Moser v. Western Harness Racing Ass'n, 89 Cal.App.2d 1, 7, 200 P.

the absolute power of alienation or the permissible period for the vesting of an interest within the rule against perpetuities."

2d 7; Armstrong v. Adams, 102 Cal.App. 677, 684, 283 P. 871; see Wade, The Attorney's Liability for Negligence (1959) 12 Vanderbilt Law Rev. 755, 762–765; 5 Am.Jur. 336. The attorney is not liable for every mistake he may make in his practice; he is not, in the absence of an express agreement, an insurer of the soundness of his opinions or of the validity of an instrument that he is engaged to draft; and he is not liable for being in error as to a question of law on which reasonable doubt may be entertained by well-informed lawyers. See Lally v. Kuster, 177 Cal. 783, 786, 171 P. 961; Savings Bank v. Ward, 100 U.S. 195, 198, 25 L.Ed. 621; 5 Am.Jur. 335; 7 C.J.S. Attorney and Client § 143, p. 980. These principles are equally applicable whether the palintiff's claim is based on tort or breach of contract.

The complaint, as we have seen, alleges that defendant drafted the will in such a manner that the trust was invalid because it violated the rules relating to perpetuities and restraints on alienation. These closely akin subjects have long perplexed the courts and the bar. Professor Gray, a leading authority in the field, stated: "There is something in the subject which seems to facilitate error. Perhaps it is because the mode of reasoning is unlike that with which lawyers are most familiar. * * * A long list might be formed of the demonstrable blunders with regard to its questions made by eminent men, blunders which they themselves have been sometimes the first to acknowledge; and there are few lawyers of any practice in drawing wills and settlements who have not at some time either fallen into the net which the Rule spreads for the unwary, or at least shuddered to think how narrowly they have escaped it." Gray, The Rule Against Perpetuities (4th ed. 1942) p. xi; see also Leach, Perpetuities Legislation (1954) 67 Harv.L.Rev. 1349 [describing the rule as a "technicality-ridden legal nightmare" and a "dangerous instrumentality in the hands of most members of the bar"]. Of the California law on perpetuities and restraints it has been said that few, if any, areas of the law have been fraught with more confusion or concealed more traps for the unwary draftsman; that members of the bar, probate courts, and title insurance companies make errors in these matters; that the code provisions adopted in 1872 created a situation worse than if the matter had been left to the common law, and that the legislation adopted in 1951 (under which the will involved here was drawn), despite the best of intentions, added further complexities. (See 38 Cal.Jur.2d 443; Coil, Perpetuities and Restraints; A Needed Reform (1955) 30 State Bar J. 87, 88–90.)

In view of the state of the law relating to perpetuities and restraints on alienation and the nature of the error, if any, assertedly made by defendant in preparing the instrument, it would not be proper to hold that defendant failed to use such skill, prudence, and diligence as lawyers of ordinary skill and capacity commonly exercise. The provision of the will quoted in the complaint, namely, that the trust was to terminate five years after the order of the probate court distributing the property to the trustee, could cause the trust to be invalid only because of the remote possibility that the order of distribution would be delayed for a period longer than a life in being at the creation of the interest plus 16 years (the 21-year statutory period less the five years specified in the will). Although it has been held that a possibility of this type could result in invalidity of a bequest (Estate

of Johnston, 47 Cal.2d 265, 269–270, 303 P.2d 1; Estate of Campbell, 28 Cal.App.2d 102, 103 et seq., 82 P.2d 22), the possible occurrence of such a delay was so remote and unlikely that an attorney of ordinary skill acting under the same circumstances might well have "fallen into the net which the Rule spreads for the unwary" and failed to recognize the danger. We need not decide whether the trust provision of the will was actually invalid or whether, as defendant asserts, the complaint fails to allege facts necessary to enable such a determination,[3] because we have concluded that in any event an error of the type relied on by plaintiffs does not show negligence or breach of contract on the part of defendant. It is apparent that plaintiffs have not stated and cannot state causes of action with respect to the first two counts, and the trial court did not abuse its discretion in denying leave to amend as to these counts.

* * *

The judgment is affirmed.

TRAYNOR, SCHAUER, McCOMB, PETERS, WHITE and DOOLING, JJ., concur.

---

3. Defendant asserts that a provision of a will like the one quoted in the complaint could not cause a trust to be invalid unless it also appeared that there were contingent interests which could not vest within the statutory time or that the trust could not be terminated by the beneficiaries acting together within the statutory period. See Estate of Phelps, 182 Cal. 752, 759–760, 190 P. 17; Estate of Heberle, 155 Cal. 723, 726–727, 102 P. 935; Rest., Trusts, Second, § 337.

APPENDIX B

SMITH v. LEWIS

Supreme Court of California, 1975.
13 Cal.3d 349, 118 Cal.Rptr. 621, 530 P.2d 589.

MOSK, Justice.

Defendant Jerome R. Lewis, an attorney, appeals from a judgment entered upon a jury verdict for plaintiff Rosemary E. Smith in an action for legal malpractice. The action arises as a result of legal services rendered by defendant to plaintiff in a prior divorce proceeding. The gist of plaintiff's complaint is that defendant negligently failed in the divorce action to assert her community interest in the retirement benefits of her husband.

Defendant principally contends, inter alia, that the law with regard to the characterization of retirement benefits was so unclear at the time he represented plaintiff as to insulate him from liability for failing to assert a claim therefor on behalf of his client.[1] We conclude defendant's appeal is without merit, and therefore affirm the judgment.

In 1943 plaintiff married General Clarence D. Smith. Between 1945 and his retirement in 1966 General Smith was employed by the California National Guard. As plaintiff testified, she informed defendant her husband "was paid by the state * * * it was a job just like anyone else goes to." For the first 16 years of that period the husband belonged to the State Employees' Retirement System, a contributory plan.[2] Between 1961 and the date of his retirement he belonged to the California National Guard retirement program, a noncontributory plan. In addition, by attending National Guard reserve drills he qualified for separate retirement benefits from the federal government, also through a noncontributory plan. The state and federal retirement programs each provide lifetime monthly benefits which terminate upon the death of the retiree. The programs make no allowance for the retiree's widow.

On January 1, 1967, the State of California began to pay General Smith gross retirement benefits of $796.26 per month. Payments under the federal program, however, will not begin until 1983, i. e., 17 years after his actual retirement, when General Smith reaches the age of 60. All benefits which General Smith is entitled to receive were earned during the time he was married to plaintiff.

1. Defendant alternatively contends the state and federal military retirement benefits in question cannot properly be characterized as community property, and hence his advice to plaintiff was correct. As will appear, the contention is manifestly untenable in light of recent decisions by this court. (In re Marriage of Fithian (1974) 10 Cal.3d 592, 111 Cal.Rptr. 369, 517 P.2d 449; Waite v. Waite (1972) 6 Cal.3d 461, 99 Cal.Rptr. 325, 492 P.2d 13; Phillipson v. Board of Administration (1970) 3 Cal.3d 32, 89 Cal.Rptr. 61, 473 P.2d 765.)

2. A contributory plan is one in which the member contributes to his retirement fund, normally through payroll deductions. A noncontributory plan is one in which no such contributions are made.

The State Employees' Retirement System is now referred to as the Public Employees' Retirement System (Gov. Code, § 20000 et seq.).

On February 17, 1967, plaintiff retained defendant to represent her in a divorce action against General Smith. According to plaintiff's testimony, defendant advised her that her husband's retirement benefits were not community property. Three days later defendant filed plaintiff's complaint for divorce. General Smith's retirement benefits were not pleaded as items of community property, and therefore were not considered in the litigation or apportioned by the trial court. The divorce was uncontested and the interlocutory decree divided the minimal described community property and awarded Mrs. Smith $400 per month in alimony and child support. The final decree was entered on February 27, 1968.

On July 17, 1968, pursuant to a request by plaintiff, defendant filed on her behalf a motion to amend the decree, alleging under oath that because of his mistake, inadvertence, and excusable neglect (Code Civ.Proc., § 473) the retirement benefits of General Smith had been omitted from the list of community assets owned by the parties, and that such benefits were in fact community property. The motion was denied on the ground of untimeliness. Plaintiff consulted other counsel, and shortly thereafter filed this malpractice action against defendant.

Defendant admits in his testimony that he assumed General Smith's retirement benefits were separate property when he assessed plaintiff's community property rights. It is his position that as a matter of law an attorney is not liable for mistaken advice when well informed lawyers in the community entertain reasonable doubt as to the proper resolution of the particular legal question involved. Because, he asserts, the law defining the character of retirement benefits was uncertain at the time of his legal services to plaintiff, defendant contends the trial court committed error in refusing to grant his motions for nonsuit and judgment notwithstanding the verdict and in submitting the issue of negligence to the jury under appropriate instructions.[3]

The law is now settled in California that "retirement benefits which flow from the employment relationship, to the extent they have vested, are community property subject to equal division between the spouses in the event the marriage is dissolved." (In re Marriage of Fithian (1974) supra, 10 Cal.3d 592, 596, 111 Cal.Rptr. 369, 371, 517 P.2d 449, 451, citing Waite v. Waite (1972) supra, 6 Cal.3d 461, 99 Cal.Rptr. 325, 492 P.2d 13; Phillipson v. Board of Administration (1970) supra, 3 Cal.3d 32, 89 Cal.Rptr. 61, 473 P.2d 765; Benson v. City of Los Angeles (1963) 60 Cal.2d 355, 33 Cal.Rptr. 257, 384 P.2d 649; French v. French (1941) 17 Cal.2d 775, 112 P.2d 235; Crossan v. Crossan (1939) 35 Cal.App.2d 39, 94 P.2d 609.) Because such

---

3. The jury was instructed as follows: "In performing legal services for a client in a divorce action an attorney has the duty to have that degree of learning and skill ordinarily possessed by attorneys of good standing, practicing in the same or similar locality and under similar circumstances."

"It is his further duty to use the care and skill ordinarily exercised in like cases by reputable members of his profession practicing in the same or a similar locality under similar circumstances, and to use reasonable diligence and his best judgment in the exercise of his skill and the accomplishment of his learning, in an effort to accomplish the best possible result for his client."

"A failure to perform any such duty is negligence."

"An attorney is not liable for every mistake he may make in his practice; he is not, in the absence of an express agreement, an insurer of the soundness of his opinions."

benefits are part of the consideration earned by the employee, they are accorded community treatment regardless of whether they derive from a state, federal, or private source, or from a contributory or noncontributory plan. (10 Cal.3d at p. 596, 111 Cal.Rptr. 369, 517 P.2d 449.) In light of these principles, it becomes apparent that General Smith's retirement pay must properly be characterized as community property.[4]

We cannot, however, evaluate the quality of defendant's professional services on the basis of the law as it appears today. In determining whether defendant exhibited the requisite degree of competence in his handling of plaintiff's divorce action, the crucial inquiry is whether his advice was so legally deficient when it was given that he may be found to have failed to use "such skill, prudence, and diligence as lawyers of ordinary skill and capacity commonly possess and exercise in the performance of the tasks which they undertake." (Lucas v. Hamm (1961) 56 Cal.2d 583, 591, 15 Cal.Rptr. 821, 825, 364 P.2d 685, 689.) We must, therefore examine the indicia of the law which were readily available to defendant at the time he performed the legal services in question.

The major authoritative reference works which attorneys routinely consult for a brief and reliable exposition of the law relevant to a specific problem uniformly indicated in 1967 that vested retirement benefits earned during marriage were generally subject to community treatment.[5] (See, e. g., Note, Pensions, and Reserve or Retired Pay, as Community Property, 134 A.L.R. 368; 15 Am.Jur.2d, Community Property, § 46, p. 859; 38 Cal. Jur.2d, Pensions, § 12, p. 325; 10 Cal.Jur.2d, Community Property, § 25, p. 692; 1 Cal.Family Lawyer (Cont.Ed.Bar 1962) p. 111; 4 Witkin, Summary of Cal.Law (1960) pp. 2723–2724; cf. 41 C.J.S. Husband and Wife § 475, p. 1010 & fn. 69 and 1967 Supp. p. 1011.) A typical statement appeared in The California Family Lawyer, a work with which defendant admitted general familiarity: "Of increasing importance is the fact that pension or retirement benefits are community property, even though they are not paid or payable until after termination of the marriage by death or divorce." (1 Cal.Family Lawyer, supra, at p. 111.)

Although it is true this court had not foreclosed all conflicts on some aspects of the issue at that time, the community character of retirement benefits had been reported in a number of appellate opinions often cited in the literature and readily accessible to defendant. (Benson v. City of Los Angeles (1963) supra, 60 Cal.2d 355, 33 Cal.Rptr. 257, 384 P.2d 649; French v. French (1941) supra, 17 Cal.2d 775, 112 P.2d 235; Cheney v. City & County of San Francisco (1936) 7 Cal.2d 565, 61 P.2d 754; Williamson v. Williamson (1962) supra, 203 Cal.App.2d 8, 21 Cal.Rptr. 164; Estate of Manley (1959) 169 Cal.App.2d 641, 337 P.2d 487; Estate of Perryman

4. The fact General Smith will not receive any portion of the federal benefits until he reaches the age of 60 does not affect their community character. Though his right to the payments remained unmatured at the time of the divorce, it had fully vested. (In re Marriage of Fithian (1974) supra, 10 Cal.3d 592, 596, 111 Cal. Rptr. 369, 517 P.2d 449, fn. 2; Williamson v. Williamson (1962) 203 Cal. App.2d 8, 11, 21 Cal.Rptr. 164.)

5. In evaluating the competence of an attorney's services, we may justifiably consider his failure to consult familiar encyclopedias of the law. (People v. Ibarra (1963) 60 Cal.2d 460, 465, 34 Cal.Rptr. 863, 386 P.2d 487.)

(1955) 133 Cal.App.2d 1, 283 P.2d 298; Crossan v. Crossan (1939) supra, 35 Cal.App.2d 39, 94 P.2d 609.) In *Benson,* decided four years before defendant was retained herein, we stated directly that "pension rights which are earned during the course of a marriage are the community property of the employee and his wife." (60 Cal.2d at p. 359, 33 Cal.Rptr. at p. 259, 384 P.2d at p. 651.) In *French,* decided two decades earlier, we indicated that "retire[ment] pay is community property because it is compensation for services rendered in the past." (17 Cal.2d at p. 778, 112 P.2d at p. 236.) The other cases contain equally unequivocal dicta.

We are aware, moreover, of no significant authority existing in 1967 which proposed a result contrary to that suggested by the cases and the literature, or which purported to rebut the general statutory presumption, as it applies to retirement benefits, that all property acquired by either spouse during marriage belongs to the community. (Civ.Code, § 5110, as amended Jan. 1, 1970; formerly Civ.Code, § 164.)

On the other hand, substantial uncertainty may have existed in 1967 with regard to the community character of General Smith's *federal* pension. The above-discussed treatises reveal a debate which lingered among members of the legal community at that time concerning the point at which retirement benefits actually vest.[6] (See also Kent, Pension Funds and Problems Under California Community Property Laws (1950) 2 Stan.L.Rev. 447; Note, Community Property: Division of Expectancies as Community Property at Time of Divorce (1942) 30 Cal.L.Rev. 469.) Because the federal payments were contingent upon General Smith's survival to age 60, 17 years subsequent to the divorce, it could have been argued with some force that plaintiff and General Smith shared a mere expectancy interest in the future benefits. (See French v. French (1941) supra, 17 Cal.2d 775, 778, 112 P.2d 235; but see fn. 4, *ante.*) Alternatively, a reasonable contention could have been advanced in 1967 that federal retirement benefits were the personal entitlement of the employee spouse and were not subject to community division upon divorce in the absence of express congressional approval. In fact, such was the conclusion reached in 1973 by Judge B. Abbott Goldberg in his scholarly article Is Armed Services Retired Pay Really Community Property? (1973) 48 State Bar Journal 12. Although we rejected Judge Goldberg's analysis in In re Marriage of Fithian (1974) supra, 10 Cal.3d 592, 597, 111 Cal.Rptr. 369; 517 P.2d 449, footnote 2, the issue was clearly an arguable one upon which reasonable lawyers could differ. (See Sprague v. Morgan (1960) 185 Cal.App.2d 519, 523, 8 Cal.Rptr. 347; Annot., 45 A.L. R.2d 5, 15.)

Of course, the fact that in 1967 a reasonable argument could have been offered to support the characterization of General Smith's federal benefits as separate property does not indicate the trial court erred in submitting the issue of defendant's malpractice to the jury. The *state* benefits, the large majority of the payments at issue, were unquestionably community property according to all available authority and should have been claimed as such. As for the *federal* benefits, the record documents defendant's failure to conduct any reasonable research into their proper characterization under community

6. Indeed this debate may, to some extent, continue today. See, e. g., In re Marriage of Wilson (1974) 10 Cal.3d 851, 112 Cal.Rptr. 405, 519 P.2d 165.

property law.[7] Instead, he dogmatically asserted his theory, which he was unable to support with authority and later recanted, that all noncontributory military retirement benefits, whether state or federal, were immune from community treatment upon divorce. The jury could well have found defendant's refusal to educate himself to the applicable principles of law constituted negligence which prevented him from exercising informed discretion with regard to his client's rights.

As the jury was correctly instructed, an attorney does not ordinarily guarantee the soundness of his opinions and, accordingly, is not liable for every mistake he may make in his practice. He is expected, however, to possess knowledge of those plain and elementary principles of law which are commonly known by well informed attorneys, and to discover those additional rules of law which, although not commonly known, may readily be found by standard research techniques. (Lucas v. Hamm (1961) 56 Cal.2d 583, 591, 15 Cal.Rptr. 821, 364 P.2d 685; Lally v. Kuster (1918) 177 Cal. 783, 786, 171 P. 961; Floro v. Lawton (1960) 187 Cal.App.2d 657, 673, 10 Cal. Rptr. 98; Sprague v. Morgan (1960) supra, 185 Cal.App.2d 519, 523, 8 Cal. Rptr. 347; Armstrong v. Adams (1929) 102 Cal.App. 677, 684, 283 P. 871.) If the law on a particular subject is doubtful or debatable, an attorney will not be held responsible for failing to anticipate the manner in which the uncertainty will be resolved. (See, e. g., Sprague v. Morgan (1960) supra.) But even with respect to an unsettled area of the law, we believe an attorney assumes an obligation to his client to undertake reasonable research in an effort to ascertain relevant legal principles and to make an informed decision as to a course of conduct based upon an intelligent assessment of the problem. In the instant case, ample evidence was introduced to support a jury finding that defendant failed to perform such adequate research into the question of the community character of retirement benefits and thus was unable to exercise the informed judgment to which his client was entitled. (See fn. 7, *ante*.)

We recognize, of course, that an attorney engaging in litigation may have occasion to choose among various alternative strategies available to his client, one of which may be to refrain from pressing a debatable point because potential benefit may not equal detriment in terms of expenditure at time and resources or because of calculated tactics to the advantage of his client. But, as the Ninth Circuit put it somewhat brutally in Pineda v. Craven (9th Cir. 1970) 424 F.2d 369, 372: "There is nothing strategic or

---

7. At trial defendant testified that prior to the division of property in the divorce action, he had assumed the retirement benefits were not subject to community treatment, despite the fact General Smith had already begun to receive payments from the state; that he did not at that time undertake any research on the point nor did he discuss the matter with plaintiff; that subsequent to the divorce plaintiff asked defendant to research the question whereupon defendant discovered the *French* case which contained dictum in support of plaintiff's position; that the *French* decision caused him to change his opinion and conclude "that the Supreme Court, when it was confronted with this [the language in *French*] may hold that it [vested military retirement pay] is community property." On the basis of *French* defendant filed his unsuccessful motion to amend the final decree of divorce to allow plaintiff an interest in the retirement benefits. Defendant admitted at trial, "I would have been very willing to assert it [a community interest] on her behalf had I known of the dictum in the *French* case at the time."

tactical about ignorance * * *." In the case before us it is difficult to conceive of tactical advantage which could have been served by neglecting to advance a claim so clearly in plaintiff's best interest, nor does defendant suggest any. The decision to forego litigation on the issue of plaintiff's community property right to a share of General Smith's retirement benefits was apparently the product of a culpable misconception of the relevant principles of law, and the jury could have so found.

Furthermore, no lawyer would suggest the property characterization of General Smith's retirement benefits to be so esoteric an issue that defendant could not reasonably have been expected to be aware of it or its probable resolution. (Lucas v. Hamm (1961) supra, 56 Cal.2d 583, 15 Cal.Rptr. 583, 15 Cal.Rptr. 821, 364 P.2d 685.) In *Lucas* we held that the rule against perpetuities poses such complex and difficult problems for the draftsman that even careful and competent attorneys occasionally fall prey to its traps. The situation before us is not analogous. Certainly one of the central issues in any divorce proceeding is the extent and division of the community property. In this case the question reached monumental proportion, since General Smith's retirement benefits constituted the only significant asset available to the community.[8] In undertaking professional representation of plaintiff, defendant assumed the duty to familiarize himself with the law defining the character of retirement benefits; instead, he rendered erroneous advice contrary to the best interests of his client without the guidance through research of readily available authority.

Regardless of his failure to undertake adequate research, defendant through personal experience in the domestic relations field had been exposed to community property aspects of pensions. Representing the wife of a reserve officer in the National Guard in 1965, defendant alleged as one of the items of community property "the retirement benefits from the Armed Forces and/or the California National Guard." On behalf of the husband in a 1967 divorce action, defendant filed an answer admitting retirement benefits were community property, merely contesting the amount thereof. In 1965 a wife whom he was representing was so insistent on asserting a community interest in a pension, over defendant's contrary views, that she communicated with the state retirement system and brought to defendant correspondence from the state agency describing her interest in pension benefits. And representing an army colonel, defendant filed a cross-complaint for divorce specifically setting up as an item of community property "retirement benefits in the name of the defendant with the United States Government." It is difficult to understand why defendant deemed the community property claim to pensions of three of the foregoing clients to deserve presentation to the trial court, but not the similar claim of this plaintiff.

In any event, as indicated above, had defendant conducted minimal research into either hornbook or case law, he would have discovered with modest effort that General Smith's state retirement benefits were likely to be treated as community property and that his federal benefits at least argu-

8. It is undisputed that the only assets the parties had to show as community property after 24 years of marriage, aside from General Smith's retirement benefits, were an equity of $1.800 in a house, some furniture, shares of stock worth $2,800, and two automobiles on which money was owing.

ably belonged to the community as well. Therefore, we hold that the trial court correctly denied the motions for nonsuit and judgment notwithstanding the verdict and properly submitted the question of defendant's negligence to the jury under the instructions given. (See fn. 3, *ante*.) For the same reasons, the trial court correctly refused to instruct the jury at defendant's request that "he is not liable for being in error as to a question of law on which reasonable doubt may be entertained by well informed lawyers." Even as to doubtful matters, an attorney is expected to perform sufficient research to enable him to make an informed and intelligent judgment on behalf of his client.[9]

* * *

Defendant's remaining contentions of error are without merit and require no further discussion.

The judgment is affirmed.

WRIGHT, C. J., and TOBRINER, SULLIVAN and BURKE,* JJ., concur.

CLARK, Justice (dissenting).

I dissent.

The evidence is insufficient to prove plaintiff lost $100,000 from her lawyer's negligence in 1967. There is no direct evidence a well-informed lawyer would have obtained an award of the husband's pensions in the wife's divorce, nor does the record provide such inference. Rather, the state of the law and the circumstances of the parties reveal lawyer Lewis reached a reasonable result for his client in 1967.

To establish liability for negligence, a plaintiff must show defendant's negligence contributed to injury so that "but for" the negligence the injury would not have been sustained. If the injury would have occurred anyway —whether or not the defendant was negligent—the negligence was not a cause in fact. (4 Witkin, Summary of Cal.Law (8th ed. 1970) § 622, pp. 2903–2904; Rest. 2d Torts (1966) § 432; Prosser, The Law of Torts (4th ed. 1971) p. 236 et seq.) "It is not enough merely to show that the probabilities were evenly divided. The evidence must be such that it could be found the balance of probabilities was in plaintiff's favor. (Prosser, 'Proximate Cause in California,' 38 Cal.L.Rev. 369, 378–379.)" (Singh v. Frye (1960) 177 Cal.App.2d 590, 593, 2 Cal.Rptr. 372, 374.)

This fundamental principle is reflected in legal malpractice cases. Prior to today's majority opinion, a lawyer was "not liable for being in error as to a question of law on which reasonable doubt may be entertained by well-informed lawyers. [Citations.]" (Lucas v. Hamm (1961) 56 Cal.2d

9. The principal thrust of the dissent is its conclusion (*post*, p. 637 of 118 Cal.Rptr. p. 605 of 530 P.2d) that "even assuming that defendant was negligent in failing to research the pension questions, the record does not furnish a balance of probabilities that his negligence—rather than the uncertain status of the law and the availability of uncontested alimony— caused plaintiff to lose a $100,000 pension award." Whether defendant's negligence was a cause in fact of plaintiff's damage—an element of proximate cause—is a factual question for the jury to resolve. * * *

* Retired Associate Justice of the Supreme Court sitting under assignment by the Chairman of the Judicial Council.

583, 591, 15 Cal.Rptr. 821, 825, 364 P.2d 685, 689.)   The rule has been variously stated: "It has frequently been held that a lawyer is not liable for lack of knowledge as to the true state of the law where a doubtful or debatable point is involved." (Sprague v. Morgan (1960) 185 Cal.App.2d 519, 523, 8 Cal.Rptr. 347, 350.)   Or, a lawyer "is not holden for errors in judgment nor in cases where well-informed attorneys entertain different views concerning a proposition of law which has not been settled." (Floro v. Lawton (1967) 187 Cal.App.2d 657, 673, 10 Cal.Rptr. 98, 108, quoting from 69 N.J.L.J. 265.)   It should be noted the foregoing statements go beyond lawyer *negligence,* going to the ultimate question of *liability*—he shall not be "liable" or "holden" for the errors.

The advice or services performed by the lawyer may be rendered erroneous by subsequent decisions, but if his contemporaries could reasonably have been expected to have performed in the same manner, it is illogical to assume the client would have gained more by having chosen another lawyer. The point is illustrated by the reasoning in Lucas v. Hamm, *supra,* 56 Cal. 2d 583, 593, 15 Cal.Rptr. 821, 826, 364 P.2d 685, 690, involving a lawyer who prepared a will violating the rule against perpetuities. The court compared his position with that of a nonnegligent lawyer, stating there was no liability because "an attorney of ordinary skill acting under the same circumstances might well have 'fallen into the net which the Rule spreads for the unwary' and failed to recognize the danger."

When we consider the law existing in 1967 and the circumstances of the parties, it cannot be concluded on the record before us that it was probable another lawyer would have obtained pension rights for plaintiff in addition to the award obtained for her by defendant.

As the majority opinion points out, when defendant was employed to procure the divorce in 1967, the law was clear that, other than military retirement payments, pension *payments* constituted community property. (E. g., Benson v. City of Los Angeles (1963) 60 Cal.2d 355, 359, 33 Cal.Rptr. 257, 384 P.2d 689; 4 Witkin, Summary of Cal.Law (7th ed. 1960) pp. 2733–2734.)   However, *no reported California case prior to 1967 stated that a court was empowered to award an employee's future pension benefits to his spouse in a divorce action.* To the contrary, there were strong indications from statutory and case authorities that such an award could not be obtained. Further, in every reported case where a spouse sought award of the employee's pension, that spouse lost.[1]

---

1. Crossan v. Crossan (1939) 35 Cal. App.2d 39, 94 P.2d 609, did not involve an award of the employee's pension payments or benefits. In *Crossan* the employee's contributions to the pension fund were subject to withdrawal if his employment was terminated. The court held the divorce court could take into account the employee's interest in the fund and award his spouse more than one-half of the remaining community property to compensate for the contributions. There is no language in *Crossan* suggesting that an employee's pension *benefits* could be awarded to the spouse.

Crossan is not helpful to plaintiff because the husband's contributions for retirement had been refunded several years prior to the divorce. Moreover, even if the contributions had not been previously withdrawn, *Crossan* would not have aided her significantly in an attempt to recover additional property because plaintiff received substantially all of the community property other than the pensions.

Let us examine the hurdles faced by a 1967 lawyer seeking the pensions now claimed by plaintiff.[2]

[The dissenter then listed the hurdles for a spouse seeking to recover an employee's pension in 1967: The case law doctrine that in a divorce action pensions could be considered only if the benefits were more than an expectancy (here, two were contingent on survival); case law indicating that a spouse could not have a vested right in an employee's pension because it would interfere with the employer's interest; statutes exempting pensions from court process and prohibiting their assignment; case law suggesting that alimony award and modification was the proper method of remedying any imbalances arising from the husband's receipt of pension benefits; substantial doubt whether federal military pensions constituted community property that could be disposed of in a divorce action (which the majority had recognized); the husband had retired under a state statute that adopted federal law.]

* * *

VICTORY?

Assuming defendant fully researched the question whether the pensions could be obtained and further assuming his analysis of the authorities led him to forecast this court's decisions in Phillipson v. Board of Administration, *supra*, 3 Cal.3d 32, 89 Cal.Rptr. 61, 473 P.2d 765, Waite v. Waite (1972) 6 Cal.3d 461, 99 Cal.Rptr. 325, 492 P.2d 13, and In re Marriage of Fithian, *supra*, 10 Cal.3d 592, 111 Cal.Rptr. 369, 517 P.2d 449, it does not follow that he should have pursued an award of the pensions. Although defendant by litigating the awardability of pensions would perhaps have performed a valuable service to the State of California by attempting to settle the law, the lawyer's first duty is to his client's best interest—not to the resolution of uncertain legal questions.

Considering the circumstances of this case, including the alimony obtained, expensive litigation by counsel to recover pensions would have gained the client little—if anything—above that obtained in the uncontested action. And, in view of the uncertainty in the law and the risk that the litigation might result in a net loss, pursuit of the pensions would have been an unrealistic alternative. After his retirement, the husband worked as an automobile salesman receiving commissions of approximately $300 per month. Plaintiff had been earning the same amount shortly before. Plaintiff informed defendant that her husband received $645 monthly pension from the National Guard. Under the divorce decree, plaintiff obtained substantially all of the community property for herself and her son, and was awarded $300 per month alimony and $100 per month child support for her son who was then 18. It is apparent that plaintiff would receive more than one-half of the expected joint incomes of the spouses from the pension payment and salaries.

---

2. In doing so, we must assume that any claim by plaintiff would have been opposed by competent counsel. To assume otherwise in a malpractice action would place a burden on the lawyer to have made claims of such doubtful merit that the only hope of success would have been lack of opposition. Certainly, we should not encourage lawyers to make such claims, much less impose a duty to engage in the questionable practice.

Setting aside alimony awards because of error in the division of community property, this court has recognized the direct relationship between the two awards. (See v. See (1966) 64 Cal.2d 778, 786, 51 Cal.Rptr. 888, 415 P.2d 776; French v. French, *supra*, 17 Cal.2d 775, 778, 112 P.2d 235; cf. In re Marriage of Wilson (1974) 10 Cal.3d 851, 856, 112 Cal.Rptr. 405, 519 P.2d 165.) The relationship is emphasized in Kinsey v. Kinsey, *supra*, 231 Cal.App.2d 219, 222, 41 Cal.Rptr. 802, 805, in the pension context: "Manifestly, it would be grossly inequitable to permit plaintiff to retain the benefits of the property settlement and the alimony payments as provided by the terms of the interlocutory judgment entered after the default hearing that resulted from the stipulation of the parties, and also now to permit her to 'modify' this agreement in such fashion as to entitle her as a matter of right to one-half of defendant's future income in the event of his retirement. Plaintiff's present alimony award is subject to future modification and is ample protection for her future right to share in any income her husband may receive by reason of his pension payments."

Because of the relationship between community property and alimony awards, it was to be anticipated that had defendant succeeded through litigation in establishing a right to assignment of the pensions, the alimony award would have been *greatly reduced* or *eliminated altogether* and the award of the remaining community property possibly altered. Although an award of part of the pension would no doubt have been more valuable than an alimony award of equal amount, the benefit pales in significance when viewed in light of the uncertainty of the law and the large expense required to establish the right to assignment. Further, litigation would have created the risk that a court might conclude not only that pensions did not constitute awardable community property but also, based on the relative earning abilities of the spouses, alimony should be less than $300.

CONCLUSION

Given the uncertain status of the law, the circumstances of the parties, and the close relationship between property division and alimony payment, an ethical, diligent and careful lawyer would have avoided litigation over pension rights and instead would have sought a compensating alimony award for any inequity, as expressly suggested by Kinsey v. Kinsey, *supra*, 231 Cal.App.2d 219, 222, 41 Cal.Rptr. 802, and Williamson v. Williamson, *supra*, 203 Cal.App.2d 8, 12, 21 Cal.Rptr. 164.[4] So far as appears, defendant secured such compensating award.

Accordingly, even assuming that defendant was negligent in failing to research the pension questions, the record does not furnish a balance of probabilities that his negligence—rather than the uncertain status of the law and the availability of uncontested alimony—caused plaintiff to lose a $100,000 pension award.

4. The possibility of effectively dealing with the pension in this manner was apparently unavailable to counsel in Phillipson v. Board of Administration, *supra*, 3 Cal.3d 32, 89 Cal.Rptr. 61, 473 P.2d 765, the first case to recognize assignability of pensions. There the employee had fled the jurisdiction apparently taking all of the community property funds other than his contributions to the pension fund. (3 Cal.3d at p. 38, fn. 2, 89 Cal.Rptr. 61, 473 P.2d 765.)

I would adhere to the rule of Lucas v. Hamm, *supra,* 56 Cal.2d 583, 591, 15 Cal.Rptr. 821, 825, 364 P.2d 685, 689, that an attorney is not liable for errors on issues "on which reasonable doubt may be entertained by well-informed lawyers." As shown above, such an issue was presented Attorney Lewis in 1967 concerning recovery of unpaid pension benefits in a divorce action. Further, the law applicable to federal pension benefits also presented such an issue, applicable not only to the federal pension but also to the state pension by section 228 of the Military and Veterans Code.[5]

The majority limits *Lucas* to "esoteric" cases. (Ditto Op., p. 628 of 118 Cal.Rptr., p. 596 of 530 P.2d.) Even assuming *Lucas* to be so limited, the hurdles discussed above certainly make the instant case as "esoteric" as *Lucas.* As pointed out by Professor Leach in his classic 1938 article, Perpetuities in a Nutshell, 51 Harv.L.Rev. 638, 669–670, violation of the rule against perpetuities—the claimed malpractice in *Lucas*—may be avoided by use of a simple standard clause placed in every will. The 22 pages of legal discussion since 1967 by this court establishing awardability of pensions generally, of statutory pensions, and of military pensions (Phillipson v. Board of Administration, *supra,* 3 Cal.3d 32, 39–50, 89 Cal.Rptr. 61, 473 P. 2d 765; Waite v. Waite (1972) 6 Cal.3d 461, 469–472, 99 Cal.Rptr. 325, 492 P.2d 13; In re Marriage of Fithian, *supra,* 10 Cal.3d 592, 596–604, 111 Cal. Rptr. 369, 517 P.2d 449) attest to the complexity of the pension issues.

I would reverse the judgment.

McCOMB, J., concurs.

5. Careful counsel confronted with a pension question would customarily start their research with the statutory basis, if any, of the pension. Certainly all careful counsel would eventually look for the statutory basis. It is regrettable that, in a case upholding an attorney malpractice judgment on a theory of failure to research, the majority fails to even mention the statute establishing one of the pensions and containing provisions contrary to part of the majority's analysis.

APPENDIX C

Recent Case Note

40 Texas L.Rev. 1046 (1962).
[Copyright 1962, Texas Law Review. Reproduced with permission.]

ATTORNEY-CLIENT—NEGLIGENCE—AN ATTORNEY MAY BE LIABLE TO
THIRD PARTIES FOR MALPRACTICE WITHOUT PRIVITY OF CONTRACT.
Lucas v. Hamm, 56 Cal.2d 583, 364 P.2d 685 (1961).

Plaintiffs, beneficiaries under a will, sued the testator's attorney to recover an alleged $75,000 loss resulting from his defective preparation of the testator's will. Under the will the plaintiffs were to receive in trust fifteen per cent of the residue of the testator's estate. In drafting the will, however, the defendant included in the trust provision phraseology which violated the statutes relating to perpetuities and restraints on alienation. On a general demurrer the superior court dismissed the complaint on the ground of lack of privity. *Affirmed on other grounds*. An absence of privity between the attorney who drafted a will and its beneficiaries does not bar a tort action against the attorney for negligence in the will's preparation.

The liability of the attorney for errors in the practice of his profession has been a frequent subject of litigation. Although the early English and American courts imposed liability upon the lawyer only for errors of gross negligence,[1] recent decisions indicate that the relationship of trust and confidence[2] between client and attorney imposes upon the latter a duty to exercise the same degree of skill and diligence commonly posessed and exercised by attorneys in similar practice in the jurisdiction.[3] Since the courts

1. See Pearson v. Darrington, 32 Ala. 227 (1858); Cox v. Livingston, 2 Watts & Serg. 103 (Penn.1841); Annot., 45 A.L.R.2d 5, 11 (1956). In Texas, the standard of gross negligence applied to the attorney's relationship with his client by the supreme court in Oldham v. Sparks, 28 Tex. 425 (1860), has never been expressly overruled. Later cases which recited the standard of gross negligence seemed to define it as the reasonable care and diligence lawyers ordinarily practice. The attorney is held "to the exercise of reasonable care and diligence and the want of either constitutes gross negligence." Fox v. Jones, 14 S.W. 1007 (Tex.Civ. App.1889). See also Morrill v. Graham, 27 Tex. 646 (1864); Patterson & Wallace v. Frazer, 79 S.W. 1077 (Tex. Civ.App.), *rev'd on other grounds* 100 Tex. 103, 94 S.W. 324 (1904). Later Texas civil appeals decisions seem to adopt the standard of reasonable care. See Great American Indem. Co. v. Dabney, 128 S.W.2d 496, 501 (Tex.Civ.

App.1939, error dism'd judgm't correct); Lynch v. Munson, 61 S.W. 140 (Tex.Civ.App.1910) (dictum) ("An attorney * * * is required to possess such legal knowledge and to exercise such skill and diligence as men of the legal profession commonly employ.")

2. This relationship is contractual in nature, substantially that of agency. See Mechem, Agency § 76 (4th ed. 1952).

3. The standard of professional liability involves two elements, the degree of skill and knowledge a lawyer is required to possess, and the care with which he is required to exercise the requisite skill and knowledge. The standard of skill and knowledge of the lawyer will vary, perhaps, with three factors: (1) It will vary with the locality of his practice. See Pitt v. Yalden, 4 Burr 2060, 98 Eng.Rep. 74 (K. B.1767); Fenaille v. Desplaux, 44 N. J.L. 286 (Sup.Ct.1882). *But see* Com-

impose this standard of care upon the attorney in the interest of public policy [4] and also find it implicit in the contractual relationship of lawyer and client,[5] the client generally has his choice of suing in tort for negligence or for a breach of contract.[6] In either case, the client has the burden of proving that his attorney failed to exercise the proper degree of care, and that this failure resulted in his actual injury.[7] Determination of the client's injury is relatively simple if the attorney's negligence has caused the loss of a liquidated claim, such as a testamentary benefit or an enforceable debt.[8] If his loss is an unliquidated claim, as in an action for personal injury, the plaintiff's burden of proof is exceedingly more difficult.[9] While the strong majority view requires the client to prove his original cause of action to the satisfaction of the present jury,[10] some courts demand evidence to demonstrate as a matter of law that his original cause of action probably would have been successful.[11]

In the instant case, the liability of the lawyer for malpractice was extended to third party beneficiaries who were actual strangers to the attorney-client relationship.[12] In so doing, the California court unleashed anoth-

---

ment, 26 Tenn.L.Rev. 527 (1959). (2) It will vary with the type of his practice. Cox v. Sullivan, 7 Ga. 144 (1849). (3) It will vary as to whether the law of a foreign jurisdiction is involved. See Fenaille v. Desplaux, *supra. But see* Degen v. Steinbrink, 202 N.Y. 477, 195 N.Y.S. 810 (1922).

Given the requisite knowledge and skill, the attorney is required to exercise reasonable care and diligence. See Annot., 45 A.L.R.2d 5, 12 (1956). Good faith alone is insufficient, Highway Ins. Underwriters v. Lufkin-Beaumont Motor Coaches, 215 S.W.2d 904 (Tex. Civ.App.1948, error ref'd n. r. e.); nor, in absence of express warranty, does the attorney insure the success of his efforts. Lucas v. Hamm, 364 P.2d 685 (Cal.1961); Sullivan v. Strout, 120 N. J.L. 304, 199 Atl. 1 (Ct.Err. & App. 1938). The attorney is liable as agent of his client for any violation of client's instructions. See Mechem, Agency § 76 (4th ed. 1952). See also Annot., 45 A.L.R.2d 5, 12–55 (1956), for outline of specific instances of attorney's liability.

4. See Prosser, Torts § 81 (2d ed. 1955); Coggin, *Attorney Negligence*, 60 W.Va.L.Rev. 225 (1958).

5. See Lucas v. Hamm, 56 Cal.2d 583, 364 P.2d 685 (1961). "The general rule with respect to the liability of an attorney for failure to properly perform his duties to his client is that the attorney, by accepting employment to give legal advice or to render other legal services, impliedly agrees to use

such skill, prudence, and diligence as lawyers of ordinary skill and capacity commonly possess and exercise in the performance of the task, which they undertake."

6. See Prosser, Torts 485 (2d ed. 1955). For discussion of the importance of the choice of the theory of action in relation to the statute of limitations, see Coggin, *Attorney Negligence*, 60 W.Va.L.Rev. 225 (1958).

7. See Vooth v. McEachen, 181 N.Y. 28, 73 N.E. 488 (1905); Niosi v. Aiello, 69 A.2d 57 (D.C.Munic.Ct.App.1949).

8. See Mardis Adm'rs v. Shackleford, 4 Ala. 493 (1842).

9. If he had no valid cause of action or if the attorney's negligence did not result in injury, the client cannot recover. See Niosi v. Aiello, 69 A.2d 57 (D.C.Munic.Ct.App.1949). Some courts have refused the client recovery for loss of a valid cause of action or claim, if the original defendant was insolvent. See Lawsen v. Sigfrid, 83 Colo. 116, 262 Pac. 1018 (1927).

10. See, *e. g.*, McLellan v. Fuller, 226 Mass. 374, 115 N.E. 481 (1917); Annot., 45 A.L.R.2d 5, 10–11 (1956).

11. See Annot., 45 A.L.R.2d 5, 10–11 (1956).

12. 56 Cal.2d 583, 364 P.2d 685 (1961).

er assault upon the crumbling "citadel of privity." [13]   Although the rule of *White v. Winterbottom* [14] has been overruled in other areas of tort law,[15] it has continued to exercise great influence in determining the attorney's liability for his negligence.   In absence of fraud, collusion, or malicious or tortious conduct, the prevailing view is that in absence of privity a lawyer is not liable to third parties for negligence in his practice.[16]   Earlier, the Supreme Court of California strongly expressed this view in *Buckley v. Gray*.[17] This view remained unquestioned in California, as elsewhere, until the recent case of *Biakanja v. Irving*.[18]   The Supreme Court of California then upheld the right of a devisee of an improperly attested will to recover his lost testamentary benefit from the notary public, who had drafted the will. The notary, an unlicensed practitioner of law, had prepared the will at the request of the testator.   The court denied the defense of privity in this action for a purely intangible or economic loss only after a careful weighing of various policy considerations.   As stated by the court:

> The determination whether in a specific case the defendant will be held liable to a third person not in privity is a matter of policy and involves the balancing of various factors, among which are the extent to which the transaction was intended to affect the plaintiff, the foreseeability of harm to him, the degree of certainty that the plaintiff suffered injury, the moral blame attached to the defendant's conduct and the policy of preventing future harm.[19]

While the holding of *Buckley v. Gray* was seriously undermined by the decision in *Biakanja v. Irving*, it was not expressly overruled.   Many believed that the defense of privity was still available to the licensed members of the legal profession, while denied to unauthorized practitioners of law.[20] The invalidity of this explanation was revealed in the instant case when the supreme court directly overruled *Buckley v. Gray*.   Quoting from the opinion of the court:

> The extension of his [attorney's] liability to the beneficiaries injured by a negligently drawn will does not place an undue burden on the profession.   * * *   The fact that the notary public involved in *Biakanja* was guilty of unauthorized practice of law was only a minor factor in determining that he was liable.[21]

On its facts, the instant decision is limited to the situation involving a third party who was an intended beneficiary of the relationship between at-

13. Ultramares Corp. v. Touche, 255 N. Y. 170, 174 N.E. 441 (1931).

14. 10 M. & W. 109, 152 Eng.Rep. 402 (Ex.1842).

15. . . . Prosser, *The Assault Upon the Citadel*, 69 Yale L.J. 1099 (1960); Seavey, *Actions for Economic Harm, A Comment*, 32 N.Y.U.L.Rev. 1242 (1957).

16. See, *e. g.*, Jacobsen v. Overseas Tankship Corp., 11 F.R.D. 97 (E.D.N. Y.1950); Kasen v. Morrell, 18 Misc. 158, 183 N.Y.S.2d 928 (1959); * * *

17. 110 Cal. 339, 42 Pac. 900 (1895).

18. 49 Cal.2d 647, 320 P.2d 16 (1958).

19. *Id.* at 50, 320 P.2d at 19.

20. See Seavey, *Caveat Emptor*, 38 Texas L.Rev. 439, 440 (1960); Comment, 14 U.Miami L.Rev. 124 (1959).

21. 364 P.2d at 688.

torney and client.[22] The liability of the attorney to adverse parties who were injured by his action in behalf of his client was not involved. The importance to the legal profession and to the public of energetic, unhampered defense and promotion by lawyers of their clients' interest might demand a different approach in this situation.[23] But such a consideration cannot apply to an action by a third party beneficiary, who has been deprived of the benefit intended by the client due to the negligence of the attorney. Hopefully, this decision marks the beginning of the gradual elimination of privity as a bar to a negligence action against an attorney by such a third party beneficiary. Disagreement exists as to the actual justification for the retention of the defense of privity in this aspect of tort liability. Some attribute it to the hesitancy of the courts to open their doors to unrestrained third party actions for "intangible" or "economic" injury, thus encouraging remote parties to the original contractual relationship to sue for speculatory loss.[24] Others seek to rationalize this defense as a mode of protection for the legal profession.[25] Neither explanation seems to justify its retention. As a defensive mechanism for the attorney, the concept of privity seems imprecise and illogical in its application. It allows the attorney to be held liable for negligence in his trial work, his preparation of contracts, and other legal instruments, when the consequence of his negligence falls directly on the client. Yet it allows him to be careless in his handling of trusts and wills, since here the loss results not to the client, but to a person intended by the client to be a third party beneficiary. Moreover, the availability of reasonably inexpensive malpractice insurance makes it unnecessary for an innocent third party to bear the brunt of the lawyer's negligence as a shield of the legal profession against large, unpredictable liabilities.

Also, the problem of remoteness in third party beneficiary actions for mere economic loss does not present an insurmountable difficulty. One solution is the balancing test followed by the Supreme Court of California.[26] Perhaps a simpler answer is to apply the usual negligence-foreseeability standard as to event, person, and injury. No serious problem as to remoteness should develop if a plaintiff must prove that the attorney could reasonably have foreseen at the time of his negligent conduct an injury which is of the same general character as that which occurred and which endangers an intended beneficiary in the position of the plaintiff.

Estil A. Vance, Jr.

22. *Ibid.*

23. See Stayton, *Cum Honore Officium,* 19 Tex.B.J. 765 (1956); Comment, 44 A.B.A.J. 1159, 1160 (1958).

24. See Buckley v. Gray, 110 Cal. 339, 42 Pac. 900 (1895); *cf.* Ultramares Corp. v. Touche, 252 N.Y. 170, 174 N. E. 441 (1931). For a critical discussion of this view as to the liability of a manufacturer, see Seavey, *Action for Economic Harm, A Comment,* 32 N.Y.U.L.Rev. 1242 (1957).

25. See Comment, 14 U.Miami L.Rev. 124 (1959).

26. Lucas v. Hamm, 56 Cal.2d 583, 364 P.2d 685 (1961); Biakanja v. Irving, 49 Cal.2d 647, 320 P.2d 16 (1958).

APPENDIX D

Sample Office Memorandum

In the following ten pages is a comprehensive office memorandum prepared to illustrate how the *Peters v. Simmons* case might have looked to a young associate in the office of the defendant's attorney. This memorandum has been prepared for illustrative purposes only; it is not part of the file in the actual case, excerpts from which are reproduced in Appendix E, following.

TITLE: <u>Peters v. Simmons</u>—Attorney malpractice—Statute of Limitations

REQUESTED BY: [Prepared for illustrative purposes only]

SUBMITTED BY: Glenna S. Hall

DATE SUBMITTED:

QUESTIONS PRESENTED

In a suit against an attorney for malpractice, does the applicable statute of limitations begin to run on the date of the alleged negligent action, and thus bar an action commenced more than three years after such date, or does it begin to run on the date of discovery of the negligent action, and thus not serve as a defense where the date of discovery falls within the three-year period?

1. Do mandatory precedents require a lower court to apply the three-year limitation period for actions on contracts not in writing, RCW 4.16.080(3), with the period beginning to run as of the time of the breach of duty?

2. Assuming that the answer to question 1 is affirmative, will our supreme court extend the date of discovery rule to an action against an attorney for malpractice?

    a. Do Washington precedents conclusively characterize an attorney malpractice action as an action on contract so that the three-year limitation period governing actions for negligence, RCW 4.16.080(2), with the period beginning to run from discovery, will be held to be inapplicable?

b. When does an action against an attorney for
malpractice "accrue" within the meaning of
the general statute on limitations, RCW
4.16.010?

BRIEF ANSWER

Defendant should be successful, at least at the trial court level, in
asserting the statute of limitations defense. The Washington court has
stated that attorney malpractice actions are grounded on contract and that
the statute of limitations begins to run on the date the allegedly negligent
act was committed. Even though other jurisdictions have recently tended to
abandon this doctrine, the Washington precedents are mandatory upon a trial
court in this state, and a motion for summary judgment should be granted.
The probability of a change in the doctrine at the supreme level, however,
should be anticipated. The Washington court has recently applied the date
of discovery rule in malpractice actions against other types of professionals, and likely will decide to do so in regard to attornies, especially
now that courts of other jurisdictions have applied the discovery rule to
attorney malpractice actions. The discovery rule could be so extended by
the Washington court on the basis of any of the following rationales: that
such actions sound in tort, or that a cause of action for breach of contractual duty does not arise until more than nominal harm occurs, or that public
policy requires the application of the discovery rule.

STATEMENT OF FACTS

Our client, an attorney, is being sued for his alleged negligence in
failing to obtain the signature of a corporate officer as a personal guarantor on a contract for purchase of plaintiff's business. This instrument was
signed in May 1969, more than three years prior to the commencement of the
action against our client on July 17, 1974. The complaint does not allege
the date when plaintiffs discovered that the corporate officer was not bound
by the contract, but the trial court dismissed with prejudice plaintiffs'
action against the corporate officer on June 19, 1974. You have asked me to

determine whether the applicable statute of limitations can be successfully

interposed as a defense against plaintiff's action against our client and,

specifically, whether a motion for summary judgment against plaintiff based

on this affirmative defense is likely to be granted.

                        APPLICABLE STATUTES

        4.16.010 <u>Commencement of actions limited--</u>
<u>Objections, how taken</u>. Actions can only be commenced
within the periods herein prescribed after the cause of
action shall have accrued, except when in special cases a
different limitation is prescribed by statute; but the
objection that the action was not commenced within the
time limited can only be taken by answer or demurrer.

        4.16.080 <u>Actions limited to three years</u>. Within three
years:
        (1) . . .
        (2) An action for taking, detaining, or injuring per-
sonal property, including an action for the specific
recovery thereof, or for any other injury to the person or
rights of another not hereinafter enumerated;
        (3) An action upon a contract or liability, express or
implied, which is not in writing, and does not arise out of
any written instrument;
        (4) An action for relief upon the ground of fraud, the
cause of action in such case not to be deemed to have
accrued until the discovery by the aggrieved party of the
facts constituting the fraud; . . .

                        <u>Discussion</u>

    Although the <u>Peters</u> complaint does not allege the date on which plain-

tiffs discovered defendant's alleged negligence, it is apparent that plain-

tiffs must rely on the contention that the statute of limitations did not

begin to run until the date they discovered our client's alleged negligence.

We must contend, on the other hand, that the statute began to run at the

time the purchase contract was signed--the date of the act complained of.

1. <u>Mandatory precedents will require the lower court to rule that the</u>
    <u>limitation period began to run as of the time of the breach of duty.</u>

    The Washington courts have stated on numerous occasions that in mal-

practice actions against attorneys, the applicable statute of limitations

begins to run on the date the negligent act occurred. Indeed, Washington

appellate courts have never deviated from this rule. The reasoning of the

early cases was that the relationship between attorney and client was of a

contractual nature, <u>Isham v. Parker</u>, 3 Wash. 755, 29 P. 835 (1892); <u>Schirmer</u>

<u>v. Nethercutt</u> 157 Wash. 172, 288 P. 265 (1930), and that any action against

the attorney grew out of his breach of duty, thus starting the statute
running at the time of the breach. Cornell v. Edson, 78 Wash. 662, 139 P.
602 (1914). The breach of duty required to start the limitations period has
been characterized as those acts of defendant (or failure to act) that
result in harm to plaintiff. Jones v. Gregory, 125 Wash. 46, 215 P. 63
(1923); Smith v. Berkey, 134 Wash. 348, 235 P. 793 (1925). The court appears to have assumed that commencement of the limitation period was deferred until discovery only if the action was grounded in fraud or involved
fraudulent concealment and was thus governed by the fraud section, now
codified as RCW 4.16.080(4) (expressly provides action does not accrue until
discovery of facts constituting fraud). Cornell, supra; Smith, supra. And,
according to the court in Cornell, application of the fraud statute is
restricted to situations in which a party is seeking to be relieved of some
obligation or liability he was induced to assume or undertake because of a
fraudulent act. In the most recent opinion of this series, Busk v. Flanders,
2 Wn. App. 526, 468 P.2d 695 (1970), the appeals court quoted the Cornell
rationale and indicated that the Washington rule remains that, absent fraudulent concealment, the cause accrues at the time of the breach of duty.

In the Peters case the plaintiffs have not alleged fraud or fraudulent
concealment. There being no other distinguishing feature apparent, the
Cornell line of decisions will be mandatory on a Washington trial court.
They are authority for our client's position, then, that the plaintiff's
cause of action accrued at the time of Mr. Simmons' alleged breach of
duty--namely, on the date that the purchase contract was signed without the
president's personal guaranty. The complaint and plaintiff's answers to
our interrogatories reveal that the action was commenced more than three
years after that date. Therefore, a trial court will be required to grant
a judgment of dismissal.

2. The supreme court will probably extend the discovery rule to attorney
    malpractice actions.

The matter will not be this simple on appeal, and an order of dismissal will probably be reversed if an appeal reaches the supreme court. Two
factors enter into this conclusion: first, the line of Washington deci-

sions on which we must rely has serious weaknesses and may not survive the critical scrutiny of the supreme court; and second, the supreme court has allowed plaintiffs in actions against many professionals other than lawyers to use the discovery rule, and the modern trend throughout the country has been to use the discovery rule in malpractice actions involving all professionals.

2(a). The supreme court has not consistently characterized attorney mal-
       practice actions as contract-based.

A primary difficulty with reliance on the Cornell line of decisions is that we must insist on a formalistic characterization of an attorney malpractice action as an action based on breach of a contractual duty rather than one based on negligence. Although language from the Cornell opinion that is often quoted supports this distinction, the contract analysis has been undermined by the Washington court in subsequent opinions in both attorney malpractice cases and malpractice cases involving other professionals.

The doctrine that the statute begins to run upon breach can be considered to flow from the Washington court's decision in Cornell v. Edson, 78 Wash. 662, 139 P. 602 (1914). In the Cornell case, plaintiff had employed the defendant attorney to prosecute plaintiff's claim against an insurance company. During the conduct of that trial, defendant, without plaintiff's knowledge, took a voluntary nonsuit but led plaintiff to believe the judge had found against plaintiff. By the time plaintiff learned of his attorney's action (four weeks prior to his commencing the action against the attorney), the limitations period had run on his original claim. In the malpractice action, the defendant attorney successfully moved for judgment on the pleadings, based on the statute of limitations defense. On appeal, plaintiff argued that his action was grounded on fraud, so that under the fraud limitations statute, the cause did not accrue until the discovery of the facts constituting the fraud. The court firmly rejected this argument with the narrow characterization of fraud actions previously mentioned. As to fraudulent concealment, the court said:

> No action lies for concealment unless the law imposes the
> duty of disclosure. In this case, the duty is one growing
> out of the relation between the parties, and that rela-
> tion is one based upon contract. . . . and . . . a cause
> of action based upon the breach of contract accrues when
> the contract is violated and not when the violation is
> discovered.

78 Wash. at 665 (Emphasis supplied.)

In the next case in the series, Jones v. Gregory, 125 Wash. 46, 215
P. 63 (1923), the plaintiff was suing her attorneys because of their alleged
negligence in advising her in regard to the distribution of her late husband's estate. Following a trial court decree giving half of the estate
to collateral relatives, the same attorneys were able to get the decree
reversed. Subsequently, however, the supreme court reversed the latter
action. Plaintiff commenced suit against the attorneys more than three
years after the original decree. The defendants' demurrer based on the
statute of limitations was sustained, and plaintiff appealed, claiming that
the efforts of the attorneys to remedy their original error had delayed the
starting of the running of the statute. This argument, too, was rejected
by the court, which looked to the time of the acts resulting in the damage.
The court did not analyze the action as one involving contract.

The weakening of the contract analysis continued in Smith v. Berkey,
134 Wash. 348, 235 P. 793 (1925). Again rejecting the discovery rule, the
court cited Cornell and two other cases (not involving attorney malpractice) where unsuccessful arguments had been based on the fraud statute of
limitations. One of these decisions, Golden Eagle Mining Co. v. Imperator-
Quilp Co., 93 Wash. 692, 161 P. 848 (1916), was not a contract action at
all, but rather a trespass action.

In the last supreme court decision on the point, Schirmer v. Nethercutt,
157 Wash. 172, 288 P. 265 (1930), the court summarily rejected the argument
that the two-year limitation period established by the provision now codified as RCW 4.16.130 (for actions not otherwise provided for) applied to an
action against an attorney for damages for breach of duty. The court said:

> In a very early case decided by this court,
> Isham v. Parker, 3 Wash. 755, 29 Pac. 835, a malpractice
> suit against an attorney, it was held that such actions
> are based on breach of contract. The cause of action is
> founded on the breach of duty, not on the consequential

> damage, and the subsequent accrual or ascertainment
> of such damage gives no new cause of action. 37 C.J. 863.
>   It is a closed question in this state, for we have
> consistently held that such actions are based on breach
> of contract and controlled by the statute relating to
> the breach of a contractual relation, governed by the
> three-year statute of limitations. Cornell v. Edsen, 78
> Wash. 662, 139 Pac. 602, 51 L. R. A. (N. S.) 279; Jones
> v. Gregory, 125 Wash. 46, 215 Pac. 63; Smith v. Berkey,
> 134 Wash. 348, 235 Pac. 793.

157 Wash. at 180.

The opinion in Busk v. Flanders, 2 Wn. App. 526, 468 P.2d 695 (1970), represents the most recent restatement of the Cornell rule. The decision in Busk, however, is not directly on point. The Busk case resulted from a series of misadventures. Plaintiff had initially engaged the defendant attorney to sue defaulting mortgagors, who successfully defended on the ground that the brokerage firm that arranged the transaction had set up a usurious loan. Only after this judgment was finally affirmed in the supreme court did the attorney advise plaintiff that he might have a cause of action against the brokerage firm; by that time, the statute of limitations had barred that claim. Still later, plaintiffs discovered that at the time of the original litigation, the defendant attorney had also been the attorney for the brokerage firm. Plaintiff sued, alleging, inter alia, that defendant had breached his duty by neither bringing suit against the brokers as soon as he had notice of the usurious transaction nor informing plaintiff of the conflict of interest and withdrawing from the case. Defendant asserted the statute of limitations, and a summary judgment of dismissal was granted. On appeal plaintiff claimed that the case was governed by the six-year statute of limitations governing written contracts (based on a letter written after the initial trial court decision). This contention was rejected. The court observed that attorney malpractice actions might also be analyzed as tort actions, although this would not affect the applicability of the three-year statute. The court points out that the appellant did not attempt to assert the discovery rule in this appeal. Thus, discussion of the Cornell rule was clearly dicta.

No recent Washington decision has rested on the Cornell rule. Its bedrock, namely a view of the attorney malpractice action as flowing from

breach of a contractual duty, has been severely undermined, since at least
one recent Washington decision has analyzed the action as one sounding in
tort. Ward v. Arnold, 52 Wn. 2d 581, 328 P.2d 164 (1958) (statute of
limitations not in issue). Indeed, one of the earliest opinions said to
have established the contract analysis, Isham v. Parker, 3 Wash. 755, 29 P.
835 (1892), actually analyzed the attorney malpractice counterclaim in
terms of negligence. (The confusion probably results from the fact that the
bulk of the long opinion deals with the attorney's contract-based claim
against the defendant client.) Thus, the foundation has already been laid
for extending the recently developed, negligence-based discovery rule to
malpractice actions against attorneys, by characterizing them as negligence
actions.

2b. The supreme court could hold that attorney malpractice actions "accrue"
     when harm is suffered, particularly if such actions are viewed as negli-
     gence-based as well as contract-based.

The meaning of "accrued" as used in the general limitations statute,
RCW 4.16.010, has not been addressed directly or analytically in these
decisions. In Cornell itself, the parties appear to have believed that the
only basis for extending the limitations period would be to plead fraud,
thereby triggering the discovery rule of the fraud limitations statute.
The parties apparently did not argue, and the court did not discuss, the
possibility of a discovery rule flowing from the working of the general
statute of limitations section, which states, "Actions can only be commenced within the periods herein prescribed after the cause of action shall
have accrued . . . " (Emphasis supplied.) Thus, Cornell addressed primarily whether the fraud limitations statute was applicable, and assumed
without discussion that if it was not, the cause accrued upon breach, not
discovery. It did not deal directly with the problem of the unknown cause
of action.

Again, in Jones v. Gregory, the nature of accrual of an action was not
well argued. Appellant's brief reveals that she was attempting to argue
that during the period when defendants had cured their error, she had
suffered no harm and thus did not have a cause of action, thereby delaying
the accrual of her action (under the predecessor to RCW 4.16.010) until the

final supreme court order. Brief of Appellant at 12-13. Although the
court cited <u>Cornell</u> in rejecting the argument, it relied primarily on
<u>Wilcox v. Executors of Plummer</u>, 4 Peters (U.S.) 172 (1830), thus apparently
applying the then generally accepted rule that a cause of action based on
breach of contractual duty accrues at the time of the breach of duty, not
when damage develops--that is, actually occurs--(as for negligence actions).
The <u>Wilcox</u> court had, in fact, assumed (correctly) that a cause accrues at
the time an action could be instituted, and had taken for granted that in
an action on contract that time was when the breach occurred--with or
without harm.

As for <u>Schirmer</u>, which was extensively quoted in <u>Busk</u>, the question
decided had nothing to do with a choice between a date-of-discovery rule
and a date-of-the-act rule, and thus the court's discussion of accrual was
dictum, as in <u>Busk</u> itself. Thus, the accrual question may still be an open
question in the attorney malpractice setting.

As noted by the U.S. Supreme Court in <u>Wilcox</u>, <u>supra</u>, an action does
not accrue until it first can be brought. This doctrine was acknowledged
in <u>Lindquist v. Mullen</u>, 45 Wn. 2d 675, 277 P.2d 724 (1954), as follows:
"[N]egligence which does not produce harm is not actionable, and a cause of
action cannot accrue until injury has been sustained." 45 Wn. 2d at 677.
This is the analysis that the court appears to have rejected in the <u>Jones</u>
case but that likely underlies the increasing use of the discovery rule in
professional malpractice actions in Washington. See, <u>e.g.</u>, <u>Ruth v. Dight</u>,
75 Wn. 2d 660, 453 P.2d 651 (1969) (physician) (overruling <u>Lindquist v.</u>
<u>Mullen</u>, 45 Wn. 2d 675, 277 P.2d 724 (1954), wherein the court, relying on
the <u>Cornell</u> rule, had refused to construe RCW 4.16.010 as incorporating
discovery rule to define accrual of action); <u>Kuhndahl v. Barnett</u>, 5 Wn.
App. 227, 486 P.2d 1164, <u>pet. for rev. denied</u>, 80 Wn. 2d 1001 (1971) (land
surveyor).

<u>On an appeal, the trend in other jurisdictions and policy arguments</u>
<u>are contrary to our client's position.</u>

This trend has been noted in other jurisdictions, and there attorneys
have not escaped the workings of the discovery rule. See, <u>e.g.</u>, <u>Neel v.</u>

<u>Magana, Olney, Levy, Cathcart & Gelfand</u>, 6 Cal. 3d 176, 98 Cal. Rptr. 837, 491 P.2d 429 (1971); <u>Edwards v. Ford</u>, 279 So.2d 851 (Fla. 1973); <u>Downing v. Vaine</u>, 228 So.2d 622 (Fla. Ct. App. 1969), <u>appeal dismissed</u>, 237 So.2d 767 (Fla. 1970); <u>Kohler v. Wollen, Brown & Hawkins</u>, 15 Ill. App. 455, 304 N.E.2d 677 (1973); <u>Mumford v. Staton, Whaley & Price</u>, 254 Md. 697, 255 A.2d 359 (1969). In all these cases the date of discovery determined the accrual of a cause of action for attorney malpractice.

To some courts, indeed, a liberal application of the statute of limitations was particularly important where attorney malpractice was involved, since, as they reasoned, to allow attorneys an immunity not enjoyed by other professionals severely undermines public respect for the legal profession. For example, the court in <u>Neel</u> poses the issue in the most damaging way: "[W]hether members of the legal profession should enjoy a preference as to the date when they may successfully bar adverse claims under the statute of limitations." 491 P.2d at 424. It appears to be felt that where the professions are concerned, information is appreciably more in the control of the specialists than of their clients, and harm may have been suffered that will go unrevealed for longer than the ordinary limitations period. These and other policy considerations may well be viewed by the Washington court as overbalancing the desire to bar stale claims.

CONCLUSION

In my opinion, the outlook for our client is mixed. He will probably prevail at the trial court level. If we do succeed in obtaining a summary judgment and plaintiff appeals, I think it likely that the supreme court could be convinced to overturn <u>Cornell</u> once and for all, since we have virtually no policy argument to advance beyond the desirability of barring stale claims and, perhaps, the skyrocketing costs of liability insurance. Plaintiff is seeking upwards of $32,000 in damages and is therefore likely to appeal.

Respectfully submitted,

APPENDIX E

File On Motion for Summary Judgment

PETERS v. SIMMONS

Supreme Court of Washington, 1976.
87 Wash.2d 400, 552 P.2d 1053.

(Opinion reproduced in text note 6 following Chapter 3).

In the following pages are reproduced the substantively significant documents that were available to the lower court judge who granted the motion for summary judgment in the *Peters* case.

After reading the defendant's and plaintiffs' memoranda as filed in the lower court,* consider how you might have changed each had you had the opportunity to edit them. Consider, for example: Are they written in a clear and concise style? Try editing them to communicate the same information and arguments in as few words as possible. Is the form used for each the most effective form for the particular arguments? Can you write useful headings for the argument in plaintiffs' memorandum? Are quotations used effectively in the two memoranda? Given the question presented by defendant's motion for summary judgment, are all the facts stated in plaintiffs' memorandum significant? Compare the statement of facts in the appeal court's opinion. The basic argument in plaintiffs' memorandum (at page 10) is that the court should "adopt the date of discovery rule." Could the argument have been more appropriately phrased? See text note 2 following Chapter 2.

In the appellants' brief on appeal, counsel further developed the arguments presented to the lower court in plaintiffs' memorandum. Counsel for respondent argued a jurisdictional point, a procedural point (the Peters' affidavit should be disregarded because not in the form required by the governing summary judgment rule), an affirmative argument based on old precedents, and, in responding to appellants' brief, that the plaintiff "did not allege any fraud, concealment, or ignorance and later discovery which might have served to toll the operation of the statute until the time of discovery" so that "the issue so forcefully argued by respondent is not presented by the pleadings." Respondent's brief at 12. Does the court acknowledge this argument? If you had drafted appellants' reply brief, how would you have responded to this argument?

---

* Page numbering in the memoranda differs from the numbering in the originals because the original documents are on legal-size paper.

1   SUPERIOR COURT OF WASHINGTON FOR KING COUNTY

2 D. E. PETERS and PHYLLIS PETERS,)

3   Plaintiff,   )   NO. 783005

4 -vs-   )

5 J. LAEL SIMMONS,   )   SUMMONS

6   Defendant.   )

7

8 THE STATE OF WASHINGTON to the said

9   J. LAEL SIMMONS

10   Defendant

11   YOU AND EACH OF YOU ARE HEREBY SUMMONED to appear within twenty (20)

12 days after service of this summons, exclusive of the day of service, if

13 served within the State of Washington (or within sixty (60) days if served

14 without the State of Washington, exclusive of the day of service), and

15 defend the above entitled action by serving a copy of your written appear-

16 ance or defense upon the undersigned. If you fail to appear and defend,

17 judgment will be rendered against you, according to the demand of the com-

18 plaint, which has been or will be filed with the clerk of court, or a copy

19 of which is herewith served upon you.

20   CASEY, PRUZAN, KOVARIK & SHULKIN

21   BY

22   David G. Shenton
                                   Attorneys for Plaintiffs

23

24

25

26

27

    Summons

SUPERIOR COURT OF WASHINGTON FOR KING COUNTY

D. E. PETERS and PHYLLIS PETERS,	)	
Plaintiff,	)	NO. 783005
-vs-	)	
J. LAEL SIMMONS,	)	COMPLAINT FOR DAMAGES
Defendant.	)	

COME NOW the plaintiffs and for a statement of claim against defendant allege:

I.

Plaintiffs and defendant are residents of King County, State of Washington.

II.

Defendant is and was at the time in question an attorney at law licensed to practice in the State of Washington.

III.

Plaintiffs hired defendant to do legal work for them in connection with the sale of their business and defendant received the compensation he requested for all work performed.

IV.

Defendant performed said work in a negligent manner and plaintiffs have been damaged in the sum of $32,366.74 plus interest at 8% from October, 1970.

WHEREFORE, plaintiffs pray for judgment against defendant in the sum of $32,366.74 plus interest, plus their costs of suit to be taxed herein and

Complaint - Page 1.

1   such other relief as the court may deem just in the premises.

2   DATED this _____ day of July, 1974

3   CASEY, PRUZAN, KOVARIK & SHULKIN

4

5   By _____
                                      David G. Shenton of
6   Attys for Plaintiffs

7

8

9

10

11

12

13

14

15

16

17

18

19

20

21

22

23

24

25

26

27

Complaint - Page 2.

IN THE SUPERIOR COURT OF THE STATE OF WASHINGTON FOR KING COUNTY

D. E. PETERS and	)	
PHYLLIS PETERS,	)	
Plaintiffs	)	No. 783005
	)	
vs.	)	ANSWER AND AFFIRMATIVE DEFENSE
	)	
J. LAEL SIMMONS,	)	
Defendant	)	

COMES NOW the defendant and in Answer to plaintiffs' Complaint, ADMITS DENIES AND ALLEGES as follows:

I.

Admits each allegation of paragraph I.

II.

For lack of information as to what time is referred to, defendant denies each allegation of paragraph II.

III.

Defendant denies each allegation of paragraph III, EXCEPT defendant admits having on occasion performed legal service in matters in which plaintiffs were involved and that he was paid for all work performed.

IV.

For lack of information as to what work is referred to in paragraph IV of the Complaint, the defendant denies each allegation thereof and specifically denies that plaintiffs have been damaged in any sum whatsoever.

BY WAY OF FURTHER ANSWER AND AFFIRMATIVE DEFENSE, DEFENDANT ALLEGES:

ANSWER AND AFFIRMATIVE DEFENSE -1-

1   V.

2   If defendant performed any work for the plaintiffs in a negligent

3 manner, then action for the same is barred by the statute of limitations,

4 R.C.W. 4.16.080.

5   WHEREFORE, defendant prays that the Complaint be dismissed with

6 prejudice.

7

8   Phil McIntosh, Attorney for

9   Defendant

10

11

12

13

14

15

16

17

18

19

20

21

22

23

24

25

26

27

ANSWER AND AFFIRMATIVE DEFENSE -2-

IN THE SUPERIOR COURT OF THE STATE OF WASHINGTON FOR KING COUNTY

D. E. PETERS and   )
PHYLLIS PETERS,   )
               Plaintiffs)   No. 783005
)
        vs.   )   DEFENDANT'S FIRST SET OF INTERROGATORIES
)   PROPOUNDED TO PLAINTIFFS
J. LAEL SIMMONS,   )
               Defendant)
_____

        IN ACCORDANCE with Rule 33 of the Civil Rules of the Superior Court

of the State of Washington, you will please answer the following interroga-

tories, fully and separately, under oath, within twenty (20) days after the

date of service of these interrogatories upon you or your attorney.

INTERROGATORY #1: When did plaintiffs hire defendant to do the legal work

referred to in paragraph III of the Complaint?

ANSWER: 1969

INTERROGATORY #2: What was the legal work that defendant was hired to do?

ANSWER: Draft purchase agreement and secure personal guarantee of corporate

purchaser's President.

INTERROGATORY #3: What was the work which defendant performed?

ANSWER: Drafted purchase agreement.

INTERROGATORY #4: Please state in complete detail, each action or failure

to act on the part of the defendant that constituted the "negligent manner"

referred to in paragraph IV of the Complaint.

INTERROGATORIES TO PLAINTIFFS   -1-

1   ANSWER: Defendant failed to secure personal guarantee of John Fisk,

2   President of purchasing corporation.

3

4   INTERROGATORY #5: In reference to the damage referred to in paragraph

5   IV of the Complaint, please specify as follows:

6   a) What are each of the items of damage?

7   b) When did each of those items of damage occur?

8   ANSWER: Damage is unpaid principal balance of Purchase Agreement plus

9   accrued interest.

10

11   DATED at Seattle, Washington this 26th day of August, 1974.

12

13   _____
                                            Phil McIntosh, Attorney for
14   Defendant

15

16

17

18

19

20

21

22

23

24

25

26

27

    INTERROGATORIES TO PLAINTIFFS -2-

1 State of Washington)
)   ss.
2 County of K I N G)

3

4   D. E. PETERS, being first duly sworn on oath deposes and says:

5   That he is the party to whom the within and foregoing interro-

6 gatories are addressed; that he has read and made answer to the same;

7 knows the contents thereof and believes the same to be true.

8

9   _____
                                           D. E. P E T E R S
10

11
       SUBSCRIBED AND SWORN to before me this ____ day of
12
       _____, 1974.
13

14

15   _____
                                           NOTARY PUBLIC in and for the State
16   of Washington, residing at

17

18

19

20

21

22

23

24

25

26

27
       INTERROGATORIES TO PLAINTIFFS -3-

IN THE SUPERIOR COURT OF THE STATE OF WASHINGTON FOR KING COUNTY

D. E. PETERS and   )
PHYLLIS PETERS,   )
            Plaintiffs)   No.   783005
)
    vs.   )   DEFENDANT'S SECOND SET OF INTERROGATORIES
)   PROPOUNDED TO PLAINTIFFS
J. LAEL SIMMONS,   )
            Defendant)

IN AMPLIFICATION OF YOUR ANSWERS TO DEFENDANT'S FIRST SET OF INTERROGA-
TORIES AND IN ACCORDANCE WITH RULE 33 OF THE CIVIL RULES OF THE SUPERIOR
COURT OF THE STATE OF WASHINGTON, YOU WILL PLEASE ANSWER THE FOLLOWING
INTERROGATORIES, FULLY AND SEPARATELY, UNDER OATH, WITHIN TWENTY (20) DAYS
AFTER THE DATE OF SERVICE OF THESE INTERROGATORIES UPON YOU OR YOUR ATTORNEY.

INTERROGATORY #1a: When was the "purchase agreement" referred to in your
answer to interrogatory #3 drafted?

    A. This is within defendant's knowledge, as he drafted said
agreement.

INTERROGATORY #2a: What date did each action or failure to act on the part
of the defendant that constituted the "negligent manner" referred to in
paragraph IV of the Complaint occur?

    A. May, 1969.

INTERROGATORY #3: Please answer interrogatory #5 as propounded in
defendant's first set of interrogatories by stating:

    (1) What is the amount of each of the items of damage?

    A. $32,366.74 plus interest.

SECOND SET OF INTERROGATORIES
    -1-

1   (2) On what date did each of those items of damage occur?

2   A. No payments made on purchase agreement since October, 1970.

3
     DATED at Seattle, Washington this 16th day of September, 1974.
4

5   _____
                                     Phil McIntosh, Attorney for
6   Defendant

7   State of Washington)
) ss.
8   County of K I N G   )

9   D. E. PETERS, being first duly sworn on oath deposes and says:

10   That he is the party to whom the within and foregoing interrogatories

11   are addressed; that he has read and made answer to the same; knows the

12   contents thereof and believes the same to be true.

13

14   _____
                                         D. E.   P E T E R S
15
     SUBSCRIBED and sworn to before me this _____ day of
16
     _____, 1974.
17

18

19   _____
                                     NOTARY PUBLIC in and for the State
20   of Washington, residing at Redmond

21

22

23

24

25

26

27
     SECOND SET OF INTERROGATORIES
          -2-

IN THE SUPERIOR COURT OF THE STATE OF WASHINGTON FOR KING COUNTY

D. E. PETERS and
PHYLLIS PETERS,
 	
  Plaintiffs
 	
  vs.
 	
J. LAEL SIMMONS,
 	
  Defendant
	No. 783005
	
	DEFENDANT'S MOTION FOR SUMMARY
	JUDGMENT OF DISMISSAL

DEFENDANT MOVES that he be granted a summary judgment of dismissal of the above-entitled cause. This motion is based upon the file and record, including the following items:

I. Plaintiffs' Complaint for Damages.

II. Defendant's Answer and Affirmative Defense.

III. Defendant's First Set of Interrogatories Propounded to Plaintiffs and the Answers thereto.

IV. Defendant's Second Set of Interrogatories Propounded to Plaintiffs and the Answers thereto.

    DATED this _____ day of October, 1974.

               Phil McIntosh, Attorney for
               Defendant

1   IN THE SUPERIOR COURT OF THE STATE OF WASHINGTON FOR KING COUNTY

2

3   D. E. PETERS and   )
    PHYLLIS PETERS,   )
)   No.   783005
4   Plaintiffs   )
)   DEFENDANT'S MEMORANDUM ON MOTION FOR
5   vs.   )
)   SUMMARY JUDGMENT OF DISMISSAL
6   J. LAEL SIMMONS,   )
)
7   _____Defendant_____   )

8
    DEFENDANT has moved for summary judgment of dismissal of the above
9
    cause. The grounds for such dismissal are that the action is barred by
10
    the statute of limitations.
11
    The Complaint alleges that the Defendant as an attorney at law was
12
    employed by Plaintiffs to do certain legal work for them and that the said
13
    work was done in a negligent manner, to the damage of the Plaintiffs, for
14
    which they seek recovery.
15
    The Defendant's Answer denies any negligence or damage to the Plain-
16
    tiffs and further, by way of affirmative defense, contends that the action
17
    is barred by the statute of limitations.
18
    Interrogatory #2a of Defendant's Second Set of Interrogatories Pro-
19
    pounded to Plaintiffs, and the Answer thereto submitted by Plaintiffs,
20
    is as follows:
21
        INTERROGATORY #2a: What date did each action or failure
22   to act on the part of the defendant that constituted the
        "negligent manner" referred to in paragraph IV of the
23   Complaint occur?

24   A. May 1969.

25   R.C.W. 4.16.010 provides as follows:

26

27

DEFENDANT'S MEMORANDUM ON MOTION
        -1-

1

2 "4.16.010 COMMENCEMENT OF ACTIONS LIMITED - OBJECTIONS HOW TAKEN.
Actions can only be commenced within the periods herein prescribed
after the cause of action shall have accrued, except when in special
3 cases a different limitation is prescribed by statute; but the objection that the action was not commenced within the time limited
4 can only be taken by answer or demurrer."

5 "4.16.080 ACTIONS LIMITED TO THREE YEARS. Within three
years: ....

6

(3) An action upon a contract or liability, express or implied,
7 which is not in writing, and does not arise out of any written
instrument; ....."

8

9 In the case of Busk v. Flanders, 2 Wn. App. 526, 468 P.2d 695, at

10 page 530, the applicability of the statute of limitations to legal mal-

11 practice actions was confirmed in the following words:

12 "The Supreme Court of Washington has consistently applied the
3-year statute of limitations to malpractice cases. This rule
13 was decisively announced in Schirmer v. Nethercutt, 157 Wash. 172,
179, 288 P. 265 (1930), when the court stated:

14

In a very early case decided by this court, Isham v. Parker,
15 3 Wash. 775, 29 Pac. 835, a malpractice suit against an
attorney, it was held that such actions are based on breach
16 of contract. The cause of action is founded on the breach of
duty, not on the consequential damage, and the subsequent
17 accrual or ascertainment of such damage gives no new cause of
action 37C.J. 865.

18

It is a closed question in this state, for we have consistently
19 held that such actions are based on breach of contract and controlled by the statute relating to the breach of a contractual
20 relation, governed by the three-year statute of limitations.
Cornell v. Edsen, 78 Wash. 662, 139 Pac. 602, 51 L.R.A. (N.S.)
21 279; Jones v. Gregory, 125 Wash. 46, 215 Pac. 63; Smith v.
Berkey, 134 Wash. 348, 235 Pac. 793.

22

(1) Regardless of whether the basis for the claimed malpractice is
23 a breach of a contractual relationship so that the applicable statute
of limitations is RCW 4.16.080(3) as was determined by the trial
24 court, or that the wrong complained of is negligence so that the
statute to be applied is RCW 4.16.080(2), the cause of action is
25 governed by a 3-year statute of limitations."

26

27

DEFENDANT'S MEMORANDUM
-2-

1 CONCLUSION

2   1. The record discloses that the action is for negligence claimed

3 to have occured more than three years prior to the commencement of the

4 action.

5   2. The action is barred by the statute of limitations.

6   3. Judgment of dismissal with prejudice should be granted.

7

8   Respectfully submitted,

9

10

11   _____
                                       Phil McIntosh, Attorney for
                                       Defendant

12

13

14

15

16

17

18

19

20

21

22

23

24

25

26

27

DEFENDANT'S MEMORANDUM
    -3-

1   SUPERIOR COURT OF WASHINGTON FOR KING COUNTY

2

3 D. E. PETERS and PHYLLIS PETERS,   )

)

4   Plaintiffs,   )   No.   783005

)

5   v.   )   AFFIDAVIT OF DELMER E. PETERS

)

6 J. LAEL SIMMONS,   )

)

7   Defendant.   )

)

8

9 STATE OF WASHINGTON   )

)   ss

  COUNTY OF KING   )

10   DELMER E. PETERS, being first duly sworn upon oath, deposes

11 and says:

12   That he is one of the plaintiffs in the within action, who is com-

13 petent to be a witness herein, and has personal knowledge of the facts

14 herein stated.

15   I have read the statement of facts contained in pages 1, 2, and

16 3 of plaintiffs' brief in opposition to defendant's motion for summary

17 judgment of dismissal and hereby state and allege that the facts as

18 recited therein are true and correct.

19

20

21   Delmer E. Peters

22 SUBSCRIBED AND SWORN to before me this ____ day of December, 1974.

23

24   NOTARY PUBLIC in and for the State

25   of Washington, Residing at Redmond

26

27

  Affidavit of D.E. Peters

  Page 1

SUPERIOR COURT OF WASHINGTON FOR KING COUNTY

1

2

D. E. PETERS and PHYLLIS PETERS)
3   )
                    Plaintiffs,   )   No.   783005
4   )
        vs.   )   PLAINTIFFS' BRIEF IN OPPOSITION
5   )   TO DEFENDANT'S MOTION FOR
    J. LAEL SIMMONS,   )   SUMMARY JUDGMENT OF DISMISSAL
6   Defendant.   )
)

7

8   STATEMENT OF FACTS

9   Prior to May 1, 1969, plaintiffs engaged in negotiations with John

10 Fisk, President of Bellevue Enterprises, Inc., for the purchase by Bellevue

11 Enterprises, Inc., of plaintiffs' wholly owned business, the Mercer Island

12 Taxi Company. Pursuant to these negotiations J. Hartley Newsum, the attor-

13 ney for the purchaser, prepared the initial draft of an agreement for the

14 purchase of plaintiffs' business by Bellevue Enterprises, Inc.

15   The initial draft was forwarded to defendant who made a number of

16 changes in pen and pencil. In particular, defendant included a signature

17 line for the personal signature of the purchaser's president as guarantor

18 of the purchaser's obligation. Defendant made this change pursuant to

19 plaintiffs' instruction that, in addition to drafting a purchase agreement,

20 defendant was to secure the personal guarantee of Fisk, the purchaser's

21 president.

22   Defendant thereafter prepared the final draft of the purchase agree-

23 ment. Defendant failed to include in the final draft a guaranty clause

24 or a signature line for the signature of Fisk as guarantor of the pur-

25 chaser's obligation. Although defendant had informed plaintiffs to the

26

27

Pls. Brief in Opposition
Page 1

1 contrary, defendant also failed to inform either Fisk or the purchaser's

2 attorney that plaintiffs wanted Fisk to sign the purchase agreement as

3 guarantor of the purchaser's obligation.

4   On May 19, 1969, the purchase agreement was executed in the office of

5 the purchaser's attorney by the plaintiffs and by Fisk, who signed the

6 agreement on behalf of the purchaser. Prior to the May 19, 1969 meeting,

7 Fisk had signed the agreement in the office of the purchaser's attorney.

8 At the meeting Fisk signed the agreement a second time at defendant's

9 request without any accompanying words for the sole purpose of identifying

10 his first signature for the defendant who notarized the signatures of the

11 parties to the purchase agreement.

12   No payments were made under the purchase agreement after October 1,

13 1970. The principal balance due and owing is $32,366.74. Under the pur-

14 chase agreement the unpaid balance draws interest at the rate of eight (8)

15 percent per annum. Bellevue Enterprises, Inc. has been declared insolvent

16 and no distribution to creditors was made.

17   On January 14, 1971, defendant filed an action on the purchase agree-

18 ment entitled Peters v. Bellevue Enterprises, Inc. and John Fisk, King

19 County Superior Court No. 732995. On November 11, 1972, defendant with-

20 drew as plaintiffs' counsel and consented to the substitution of plaintiffs'

21 present counsel. On November 26, 1973, the court signed an order of volun-

22 tary dismissal after plaintiffs' substituted counsel had moved at the trial

23 of the case for a dismissal under CR 41(a) (2), following the citation by

24 opposing counsel of Washington case law indicating that the Washington

25 Statute of Frauds barred the admission of parol evidence to prove that

26 Fisk had signed the purchase agreement as a guarantor.

27

Pls. Brief in Opposition
Page 2

1   Plaintiffs' substituted counsel then commenced an action entitled

2   Peters v. Fisk, King County Superior Court No. 773694, for reformation of

3   the purchase agreement to conform with the parties' intent that Fisk was

4   to be a guarantor of the purchaser's obligation. On June 19, 1974, the

5   court dismissed plaintiffs' action with prejudice. The court found that

6   during the May 19, 1969 meeting and all prior negotiations defendant never

7   told Fisk or the purchaser's attorney that Fisk's signature as a guarantor

8   would be required on the purchase agreement. Second, the plaintiffs and

9   Fisk made no independent agreement for a personal guarantee by Fisk of the

10   purchaser's obligation. Third, after the defendant made the changes in the

11   initial draft, the revised draft was never shown to Fisk or the purchaser's

12   attorney. Fourth, the defendant's failure to inform either Fisk or the

13   purchaser's attorney that plaintiffs wanted Fisk to sign the purchase agree-

14   ment as a guarantor formed the basis for a unilateral mistake of fact by

15   plaintiffs. Fifth, there was no mutual mistake of the parties to the

16   purchase agreement regarding the personal assumption of the purchaser's

17   obligation by Fisk as guarantor. On this basis, the court concluded there

18   was no binding agreement between the plaintiffs and Fisk concerning the

19   assumption of the purchaser's obligation by Fisk as guarantor. On July 17,

20   1974, plaintiffs filed the present action against defendant for damages

21   in the sum of $32,366.74, plus eight (8) percent interest from October 1,

22   1970.

23   PLAINTIFFS' ARGUMENT

24   In this attorney's malpractice action, the court should adopt the rule

25   that the applicable three year statute of limitations, RCW 4.16.080(3),

26   does not begin to run until the plaintiff discovered or should have dis-

27   covered the defendant's negligent act. The court should reject the present

Pls. Brief in Opposition
Page 3

1 Washington rule that in attorney's malpractice actions the statute of

2 limitations begins to run on the date of the negligent act. The case law

3 on which the present rule is based is outdated and inappropriate. More

4 recent Washington malpractice cases involving other professions have

5 applied the date of discovery rule proposed herein. See, e.g., Ruth v.

6 Dight, 75 Wn.2d 660, 453 P.2d 651 (1969) (physician's malpractice action);

7 Kundahl v. Barnett, 5 Wn.App. 227, 486 P.2d 1164, pet. for rev. denied,

8 80 Wn.2d 1001 (1971) (land surveyor's negligence action); Janisch v. Mullins,

9 1 Wn.App. 393, 461 P.2d 895 (1969), rev. dismissed, 78 Wn.2d 997 (1970)

10 (physician's malpractice action). The date of discovery rule adopted in

11 the medical malpractice cases was codified as 4.16.350 in 1971. Laws of

12 1971, Ch. 80, §1. 4.16.350 provides that an action against a hospital

13 or a member of the healing arts

14   "based upon alleged professional negligence shall be com-
    menced within (1) three years from the date of the alleged

15   wrongful act, or (2) one year from the time that plaintiff
    discovers the injury or condition was caused by the wrongful

16   act, whichever period of time expires last."

17 The recent Washington malpractice cases involving other professions are

18 consistent with several attorney malpractice cases from other jurisdictions

19 which adopt the date of discovery rule. See, e.g., Neel v. Magana, Olney,

20 Levy, Cathcart & Gelfand, 98 Cal. Rptr. 837, 491 P.2d 429 (1971); Downing

21 v. Vaine, 228 So.2d 622 (Fla. Ct. App. 1969), appeal dismissed, 237 So.2d

22 767 (Fla. 1970); Mumford v. Staton, Whaley & Price, 255 A.2d 359 (Md.

23 1969).

24   The date of the act rule presently applied by Washington courts in

25 attorney malpractice cases is based upon the following rationale. An

26 attorney's duty to a client is

27 Pls. Brief in Opposition
Page 4

1   "one growing out of the relation between the parties, and
2   that relation is one based upon contract. The relation, it
   is true, is fiduciary, but that does not disturb the fact
3   that it is contractual, and that a cause of action based upon
   the breach of the contract accrues when the contract is violated and not when the violation is discovered." <u>Cornell v.</u>
4   <u>Edsen</u>. 78 Wn. 662, 665, 136 P. 602 (1914)

5   The expressed purpose of the common law, however, is to strike a

6 balance between the harm to the plaintiff of being deprived of a remedy

7 versus the harm to the defendant of being sued. <u>Ruth v. Dight</u>, 75 Wn.2d

8 at 665; <u>Janisch v. Mullins</u>, 1 Wn.App. at 399.

9   "But what happens to the concepts of fundamental fairness and
   the common law's purpose to provide a remedy for every genuine
10   wrong when, from the circumstances of the wrong, the injured
   party would not in the usual course of events know that he had
11   been injured until long after the statute of limitations had
   cut off his legal remedies?" <u>Ruth v. Dight</u>, 75 Wn.2d at 665.
12

13 Concluding that the accrual of a cause of action under RCW 4.16.010 is

14 left to the courts to determine, the Washington Supreme Court stated:

15   "But in reading RCW 4.16.010, as it speaks of the accrual of a
   cause of action, along with subsection RCW 4.16.080(2), prescribing the kind and classes of actions which are limited to 3 years.
16   . . we note that the time fixed for calculating the accrual of
   the cause of action becomes general instead of specific, and
17   could as readily be said to commence with the reasonable discovery
   of the injury as with the occurrence of the event or omission
18   which produced the alleged injury. . . . Thus, a fair resolution
   of the dilemma involves both a preservation of limitations on the
19   time in which the action may be brought and a preservation of the
   remedy, too, where both parties are blameless as to delay in dis-
20   covery of the asserted wrong." <u>Id</u>. at 666-67.

21 Relying upon this rationale, the Court in <u>Ruth</u> overturned the date of

22 the act rule in medical malpractice cases and adopted the date of dis-

23 covery rule. <u>Id</u>. at 667-68. Preservation of the client's remedy until

24 the date of discovery of an attorney's wrongful act should be mandatory

25 where the attorney, but not the client, is not blameless as to the delay

26 in the client's discovery of the asserted wrong.

27

Pls. Brief in Opposition
Page 5

1   The principles applicable in other types of professional malpractice

2   cases to determine the accrual of a cause of action are equally applicable

3   in attorney's malpractice cases. Holding that an action for negligent

4   breach of duty against a land surveyor accrued for purposes of the

5   statute of limitation upon discovery of the negligence, Kundahl v. Barnett,

6   supra, stated:

7   "We see no distinction between the medical and other professions
        insofar as application of the discovery rule is concerned. Al-
8   though the damages resulting from medical malpractice are more
        personal in character, the pecuniary loss caused by malpractice
9   in the other professions can be as great or greater. In this
        case it is illogical to charge respondents with the obligation of
10   retaining the services of another surveyor to prove out the stakes
        which appellant Elrod placed. That would be the only way that re-
11   spondents could discover the error; unless, of course, the second
        surveyor was in error, calling for a third survey, and so on ad
12   infinitum." 5 Wn.App. at 231.

13 Similarly,the Court of Appeals in Janisch v. Mullins, supra, quoted with

14 approval the following statement:

15   "On a theoretical basis it is impossible to justify the applica-
        bility of the discovery rule to one kind of malpractice and not
16   to another. The reason for the application of the discovery rule
        is the same in each instance. It is manifestly unrealistic
17   and unfair to bar a negligently injured party's cause of action
        before he has had an opportunity to discover that it exists."
18   1 Wn.App. at 401.

19   Unlike malpractions [sic] against doctors and land surveyors, which have

20 been held to sound in tort and therefore to be governed by RCW 4.16.080(2),

21 malpractice actions against attorneys have been held to sound in contract

22 and therefore to be governed by RCW 4.16.080(3). RCW 4.16.080(3), however,

23 is no more specific than RCW 4.16.080(2) concerning when a cause of action

24 accrues. Both sections are equally silent on the subject. Thus the reason-

25 ing of the recent Washington professional malpractice cases which hold that

26 a malpractice action in tort accrues on the date of discovery of the wrong

27 Pls. Brief in Opposition
    Page 6

1   is equally applicable to the determination of the date of accrual of a

2   malpractice action in contract.

3   The cases from other jurisdictions which have adopted the date of dis-

4   covery rule to determine the date of accrual of an attorney malpractice

5   action have relied upon three basic policy considerations. First, a lay

6   client necessarily is placed in a position of trust in relation to his or

7   her attorney because the client cannot evaluate the attorney's judgment or

8   performance. Hence, a client should not be denied a remedy when his or her

9   attorney negligently violates that trust if the violation could not have

10 been discovered within a particular statutory period running from the date

11 of the attorney's negligent act. Second, regardless of whether a pro-

12 fessional relationship is classified as contractual or non-contractual, the

13 same rules concerning the accrual of a professional malpractice action

14 should be applied to all professions because all professional malpractice

15 actions are grounded upon a negligent breach of duty. Attorneys should not

16 be allowed to remain a favored professional group by the courts. Third, if

17 a client is not given a reasonable opportunity to bring an attorney mal-

18 practice action, the assertion by the attorney of the statute of limitations

19 as a bar to the client's action impugns the integrity of the legal pro-

20 fession.

21   The following cases from other jurisdictions, all of which applied

22 the date of discovery rule to determine the accrual of the plaintiff's

23 action, further explore these policy considerations in relation to attorney

24 malpractice actions. In Downing v. Vaine, 228 So.2d 622 (Fla.Ct.App. 1969),

25 appeal dismissed, 237 So.2d 767 (Fla. 1970), the court considered the fact

26 that a client has no way of knowing he or she has been injured to be deter-

27 minative.
    Pls. Brief in Opposition
    Page 7

1   "We find it impossible to rationalize how an injured client
2   can be required to institute an action within a limited
    time after his cause of action accrues if he has no means of
3   knowing by the exercise of reasonable diligence that the
    cause of action exists. It occurs to us that one should be
    held in fault for failing to timely exercise a right only if
4   he knows, or by reasonable diligence should have known, that such
    right existed." 228 So.2d at 625.
5
    In Mumford v. Staton, Whaley & Price, 255 A.2d 359 (Md. 1969), the
6
court concluded that although attorney-client relationships are contractual,
7
all professional groups must be treated the same:
8
9   "[W]e think the fact that liability is grounded on the negligent
    breach of duty permits the application of legal principles usually
    reserved to the field of torts, such as the discovery rule with
10   regard to limitations." 255 A.2d at 363.

11 The court went on to state that courts should never favor attorneys over

12 other professional groups:

13   "[W]e cannot now make favored litigants of attorneys by applying
    a less stringent rule to members of the legal profession than to
14   doctors or surveyors. It would appear that in recent years the
    trend has been for courts, in applying limitations to professional
15   malpractice cases, not to become too concerned as to whether the
    action is grounded in contract or tort, but rather to focus attention
16   on the fact that it is the failure to perform one's professional
    duties with reasonable skill and diligence which gives rise to the
17   cause of action, whether it be a negligent breach of contract or
    otherwise. Since such actions share the common gravamen of negli-
18   gence, limitations should be applied in the same manner to all suits
    for professional malpractice, even though the relationship between
19   the parties be contractual, as in the case at bar." 228 So.2d at 367.

20   In Neel v. Magana, Olney, Levy, Cathcart & Gelfand, 98 Cal. Rptr. 837,

21 491 P.2d 421 (1971), the California Supreme Court overruled the date of the

22 act rule and adopted the date of discovery rule to determine the accrual

23 of an attorney malpractice action. The court articulated three determinative

24 factors to support its decision. First, an attorney has a professional

25 obligation to perform his or her work using the skill and prudence commonly

26 exercised by those in the legal profession. Second, the layman is unable

27 to detect misapplications of the law by the professional and often lacks
Pls. Brief in Opposition
Page 8

1 the opportunity to do so. Third, the failure of an attorney to disclose

2 a negligent act to a client is itself a breach of the attorney's fiduciary

3 duty to the client.

4   Concluding that postponement of the accrual of a malpractice action

5 until the client discovered the wrong would uphold the attorney's duty of

6 disclosure, the California court stressed that attorneys should not be

7 favored litigants.

8   "An immunity from the statute of limitations for practitioners
       at the bar not enjoyed by other professions is itself suspicious,
9   but when conferred by former practitioners who now sit upon the
       bench, it is doubly suspicious. We therefore hold that in an
10   action for professional malpractice against an attorney, the cause
       of action does not accrue until the plaintiff knows, or should know,
11   all material facts essential to show the elements of that cause of
       action. 491 P.2d at 430.

12 The court stated that a contrary holding would harm the integrity of

13 the legal profession.

14   "[W]hen an attorney raises the statute of limitations to occlude [sic]
15   a client's action before that client has had a reasonable oppor-
       tunity to bring the suit, the resulting ban of the action not
16   only starkly works an injustice upon the client but partially
       impugns the very integrity of the legal profession." Id. at 431.

17 The Washington Court of Appeals made a parallel observation concerning

18 the preservation of professional integrity in Janisch v. Mullins, 1 Wn.App.

19 393, 461 P.2d 895 (1969), rev. dismissed, 78 Wn.2d 997 (1970).

20   "[W]e give special weight to the necessity of protecting the
21   integrity of the relation of trust and confidence that must
       prevail between physician and patient to best promote proper
22   treatment and diagnosis of the patient's condition. We should
       not interpret the limitation statute in a manner that will cause
23   the patient to distrust his physician or to be under the necessity
       of continually checking on him in order to avoid a possible loss
24   of remedy in the event of malpractice." 1 Wn.App. at 400-401.

25

26

27
    Pls. Brief in Opposition
    Page 9

CONCLUSION

An examination of the policy considerations underlying the right of a client to bring a malpractice action against his or her attorney indicates that adoption of the date of discovery rule to determine the accrual of an attorney malpractice action would strike a better balance between the harm to the client of being deprived of a remedy versus the harm to the attorney of being sued. Continued application of the date of the act rule would unduly favor attorneys and disregard the needs of clients and the purposes of malpractice actions in general.

> "Today, then, is no time to perpetuate an anachronistic interpretation of the statute of limitations that permits the attorney to escape obligations which other professionals must bear. The legal calling can ill afford the preservation of a privilege born of error, subject to almost universal condemnation, and in present-day society, anomalous." Neel v. Magana, Olney, Levy, Cathcart & Gelfand, 491 P.2d at 433.

In the present case, the defendant controlled the litigation of the plaintiffs' contract dispute for more than three years after the date of the defendant's negligence. Moreover, until the plaintiffs' litigation to enforce the alleged contractual guarantee against Fisk was unfavorably concluded in 1974, the plaintiffs were unable to determine that the defendant had been negligent. Thus, if the date of the act rule is applied to determine the accrual of the plaintiffs' malpractice action, plaintiffs would be deprived of a reasonable opportunity to exercise their legal remedy for redress of the harm suffered as a result of the defendant's negligence.

Accordingly, plaintiffs respectfully request the court to adopt the date of discovery rule to avoid the inequity of a complete denial to plaintiffs of any legal remedy against defendant. Further, the plaintiffs

Pls. Brief in Opposition
Page 10

1 respectfully request the court to deny defendant's motion for summary

2 judgment because, applying the date of discovery rule to the facts of

3 this case, plaintiffs properly commenced their malpractice action

4 against defendant within the required three year period of limitation.

5   DATED this _____ day of December, 1974.

6   CASEY, PRUZAN, KOVARIK & SHULKIN

7

8   By:_____

9   David G. Shenton
          Of Attorneys for Plaintiffs

10

11

12

13

14

15

16

17

18

19

20

21

22

23

24

25

26

27

Pls. Brief in Opposition
Page 11

APPENDIX F

Rules of the United States Supreme Court

Rule 40. Briefs—In general

1. Briefs of an appellant or petitioner on the merits shall be printed as prescribed in Rule 39, and shall contain in the order here indicated—

(a) A reference to the official and unofficial reports of the opinions delivered in the courts below, if there were such and they have been reported.

(b) A concise statement of the grounds on which the jurisdiction of this court is invoked, with citation to the statutory provision and to the time factors upon which such jurisdiction rests.

(c) The constitutional provisions, treaties, statutes, ordinances and regulations which the case involves, setting them out verbatim, and citing the volume and page where they may be found in the official edition. If the provisions involved are lengthy, their citation alone will suffice at this point, and their pertinent text shall be set forth in an appendix.

(d)(1) The questions presented for review, expressed in the terms and circumstances of the case but without unnecessary detail. The statement of a question presented will be deemed to include every subsidiary question fairly comprised therein.

(2) The phrasing of the questions presented need not be identical with that set forth in the jurisdictional statement or the petition for certiorari, but the brief may not raise additional questions or change the substance of the questions already presented in those documents. Questions not presented according to this paragraph will be disregarded, save as the court, at its option, may notice a plain error not presented.

(e) A concise statement of the case containing all that is material to the consideration of the questions presented, with appropriate references to the appendix, e. g., (A. 12) or to the record, e. g., (R. 12).

(f) In briefs on the merits, or in any briefs wherein the argument portion extends beyond twenty printed pages, a summary of argument, suitably paragraphed, which should be a succinct, but accurate and clear, condensation of the argument actually made in the body of the brief. It should not be a mere repetition of the headings under which the argument is arranged.

(g) The argument, exhibiting clearly the points of fact and of law being presented, citing the authorities and statutes relied upon.

(h) A conclusion, specifying with particularity the relief to which the party believes himself entitled.

2. Whenever, in the brief of any party, a reference is made to the appendix or the record, it must be accompanied by the appropriate page number. When the reference is to a part of the evidence, the page citation must be specific. If the reference is to an exhibit, both the page number at which the exhibit appears and at which it was offered in evidence must be indicated, e. g., (Pl.Ex. 14; R. 199, 2134).

3.   The brief filed by an appellee or respondent shall conform to the foregoing requirements, except that no statement of the case need be made beyond what may be deemed necessary in correcting any inaccuracy or omission in the statement of the other side, and except that items (a), (b), (c) and (d) need not be included unless the appellee or respondent is dissatisfied with their presentation by the other side.

4.   Reply briefs shall conform to such portions of this rule as are applicable to the briefs of an appellee or respondent, but need not contain a summary of argument, regardless of their length, if appropriately divided by topical headings.

5.   Briefs must be compact, logically arranged with proper headings, concise, and free from burdensome, irrelevant, immaterial, and scandalous matter.   Briefs not complying with this paragraph may be disregarded and stricken by the court.

APPENDIX G

Summary of an Oral Argument Before the United States Supreme Court

BURNS v. ALCALA

Supreme Court of the United States, 1975.
420 U.S. 575, 95 S.Ct. 1180, 43 L.Ed.2d 469.

Reproduced from 43 U.S.L.W. 3409 (1975) with permission.

[Copyright, 1974, The Bureau of National Affairs, Inc.]

The Honorable Richard C. Turner, Attorney General of the State of Iowa, argued for the petitioners, state and local welfare directors in Iowa, who denied AFDC benefits to the respondent, three unmarried pregnant women who were otherwise qualified for AFDC assistance. Turner stated that there are two issues in the case. The first issue is whether a pregnant woman can be considered a mother before her child is born. He stated that the second issue is whether a pregnant woman can be considered a parent, within the meaning of the Act, prior to the birth of her child. Turner argued that if a pregnant woman has no obligation to support her fetus, under the reasoning of King v. Smith, 392 U.S. 309 (1968), she could not be held to be a parent.

The Chief Justice: "You mean no legal obligation, don't you?"

Turner: "Yes sir."

Turner cited the dissent of Judge Pell in Wilson v. Weaver, 499 F.2d 155, 42 LW 2634 (CA 7 1974). Judge Pell stated that neither the mother nor the father is a "parent" before a child is born. Turner said that even the real father has no duty of support prior to the birth of the child. Moreover, he argued that if a woman can legally abort her fetus, how can she have a duty to support it.

However, assuming for the sake of argument that she has a duty, Turner stated that a woman and her fetus are not a "family," and it is families, not individuals as such, that are entitled to AFDC.

The ultimate question in this case, according to Turner, is whether a fetus is a "dependent child." Dependent child is defined in 42 U.S.C. § 606 (Section 406 of the Social Security Act), to mean "a needy child * * * who has been deprived of parental support or care by reason of the death, continued absence from the home, or physical or mental incapacity of a parent, and who is living with [certain defined relatives] in a place or residence maintained by one or more of such relatives as his or their own home * * *." Turner stressed the word "own home." "There's a far cry between a home and a womb," Turner declared. He argued that unless the child is living within a home, it's not a "child" within the meaning of the statute.

In February 1971, for the first time, according to Turner, HEW published a rule that made it optional for the states to pay AFDC benefits on behalf of unborn children. There is some indication, however, that, as far

back as 1946 an ADC (the name was changed in 1950) manual recognized such an optional right of the states. Nevertheless, at the end of 1971, about one-third of the states and the District of Columbia continued to make AFDC benefits available on behalf of unborn children.

The following year, according to Turner, Congress considered amending the Act to make it clear that unborn children are not "dependent" children within the meaning of the Act. The proposal did not pass, and the issue has been heavily litigated since. Of the six circuit courts that have considered the question, Turner conceded that only one, the Second Circuit, has upheld his position. Turner stressed, however, that the Second Circuit, in Wisdom v. Norton, 43 LW 2173 (CA 2, October 11, 1974), had the benefit of the opinions of four of the other circuits, but that the Fifth Circuit, which filed its opinion in December, did not have the benefit of Wisdom. He contended that the Second Circuit opinion in Wisdom is very well reasoned.

Turner reviewed the reasons cited by the courts that have held that unborn children are eligible for AFDC benefits. He was interrupted, however, by the following questions:

Mr. Justice Rehnquist: "Your opponent's contention is that if the unborn are indeed eligible under the Act, the extension of benefits to them is mandatory and the states do not have an option. Do you agree or disagree?"

Turner: "Yes, if an unborn is eligible, assistance to him is mandatory and there is no option."

Mr. Justice Rehnquist: "Then you disagree with HEW's approach?"

Turner: "Yes I do."

The Chief Justice: "Then you also disagree with Wisdom. Wisdom said that the regulation is valid."

Turner: "Yes, that's correct. I agree that the regulation is invalid."

In an exchange of several questions and answers with the Chief Justice, Turner agreed that HEW has never really thought that the Act included unborn children, but he again disagreed with HEW's contention that the statute is optional.

Turner argued that the statute should be construed according to its plain meaning, and that one shouldn't actively search for ambiguities in the law if a statute is clear. In fact, he stated that it's not even necessary to consult HEW regulations if the statute is clear. He contended that the pertinent section of the Social Security Act is quite clear in prescribing that a recipient of AFDC benefits must be living. He drew the Court's attention again to Judge Pell's dissent in Wilson in which he cites many sections of the Act and its amendments that use language which would be inoperative if applied to a child not yet born.

Turner also cited the contention made in Wisdom that references to "child" in normal parlance always mean a living child. A child that has already been born is never modified by "unborn." One doesn't say "I have three children," but rather "I have two children and one on the way."

Mr. Justice Stewart: "A woman can be said to be great with child."

Turner: "Yes, sir, that's true. But that's unordinary language. At least in Iowa it is."

The Chief Justice: "This Court has held that a fetus in embryo is not a legal person. Is this of any significance?"

Turner: "Yes sir, it is. Roe v. Wade held that an unborn child is not a person."

Mr. Justice Stewart: "Within the meaning of the Fourteenth Amendment."

Turner: "Yes, sir."

Turner argued that if under Roe v. Wade a state is not permitted to abridge the right to privacy of a woman who wants to abort her fetus, how can it possibly impose on her the obligation of a parent to support the fetus.

Professor Robert Bartels of the College of Law of the University of Iowa argued for the respondents. Bartels opened his argument by stating that he agreed with the attorney for the petitioners that the issue is purely one of statutory interpretation. The sole question is whether an unborn child is "dependent" under Section 406(a) of the Social Security Act. If a fetus is a dependent child, under prior decisions of the Court the states must make pregnant women eligible for AFDC aid for their unborn children. If not, no state is permitted to receive or use federal funds for such purposes.

Mr. Justice Stewart: "You agree that the HEW regulation is invalid in either event. It can't be optional, that is."

Bartels: "That's correct. It cannot be optional." Bartels stated that HEW has adopted a new position in its amicus brief before the Court. Its position appears to be that an unborn child is not in fact a dependent child, but that the Secretary has rulemaking authority extensive enough to justify a rule making AFDC assistance to the unborn optional with the states.

Mr. Justice Brennan: "In the states that have opted to pay pregnant women, how is the computation made?"

Bartels: "It varies from state to state. There's nothing in the Act prescribing the scheme to be used."

Mr. Justice Brennan: "Is it done as if the child had been born?"

Bartels: "It is in some states, but in California, for example, a woman receives a smaller amount for an unborn child than she does for one that has been born."

Mr. Justice Rehnquist: "Wouldn't there be a difficulty with this under Townsend v. Swank [404 U.S. 282, 40 LW 4080 (1971–]? If an unborn child is a child, how can the states distinguish among them in making payments?"

Bartels: "Under Dandridge v. Williams [397 U.S. 471, 38 LW 4277 (1970)], the states can distinguish. States have very wide discretion in making reasonable distinctions among their citizens to reflect different needs among different groups."

The Chief Justice: "You do not think that the federal contribution mandates uniform treatment?"

Bartels: "No sir."

The Chief Justice: "What cases do you rely on?"

Bartels cited Jefferson v. Hackney, 406 U.S. 535, 40 LW 4585 (1972), and stated that federal standards are mandatory as to eligibility only, not as to the amount of the benefits or differences in them.

Mr. Justice Rehnquist: "Suppose you win. Can Iowa then say that it recognizes the Supreme Court's decision and that it will allow $50 per month for a living child and $1 per month for an unborn child?"

Bartels: "The state could make a distinction, but $1 per month might not be reasonable in light of the financial requirements in caring properly for a pregnant woman and her fetus."

Mr. Justice Stewart: "Does the statute say it has to be reasonable?"

Bartels: "No, it's a constitutional requirement."

Mr. Justice Stewart: "Where in the Constitution?"

Bartels: "The Equal Protection Clause of the Fourteenth Amendment."

Mr. Justice Stewart: "That's not what the Constitution says."

Bartels: "Not directly, but I understand that to be the case on the basis of the way it has been interpreted by this Court."

Mr. Justice Powell: "Will the age of the fetus make any difference?"

Bartels: "No, but the most logical point from which to begin payment of benefits would be the point of proof of conception or quickness."

Mr. Justice Blackmun: "What justification would viability have as a point of entitlement? If a fetus is a child within the meaning of the statute, it's just as much one before quickness as it is after."

Bartels: "Correct, but quickness is traditional."

Mr. Justice Blackmun: "The Internal Revenue Code has never allowed a dependency exemption for a fetus."

Bartels: "Your honor, I don't think that has much to do with this case."

Mr. Justice Blackmun: "Well, you certainly didn't cite it." Mr. Justice Blackmun then quoted pertinent sections of the Internal Revenue Code.

Bartels: "The purposes of AFDC assistance are entirely different from the dependency exemption sections of the Internal Revenue Code."

The Chief Justice: "Both take into account the expenses of rearing a child."

Bartels: "Yes, but as an administrative matter, for the collection of taxes, Congress may have decided that it's administratively better to have a live child. Also, the expenses for an unborn child are less than those for a living child."

Bartels contended that the pertinent statutory provision is unclear. The great majority of federal judges who have passed on it have found it unclear. Accordingly, one must look to the legislative purposes and longstanding HEW interpretation in construing it. He noted that the Court has rejected HEW's "optional" argument in Townsend v. Swank, supra, and Carleson v. Remillard, 406 U.S. 598, 40 LW 4624 (1972).

Mr. Justice Brennan: "You would agree that if the Act does not include a fetus, the HEW regulation is invalid?"

Bartels: "Yes, that's correct, your honor."

Bartels stated that the evidence clearly establishes a relationship between prenatal and postnatal care. In response to a question from the Chief Justice about whether there are programs for prenatal care, Bartels cited Title V of the Social Security Act. The Chief Justice said that the passage of Title V demonstrates that Congress was aware of the problem of prenatal care. In response, Bartels stated that Title V talks about mother and child and has been interpreted to include the fetus. In other words, it covers both the born and the unborn. He continued, "as the First Circuit suggested, it's incongruous for Congress to have extended both Titles IV and V to the born and to have included the unborn in only Title V."

In 1950, Bartels stated, Congress amended the Social Security Act by adding, among other things, Section 402(a)(10). Additionally, it changed the name of the Aid to Dependent Children program to Aid to Families of Dependent Children. This change reflects the fact that for the first time the definition of "aid to dependent children" in Section 406(b) of the Act included funds to meet the needs of the parent or other relatives with whom eligible "dependent children" were living.

The Chief Justice: "Do you read much significance into the addition of caretaker relatives in 1950?"

Bartels: "No special significance, but the addition of Section 402(a)(10) required, as this Court has held, that the state had to pay everyone eligible under the Act."

Mr. Justice Stewart: "Since the addition of that section there can't be an option anymore."

Bartels: "That's correct; there is no authority for an option in the Act."

Bartels claimed that administrative interpretation to include unborn children goes back to at least 1941.

Mr. Justice Brennan: "Was 1941 the first time such an opinion was expressed administratively?"

Bartels: "The 1941 statement was the first officially expressed view, but it was under consideration prior to that."

Bartels devoted the balance of his time to rebutting two contentions made by the petitioners. He denied that there are satisfactory alternatives available to pregnant women. He cited the Iowa county relief program and said that it is not only totally discretionary with the counties in Iowa, but the aid extended under it is typically not equivalent to AFDC benefits. Additionally, he contended that food stamps are not a suitable alternative. In fact, AFDC recipients are eligible for food stamps too.

Bartels also argued that the petitioners' citation of Jefferson v. Hackney, supra and Dandridge v. Williams, supra, is entirely inappropriate. These cases have nothing to do with this case. The issue in this case is eligibility, and not the amount of assistance.

In summary, Bartels said that the statutory purpose of the AFDC program, the 1950 amendments to the Social Security Act, and the long-standing administrative interpretation of the AFDC program mandate AFDC benefits on behalf of the unborn.

In rebuttal, Turner stressed the significance of the fact that while Title V of the Social Security Act provides for prenatal care, Title IV of the Act does not. He stated that Congress was not unmindful of the fact that in some cases pregnant women need health care, but did not expressly provide for it in Title IV.

Mr. Justice White: "How much will this case mean to Iowa?"

Turner: "I don't know, although in another case, involving Georgia. I think, it meant $6.8 million."

Finally, Turner objected to the Court's consideration of the 1940 and 1941 Bureau of Public Assistance Memoranda, contained in the addenda to the respondents' brief, that officially interpret "dependent child" to include a fetus. He stated that he did not think that the memoranda were a part of the record made in the district court, but under questioning from Mr. Justice Marshall he admitted that he had not examined completely that record and therefore could not say definitively that such was the case.

INDEX

SHEPARD'S CITATIONS—Cont'd
Described, in general, 95.
Federal Law Citations in Selected Law Reviews, 160.
Law Review Citations, 177.
Ordinances, 217.
Restatements, 162.
Statute editions, 186, 200–201.

SHEPARD'S FEDERAL CIRCUIT TABLE (1960–1971), 159.

SHEPARD'S ORDINANCE LAW ANNOTATIONS, 217.

SIGNIFICANT FACTS, 8, 26–28, 51–52, 116–117.

SLIP LAWS, 182.

SOUTHEASTERN REPORTER (S.E., S.E.2D), 12.
See Reports and Reporters.

SOUTHERN REPORTER (SO., SO.2D), 12.
See Reports and Reporters.

SOUTHWESTERN REPORTER (S.W., S.W.2D), 12.
See Reports and Reporters.

SPADING, DEFINED, 244.

STAR PAGING, 79.

STARE DECISIS
See Common Law.

STATISTICAL AND SURVEY DATA, 178.

STATUTES
See Annotated Codes; Codes; Legislation.

STATUTES AT LARGE (STAT.), 181–182, 185, 187.

STONE, JULIUS
"The Ratio of the Ratio Decidendi," quoted, 52–53.

SUB–ANALYSIS, ANALYSIS TABLES, 95, 120.

SUBSTANTIVE DECISION
See Precedents.

SUPREME COURT DIGEST, 155.
See Digests.

SUPREME COURT REPORTER (S.CT.) 106.
See Reports and Reporters.

SYLLABUS
See Opinions of Courts.

SYNTHESIS
See Opinions of Courts.

TABLES APPROACH TO RESEARCH
See Research Techniques.

TAPP RULE
See Research Techniques.

TEXTS, TREATISES
Citation forms, 246.
Described, in general, 13, 93.
Finding and evaluating, 124–126.
Student texts, limitations, 13, 126.

TEXTUAL REPORTING
See Legal Writing.

TOPIC APPROACH TO RESEARCH
See Research Techniques.

TOPICAL LAW REPORTS
See Looseleaf Services.

TREATISES
See Texts, Treatises.

TRIAL COURTS
See Memoranda; Opinions of Courts; Precedents.

TRIAL DE NOVO, 4, 253.

UNIFORM LAWS ANNOTATED, MASTER EDITION, 200.

UNIFORM STATUTES, 172, 188.

UNIFORM SYSTEM OF CITATION, A
See Blue Book.

UNITED STATES CITATIONS, 158.
See Citations; Shepard's Citations.

UNITED STATES CODE (U.S.C.).
See Codes.

UNITED STATES CODE AND CONGRESSIONAL SERVICE, 201.

UNITED STATES CODE ANNOTATED (U.S.C.A.)
See Annotated Codes.